Becoming Human

Literature and Philosophy

A. J. Cascardi, General Editor

This series publishes books in a wide range of subjects in philosophy and literature, including studies of the social and historical issues that relate these two fields. Drawing on the resources of the Anglo-American and Continental traditions, the series is open to philosophically informed scholarship covering the entire range of contemporary critical thought.

ALREADY PUBLISHED:

J. M. Bernstein, *The Fate of Art: Aesthetic Alienation from Kant to Derrida and Adorno*
Peter Bürger, *The Decline of Modernism*
Mary E. Finn, *Writing the Incommensurable: Kierkegaard, Rossetti, and Hopkins*
Reed Way Dasenbrock, ed., *Literary Theory After Davidson*
David P. Haney, *William Wordsworth and the Hermeneutics of Incarnation*
David Jacobson, *Emerson's Pragmatic Vision: The Dance of the Eye*
Gray Kochhar-Lindgren, *Narcissus Transformed: The Textual Subject in Psychoanalysis and Literature*
Robert Steiner, *Toward a Grammar of Abstraction: Modernity, Wittgenstein, and the Paintings of Jackson Pollock*
Sylvia Walsh, *Living Poetically: Kierkegaard's Existential Aesthetics*
Michel Meyer, *Rhetoric, Language, and Reason*
Christie McDonald and Gary Wihl, eds., *Transformations in Personhood and Culture After Theory*
Charles Altieri, *Painterly Abstraction in Modernist American Poetry: The Contemporaneity of Modernism*
John C. O'Neal, *The Authority of Experience: Sensationist Theory in the French Enlightenment*
John O'Neill, ed., *Freud and the Passions*
Sheridan Hough, *Nietzsche's Noontide Friend: The Self as Metaphoric Double*
E. M. Dadlez, *What's Hecuba to Him? Fictional Events and Actual Emotions*
Hugh Roberts, *Shelley and the Chaos of History: A New Politics of Poetry*
Charles Altieri, *Postmodernisms Now: Essays on Contemporaneity in the Arts*
Arabella Lyon, *Intentions: Negotiated, Contested, and Ignored*
Jill Gordon, *Turning Toward Philosophy: Literary Device and Dramatic Structure in Plato's Dialogues*
Michel Meyer, *Philosophy and the Passions: Toward a History of Human Nature*. Translated by Robert F. Barsky
Reed Way Dasenbrock, *Truth and Consequences: Intentions, Conventions, and the New Thematics*
David P. Haney, *The Challenge of Coleridge: Ethics and Interpretation in Romanticism and Modern Philosophy*
Alan Singer, *Aesthetic Reason: Artworks and the Deliberative Ethos*
Tom Huhn, *Imitation and Society: The Persistence of Mimesis in the Aesthetics of Burke, Hogarth, and Kant*
Jennifer Anna Gosetti-Ferencei, *The Ecstatic Quotidian: Phenomenological Sightings in Modern Art and Literature*
Max Statkiewicz, *Rhapsody of Philosophy: Dialogues with Plato in Contemporary Thought*
David N. McNeill, *An Image of the Soul in Speech: Plato and the Problem of Socrates*
Alan Singer, *The Self-Deceiving Muse: Notice and Knowledge in the Work of Art*

Becoming Human

Romantic Anthropology *and the* Embodiment of Freedom

Chad Wellmon

The Pennsylvania State University Press
University Park, Pennsylvania

Library of Congress Cataloging-in-Publication Data

Wellmon, Chad, 1976-
Becoming human : romantic anthropology and the embodiment of freedom / Chad Wellmon.
   p.   cm.—(Literature and philosophy)
Includes bibliographical references and index.
Summary: "Examines the crisis of a late eighteenth-century anthropology as it relates to the emergence of a modern consciousness that sees itself as condemned to draw its norms and very self-understanding from itself"—Provided by publisher.
   ISBN 978-0-271-03734-9 (cloth : alk. paper)
   ISBN 978-0-271-04852-9 (pbk : alk. paper)
   1. Philosophical anthropology—History.
      2. Civilization, Modern.
         3. Freedom—Philosophy.
            4. Human beings.
               I. Title.

BD450.W45   2010
128—dc22
2010024358

Copyright © 2010 The Pennsylvania State University
All rights reserved
Printed in the United States of America
Published by The Pennsylvania State University Press,
University Park, PA 16802-1003

It is the policy of The Pennsylvania State University Press to use acid-free paper. Publications on uncoated stock satisfy the minimum requirements of American National Standard for Information Sciences—Permanence of Paper for Printed Library Material, ANSI Z39.48-1992.

For my mother

Contents

Acknowledgments ix

Introduction: On the Possibility of Critique and the Failure of Anthropology 1

Part One: The Historical Problem

1. Proto-anthropology and the Discovery of Reflexivity 15

Part Two: A Provisional (Kantian) Solution

2. Cultivating Freedom: Kant's Affective Ethics 49
3. Freedom, Between Nature and Reason: Kant's Pragmatic Anthropology 99
4. Testing the Human: Kant and Forster on the Differences of Race and the Possibilities of Culture 138

Part Three: Three Responses to Kant

5. *Poesie* as Anthropology: Schleiermacher, Colonial History, and the Ethics of Ethnography 193
6. Lyrical Feeling: Novalis's Anthropology of the Senses 213

7. The Body of Language: Goethe, Humboldt, and the "Lively Gaze"   236

Conclusion   274

Notes   281
Bibliography   307
Index   323

Acknowledgments

This book is the product of countless discussions and interactions that began during my graduate studies at UC Berkeley. Pheng Cheah, Bob Holub, Martin Jay, Tony Kaes, Claire Kramsch, and Hinrich Seeba were all invaluable mentors. Scott Denham, Stefani Engelstein, Hansford Epes, Terry Pinkard, Paul Reitter, Michael Taylor, and Astrid Weigart are owed a special debt of gratitude for taking the time to read parts or all of this manuscript. I would especially like to thank my colleagues at the University of Virginia for their energy, ideas, and reading: Ben Bennett, Asher Biemann, Beth Bjorklund, Jeff Grossman, Richard Handler, Jannette Hudson, Paul Jones, Volker Kaiser, Lorna Martens, Chuck Mathewes, Bill McDonald, Allan Megill, John O'Brien, Brad Pasanek, Sophie Rosenfeld, Siva Vaidhyanathan, Renate Voris, and Josh Yates. Matthew Puffer became my most critical and valued reader in the last stages of this project. I thank Brooks, who is always there and is my best reader. Finally, I dedicate this book to my mother, Suzie Fryar, who read to me from the beginning but is not here to read this book.

I appreciate the permissions afforded by *Eighteenth-Century Studies, Studies in Romanticism,* and the *German Quarterly* to incorporate revised versions of articles that appeared in those journals: Portions of chapter 2 first appeared as "Kant and the Feelings of Reason," *Eighteenth-Century Studies* 42, no. 4 (2009): 557–80. Copyright © 2009 The Johns Hopkins University Press. An earlier version of chapter 5 appeared as "*Poesie* as Anthropology: Schleiermacher, Colonial History, and the Ethics of Ethnography," *German Quarterly* 79, no. 4 (2006). An earlier version of chapter 6 appeared as "Lyrical Feeling: Novalis's Anthropology of the Senses," *Studies in Romanticism* 47, no. 4 (2008): 453–78.

Introduction

On the Possibility of Critique and the Failure of Anthropology

Around 1800 Immanuel Kant stated that his philosophy posed three questions: What can I know? What can I do? What can I be permitted to hope for? He then added a fourth that he claimed would subsume them all: What is the human being? This last question, he suggests, could be answered by a new science of the human, a science that had come to be called anthropology. The late eighteenth-century convergence of medicine, natural science, philosophy, literature, and history around the figure of the *anthropos*—as an embodied, natural object—had made such a science possible. By 1800, however, this science was already in crisis. A solitary, monolithic discipline called anthropology had not yet emerged; instead, there were multiple and competing anthropologies. The distinctions that had come to ground Enlightenment modernity, distinctions between nature and culture, body and mind, human and animal, European and non-European, had become too capacious, too unstable for a science that was to answer the question of the human. If, as Friedrich Schlegel wrote, we don't even know "what the human is,"[1] then what object could ever ground a science of the human? What Kant invoked was less a discipline than a conceptual problem.

In his seminal essay "The Impact of the Concept of Culture on the Concept of Man," Clifford Geertz suggests that twentieth-century anthropology never escaped this crisis. To distinguish between what is "natural, universal, and constant in man and what is conventional, local, and variable" has been the task of anthropological inquiry since its disciplinary origins in eighteenth-century Europe.[2] Geertz wonders what we are to conclude about "human nature" from, for example, his studies of the Balinese. Are we to conclude that differences between cultures are merely "incidental," differences only of customs? Or should we conclude that human beings are simply what their cultures make of them? If the latter holds, suggests Geertz, the individual "dissolves, without residue, into his time and place, a child and perfect captive of his age" and becomes "conscripted" into the large, weary march of historical progress and determinism.

I argue that the conceptual problem of twentieth-century cultural anthropology has a long history—one that historians and students of contemporary cultural anthropology could not glean from Geertz's caricature of "the Enlightenment view of man"[3] as presupposing an immutable human nature. In fact, the historical and conceptual collision of a post-Kantian philosophy and literature with the fragmented discourse of anthropology around 1800 laid bare the conceptual architecture of a seemingly impossible discipline. It revealed a mode of thought in which the subject becomes entangled in thoroughly self-referential forms of knowledge. Kant, Friedrich Schlegel, Novalis, Schleiermacher, Goethe, and Wilhelm von Humboldt make clear the ironies, which have confounded the discipline of anthropology from its inception, of a mode of thought in which the human being is both the object and subject of observation. Anthropology becomes the necessary but formidable conjuncture of an account of what the human being is and a corresponding account of what it should become. In *Becoming Human* I argue that the crisis of late eighteenth-century anthropology marks the emergence of a modernity—and by "modernity" I mean the world of philosophical and literary discourse and social relations created in the wake of Kant and the late Enlightenment—that sees itself as condemned to draw its norms and very self-understanding from itself. Kant's fourth question invokes a disciplinary failure and a particular mode of anthropological thinking that has come to characterize the subject of modernity. Modernity so understood becomes fully modern when it becomes fully reflexive, that is to say, when it becomes deeply sensitive to the paradoxical and possibly futile nature of the modern project itself.

In *Becoming Human* I tell the story of modernity as an anthropological mode of thought. For modern European thought anthropology is not just the discipline of ethnographic inquiry into the diversity of human beings. Its question is modernity's question: what is the human? For many, however, the question of the human has become hopelessly tethered to a thoroughly rational, self-determining subject. From Marx, Nietzsche, and Freud to Heidegger, Derrida, and Foucault, thinkers have plotted the failures and blind spots of the modern, autonomous self. The philosophical project of Enlightenment modernity has long since been revealed as a fiction grounded in the ruse of a Cartesian cogito that, even in its doubt, was always naïve about the power of reason. This particular narrative is, as Robert Pippin puts it, suspicious of the sort of human that modern democratic societies seem to require.[4] The modern self, they contend, has been scattered amidst the ruins of an Enlightenment reason that imagined itself pure and autonomous.

Recently, scholars of the Enlightenment and the broader eighteenth century have begun to tie the emergence of anthropology as a discipline to a more complex account of Enlightenment reason. This work has sought to undo the narrative that caricatures Enlightenment reason as blind to the exigencies of life and numb to the particularity of experience. I continue the revision of the European Enlightenment in this book by focusing on the impurity of reason, but I do not provide a history of the discipline of anthropology as we know it today; instead, I articulate a particular mode of anthropological thinking that we have come to associate with modernity. Anthropology's crisis of self-recognition epitomizes the critical project of modernity that since its self-proclaimed inception has been obsessed with its own operations.

Highlighting how Kant, Novalis, Schleiermacher, Wilhelm von Humboldt, Friedrich Schlegel, and Goethe confronted and sought to transcend the conceptual architecture of an anthropology in crisis, I emphasize the critical potential of an Enlightenment modernity that many dismiss as a monolithic and imperializing ideology. I suggest how the possibility of critique emerges within the tension between the empirical and transcendental functions of anthropology, between questions about what the human being is and what the human being should or could become.

Foucault's ambivalent embrace of Kant offers an especially useful frame for the inextricable link between this particular anthropological mode of thought and modernity. In this introduction I consider, however briefly, the possibilities of a Kantian critique that Foucault found promising. In the chapters that follow I articulate something similar. I will outline the perils and promises of a critique that operates between the conjuncture of the empirical and the transcendental. In his discussion of Kant's "Beantwortung der Frage: Was ist Aufklärung?" Foucault offers a hesitant embrace of what he saw as the promise of Kant's legacy. Kantian critique, he suggests, offers us not a "permanent body of knowledge" or doctrine but a particularly modern ethos or attitude. For Foucault, the promise of critique lies in an analysis of the historical conditions that limit the human and the possibilities of exceeding these limits. "Criticism is no longer going to be practiced in the search for formal structures with universal value, but rather as a historical investigation into the events that have led us to constitute ourselves and to recognize ourselves as subjects of what we are doing, thinking, saying. In that sense, criticism is not transcendental, and its goal is not that of making a metaphysics possible."[5] What is the *ethos* of modernity, then, that Foucault claims to have found in Kantian critique? The transcendental aspirations of Kantian critique, as they are often portrayed, would not seem to align with the goals of Foucault's critical project. Is not Kantian critique a fundamentally transcendental project?

On the one hand, Kant envisions a critique that would "guard against error" and "serve the determinations of boundaries" by marking the limits of knowledge. This is a philosophy that "reins in" human reason.[6] Critique as transcendental philosophy does aim to show that all experience or representation of objects is fundamentally governed by self-legislated rules. This is the philosophy of the finitude of reason. On the other hand, Kant also speaks of philosophy as a process, as a move away from philosophy as a metaphysics with positive principles and toward philosophy according to its cosmopolitan concept (*Weltbegriff*). According to this cosmopolitan conception of philosophy, we learn to "philosophize," to "exercise the talent of reason." But this exercise of reason, this process of philosophizing is, he insists, carried out according to an end, according to the "relation of all cognition to the essential ends of the human race" (A839/B867). Kantian critique, then, seems to have two registers, an empirical demand on a historical subject and a transcendental argumentative claim. Whereas the latter is synonymous with a form of transcendental argumentation or critical philosophy that considers the conditions of possibility of knowledge, the former is more concerned with present possibilities and effects. This is the aspect of critique that makes the imperative of Kant's Enlightenment essay possible: "Have courage to make use of your own reason."[7] With this double character in mind, Kant's revision of the ancient imperative *sapere aude* is, on the one hand, a confident exhortation to make use of the autonomy of reason, to self-legislate. On the other hand, however, it is a two-pronged warning: to ignore this imperative is to remain under the sway of dogmatism (be it philosophical, religious, or political), but to heed it is to recognize that the only thing we can rely on in modernity is our own self-legislated claims, our own autonomy. To heed the ancient imperative in the Kantian sense is to become modern. In this second, more qualified instance, critique takes shape as enlightenment.

This discussion points to a more complex form of critique. Critique operates between its transcendental aspirations—to ground the conditions of knowledge—and its more immediate imperatives addressed to a historical subject. There is, therefore, a more qualified, empirical notion of critique. Kant, of course, goes to great lengths to keep these two realms, the empirical and the transcendental, separate. This tension is evident in the preface to the *Kritik der reinen Vernunft,* when he writes, "Our age is the genuine age of critique to which everything must submit itself."[8] The epoch of critique is located in a specific time, our time, and not displaced or projected into some transhistorical realm. The pronoun "our" locates critique in a particular historical moment. But the imperative to subordinate everything to critique expresses another element of the project: it is unabashedly directed toward a possible but always deferred enlightenment and toward a future that could be radically different from the present. Kant's distinction of critique from an epistemological knowledge project, from a project that would concern itself simply with constitutive claims about reality, points to a form of critique akin to an attitude toward the present made possible by a hopeful embrace of the future, a future that imagines the world otherwise. The paradox of these two aspects of critique arises from the fact that Kant bases his transcendental philosophy (including his transcendental doctrine of the faculties) on the finite human being. For Kant, critique, as both a transcendental philosophy and a more limited imperative, is necessary for our reason, for us as human beings not only to philosophize but to become human. And it is necessary because of the fundamental finitude of our cognitive faculties. Kant acknowledges these imperatives from the start of his project.

This second, more limited form of critique is the one that Foucault wants to cultivate. Foucault's seeming embrace of Kant has struck some as odd, since in *The Order of Things* he accuses Kant of having awakened philosophy from its dogmatic slumber only to have lulled it back into its "anthropological sleep," a sleep in which the human being is both the object of empirical inquiry and the transcendental ground of all knowledge.[9] Habermas reconciles Foucault's seemingly contradictory accounts of

Kant and the Enlightenment tradition by simply dismissing them as the exhausted surrender to the modernity Foucault fought to undo. I, however, read this ambivalent embrace as a function of the fundamental tension that burdened anthropological thinking from 1800 on: the tension between the empirical and the transcendental, between the human being as the object of observation and the transcendental ground of such observation. The modern ethos that Foucault admires in Kant has its conceptual origins in the post-Baconian, post-Kantian articulation of anthropology's conceptual paradoxes. I investigate the approaches of several key figures to this tension between the empirical and transcendental that is most acute and perhaps most productive subsequent to the Kantian radicalization of an Enlightenment anthropology, namely, around 1800. The paradoxes of the self-referential subject crystallize in a moment of crisis for anthropology, while simultaneously forcing a moment of recognition that would irreversibly shape modernity. In this book I try to recover a notion of critique that emerges from a modernity that, as Habermas puts it, sees itself "condemned to draw on itself" for its own self-understanding and norms.[10] Modernity is the epoch in which the human being is condemned to justify itself.

Kant frames this paradox pragmatically by offering a provisional response to the crisis of anthropology. He presents an anthropological mode of thought that makes claims about not only what the human is but what it ought to become.[11] Appropriately, the post-Kantian figures that I consider in the following chapters ask whether such normative claims of anthropology can be compelling. The primary figures in this book, then, were key participants less in the discipline that would become anthropology than in that more profound mode of anthropological thinking that Foucault calls modernity. They radicalize the very conceptual architecture that burdened the discipline of anthropology even in its early, fragmented form.

The Argument

In *Becoming Human* I sketch how the conceptual paradox of Enlightenment anthropology crystallized in Kantian and post-Kantian critiques of a certain anthropological mode of thinking. The story I tell focuses on the tension between two forms of critique, one empirical and one transcendental. They collide most clearly in a post-Kantian critique (but not necessarily overcoming) of a particular mode of anthropological thinking. Immanuel Kant and those immediately following him made clear the ironies and obstacles facing a science in which the human being is both the object and subject of observation. They reveal the crisis of anthropology as the irreducible tension between the empirical and the transcendental, the natural and the moral.

In recent years, the discourse if not the discipline of anthropology has become a paradigm for studying the eighteenth century, so much so that scholars have spoken of an "anthropological Enlightenment." The common characterization of eighteenth-century anthropology as the devaluation of the soul,[12] however, is indicative of the conceptual limitations of such a paradigm. Until recently most scholarship has limited eighteenth-century anthropology to a medical discourse and its discursive traces in various cultural forms from literature to politics.[13] Whereas a physiologically oriented anthropology might be of primary importance for a broader history of the discipline, I am more interested in the particular mode of thinking that led to the late eighteenth-century declaration of "crisis" in anthropology that preceded any institutional discipline of anthropology. Scholars have only recently begun to consider these tensions in eighteenth-century anthropology between the more physiological-medical anthropology of Ernst Platner and the so-called philosophical physicians, on the one hand, and the emergence of a comparative anthropology characterized by a normative or cultural-philosophical orientation, on the other. As Jörn Garber and Thomas Heinz put it in their innovative collection, the nascent discipline of anthropology moves between the poles of "*physis* and norm."[14] My reading of what we could call a Kantian or romantic anthropology locates the promise of critique at precisely this juncture, in the reciprocation between the empirical observation of what the human being is and the normative claim of what the human being should be. Consequently, in the following chapters I am not, fundamentally at least, interested in the explicit topics of anthropology but in the very form of anthropological questions. I consider how the paradoxes of self-implication inherent in this emergent "science of the human," in which the human being is both the subject and object of inquiry, manifest themselves in a range of questions. The confusions and tensions of an anthropological mode of thinking—the endless reduplication of anthropological inquiry—were not just theoretical paradoxes; they were also ethical problems.

In light of such scholarship, I have four main aims. First, I wish to outline how the shift in anthropology from a medical to a cultural science led to a conceptual crisis and the proliferation of anthropologies. Initially, anthropology was a medical discourse concerned with the relationship of the mind to the body. As the so-called *philosophical physicians*—doctors more interested in the animal nature of the human being than its metaphysical possibilities—became more influential, the material character of psychic and cognitive processes became more accepted. Anthropology was understood as the meeting of physiology and psychology. Toward the end of the century, however, these medical concerns became increasingly bound up with moral and cultural concerns. Questions about the animal nature of the human being became so intertwined with questions about the rational nature of the human being that by 1800 anthropology was wavering between the poles of the material and the normative. In 1795 Wilhelm von Humboldt called for a comparative cultural anthropology that would organize itself around the very conundrum that had come to define anthropology: the tension between the empirical and transcendental. The medical anthropology of the previous decades had become a cultural anthropology that began to recognize its conceptual problems.

Second, I wish to demonstrate that this conceptual shift from a medical to a cultural anthropology can be observed most clearly, and perhaps most surprisingly, in the work of Immanuel Kant. Kant lectured on anthropology for almost thirty years and eventually published *Anthropologie in pragmatischer Hinsicht* (*Anthropology from a Pragmatic Point of View*) in 1798. Kant's idiosyncratic anthropology—idiosyncratic in the sense that it was, from the start, positioned in opposition to more mainstream anthropological inquiry—was concerned not with what nature could make of the human but what the human being could make of itself. And for Kant, the discipline of anthropology was meant to orient and guide the individual toward becoming human. Anthropology was pedagogy for the human race. Kant's radical cultural anthropology confused empirical, scientific, and normative questions. By inserting Kant's anthropology into the larger context of eighteenth-century anthropology, I reread Kant's philosophy, which was until recently often derided as hopelessly formal and abstract, as bound up with anthropological, historical, and pedagogical concerns.

But, more centrally, I locate the conceptual paradox of a modern anthropological mode of thought in what might paradoxically, but appropriately, be termed Kant's promise of a teleological anthropology.

Third, I intend to survey the challenges to Kant's provisional solution to the problem of anthropology by Friedrich Schleiermacher, the father of modern hermeneutics; Friedrich Schlegel, the literary critic; Goethe; Novalis; and Wilhelm von Humboldt, the statesman and founder of the modern research university. I chose these figures for their interest in the recursive character of anthropology—that is, they all examine how the human subject of anthropology is always implied in the object of anthropology. If Kant's pragmatic anthropology posed two questions—what is the human? and what should the human become?—the recursive or reflexive character of the "science of the human" led Novalis to pose a third question: what does the human as a natural being make of the human? The distinctions that Kant and previous anthropologies had made between sciences of the body and sciences of reason are collapsed into a single form of inquiry. With the rise of the life sciences and the subsequent naturalization of the human body during the eighteenth century, the rational human being becomes a natural being as well. At the juncture of a Kantian critical philosophy and the emergent life sciences, romantic anthropology asks how anthropology and modern forms of knowledge can account for these processes of mutual formation that always fold back upon themselves.

Finally, I intend to describe a semantic and ethical shift in the category "human" that took place around 1800. Long before modernism's challenge to the rational self, eighteenth-century anthropology had given the Cartesian cogito a body. This anthropological shift makes possible different ways of thinking about universality and normativity. Claims of what the human *is* are reshaped and reformulated in, for example, the self-reflexive ethnography of Schleiermacher and Humboldt, the reformulation of a hierarchy of the senses by Novalis, and the moral technologies and disciplines of Kant's anthropologically inflected ethics. While the figures in this book do not abandon Enlightenment notions of the human, they place these notions under increasing scrutiny. We must then ask how we might conceive of the human as a norm with both a universal force and an anthropological flexibility. Can normative claims be compelling if they are recursively articulated, reformulated, and revised?

In the first chapter, "Proto-anthropology and the Discovery of Reflexivity," I outline the conceptual framework of eighteenth-century anthropology and how its fragmented and centrifugal character threatened its disciplinary aspirations from the beginning. I show how a crisis was precipitated by the shift from a medical discourse interested in the mind-body relationship to a broader discourse concerned with the diversity of peoples, races, and cultures. By 1800 there was no simple, monolithic discipline of anthropology; instead, there were multiple anthropologies. The only conceptual center was the tension between the empirical and the transcendental, between the reduplication of the subject in the object of study.

In the second chapter, "Cultivating Freedom: Kant's Affective Ethics," I explore Kant's ethics as integral to this anthropological mode of thought and to the articulation of the limits of anthropology. Whereas scholarship has tended to view Kant's moral philosophy as simply metaphysical and hopelessly formal, in this chapter I explore it in a more pragmatic light. Building on recent work in Kant studies that emphasizes an embodied Kantian reason, I argue that Kant's notion of freedom required not metaphysical insight but a hard-won and technically crafted attitude. Freedom is not a metaphysical discovery but a practical disposition that, in the end, needs anthropological insights to guide and cultivate individuals. We see this complex moral education in Kant's elaborate descriptions of the best moral techniques and exercises. He details the proper and most effective methods for training "the young boys" who aspire to moral maturity. Thus, there is not just a metaphysics of morals but a discipline of morality. Critique and enlightenment are not, primarily at least, a set of doctrines or deductions but a particular mode of thought or attitude.

Against this broader backdrop of eighteenth-century anthropology, in chapter 3, "Freedom, Between Nature and Reason: Kant's Pragmatic Anthropology," I argue that Kant's own *Anthropologie* is initially concerned with the possibility and theoretical problems of anthropological inquiry in general. In a move indicative of eighteenth-century anthropology, however, Kant brackets such concerns and transforms anthropology from a theoretical to a practical discipline in an attempt to resolve the tension between the empirical and transcendental. Kant's pragmatic anthropology offers a blueprint of the future not just for the individual but for the entire human race, through its appeal to a seemingly paradoxical anthropological teleology. Its goal is to form a sensible creature into a moral being. Anthropology becomes a science of culture and charts a normative path through which the individual might become human.

In chapter 4, "Testing the Human: Kant and Forster on the Differences of Race and the Possibilities of Culture," I consider how this transformation of anthropology into a historical and pedagogical undertaking was driven by debates on race and human diversity. Race, for a number of figures, was the decisive conceptual issue that moved anthropology from a discussion of the individual body to a discussion of culture and thus to the conceptual architecture of the entire discipline in which the human being as observer is always bound to the human being as observed. For Kant, as well as for the naturalist Georg Forster, the scientist J. F. Blumenbach, and a host of other figures, the debates about race were ultimately concerned with reconciling the universal claims of the human with the diversity of human beings. For Kant and Forster at least, the possibility of a common humanity was basically a problem of narration. How, they ask, can humankind be narrated? How can a common story be found or told amidst the multiplicity of human beings? Anthropology inherits the narrative task of weaving human beings together through an imagined past and future. Kant turns to an aesthetic and reflective act, narration, to reconcile the empirical and transcendental.

In the fifth chapter, "*Poesie* as Anthropology: Schleiermacher, Colonial History, and the Ethics of Ethnography," I not only uncover the anthropological beginnings of modern hermeneutics but locate one of the earliest and most devastating critiques of eighteenth-century anthropology's failure. Schleiermacher wrote a fragmentary ethnography of New South Holland (modern-day Australia) that took aim at the entire tradition of travel writing as it had been practiced up to his day. In his attempt to reconcile Enlightenment universality with the particularity of ethnography, Schleiermacher's early work anticipates the task of his hermeneutic philosophy: relating the particular to the universal, the individual to the human. Schleiermacher the anthropologist and ethnographer precedes Schleiermacher the father of hermeneutics. But the fragmented state of his own project seems to highlight the very impossibility of bringing a romantic anthropology to completion. The human being is an ever-changing form.

The tensions of this anthropological mode of thought are nowhere more evident than in Novalis's rethinking of the senses. In chapter 6, "Lyrical Feeling: Novalis's Anthropology of the Senses," I consider how anthropology transforms the relationship of sensibility and reason into a broader theory of modernity. By redefining sensibility so as to undo oppositions of nature and culture, *physis* and norm, Novalis radicalizes the reflexive structure of anthropology as an ethical response to a perceived fragmentation of the senses and modern humanity in general. In this chapter I focus on Novalis's poetic and philosophical reframing of the basic problem of anthropology. His anthropology of the senses highlights the inherently reflexive conundrum of an anthropological mode of thought in which the cognizing human being is always bound up with the sensing human being.

In the final chapter, "The Body of Language: Goethe, Humboldt, and the 'Lively Gaze,'" I look to Wilhelm von Humboldt's early theoretical reflections on anthropology and his travels to the Basque country of Spain as a radical expansion of Kant's anthropological thinking and a distillation of what I term romantic anthropology. It traces the beginnings of this anthropology from Humboldt and Goethe's collaborative dissection of human corpses in Jena in 1794 to Humboldt's work on a Basque grammar. Over a period of less than a decade Humboldt had traded bodies for words. In this transition we find an attempt to rescue a type of anthropological thinking from its conceptual impossibility. In Humboldt's observations of local dance traditions and linguistic differences in the Basque country, we observe the emergence of a mode of thought driven to relate the particularity of the individual to a more universal category called the human through a fundamentally reflexive mode of thought.

This book is in part a recovery effort. In it I set out to unearth that particular form of Enlightenment critique that Foucault so ambivalently embraced. In it I do not trace the emergence of anthropology as a discipline, nor do I take up Foucault's own critical project. Instead, I locate the ethos of modernity, of which Foucault speaks, in anthropology's early moment of crisis. If, as Foucault argued in *The Order of Things*, Kant lulled modernity into its great anthropological sleep, in *Becoming Human* I counter that our slumber has been restless and fitful from the beginning.

PART ONE

The Historical Problem

I

Proto-anthropology and the Discovery of Reflexivity

The Sources of Anthropology

The eighteenth century witnessed the emergence of an array of sciences, from the life sciences and psychology to various forms of *schöne Wissenschaften*, such as aesthetics, history, and poetics.[1] Gottfried Immanuel Wenzel (1754–1809), a professor of philosophy from Linz, anticipated a science that would integrate them all: "the study of the human" or anthropology. This science of the future was gaining in significance daily, and it would soon be able to focus on that one object that had thus far escaped all sciences, the human being.[2] This new object of science, however, would require radically different kinds of knowledge, because "nothing is closer to the human being than he himself": "No knowledge is more interesting and more important than the knowledge of our nature, but no other knowledge poses more problems that must be overcome. The observer and the object of the observation are one thing; the human being is judge and party at the same time."[3]

From its conceptual beginnings, the science of anthropology was defined by the question of observation, and this doubling of the human being as subject and object of observation entailed significant difficulties as well as advantages. On the one hand, the reduplication elides the distance between subject and object of observation assumed central to modern, Baconian science. The problem of anthropology was from its beginning a problem of observation. The various topics often associated with anthropology—the mind-body problem, the rehabilitation of sensibility, ethnography and comparison—are undergirded by questions of observation, of how the human being can be viewed from different perspectives. It is not the case that the human being exists somewhere between mind and body, for example, but rather that the human being can be observed from multiple perspectives. This is the problem of self-reflexivity. But on the other hand, anthropology offers a reference point, the human being, from which to unify a variety of sciences that lacked uniform or even complementary methods of organizing knowledge. To pose the question "What is the human being?" is to cast all forms of inquiry back toward a figure of knowledge, the human being, that must increasingly be observed as subject to both physical and metaphysical demands. This second aspect takes reflexivity, which from a modern, Baconian perspective is a threat, and reconceives it as an advantage. If a Baconian modernity leads to what we might today call disciplinary specialization and fragmentation, then a "science of the human being" promises a way of unifying increasingly distinct ways of knowing. By 1800 Wenzel, as well as innumerable other German scientists and observers of all stripes, from biologists and doctors to philosophers and poets, had come to call this nascent science of the human being anthropology.

It should be noted that in eighteenth-century Germany there was no singular, monolithic discipline known as anthropology.[4] In what he calls his "attempt" to write an anthropology, Johann Ith warns that a science of the human being "is still so new and even still emerging! . . . We are just now beginning to collect and form its dispersed fragments into a scientific system. There is still no consensus about the actual concept of this science, its domain, its elements, its methods."[5] The temporal character of late eighteenth-century anthropology, if we can speak of such a thing, was at best ambiguous. Its defenders and detractors alike referred to it as a science of the future. More recently, scholars have referred to its "lack of potential as an academic discipline"[6] or an organizing concept. It was always a science in the making. For this reason I will refer to the earliest forms of this science of the human being as "proto-anthropology,"[7] to avoid confusing it with the discipline of anthropology that took institutional shape in the early twentieth century and to avoid implying that the anthropological mode of thought extant in eighteenth-century Germany was a fully articulated distinct discipline.

Throughout the eighteenth century proto-anthropology came to be aligned with a particular form of philosophy.[8] Georg Gustav Fülleborn, for example, framed it as a practical philosophy:

> Through the combined efforts of systematic thinkers and empirical observers practical philosophy achieved daily more content and

form. . . . Anthropology was treated in all parts and relationships and in all manners. Everywhere one demanded that philosophy be conducted for life: the attention to natural history, philosophy of history, history of humanity, aesthetics and pedagogy was part fruit, part impetus of a practical spirit in philosophy that became ever more universal, and emboldened the philosopher to search everywhere for new objects of inquiry with which one could enrich their science and make it useful for life.[9]

Proto-anthropology integrated various sources and forms of knowledge in order to produce a more *practical* knowledge, a knowledge "for life." By linking the study of the human being to "life," proto-anthropology bracketed the extreme forms of Cartesian dualism that undergirded *pure* theoretical inquiry and disjoined knowledge from the world of practical being. Similarly, the figures discussed in the following chapters bracket such dualisms in one way or another for their own practical reasons. For Fülleborn, an anthropological mode of inquiry implied less a particular method than a particular attitude toward scientific inquiry, namely, that the scientific work of various fields could be integrated around a more practical interest in the human being. Above all, it projected itself as a possible science whose knowledge would be both of and for the human being. And its correlative claim is that the scientific observer is always bound to the object being observed. Emerging out of the confluence of seemingly incongruent modes of inquiry—from medicine, chemistry, and biology to literature, history, and philosophy—proto-anthropology was less a clearly defined discipline during this period, and more a developing web of methods and techniques for knowing and being in the world.[10] Each of these, individually and collectively, were concerned with establishing modes of observation that could link various extant sciences.

Proto-anthropology connected its imperative to conduct all scientific inquiry "for life" to another equally significant imperative of this anthropological mode of thought: to bracket metaphysical problems. This "temporary" and provisional bracketing gesture reinforced the future-oriented character of proto-anthropology, which in turn allowed a more fully articulated anthropology to emerge between the poles of the physical and the metaphysical. Its double character—its concern with the mind and the body—derived both from its orientation between these poles and its bracketing of questions about the ontological basis of the mind-body relationship. Proto-anthropology offered a unified alternative to the separate inquiries of metaphysics or theology (with their attention to formal and final causality) and natural or physical science (with their focus upon efficient and material causes). Its bracketing gesture, however, necessitated the deferral of its disciplinary status to some indefinite future in which a solution to the mind-body problem might be possible, a future in which the human being might be whole. In this sense, proto-anthropology was more akin to a task than a distinct discipline.

Proto-anthropology's temporal ambiguity—it was a science that was always becoming—is tied not only to the status of a possible discipline but to the increasing uncertainty regarding its object of study, the human being. If, as Friedrich Schlegel writes, "we don't know what the human is," what then grounds modernity's distinctions of human and animal, nature and culture, reason and body, European and non-European? From what perspective could anthropology even deploy the category "human" given the problem of reduplication? How can the category of the human be normatively compelling without being subordinated to antecedent norms—that is, what type of normativity, what conception of "the human" emerges from this proto-anthropology? The absence of a distinct eighteenth-century discipline of anthropology marks, therefore, a more fundamental concern with the tension between normativity and observation.

In this chapter I outline how a particular mode of anthropological thought—what I call proto-anthropology—can helpfully frame a range of theoretical problems that have come to characterize a late Enlightenment, European modernity, above all, problems of ethical belonging and freedom. Many contemporary narratives argue that modernity crystallizes around a subject-object relationship in which the observing subject is, depending on the narrator, either freed or condemned to observe itself observing. My contention is that if *anthropology* names anything, it names the problem of modernity: the doubling of the human being as *both* the subject who observes and object being observed.

The reduplication of subject and object epitomizes not just a particularly modern discipline, anthropology, but a modernity that since its self-proclaimed inception has been obsessed with its own operations. The self-reflexive structures of anthropology can be seen as the self-reflective ironies of modernity. Modernity's insistent self-reflexivity, however, only highlights the proliferation of perspectives and the multiplication of different ways of knowing and relating to the world. Despite more pessimistic accounts of Enlightenment modernity, such as Max Horkheimer and Theodor Adorno's *Dialectic of Enlightenment*, these epistemological crises also make possible different forms of knowledge. The primacy of proto-anthropology, for example, coincided with a rehabilitation of sensibility and a resignification of the human body.[11] The increasingly reflexive character of reason returns the human being not just to his or her own rational activity but to his or her body as well. To study the human being, to engage in a science of the human, was, as the mantra of eighteenth-century proto-anthropology went, to study the "whole of the human being."[12] It is in relation to this purpose that the difficulties multiply. To study the whole of the human being is to treat both the physical and the metaphysical simultaneously. It is to study an object about which the subject can never be objective. Or again, it is to study an object to which the subject's access is both mediated and unmediated—the object the subject studies is the subject him- or herself. Thus, anthropology figures another typically modern epistemological problem: the relationship between reason and the senses and the possibility of embodied ways of being and thinking. This particularly anthropological mode of thought gains increasing force amid the lamentations that individual human beings had become estranged from themselves, others, and nature. As we will see in the chapters to come, this inherent reflexivity also encouraged critical reflections on a European ethnographic gaze, reflections that gradually began to cast that same gaze back on the European reader and writer of ethnographies.

In order to understand how and why proto-anthropology increasingly coincided with philosophy, we first need to consider how it "burst loose from eighteenth-century European philosophy."[13] The expansion of proto-anthropology in the most literal of senses—that is, the appearance of the very word "anthropology" in book titles and essays—accelerated only in the latter part of the century and experienced a rapid growth in the century's final decade.[14] In this first chapter, I focus on texts that took the delineation of anthropology as a primary task and thus are among the first to include "anthropology" in their titles. My primary purpose is not to provide a detailed analysis of the various problems themselves around which anthropology as a science coalesced and eventually emerged as a distinct discipline; instead, I focus on how proto-anthropology was organized around the conceptual problems resulting from the doubling of the human being as the subject and object of observation.

Observation, Analogy, and Language in Proto-Anthropology

In his now eponymous lexicon of 1732, Johann Heinrich Zedler defined anthropology as the "special part of physics in which the natural condition and state of man, especially with regard to his physical and natural characteristics, are treated and explained." At this early date, anthropology concerned the physical nature of the human being. It was a physical anthropology. But, he continues, "in addition it is also to be noted that if one wants to use the word 'anthropology,' the doctrine of the moral condition of man and thus the teaching of reason is to be added to the first as well."[15] This remark forecasts tensions that later came to define proto-anthropology as a science of the human being as both a physical *and* a moral being. As Zedler's lexicon indicates, anthropology in the early eighteenth century referred primarily to the study of the human being's physical nature and only secondarily to the study of the human being as a moral or reasonable entity. In the early eighteenth century, "anthropology" simply assumed that the human being was divided between the sensible and the intelligible.

Throughout the seventeenth century, there had been debates on "anthropological" themes—concerning the biological origins of the human being, the relationship between the human being and animal, and the categorizing potential of race. By the mid-eighteenth century, however, these themes were taken up from a different perspective. The prior assumption that the human being was divided meant that to study the human being was to do so from two distinct perspectives or two sciences: metaphysics and natural science. Before the middle of the eighteenth century the human being "had no right to his own discipline, in which the various examinations of him could be unified and homogenously connected on the basis of a new definition of his ontological status and a new formulation of his relationship to other natural beings."[16] Proto-anthropology began to make the case for such a unified science.

The emergence of proto-anthropology, then, was bound up with a professed intention to observe and study the "whole human being," as both a product of nature and a product of reason. In this sense, proto-anthropology was less an attempt to unify the human being itself than it was an attempt to unify various modes of inquiries and knowledge about the human being. Only then, from a perspective of epistemic unity, might the scientist of the *anthropos* be able to observe the "whole human being."

Phillip Sloan argues that etymological inquiries into the use of the term "anthropology" in scientific contexts have "established with decisiveness" that its original use in the early modern period was within medical and, more specifically, anatomical contexts.[17] Whereas this may be true of French anthropology and even of early German anthropology, German anthropology quickly and increasingly came to refract explicitly moral concerns through its scientific analyses.[18] Proto-anthropology gradually emerged at the juncture of these methods of inquiry. Its story is one of eclecticism and profound disciplinary rearrangement. It gathers up the various means of organizing knowledge that had been the province of sundry sciences.

Broadly speaking, proto-anthropology was a "double turning-away"[19] from the rational academic metaphysics (*Schulmetaphysik*)[20] of Christian Wolff (1679–1754), on the one hand, and from a mathematically based natural science, on the other. The devaluation of Wolffian metaphysics was a function of an increasing suspicion of its underlying image of the human being as divided between a sensible nature and an intelligible one. Christian Wolff's systematic metaphysics epitomized the faculty psychology of an academic metaphysics that sought to make philosophy a rigorous science predicated upon a self-contained system derived from logical principles.[21] In his *German Metaphysics,* Wolff took mathematics as his model for logic and systematized Leibniz's metaphysics in order to transform philosophy into the foundational, theoretical discipline that would provide all other sciences with "clear concepts, sure principles, and exact methods."[22] With its deductive and demonstrative character, Wolffian metaphysics came to symbolize a form of philosophy that divided the human being into a sensible self and an intelligible one, which through reason could overcome the sensible self and ascend to metaphysical—that is, intellectual—purity.[23]

Proto-anthropology also coincided with a transition in the natural sciences away from an evaluation of nature based on deductive principles and aprioristic mechanisms toward an observation-based science of life.[24] It was an "epistemological liberation" from a seventeenth-century science grounded in physics and mathematics that "privileged categories and procedures of an abstract, systematizing, deductive, and nomological type."[25] In Germany, this epistemological shift can be traced in the reception of John Locke and, especially, his rejection of innate ideas.[26] In *An Essay Concerning Human Understanding* (1689) Locke writes:

> It is an established opinion amongst some men, that there are in the understanding certain *innate principles,* some primary notions . . . as it were stamped upon the mind of man, which the soul receives in its very first being and brings with it into the world. It would be sufficient to convince unprejudiced readers of the falseness of this supposition, if I should show (as I hope to do in the following parts of this discourse) how men, barely by the use of their natural faculties, may attain to all the knowledge they have, without help of any innate impressions.[27]

Locke's rejection of innate impressions found a welcome, if mediated, reception in Germany. These early forms of anthropology often concerned psychological matters addressed from a physiological approach.[28] The German psychologist Michael Hissmann argued that the history of new forms of perception began at that point in time "when the teaching of innate impressions began to become suspect."[29] The emergence of these alternate modes of perception, which we will consider in greater detail later, indicate a general pluralization of mental categories, a predilection for inductive over deductive analysis, and above all a commitment to sense-based observation.

Ernst Platner (1744–1818), a professor of medicine in Göttingen, who produced perhaps the most famous of eighteenth-century German texts on proto-anthropology, wrote, "All ideas originate through sensible impression. The soul has in it neither innate impressions nor thoughts. It acquires all of this through experience. . . . The origin of all ideas is then sensible experience."[30] Although the so-called German Locke,[31] Johann Nicolaus Tetens (1736–1807), argued that the proper method for studying nature is the "observational method" advanced by Locke and others, he also warned about the limitations of such a method. He doubted that it was possible to universalize particular statements of experience.[32] In order to move from the particularity of experience to more universal claims, the "observational method" relies on the scientist to compare particulars and then extrapolate from them through analogy. Truth, then, is not absolute correspondence between a proposition and a state of the world; it is analogy.

In order to gain knowledge of the world, the scientist compares sensations (*Empfindungen*) and sensual data through analogy, which then affords not certainty but probability and approximation. Analogy negotiates the relationship between the multiplicity of data collected through sense observation, on the one hand, and abstract systemization, on the other. Because the scientist deals with a multiplicity of individual and discontinuous data, he must embrace the knowledge of analogical reasoning that can only be "probable"—that is, it is more than hypothetical because it is based on the comparison of sense data, but it is less than certain because it deals with individual data.[33] The German romantic poet and philosopher Friedrich von Hardenberg (Novalis), for example, develops this "analogization" as an alternative to what he saw as the failures of the classificatory schemas of natural science.[34] Novalis grounds relationships, be they between the human being and nature, subject and object, or body and mind, not in logical categories but in analogies. Natural science does not accord to analogical relationships the same epistemological certainty it accords to logically determined relationships. Because of its epistemological uncertainty, analogy was criticized by, among others, Kant and Hegel as a poor source of knowledge.[35] For Novalis, however, analogy is a "tool" that generates new forms of organization and relationality.[36] Modeled on mathematics, Novalis's analogization draws on mathematical notions of analogy and proportion according to which analogy marks not the similarity of certain characteristics but the correspondence in relationships of two systems.[37] Thus in the series 10–6–2, the numbers are analogous because of the similarity of differences. Similarly, the two ratios 8:4 and 4:2 are analogous because of a similarity in proportions. It is not the characteristics of the terms themselves that relate the two series, but the analogous relationships between the terms.

Proto-anthropology likewise framed its rejection of academic metaphysics as an attempt to be a more practical and popular science.[38] Wenzel described proto-anthropology as the "basis for wisdom" in the sense of a wisdom that a broad public could comprehend and apply.[39] The texts of late eighteenth-century anthropology were peppered with "anthropological" examples, which, argues Kant, make the more systematic elements of anthropology accessible to all readers.[40] The exemplary impulse of anthropology is evident in the myriad examples of sickness or accident that showcase extreme or abnormal behaviors. Michael Wagner's 1794 *Beyträge zur philosophischen Anthropologie* (Contributions to Philosophical Anthropology) included sections that he refers to as "Anthropological Facts" that were summaries of "real life" stories ranging from instances of melancholy and blindness to superstition and intoxication. The inclusion of such stories and examples was thought not only to appeal to a broader reading public but also to highlight the modifications in the body that, according to Wagner, "expressed changes in the mind."[41] Such limited cases were thought to highlight analogous aspects of mind and body, though not to explain the interrelated functions.

Platner's decision to publish his book in German rather than Latin gives another indication of how anthropology's popularity and practicality were conceived: "Because my work [represents] a system of human nature . . . which we experience daily in ourselves and in others, and because all of these conditions have their own terms in our own language, in which one immediately recognizes and in that moment also experiences himself: how should I be able to transform these experiences through Latin words into the experiences and sensations of a German reader (and that is my primary intention) without having to add German words everywhere . . . and without also having to translate half of the book."[42]

For Platner, the answer to the question "What is the human?" emerges in the dispersed, daily exchanges of language. Unlike the atemporal attempts of metaphysics to address the human being as a disembodied being, anthropology, according to Platner at least, studies an object that emerges within particular moments of experience and through the very utterances of language. Anthropological knowledge emerges within time because we, as both the subject and object of this science, always appear to ourselves within time. Similarly, Gustav Fülleborn's claim that anthropology is a "philosophy of life" suggests that it is a philosophy of temporal, lived truths. However, if the truths of anthropology are temporal truths, truths that emerge in time, how can the human, as a collective entity, be evoked? To what kind of universality can anthropology lay claim?

Whereas proto-anthropology can be broadly characterized as a "turning-away" from academic metaphysics and a mathematically based natural science and even by its "popularity," it increasingly became defined by the question of observation. In the remaining sections of this chapter, I trace how three topics of this early discourse on anthropology were fundamentally questions about perspective, about the doubling of the human being as both the subject and object of observation. We will address in turn: first the challenge to the mind-body dualism, then the rehabilitation of sensibility, and finally the comparative analysis of human beings.

Recasting the Mind-Body Problem as a Problem of Observation

Proto-anthropology defined itself in large part as a response to the Cartesian mind-body problem—that is, the question of how two independent systems could communicate or interact with each other. Descartes had divided the world into two kinds of stuff: "mental substance whose essence is thought and material substance whose essence is extension."[43] Descartes argued that these two domains were causally related. Bodily states could affect ideas, and volitions could affect bodily states. What became the so-called Cartesian problem, however, concerned exactly *how* these two domains related to each other. Given the clear distinction that Descartes drew between the two, it was not clear how objects interacted. In the debates around the mind-body problem in the eighteenth century, proto-anthropology developed some fundamental philosophical questions: Is one substance more active than the other? Is one more passive than the other? Is there a common medium that might relate the two?

Eighteenth-century philosophy offered basically three solutions to the so-called Cartesian problem.[44] Occasionalists argued that both mind and body were passive and thoroughly independent, that is, they had no power to change the other's state, but that God *occasionally* intervened to coordinate ideas and bodily motions (e.g., Nicolas Malebranche's intelligible extension). Harmonists argued that God had programmed an original harmony between both substances at the moment of creation (e.g., Leibniz's preestablished harmony). According to the model of physical influx (*influxus physicus*), substances immediately affected one another. Another solution, psycho-physical parallelism, would become influential toward the end of the century. According to this solution, which drew on Spinoza's parallelism, the question of how the two realms interacted or communicated was no problem, because mind and body were simply two attributes of a more fundamental divine substance.

In his 1772 *Anthropologie für Aerzte und Weltweise* (Anthropology for Doctors and Wise Men), Ernst Platner expressed his dissatisfaction with all of these solutions and offered anthropology as a mediating model. In so doing, he managed to specify proto-anthropology's object of inquiry. Rejecting previous delimitations of anthropology to physiological concerns, he argued that anthropology should consider the human being as both a physical and a moral being. Whereas anatomy and physiology considered the human being as a machine and subsequently ignored the effect of the soul on the body, psychology (including its related sciences—logic, aesthetics, and moral philosophy) investigated the forces and character of the mind or soul as independent from the body. Anthropology, in contrast to these disciplines, would study the body and the soul in their reciprocal relationships: "Everything depends on how one defines philosophy. I think philosophy is nothing other than the science of the human being. . . . According to this concept medicine would obviously be a part of philosophy. The human being is neither body nor soul alone; he is the harmony of both."[45] Platner's *Anthropologie* was regarded in Germany throughout the eighteenth century as the "real anthropology" or "anthropology of the human being in general" because it was one of the first texts to outline a possible anthropological method.[46] The attempted erasure of the boundaries between substances is reproduced here as a blurring of scientific and epistemological boundaries. By equating anthropology with philosophy, Platner attempted to align medical questions with what were thought to be philosophical questions. Whereas Platner did offer a model for a possible resolution to the mind-body problem, his more lasting contribution was a model for epistemic consolidation, a model that encouraged doctors to think like philosophers and philosophers to think like doctors. Already in its earliest form, anthropology began to reunite what certain strands of the Enlightenment had sought to divide. Platner's anthropology rejoined mind and body as a single object of scientific investigation.

Platner's merging of mind and body and of anthropology and philosophy in medicine is predicated upon a detailed model for the interaction of substances according to which the origin of all ideas is "sensible impression." In almost mechanical terms, Platner explains how external movements cause outward impressions in sense organs that are eventually transmitted to the brain. As these outer impressions are transmitted from particular sense organs (like the eye or a finger) through nerves and their "nerve fluid" (*Nervensaft*), they eventually become internal impressions that are the basis of mental sensations or ideas.[47] Platner imbued Hume's primary and secondary impressions, which for Hume are purely psychological, with a physiological basis.[48]

Despite Platner's materialist tendencies (which he addresses more fully in an updated version of his *Anthropologie* of 1790), his model left a gap between the fundamentally mechanical character of the inner impressions and the process of cognition that turned these mere impressions into ideas.[49] He never specified the exact mechanisms or points of contact between body and mind.[50] His anthropology was marked by skepticism in two respects. One, because he claimed that all perception was caused by physiological processes in the nerves, human beings never perceived objects themselves. Internal impressions were images that "might" be related to the external objects that caused the initial movement (66). "That which thinks" is not a part of the human body (15). Two, he bracketed questions concerning the ontological grounds—or as he puts it, "what really is in fact the case"—of the mind-body relation and wrote only of the "possibility" of a real association (94). Marked by this twofold skepticism, his model could not become a "stable doctrinal edifice" for explaining the mind-body relationship (xiv). Realizing its limitations, he regarded it as only a "trial piece" for a discipline that did not even exist at the time. Such comments indicate just how tentative the appraisals of proto-anthropology were.

More than a decade after Platner's *Anthropologie* was published, Johann Karl Wezel reiterated Platner's definition of anthropology:

> Our examinations have achieved much through the fact that man has been cut into two large halves, the body has been left to the anatomist and physiologist, and the mind to the philosopher . . . but it seems to have been forgotten that both parts are of a whole and thus must stand in the most exact connection with each other. The philosopher lost himself so much in abstractions that he raised the immateriality of the soul to a point that he did away with the possibility of a physical relationship between it and the body. On the other side, the physiologist went so far with the conclusions that he drew from anatomical, chemical, and physical discoveries . . .

> beyond their limits, that he made a mental being almost unnecessary.... He considered the philosopher a foreigner and not as his coworker whom he should help and who should help him.... The physiologist complained about the ignorance of the philosopher of the bodily nature of man and called him an abstract dreamer.... The human being was torn into ... two halves.... To reconnect the band between the two separated parts of man was the purpose of a science that one called anthropology.[51]

The scientific interest in explaining the mind-body relationship was the consequence, not the source, of a more fundamental investigation into the relationships between and among various sciences. In this sense, Wezel's proto-anthropology was not a detailed explanation of the mind-body relationship but rather a descriptive matrix of possible connections that might become apparent through different methods of observation. Body and mind interacted not through so-called nerve fluids (*Nervensäfte*) or any number of other material mediums but through natural sympathies between nerves and organs. The mind-body relationship was organized around natural relationships between cognitive and bodily reactions, habituated effects and reactions. Wezel did not speculate on how exactly these interactions were possible. He simply observed that they do occur and insisted that the complex interactions could only be observed by plural methods of observation.

Proto-anthropology became a possible science, a unique field of inquiry, at the point when the reciprocity of the body and mind was seen not as an act of transcendence but as matter of finitude. To explain exactly how the mind and body interacted or to reveal the precise mechanisms or materials of their interaction was not its goal; the unity, however it might manifest itself, was a general assumption. It was a working hypothesis that conditioned the human being in the present. It served as a presupposition from which scientific inquiry could begin. Proto-anthropology did not claim to have solved the problem of what for so long had been understood as the human being's "double personality."[52] It consistently reaffirmed that it was "of all the wonders of the creation the most inexplicable."[53] Framed by its hopeful yet hesitant claims, proto-anthropology was oriented toward a future discipline that might one day elucidate not only the mind-body relationship but also the relationship of different modes of knowledge and different types of observation.

The bracketing of metaphysical questions regarding the mind-body relationship was nowhere more evident than in the work of the so-called philosophical physicians, many of whom pre-dated both Platner and Wezel. The work of the French *médecins-philosophes*—Maupertuis, Helvétius, Bordeu, and other figures of the Montpellier School of Medicine—was received and expanded upon in Germany by Albrecht von Haller.[54] He initiated a debate on stimulation (*Reitz*) and vital forces, and, in his 1752 lectures, offered an influential definition of sensibility that would be reformulated and revised throughout the century. He identified sensibility and irritability as the two primary forces of organisms. He argued that sensibility was a nervous phenomenon associated with the mind and soul and that irritability, in contrast, was a disposition to movement inherent to bodily fibers and muscles. The pathbreaking claim was Haller's insistence that irritability as a bodily phenomenon was independent of the mind or soul. This independence directly challenged dominant physiological models that subordinated the body to the mind. Haller's distinction also pointed to a differentiation within the organism itself. The work of the French medical philosophers and Haller found reception among German physicians like Michael Hissmann (1752–1784); the doctor and publisher Adam Weikard (1742–1799); the Hannover doctor and author of popular medical texts Johann Georg Zimmermann (1728–1795); and Friedrich Zückert (1737–1778).[55]

For Hissmann, any successful approach to the mind-body problem would involve a rethinking of philosophy itself: "The entire speculative philosophy becomes more instructive, productive and more perfect the more . . . earthly one thinks of man and the more materialistically one thinks of the soul. . . . The Germans were unfortunately the last [to adopt this way of thinking]. Condillac, Bonnet, Search, Helvétius, and other Englishman and Frenchmen had long ago come around. . . . Now one collects facts, one respects facts. . . . If one has facts, one has explanations."[56] Philosophy needed to be brought down to earth. Whereas Hissmann's materialism cannot be denied, it is more productively understood as an explicit rejection of what he considered the "dogmatic" assumptions of Wolffian academic metaphysics—that is, the sharp distinction between metaphysical and empirical modes of inquiry. Instead of getting caught up in proving exactly how the body and mind were related, Hissmann and these other philosophical physicians assumed an as yet unspecified relationship and sought to treat patients therapeutically in terms of an assumed unity. They took the animal nature of the human being seriously and considered any medical treatment of the human being to require attention to its material body and its complex relationship to its mind or soul.

Their therapeutic treatment of the human being involved not only the bracketing of the metaphysical problems of the mind-body relationship but an insistence that medical and philosophical modes of observation overlapped. As Zimmermann put it: "Moral and medical observations require the same spirit of observation. Whoever is capable of observing the moral human being well is capable of observing his illnesses well. . . . A true physician determines the illnesses of the body through the immediately and correctly observed signs, just as a true moralist [discerns] the dispositions of minds."[57] Philosophical physicians assumed that the empirical methods of Haller and Charles Bonnet could support both medical and moral modes of observation. Their periodicals announced their clear intention to consolidate medicine and philosophy into anthropology. *Der Arzt*, edited by Johann August Unzer, and *Der philosophische Arzt*, edited by Adam Weikard and published from 1773 to 1775, emphasized the practical treatment of the body and the soul. The "art of philosophical medicine," wrote Weikard, concerned itself with the "forces and infirmities of the understanding and the mind in order to research, to guide and through physical and moral aids to maintain them in a proper relationship."[58] Philosophical doctors studied the economy of the life forces that were thought to underlie both the mind and the body.

It would be a mistake to limit the work of these philosophical physicians to a so-called medical discourse. These philosophical physicians increasingly blurred the distinction between substances and faculties that Wolffian metaphysics had always assumed, and in that sense they bracketed the problems of Wolffian metaphysics. That bracketing was one of the presuppositions for the emergence of proto-anthropology as an independent discipline. As Wolfgang Riedel notes, by the last third of the eighteenth century, any discussion of the soul—that which Wolff had defined as an immaterial, incorruptible substance—would have to mention bodies, brains, and nerves.[59] Once this body became more than mere matter, the human being, or the potential of the human being, could become more than reason.

In this sense, Platner exemplified the approach and concerns of proto-anthropology and the philosophical doctors. His emphasis on *influx physicus,* the immediate relationship of body and mind, emphasized what he insisted was the nonmetaphysical character of this relationship in contrast to previous attempts to solve the mind-body problem. The practical assumption of a mind-body relationship effectively bracketed the metaphysical problem that had threatened to derail a more material anthropological mode of inquiry before it even began. That bracketing maneuver was simply another manifestation of the more fundamental form of proto-anthropology. That is, it turned what had been a fundamentally metaphysical question—how the two realms of mind and body interacted—into a question about observation. It deferred the metaphysical questions by embracing the figure of the human being—as both object and subject of observation—as a unifying reference point for all sorts of broader scientific questions. The mind-body problem had migrated and become instead a problem of observation. The apparent dualism of mind and body increasingly became a problem of perspective.

In 1794 Johann Ith, a philosopher in Bern, summarized the turn that proto-anthropology had taken: "When I say that anthropology is a new science, I am not unaware that the name is old. But before, anthropology was simply understood to be nothing more than the physiology of man [Ith cites Wolff as the main example of this definition]; later one began to understand this term as a science that lay in the middle between physiology and psychology."[60] Even in this mediating state, there was no perspective from which to observe the newly assumed unity. For Ith, proto-anthropology was a middle science that was not interested in speculative solutions to the mind-body problem but with articulating and relating new forms of observation. Proto-anthropology organized the newly emerging sciences and modes of inquiry. It aimed for a new kind of scientist or, as Platner put it, "the perfect doctor" in whom three methods of observation would be united: the analytical observation of the natural scientist, the speculative observation of the philosopher, and the practical observation of the physician.[61]

Observation and the Rehabilitation of Sensibility

The issue of observation also came to define what was later referred to as the rehabilitation of sensibility in the eighteenth century. The valuation of sensibility as more than the subordinate, passive faculty of Wolffian-scholastic metaphysics, however, was less a claim about the biological makeup of the human being than an increasingly common mode of thought.[62] While Wolff did claim that all faculties were merely different manifestations of a more fundamental force, he maintained a clear and distinct hierarchy. Cognition and volition were the fundamental faculties to which sensation was subordinate. In exemplary fashion, Johann Gottfried Krüger countered this claim: "If human beings had no senses, they would have no imagination. If they had no imagination, they would have no *Witz* or memory; if they had no *Witz* or memory, they would not have reason. They would, thus, have no reason if they did not have senses."[63] Proto-anthropology's arguments for a higher valuation of sensibility should be understood, then, not as an argument for sensation over reason but for their mutual relationship.[64]

We can observe this transition toward a higher valuation of sensibility in the gradual displacement of mind-body dualism by the perhaps less dualistic physical-moral pair. As a metaphysical resolution of the mind-body problem became less of a concern, the practical unity of mind and body became a functional assumption and the dualism of their substances became a functional pair. Still, the human being as an assumed unity of substances had both physical and moral functions that needed to be maintained through an economy of forces. This transition is marked semantically on a number of levels. First, proto-anthropology spoke less of a mind-body dualism than of an outside-inside pair. The human being was characterized not by a "double personality" but by complementary functions that converged in the body itself. Second, as we have already noted, proto-anthropology's discussion of the "whole of the human being" came to connote the unified organization of all human faculties. The human being began to signify the complex organization of various potentials, faculties, and abilities.

In his *Populäre Anthropologie, oder Kunde von dem Menschen nach seinen sinnlichen und geistigen Anlagen,* Carl Heinrich Ludwig Pölitz (1772–1838) wrote that human beings "stand in an immeasurable reciprocal relationship with the physical and moral world, and it is through the medium of the perceptible body, which is receptive, that [this relationship] is visible for all."[65] Here the body becomes the organizational center for the human being's interaction with nature and reason. No longer is it merely that which tethers the human being to the mechanical causality of nature. The practical assumption of the unity of the mind and body allowed the body to become the locus of perception and cognition, because, it was thought, the traces of the mind-body's interaction would be perceptible. It is important to note that this higher valuation of the body and sensation as a faculty is not a rejection of reason; it is rather a reminder that the human being possesses additional faculties besides reason. The claim is that sensibility is not a lesser faculty but itself plays a central and productive (not merely passive) role in cognition.

The Wolffian-scholastic subordination of the faculty of sensation to those of cognition and volition had meant not only the relegation of the body to mere matter but also the relegation of the mind to an otherworldly realm of metaphysics, where it was inaccessible to empirical inquiry. Wolff had divided psychology into a *psychologia rationalis* and a *psychologia empirica*. The first regarded the soul as an immaterial substance about which it could only deduce rational concepts. The second regarded the soul as matter and thus, according to the hierarchy of faculties, could only verify the concepts of its metaphysical counterpart through empirical observation.[66] By challenging this Wolffian hierarchy of the faculties, proto-anthropology's rehabilitation of sensibility meant that both physical and mental functions could become objects of inquiry. From 1750 onward, empirical psychology displaced rational psychology as the dominant mode of inquiry.[67] Not just the irritability of Haller, a strictly physiological phenomenon, but so-called obscure ideas (*dunkle Begriffe*)[68]—by which Johann Georg Sulzer, a philosopher-psychologist writing in the 1750s and 1760s, had meant dreams, desires, or prejudices—became objects of inquiry.[69] Proto-anthropology included studies of mental infirmities, mental illnesses, and a range of emotions from feelings of the self to moral feelings. If the mind and body were assumed, however inexplicably, to be related, then mental processes might manifest themselves in the body or be perceptible to the senses, that point of convergence of the human being's faculties. The obscure abilities of the mind once relegated to the nonobservable realm of metaphysics emerge within a perceivable body.

As these somatic traces of the mind-body interaction became observable, the entire semantic field of "sensibility" and "sensation" expanded. A range of terms came to signify this nebulous field: *Empfindung, Empfindungen, Sensationen, Gefühle, Sinne,* and *Sinnlichkeit*. Whatever their particular denotations—each was always highly contextualized—they all came to signify, in the most general terms, how a distinct type of knowledge was produced through the interaction of mind and body. They came to mark the increasingly blurred line between mind and body, inside and outside. In his *Allgemeine Theorie der schönen Künste* (1799), Sulzer notes how the term "sensible" had expanded from signifying that which we sense through the external senses of the body to include that which we sense through the inner senses, like love or fear.[70] For Sulzer, sensation named a form of knowledge that was distinct from cognition: "During contemplation nothing happens in the body that an idea of our own could awake; everything there [in the body] is completely quiet and calm. In contrast the state of sensation is always related to some sensible sensation. . . . Noticeable changes in the circulation of the blood and in the nerves of the bowels occur, if the soul has even a relatively strong sensation. By contemplation, in contrast, only a few nerves seem to be shaken."[71]

"Sensible" signified an immediate correspondence between a perceived (external) object and a change in ourselves as opposed to cognition, through which we perceive or become conscious of objects through concepts. Similarly, Herder and Ith defined sensibility as "the link" between mind and body, a link, however, that was proper to neither.[72] Whatever the particular terms and models, sensibility in all its semantic expansiveness came to signify the complex interaction of internal and external, mind and body. It came to connote mediation, and proto-anthropology was increasingly fashioned as that future science which would be able to account for all these as yet not fully understood interactions. For Ith, anthropology would be the study of "reason modified through sensibility."[73]

Sensibility, then, was not a monolithic term. It simply registered broader mediating functions of a range of different sensations or forms of sensibility. Michael Wagner was one of the first to specify the broader internal-external dichotomy through a distinction between inner and outer senses.[74] The outer senses registered how the human being is affected from the outside, while the inner sense registered how the human being is affected from the inside, or as he puts it, from "empirical self-consciousness."[75] He tied the outer senses to the five senses and the inner sense to one's own thoughts and emotions, or, more generally, the mind.

Proto-anthropology, however, understood these two systems of senses as two sides of the same system. It attempted to synthesize perspectives on the mind-body relationship that are reduplicated in terms of perception. The human being emerges as the point of convergence. Once the mind and body are assumed to stand in some reciprocal relationship, an alternate mode of perception becomes possible, one that integrates perceptions of external stimuli with perceptions of internal stimuli or one's own "mental play." The very functioning of the mind becomes an object of perception analogous to external objects.[76] The distinctions and semantics of outside and inside are obscured.

Proto-anthropology purposely confused the dichotomies that had come to distinguish a post-Cartesian modernity: mind and body, inner and outer. Increasingly, however, figures like Wagner and Herder came to view the articulated models of sensibility as limited. Despite his earlier attempts in his *Aesthetica* (1750/58) to establish aesthetics as a philosophical discipline or science devoted to "sensible knowledge," Alexander Gottlieb Baumgarten, for example, still relied on metaphysics—his theory of sensibility was organized around a priori deductions and speculation. A more robust philosophy of sensibility, insisted Herder, must once and for all eschew rationalist modes of thinking and attend to how particular human beings sense and think in particular contexts. Sensibility must be historicized.

In this sense Wagner described his proto-anthropology as a "history of sensation" that would account not only for the interaction of mind and body, the internal and the external, but also for how these interactions changed over time.[77] The history of the human being came to be tied up with the question of how human beings sensed, perceived, and felt through time. Herder paved the way for this historicization of sensation that rendered an ultimate solution or explanation of the mind-body problem almost superfluous. On the one hand, he insisted that every psychology—every theory about the mind-body relation—be a physiology; and on the other hand, he insisted that physiological accounts search for the origins of the human mind.[78] As we shall discuss in great detail in the following section, Herder's search for "origins" and historical unity was itself fraught with paradoxes. Still, his insistence that philosophy historicize sensibility (and cognition) proved to be decisive for the development of proto-anthropology.[79] Just as the bracketing of the metaphysical questions had led to an increasingly descriptive or phenomenological account of the human being, so too did this historicizing effort.[80] The question remained, from what perspective could the *mediating* work of the senses, both diachronically and synchronically, be observed? Proto-anthropology began to frame all dualisms, be they mind and body, inner and outer, or subject and object, as problems of observation and perspective.

Culture, Comparison, and Progress: Anthropology as Morality

In his 1791 *Anfangsgründe der medizinischen Anthropologie und der Staatsarzneikunde* (Elements of a Medical Anthropology and the Pharmacology of the State), Justus Christian Loder, doctor to both Goethe and Wilhelm von Humboldt, argued that the "vital forces" (*Lebenskräfte*) not just of the individual but of the entire state had to be properly maintained. Loder's proto-anthropology was concerned not just with the care of the individual but with the "care" and "health" of the state's entire population.[81] Loder's interest in the "proper maintenance" of the "vital forces" of entire populations signals a fundamental shift in proto-anthropology. The historicizing of human faculties allowed proto-anthropology to transpose individual human economies onto entire populations and, ultimately, onto the human species. The question "What is human?" was projected not only onto political *bodies* but, more fundamentally, onto a historical being that changed over time. The relationship of the mind to the body, for example, had to be posed not just in terms of the individual human being but in terms of the entire species. How did this relationship develop and change over time? This historicization of the anthropological question relied on a basic analogy that Franz von Paula Gruithuisen puts as follows: "Just as the individual human experiences a metamorphosis of life and the day, so too does the human species experience its period of development."[82] This underlying analogy of the development of the individual human being with a human species required both a temporalization of the human being, as noted in the previous section, and the assumption of a universal human belonging—that is, proto-anthropology's basic transposition had to assume the historical and generic continuity of the *human*. How could the categorical stability of the *human* be maintained in the face of historical difference?

Wezel argued that proto-anthropology's transition from the study of the faculties of the individual to the faculties of an entire species required a respect for "the germs [*Keime*] and purposes [*Zwecke*] of humanity."[83] Human beings cannot be studied according to their present state and conditions; instead, human beings have to be studied according to the "predispositions," "faculties[,] and forces" of the human as such.[84] These germs, purposes, and predispositions emerge and develop not within an individual human being but through the human as a historical species.[85] Almost immediately, attention to the study of the "human" diachronically and collectively ushered in teleological notions of humanity. "The individual may always grow old . . . and may resign from his march to perfection . . . ; the species, however, gradually be it here or somewhere else . . . will never miss its goal."[86] The bold assumption of a unified human species implied for most of proto-anthropology a common human destiny.

As proto-anthropology became a science of the human species, its inquiry into the individual human being was functioning on two levels. In terms of the "germs," it considered what was given to the human being. In terms of the "predispositions," it studied what the individual human being could make of these germs. While proto-anthropology continued to frame itself as a discipline of the future, it also expanded the temporal orientation of its *subject* to include past, present, and future (what the human being has been, is now and can become). In order to answer the question of what is human, proto-anthropology had to tell the story of the human being's past, present, and future, a story only possible through the assumption of a unified *humanity*. The crossing of history and anthropology introduced another complex of problems, that of narrativity. It is in this vein that Kant suggests a history of the world could only take the form of a novel (*Roman*). It is a story not of an individual, but of a collection of individuals that forms a larger community, including all of its practices and ways of thinking and being with one another, in short, a *Kultur*.

Ith writes that by considering the human being in its physical and moral dimensions proto-anthropology would ultimately be able to give an account of the human "in [his] most general relationships with the nature that surrounds him in his different places on the face of the earth, his various standpoints with respect to culture."[87] The modern German concept of culture emerged as a mediating term for both the moral-physical and the individual-species poles of anthropological inquiry. And like so many other figures in late eighteenth-century Germany, Ith ties the concept of culture to the notion of moral progress. The human being is capable of "improvement and betterment through culture."[88] Proto-anthropology's most basic transposition was facilitated by the concept of culture.

Until its conceptualization in late eighteenth-century Germany, culture had both an individual and a social dimension.[89] On the one hand, it involved the metaphorical extension of the agrarian connotations of *cultura*—from a cultivation or working of the land to a cultivation of letters, or individual ethical improvement. On the other hand, it involved an extension of this individual-ethical element to broader social forms—from the culture of the individual to the culture of societies. It connoted a unified social organization. Culture came to mark not just the improved ethics of an individual or even the cultivated ethos of a particular social group but rather "the totality of all these works, the objectified results of human creativity by which the 'natural constitution' of human individuals—their inborn needs, drives and propensities—become modified, developed and supplemented, and which is inherited by each generation from its predecessors as its legacy."[90] Culture came to name an objective material realm of its own, a realm with its own internal logic and organization. It emerged as a realm distinct from nature with its own processes of transmitting the results of individual human labor over time. The nominalization of culture as an objectified realm—the emergence of *Kultur*—signified the transmission of human work (and works) from generation to generation.

Toward the end of the century, the concept of culture became increasingly linked with a notion of progress and an ideal image of the human being. The social dimension of culture came to orient itself in terms not just of a particular social group, like Loder's state populations, but of a more universal or normative idea of what human beings as a common group could become. As Christoph Wilhelm Hufeland, one of Kant's correspondents, put it: "Only through culture will the human being become perfected."[91] Culture came to be the name for that conceptual space in which the human species progressed on its way to its own perfection. As such, it also came to signify the gap between the individual human being and the image of a perfected human species and to highlight the difference between what individual human beings were empirically observed to be and what the human species could hope to become. Culture became the realm of this historical movement from individual, imperfect being to perfected human being. From its conceptual beginnings, then, culture was marked by a fundamental contradiction. On the one hand, it signified the totality of material, objectified human works as they were passed down from one generation to the next. This empirically observable element stressed historical difference and geographical particularity. On the other hand, the concept of culture signified a transhistorical unity, a normative, ethical teleology that could only be achieved through human becoming.

The paradoxical concept of culture allowed human beings to imagine their progress toward more than natural existence. They could become cultural beings capable of transforming themselves as natural beings into a normative image of human being. As a realm not subordinate to nature, culture came to mark the space in which individuals reworked (or cultivated) their given germs and predispositions. This irreducible relationship between normativity—the presumption of some positive *human* values—and facticity—the simple fact of the particularity of human beings—framed culture from its conceptual beginnings in eighteenth-century Germany.[92]

This concept of culture owes a great deal to Herder's reconceptualization of the individual human being as an organism, which emphasized the individual's developmental capacity, and of history as a unified, organic whole, which offered new models for the development of human being as a species.[93] For Herder, a human being has individual predispositions that allow it to develop like other natural organisms. The individual's internal development, however, is influenced by external, natural forces, such as climate and geography, and the particularity of an individual's organic development results from this exchange between internal predispositions and external influences. The monism underlying Herder's entire thought blurs these inside-outside distinctions and, more generally, his organic concept of the individual. Herder's reconceptualization of history involves the temporalization of this organic development of internal-external processes. The development of the human race, or the human species, proceeds genetically—through the transference of material, objective powers and predispositions or germs—and organically—through the absorption and application of these material substrates. Herder designates the broader process of the historical and organic development of the human being as *Kultur* (he sometimes uses *Aufklärung* as a synonym for *Kultur*). As the mutual development of outside and inside, Herder refers to culture as the "second genesis" of the human being. It is the realm in which we human beings can re-create ourselves,[94] the realm in which we become human: "We are not actually human beings yet, but we are becoming human daily" (348).

This re-creation of the individual human being, however, is not, for Herder at least, a transcendence of nature. It is checked on two sides. On the one hand, the individual as a natural being always stands in relation to nature—checked by the limits of his or her material body (the germs given it by nature) and by the forces of nature. On the other hand, the development of these germs always progresses within the historical chain of development of the human species. Herder frames this tension in terms of the irreducibility of the very language of human development. To speak of the human race or human species risks subordinating the individual human being to abstract categories, because such terms are universal concepts and thus have no ontological existence. Herder likens the invocation of "humanity" (*Humanität*) to animal-ness or stone-ness (346). And yet Herder argues that the development of the individual human being can only be accounted for with respect to the interconnection of all human beings. "Not one of us has become human on our own" (346). The human being becomes human in the fullest sense of the term somewhere between these two poles. Herder's conceptual balancing act highlights one of the theoretical difficulties that the culture concept raises, namely, how to reconcile the "infinite difference" of real human beings with the normative force of the category "human"—that is, how to square an Enlightenment universality with an increasingly diverse ethnographic particularity. Herder attempted to maintain these two diverging commitments.

Herder balanced his commitment to universality and particularity by defining the difference between so-called cultured and uncultured peoples as a matter not of genetic (or generic) but of historical distinctions. He conceives of the historical development of the human species in analogy with the development of the individual human being. Just as parents and children "become one through the chain of instruction," so too does the "human race" develop into a "whole . . . through the chain of *Bildung*" (352).[95] Consequently, he never refers to plural *Kulturen*, only to one singular *Kultur*. Thus, the particularity and diversity of human beings are ultimately modalities of a universal and unified human species: "In however many forms the human race [*Menschengeschlecht*] appears on the earth, it is still one and the same human species [*Menschengattung*]" (352). For Herder, culture signifies both the distinctions and diversity of different human beings and the common culture of humanity, the co-belonging of all human beings to a single human species.

The eighteenth-century German concept of culture accommodated the conceptual linking of human diversity and unity. *Kultur* was the mediating term for the historical and geographical diversity of human predispositions or germs and, therefore, the conceptual link between the human being and the human species. By 1800 it had become the conceptual hinge for relating the ethical labor of the individual to the historical labor of the entire human race. So conceived, the concept of culture reveals how the fundamental problem of proto-anthropology—the reduplication of the subject and object of observation—engendered another tension: the tension between normativity and facticity, between the transcendental and the empirical. From what perspective, from what position, could one make normative claims about the human species? From what perspective could proto-anthropology even speak of *the* human being, *the* human species?

It is in this context that ethnographic and comparative interests of proto-anthropology emerge. To know the human being as a species is to know the dispersed germs and predispositions that are spread across the earth and among the peoples of the earth. The comparative character of physiology and anatomy, which consider body parts and functions of individual beings, becomes an anthropological comparativity once the objects of comparisons cease to be the systems of individual human beings and become rather the constitutive elements of an entire species. Proto-anthropology takes up the ethnographic task of accounting for the diversity of the human as manifest in the plurality of peoples and cultures.[96]

This comparative element of proto-anthropology was encouraged and, in part, precipitated by a mid-eighteenth-century travel literature that had become more organized and "scientific" in its observation of the variety and unity of the human. The earlier proto-anthropological texts, such as Platner's, do not consider in any detail the variety of humankind. Only later with, for example, Herder, Kant, Pölitz, Schleiermacher, and Wilhelm von Humboldt do the texts of proto-anthropology include sections on the characteristics not just of individuals but of peoples, nations, and all humanity.

The Converging Disciplines of Proto-anthropology

The foregoing three sections have outlined how the various concerns of proto-anthropology can be read as problems of perspective or the reduplication of the subject and object of observation. I have also pointed to problems of temporalization or historicization and the precipitation of a normativity-facticity paradox. In conclusion, it is useful to revisit the tenuous disciplinary status of proto-anthropology. With these concerns in mind, a short survey of the multifarious methodologies that claimed the name of anthropology provides a background against which later developments in the science gain significant relief.

In his *Populäre Anthropologie,* Pölitz wrote that it was difficult to discuss "anthropology" because its practitioners took such varied approaches. Thus, anthropology "now finds itself in a state of crisis, since Platner chose a physiological-philosophical; Schmid a teleological; Jakob a physiological and Kant a pragmatic. . . . The science itself, however, must with all these attempts win out in the end."[97] By 1800 proto-anthropology had developed at least four distinct foci: a physiological-philosophical focus that studied the harmony of mind and body, a physiological interest that focused on the physiological mechanisms of the human body, a pragmatic approach that considered the "application of the powers of nature" through freedom,[98] and a teleological form that considered the human being according to "the purposes of human predispositions."[99]

We have already discussed Platner's vision of a unified science that would require the doctor to be a philosopher and the philosopher to be a doctor. Contra Platner, Ludwig Heinrich Jakob argued that the only true anthropology was a medical one that was based solely on experience. For Jakob and other physiologically oriented proto-anthropologists, a science of the human had to avoid all questions that did not deal directly with the human body in order that such a science would not to "spring out of the field of experience and into the regions of metaphysics." "All metaphysical hypotheses are empty and irrelevant in anthropology."[100] The Kantian G. S. A. Mellin—author of the *Encyclopädisches Wörterbuch der kritischen Philosophie* (1797–1804)—defined practical or pragmatic anthropology as the study of "the unique nature and condition of the human faculty of desire, the drives, inclinations, and passions of the human being and the hindrances of exercising the moral law."[101] Such an anthropology would apply its knowledge of the human being to the "realization of particular ends."[102]

Carl Christian Erhard Schmid (1762–1812) proposed a teleological anthropology that would consider the human as a natural being in relation to a "natural purpose that is thought through the reflection of the power of judgment."[103] For Schmid, only a teleological anthropology could fulfill the promises of physical and pragmatic anthropologies, because it was the only one that would be able to integrate the "powers and highest abilities" of individual human beings with the entire human species.[104] Similarly, Ith described his own proto-anthropology in teleological terms. He argued that it would "develop rules for the entirety of human behavior out of the principles of his own being; . . . it teaches him what he is, what he should be and what he has to hope for in all eternity."[105] A teleological anthropology would be both an "empirical science" and a "philosophy of the human." It would consider the human being both as a being "in the sensible world" and as the agent of its own perfection.

For Ith and Schmid, the human being was marked by an "incomprehensible predisposition to an ever increasing perfection" (347). This "predisposition to perfection" was to be found not only in the products of the human being but in the perfection of himself, in the perfection of "all of his abilities." "This is where he knows no limits . . . What a wonderful and inexplicable creature you are, oh human! . . . Yes, he should fill out that immeasurable space between animal to God" (348). And yet, for Ith, all of these predispositions, all of these possibilities are already in "the body" and "in all of [the] relationships" in which human beings find themselves entangled. The confusion of normative and empirical claims and observations in this so-called teleological anthropology made it almost impossible to distinguish what was universal, constant, and a function of the human from what was local, particular, and a function of culture. The possibilities of the human are both given by nature and a product of the human's own labor.

Whereas recent scholarship, especially in Germany, has shown an increasing tendency to identify an anthropological orientation of the eighteenth century in general,[106] scholars have only recently begun to consider the plurality of eighteenth-century anthropologies or, more precisely, the tension between, on the one hand, a medical anthropology and, on the other hand, the emergence toward the end of the century of a more normative or cultural-philosophical anthropology. Throughout the last third of the eighteenth century, proto-anthropology moved between the two poles of "physis and norm."[107] As indicated in the discussion of the emergence of a teleological orientation, proto-anthropology adopted an increasingly normative stance, while simultaneously struggling to understand how such normative claims might themselves be part of nature.

Proto-anthropology's concerns with the physical body of the human being were increasingly interwoven with concerns regarding the cultures of the human.

The mixing of these two orientations reached an apogee in a post-Kantian Germany. Schmid and Ith published in the 1790s, well after the publication of Kant's *Kritik der reinen Vernunft* in 1781. Even Platner was forced to revise his own anthropology in the 1790s after enduring a series of attacks by Kant, who referred to Platner's anthropology as a "futile undertaking,"[108] and Pölitz, Kant's acolyte, chimed in.[109] Pölitz described his own proto-anthropology as a "treatment of the relationship of the new skepticism [i.e., the critical philosophy of Kant] to the science of anthropology."[110] Whereas Kant's pragmatic anthropology may not have been decisive or even very influential in the 1760s, 1770s, and 1780s, by 1800 his critical philosophy became increasingly important for the normative turn that proto-anthropology had taken. In his *Anthropologie in pragmatischer Hinsicht*, Kant described the so-called crisis in proto-anthropology as a decision between a physiological anthropology that considers what nature "makes" of the human being and a pragmatic anthropology that considers what human beings in freedom can and should make of themselves.[111] The very modality of Kant's formulation—the facticity of "makes" versus the normativity of "should"—condenses and foregrounds the central concerns of proto-anthropology around 1800. It was torn by a basic tension between its commitment to empirical inquiry on the one hand, and its commitment to normative possibilities of the human on the other.

As I have suggested throughout this chapter, proto-anthropology's attempt to conceive of the human being as both a physical and a moral being meant that it had always conceived of the human being as a sort of "middle-thing" between angel and animal.[112] This middle status, between the metaphysical impulses of moral being and the limits of physical being, was a function, in part at least, of the confusion about the aims and methods of proto-anthropological inquiry. The following chapters take this anthropological confusion seriously. They address proto-anthropology's paradoxes and misunderstandings of norm and fact, particular and universal, and transcendental and empirical in a post-Kantian Germany around 1800—that is, against the backdrop of Kant's critical philosophy. Kant's so-called critical philosophy presented a fundamental challenge to all prior anthropological inquiry. The confluence of an eighteenth-century proto-anthropology and a post-Kantian critical attitude, however, has ramifications not just for the history of anthropology as a discipline but also for questions about its most fundamental category, the human. What kind of normativity emerges from a science that oscillates between the empirical and the philosophical? Can anthropology produce or incite a comparative universality? These questions concern the historical possibility of a more flexible type of normativity that must navigate problems of contextuality and temporality, observation and progress.

PART TWO

A Provisional (Kantian) Solution

2

Cultivating Freedom

Kant's Affective Ethics

> Kant may well have said, whoever does not want to be reasonable, with him I want nothing to do. What would he have done, however, if someone had come to him and said he'd like to be more than reasonable.
>
> —SCHLEIERMACHER, *GEDANKEN V*

Ethical Dietetics

In 1796 Christoph Hufeland—a German doctor whose patients included Schiller, Goethe, and Herder—wrote to Kant about the art of prolonging one's life.[1] Hufeland included a copy of his latest book, appropriately if not creatively titled *Die Kunst das menschliche Leben zu verlängern* (*The Art of Prolonging Human Life*), wherein he argued that a life force organized human life and health. This life force, whose conceptual underpinnings Hufeland had adapted from Johann Friedrich Blumenbach, could be weakened, strengthened, or maintained through external influences. According to Hufeland, illness was not to be cured but prevented through a dietetics—from the Greek δίαιτα, meaning "way of living"—which he described as a strict, regimen of dietary and behavioral practices. The goal of medicine was not merely to extend life but to establish a particular "lifestyle." Hufeland was concerned with the medical and ethical health of the human being.[2]

Hufeland solicited Kant's opinion on his efforts to treat, as he put it, the whole human being, including the physical, morally—that is, Hufeland wanted Kant's opinion on whether what he termed a moral culture was indispensable for both the moral and physical perfection of the human being. In his reply, Kant expressed significant admiration for Hufeland's work, and added that he intended to write his own "dietetics" that would, citing Hufeland, address the "power of the mind over its sickly bodily sensations."[3]

Kant's promised contribution appeared as his late essay "Von der Macht des Gemüts durch den blossen Vorsatz seiner Krankhaften Gefühle Meister zu sein" (On the Power of the Mind to Be Master over Its Morbid Feelings Through Sheer Resolution), which was published in Hufeland's *Journal der praktischen Arzneikunde und Wundarzneikunde* in January 1798. Later that same year, Kant published this same essay as the third section of *Streit der Fakultäten,* where he defines a "dietetic" as the art of preventing diseases.[4] Drawing on the Greek etymology of dietetics as a "way of living" or "regimen," Kant and Hufeland's use of the term assumes that the relationship of the mind to the body is not fixed but must be cultivated and developed. The human body is not to be escaped or transcended but integrated, even if hierarchically, into the whole system of the human being. Dietetics, says Kant, aims to establish a *proper* relationship between mind and body. "Stoicism as the principle of the dietetic (*sustine et abstine*) belongs not merely to practical philosophy as a doctrine of virtue, but also to it as medicine. This is philosophical, then, when only the power of reason in the human being to be master over his sensible feelings through a self-given principle determines his way of life."[5] There is a delicate human economy organized around a normative relationship between inside and outside, reason and feeling, and body and mind and governed by a regimented cultivation of the power of the mind over the body. Throughout the essay, Kant offers dietetic advice on how one should eat, drink, and sleep—concerns that fail to comport with caricatures of Kant as preoccupied with the noumenal and pure reason. But precisely these dietetic prescriptions are intended to exemplify "resolution." Only when grounded on a rational principle, in this case a Stoic principle of *sustine et abstine* (endure and abstain),[6] can such medical advice and techniques contribute to a "healthy reason." For Kant's philosophical dietetics, then, the only moral (and thus proper) relationship between mind and body is one in which the mind masters its "sick feelings" through "philosophical" means or the consistent adherence to rational principles.[7]

Philosophical principles, however, even for Kant, remain mere principles—objective and formal—unless they are made subjectively effective. The resolute and consistent application of such rational principles is made possible subjectively—that is, made effective for individual human beings—through what he calls a particular way of thinking (*Denkungsart*) or a moral disposition. As we shall see, for Kant, the truly moral disposition is characterized by a "resolution" not to extirpate feelings as such but to shape them according to Kant's image of moral health. Kant grounds such a healthy reason in a moral disposition. Thus, a medicine grounded in moral ends prescribed by reason can be philosophical. Such principled methods would determine not just how one lives but how one relates to his or her own principles or conduct of thought. Dietetics, as a philosophically grounded medical technique, would be part of a practical philosophy, because its ultimate concern would be less the articulation of rules than the facilitation of a subjective relationship to reason. It should not be overlooked that in establishing this relationship of rational principles to physical health, Kant reframes the mind-body question of proto-anthropology in precisely normative terms. The attainment of such a normative relationship between mind and body, of a moral disposition, is inextricable from what Kant terms the "mechanisms" and "leading strings" of his ethical dietetics.[8] The purity to which his philosophical medicine aspires—the "sheer resolution" of a moral disposition—is an art, an ethical technology.

In this chapter I expand on what Ian Hunter has called Kant's "intellectual *paideia*" and consider Kant's moral philosophy in a manner that comports with both the broader tradition of Pierre Hadot's notion of philosophy as a way of life and with recent work on Kant as a virtue ethicist.[9] In particular, I bring Kant's notion of a philosophical medicine or a practical dietetics to bear on his ethics and particularly the place of feeling within his practical philosophy. In his *Kritik der praktischen Vernunft* (1788) Kant offers up a dietetic regime designed to prevent a pathological subjectivity, or what he terms solipsism. Kant's ethical dietetics assumes, as we shall see, a critique of what he considers modernity's corruption of human inclinations. In the face of modern inclinations, Kant outlines a practical dietetics that would cultivate a moral disposition by cultivating moral feelings—that is, his ethical dietetics would correct modernity's corruption of feelings and inclinations. But this ethical discipline involves not so much the extirpation of feelings as the modification of their place in the larger human economy. According to this Kantian dietetics, the human being is the unified system of what may be mistakenly considered two distinct systems: mind and body. Kant's moral regimens cultivate particular feelings as necessary and indispensable elements of moral being. All moral action requires feeling. To feel is not simply to suffer the effects of an external world or to exhibit a fundamental passivity. Rather, feeling is essential to a reason that can preserve itself.[10] This preservation of reason is bound up with the complex feelings of reason. For Kant, reason not only legislates: it needs, it feels, it suffers. And it disciplines not only the body but itself. The desires of reason, the feeling of respect and the dietetics of ethics will demonstrate a Kantian ethics concerned not only with articulating objective moral principles but with caring for and developing the moral self. A disciplined reason is an embodied reason, a reason bound to particular human beings and particular practices. And for Kant, the most important disciplinary practice involves the cultivation of moral feelings, their place in the Kantian ethical economy, and ultimately, a moral disposition.

Post-Kantian Accounts of Kant's Ethics

Such an account of Kantian ethics is at odds with more traditional readings. From Hegel to Rawls, whether dismissively or sympathetically, critics have with great regularity characterized Kant's moral philosophy as an exclusively formal project.[11] With its focus on establishing the rational grounds of moral life and the logical form of moral judgments, Kant's ethics is either, depending on the perspective, uncontaminated by sensible desires or bereft of feeling. Contemporary scholars in fields from anthropology to political theory continue to be weary of a Kantian ethics that they regard as a two-world metaphysics fixated on moral purity.[12] Echoing Hegel's famous claim that Kant's moral philosophy is nothing but an "empty formalism,"[13] contemporary detractors have suggested that Kant ignores the "visceral" elements of the human and has "no sympathy for man's natural needs."[14] In those interpretations, Kant's attention to dietetics would presumably be merely incidental, if not contradictory, to Kant's project as a whole. Kant's notion of freedom, in that light, would be synonymous with an individual autonomy that would transcend nature and subordinate the body to reason. Kant often encourages this image of a pure reason, as, for example, in his insistence in the *Streit der Fakultäten* that the mind be the "master" over "sickly feelings."[15] Inclinations and affections, it would seem, are simply tethers that bind reason to a burdensome body.

Heinrich Heine famously picked up on this in his caricature of Kant the philosopher, when he argued that Kant's life story is difficult to describe, because he had "neither a life nor a story":

> He led a mechanical, regular, almost abstract bachelor existence in a small, quiet street in Königsberg. . . . I don't even think that the great clock of the cathedral went about its daily routine in a more passionless and methodical manner than did its townsman, Immanuel Kant. Rising in the morning, coffee-drinking, writing, reading lectures, dining, walking, everything had its appointed time, and the neighbors knew that it was exactly half-past three o'clock when Immanuel Kant stepped forth from his house in his grey, tight-fitting coat, with his Spanish cane in his hand, and strolled to the little linden avenue called to this day, on his account "Philosopher's Walk." Summer and winter he walked up and down it eight times, and when the weather was dull or heavy clouds prognosticated rain, the townspeople beheld his servant, the old Lampe, trudging anxiously behind him with a big umbrella under his arm, like an image of Providence.[16]

Heine goes on, however, to connect the famed sterility and rigor of Kant's personal habits not so much to his critical philosophy as to that legion of post-Kantians, his "soul-less imitators" who mimic the ponderous style of the *Kritik der reinen Vernunft*. Heine suggests that in contrast to his progeny Kant was uninterested in dividing up the world into noumena and phenomena. Beneath his blinding irony, Heine admired what he saw as Kant's restless exercise of reason. Reason cannot be reduced to theorizing about the world. For Kant, reason was a way of life that was manifest in all those mechanical and seemingly superfluous details of his daily life. If one misses Heine's irony, one loses sight of Kant's suggestion not only that reason has needs and desires but that the moral subject of his ethics must be educated, disciplined, and formed toward freedom. One also misses the irony of Kant's ethical dietetics. What Kant deems the life of reason—a resolute commitment to the moral law—involves not only rigorous labor but a timeless decision that such a life is worth living in the first place.

Having remained under the sway of those "soul-less imitators" of whom Heine spoke, scholars too have come to see Kant's discussion of reason almost exclusively in terms of its analysis of the finitude of reason and its circumscription of reason's power.[17] What is one to make, then, of Kant's repeated claims that reason has needs, desires, and even feelings? In speaking of reason's general task in the *Kritik der reinen Vernunft*, Kant claims that reason is moved not by the mere "vanity of knowing a great deal" or the amassing of knowledge but by its "own need," a need that pushes it toward questions that cannot be answered by the empirical use of reason.[18] The human faculty of knowledge "feels a much higher need" than merely to spell out appearances.[19] Reason wants to do more than explain how things appear. It wants to set its own ends.[20]

But do not discussions of reason's needs, a moral disposition, and more generally, an ethical dietetics ultimately risk—in Kant's own terms—undermining a basic distinction of his critical philosophy? Does one not run the risk of confusing transcendental and empirical insights? Does one not risk confusing anthropology with philosophy? After all, both the *Grundlegung zur Metaphysik der Sitten* (1785) and the *Kritik der praktischen Vernunft* not only tend to exemplify the rigor and formalism for which Kantian ethics is known, they also distinguish pure morals from an impure anthropology. Purity is presumably preferable to impurity.

Purifying the Groundwork for Moral Agency

In the preface to the *Grundlegung zur Metaphysik der Sitten*, for example, Kant distinguishes between what has so far in this study been termed the pure and impure parts of ethics: "One can call all philosophy, in so far as it bases itself on grounds of experience, empirical; but philosophy, which carries forth its teaching from principles a priori, pure philosophy. . . . In this way there arises the idea of a twofold metaphysics, one of nature and one of morals. Physics will therefore have its empirical part, but also have a rational part; so too will ethics, though here the empirical part can be called specially practical anthropology, but the rational part morals proper."[21]

Just as physics has a rational and an empirical part, morals has a metaphysical and an empirical part. The metaphysical part grounds itself in a priori principles, while the empirical part is grounded in experience. For

Kant, metaphysical philosophy is pure, whereas non-metaphysical philosophy is empirical or has its sources in experience. Empirical knowledge relies, in part, on "impressions of the senses."[22] The empirical or "impure" part of morals is termed here a "practical anthropology" and is contrasted with the rational part or "morals strictly speaking."

But, if there is a morals strictly speaking, is there also a morals in a less strict sense? Most discussions of Kantian morals have tended to focus on this pure, metaphysical part because Kant appears to privilege the pure metaphysical over the impure empirical. However, the priority is given to the former in terms of the logical order, not relative value. The metaphysics of morals, he argues, must be separated from anything empirical because "the nature of science" requires that the empirical always be "carefully" separated from the rational. Just as it is necessary "to send ahead" a metaphysics of nature before an empirical physics, so too must a metaphysics of morals be "sent ahead" of a practical anthropology. The metaphysical grounds must be carefully purified or cleansed from all that is empirical, so that we may know what pure reason can accomplish and be assured of the spontaneity and self-legislating character of reason.

Reason, as Kant writes in the *Kritik der reinen Vernunft*, must be "occupied with nothing but itself"[23]—that is, reason must not rely on anything in nature as sufficient evidence for any claim. Rather, it must determine and give its own account of itself.[24] "It may be," continues Kant, that such an account-giving of reason by reason must be "carried out by all teachers of morals (whose name is legion) or only by those who feel a calling to it." This type of critical cleansing, it seems, is limited as to who can undertake it. Does the "purity" of metaphysics mark, then, not only the mode of inquiry but its proper subjects as well? While Kant exhorts his readers to recognize the force of the claims of morals, he limits the articulation of such claims only to those who are renowned as teachers or otherwise called to the task. Only those who possess a pure metaphysics of morals may then proceed to the task of an impure practical anthropology. But whence originates this call? Similar questions concerning the "destiny of the human being" will arise in the later discussion of race and Kant's pragmatic anthropology. An a priori critique of morality remains, for the present discussion at least, the purview of a pedagogical elite. But the lesson of reason—its self-determination—is one that should be recognized by all.

Kant's pedagogical elite will come up for discussion in the following sections, but one must first consider this "careful" separation of the rational and empirical parts of these scientific endeavors. The metaphysical grounds must be purified, and such a solicitation alerts the reader to the task ahead. Nothing is already pure. An act of purification must precede purity. If we are to know the limits of reason, the work of the metaphysician must always precede the empirical work of the anthropologist. In any case, this purification is a task. It is work. Purity is not a given state.

Formally, this section of Kant's text contains a series of statements, but these statements are preceded by a question of sorts: "But I ask only whether . . . ?" Its interrogative form addresses the reader and solicits a response.[25] Kant asks what the "nature of science" demands and follows his question with a series of statements, not with more questions. The text draws the reader into a certain way of taking up the problem of morals by posing a purely formal question and then laying out the work of purification to be done. The call to purify and to cleanse solicits the reader to join the movements of the ethical program, as laid out in an uninterrupted series of statements. A metaphysics of morals must be sent ahead, to do battle with the malformed student of philosophy or the uninitiated or aspiring metaphysician. For Kant, metaphysics must cleanse—or is it rather that metaphysics must be cleansed of?—all things empirical. Is metaphysics the subject or object of this purification? The transitivity of the required cleansing is unclear. Certainly, a metaphysics of morals is at least the object that "must be cleansed." Can metaphysics also be the purifying agent? If not, who or what is capable of such cleansing? And what exactly is this desired purity that Kant ascribes to his metaphysics of morals?

According to Kant, pure philosophy "sets forth its teaching" only from a priori principles, while impure philosophy appeals to experience to derive its claims. Kant insists that pure morals, morals proper, be grounded in a priori principles, which are independent of experience and necessary. They are always "valid." Experience teaches us, writes Kant, that "something may be one way, but not, that it could not be otherwise."[26] To insist on purity is to make a claim about all present and future possibilities. "It is of the utmost necessity once and for all to work out a pure moral philosophy, which has been fully cleansed of everything that may be only empirical or belong to anthropology."[27] As the ground of all normative claims, a pure moral philosophy must be established "once and for all."

This adverb clarifies the temporality of this purifying endeavor. Metaphysical cleansing is a singular event. While the a priori critique of morality occurs once, the work that anthropology does is repetitive; it persists in time. The contrasting temporalities of a pure and an impure ethics suggest that a metaphysics of morals is, for Kant, a singular occurrence, whereas anthropology is a repeated, recursive activity. The temporality of these two forms of ethical inquiry, then, implies two forms of normativity. If a metaphysics of morals is intended to articulate normative claims that are compelling outside time, what types of normative claims, if any, could anthropology articulate? What exactly are changing norms if not an oxymoronic concept? Can normative claims compel if they are repeatedly reformulated and recursively articulated?

Duty to the moral law, or here the "ground of obligation," must be sought "not in the nature of the human being, or the conditions into which he is placed" but "a priori simply in concepts of pure reason."[28] If one conceives of morality only as a set of necessary and universal laws for action (laws that must apply to everyone), then morality cannot be grounded in experience. Such a formally constructed morality is predicated on a notion of universality that is synonymous with necessity. For Kant, however, anthropology's temporality limits it to the particularity of the empirical. Experience can never ground moral norms. It teaches what is the case, not what must be the case. A morals based in anthropology would inevitably fall back on the particularities of anthropology and its delimitations of space and time. The necessity derived from a pure moral philosophy, claims Kant, arises a priori, but this commitment to a priori purity is ultimately a commitment to a certain disposition toward freedom and not a metaphysical claim about the reality of freedom itself. Kant's insistence on purity does not mean that moral philosophy must exclude anthropology, far from it. Rather, he claimed that moral norms cannot be *grounded upon* anthropological insights. While morality must not be based on anthropology—because it requires an a priori commitment to the self-legislation of reason—neither can it exclude anthropology *in toto*.[29]

Elaborating not only on the difference between moral philosophy and anthropology but also on their possible relationship, Kant writes in the *Grundlegung*:

> All moral philosophy is based entirely on its pure part, and, applied to people, it does not borrow the least thing from knowledge of him

(anthropology), but gives him, as a rational being, laws a priori, which require a judgment sharpened through experience—partly in order to distinguish in which causes they can be applied, partly in order to provide them access to the will of man and to urge the exercise of them, because man is affected by so many inclinations that although capable of the idea of a practical pure reason, he still is not so easily capable of making it concretely effective in the conduct of his life.[30]

Whereas a metaphysics of morals is based in a priori laws, the application of these moral principles and their concrete effectiveness requires knowledge of the human being or anthropology. Kant suggests that there are two types of such effectiveness. First, in order to decide in which situations to apply a priori laws, a rational agent requires a power of judgment sharpened by experience. Second, such a power of judgment sharpened by experience is needed for these a priori laws to gain access to the will. The latter question of effectiveness is more than a question of applicability. Kant is concerned about how these a priori laws can access the human will. How can a priori laws have any effect in time? Analogous forms of this question will arise later. For example, how can the idea of freedom have an effect on an individual person in time? Furthermore, how can a moral disposition be both outside time and, simultaneously, cultivated or developed?

These problems of the temporality and actuality of freedom are functions of Kant's insistence that we must presuppose our freedom, a presupposition that requires us to accept his own moral theory, which ineluctably falls back on a division of the human being into a sensible being and an intelligible one.[31] Whereas the human being can assume an attitude toward or have an idea of a practical reason, to make it effective in the conduct of his or her life is another question. The question of effectiveness concerns what Kant refers to as "cosmopolitan knowledge," which he describes as a wisdom that "shows us the ultimate purpose of human reason."[32] Cosmopolitan knowledge, the "aim" of Kant's philosophical project, concerns the ultimate purposes of reason—that is, the schematization of freedom such that it may have some effect on life as lived by human beings. And this effect of freedom appears as an affect, namely, the feeling of respect. The question becomes, what is the relationship between moral becoming and anthropological insights, given that the law of reason is supposed to be prior to anthropological knowledge?

These questions are intractable only if one insists, like those who accuse Kant of an absolute formalism, on reading Kantian morals as merely propositional—that is, either as an ethics concerned only with the propositional truth of whether noumenal and phenomenal worlds actually exist, or as an ethics devoted simply to the articulation of logical, objective moral principles. Preoccupations with the theoretical problems of Kantian ethics—that is, to focus entirely on metaphysical explanations of concepts like moral freedom (which Kant insists cannot be explained)—often fail to recognize the precise manner in which Kant privileges theoretical reason over practical reason. The "priority" of theoretical reason is one of logic, space, or time—as in an argument's premise, a structure's foundation, or a play's first act—as opposed to a "priority" that identifies one good as having greater value in a comparison of goods. Kant's ordering (perhaps better than privileging) places the theoretical groundwork below, prior to, or as a condition of the practical edifice: the practical freedom of the active moral agent. The telos, however, is found in the latter. Furthermore, a subordination of practical reason runs counter to Kant's own insistence that the moral world be actualized. There is in a real sense, then, an actual priority of practical over theoretical reason, because desire or interest drives reason itself.[33] Laying the groundwork of metaphysics is not Kant's endpoint, but rather the necessary preparatory cleansing or purifying of reason. Ultimately, Kant is concerned with the character of the moral agent.

What are the effects not only of Kant's moral concepts (most fundamentally the concept of freedom) but also of his unremitting demand for purity and the apparent degradation of the empirical? Kantian ethics cultivates a certain relationship to itself that leads to an affective disquiet. Kant's demand for purity is actually an exhortation to regard the problem of freedom from a certain position, to assume what Kant referred to as a moral disposition. Kant's account of a pure metaphysics of morals is deliberate and forceful. To borrow Hadot's words, Kant presents his readers with an existential choice, a choice to recognize, thereby actualizing, that they are either free or not.

Kant writes that if moral concepts are "to become subjectively practical, we cannot remain standing at the level of objective moral law to be admired and esteemed in relation to humanity. Rather, we must consider their representation in relation to the human being and individuals."[34] Similarly, he writes that "reason has a causality in respect to appearances:

so it must, insofar as it is reason, display its own empirical character."[35] Reason and moral concepts, ideas that might never fully correspond to any empirical object, must be considered in terms of actual human beings, not just abstract moral agents. Freedom cannot remain a conceptual claim. It must be actualized. This imperative, so often overlooked by those who insist on Kant's absolute formalism, shifts the emphasis of moral concepts from their "historical fulfillment . . . or metaphysical efforts to define it"[36] to their effect on our mode of thought and the cultivation of a moral disposition of mind. (Recall Kant's dietetics as a "way of living.") This shift in emphasis, from formal to formative, concerns how moral concepts can be adopted as maxims by agents in time. And for Kant this shift ultimately concerns the effect of the idea of freedom not just for providing rules for particular actions but as "formative" for the moral human being.[37] Given this shift in emphasis, we can ask: How does Kant's fundamental moral concept, the idea of freedom, not just give moral rules but organize the human moral economy? How does the idea of freedom have an impact on the individual moral agent in the world? Once these types of questions are posed, one is in a better position to understand Kantian ethics as the cultivation of a particular way of life.

If one thinks of freedom less from a theoretical and more from a practical perspective, a possibility that makes a lot of sense, particularly on Kantian soil, then one might better understand freedom as a hard-won presupposition, or a moral disposition, that can affect our concrete lives. If, as Thomas McCarthy puts it, moral being is to have any "purchase on human life," then an impure ethics—an ethics related to an empirical study of the human being and the mechanisms of dietetics—would be a necessary supplement to pure ethics.[38] Although the epigraph at the beginning of the chapter suggests that Schleiermacher may not have recognized it, Kantian ethics addresses the human being not only as an intelligible but also as a sensible being for whom the distinction between pure and impure is most practical, even in the Kantian sense. In fact, as I will argue, Kant addresses the finite, and radically human, sensible being and invokes an intelligible being as a regulative model of what the human being could become, not as a metaphysical claim about what the human being is.

Kant's Freedom: Transcendental and Practical

What is freedom for Kant? In the *Kritik der praktischen Vernunft*, Kant writes that the concept of freedom is the "keystone of the entire structure of a system of pure, even speculative reason."[39] Within the critical system, concepts concerning immortality or God, for example, gain their objective reality only through a concept of freedom. Freedom is the linchpin for Kant's philosophical system and more. In the *Kritik der reinen Vernunft*, he calls freedom a "need of reason."[40] Reason itself needs freedom. Underlying Kant's critical philosophy and his more general response to the question "What is the human?" is the claim that all human beings both need and desire freedom. As we will see, as a "need of reason" freedom is not only universally desirable but theoretically inscrutable—it cannot be explained by reason. Kant grounds his ethics, if not his entire critical system, on a presupposition of freedom. This presupposition, however, takes different forms throughout his critical system.

In the *Kritik der reinen Vernunft* (1781), Kant writes that a causality from freedom "must be assumed."[41] In the *Grundlegung zur Metaphysik der Sitten* (1785), he writes that freedom must be presupposed. And in the *Kritik der praktischen Vernunft*, he writes that we must simply recognize the moral law as the "fact" of reason. As Kant continued to hone his theory of freedom from the first *Critique* to the second, he increasingly emphasized not just the conceptual necessity of the idea of freedom (as in the *Kritik der reinen Vernunft*) but the actuality (*Wirklichkeit*) of freedom (as in the *Kritik der praktischen Vernunft*).[42] Before discussing the presupposition of freedom in its various forms and their relationship to the cultivation of a moral disposition in an ethical dietetics, we will find it useful to outline, however briefly, Kant's different uses of the term "freedom." Though he also writes throughout his oeuvre of a civic or political freedom, in the *Kritik der reinen Vernunft* he distinguishes between a transcendental and a practical freedom, and this distinction will frame the discussion in what follows.

In the third antinomy of the *Kritik der reinen Vernunft*, Kant writes that one can conceive of two types of causality: one according to nature and one according to freedom. A natural causality or a causality of appearances is phenomenal and based on conditions of time. According to such a causality, one must think of every event in nature as necessarily tied to a preceding event in nature. Every effect presupposes a cause, and every cause necessitates an effect *ad infinitum*. Such a natural, mechanistic causality consists, then, of an infinite chain of effects and their preceding causes. Everything in the sensible world is determined according to natural laws. If, however, there is only this natural causality, then nothing happens in nature that is not already determined by natural laws.

Such a mechanistic causality (akin to Aristotle's efficient causality) would seem to negate a causality from freedom, or freedom of the will.[43] In the face of hyper-Newtonian conceptions of mechanistic causality and the apparent impossibility of freedom in a natural (phenomenal) world, Kant does not immediately address the possibility of a freedom of the will; instead, he initially presents the possibility of freedom in a "cosmological sense"—"the faculty of beginning a state from itself."[44] In this cosmological sense, freedom would not be subject to the laws of natural causality and, thus, would not be subordinate to another cause in time. Kant refers to this alternate freedom as a "pure transcendental idea"—and as such it would correspond to nothing in nature. As a transcendental idea, such a freedom could not be derived from or refer to any object in experience, but it would allow one to conceive of a cause that is not conditioned in its causality by any previous cause or further cause.

Given that we conceive of nature according to laws of mechanistic causality, how can a person still conceive of anything outside this "absolute totality of conditions in causal relationship"?[45] (For example, how could one conceive of a transcendental freedom, an event without a cause?) In the face of this conceptual impossibility, writes Kant, reason produces the idea of an autocausality that contrasts with the causality of nature.[46] Reason "creates the idea of a spontaneity" that can act from itself.[47] The idea of transcendental freedom is posited by reason for reason's purposes. This transcendental idea of freedom is the freedom of the epistemic subject, the subject that knows and explains nature.

Kant goes on to note that "it is remarkable" that such a transcendental idea of freedom grounds freedom in another sense. Not in an active sense, but passively, transcendental freedom is the ground of what Kant terms practical freedom. Initially, he defines practical freedom as the "independence of the power of choice" from the "compulsion of sensibility."[48] Freedom in this practical sense, as related to the human will, is first a freedom *from* captivity to feelings. It signifies an independence not necessarily from nature itself but from the compulsion of nature. In contrast to the transcendental idea of freedom—an absolute freedom that spontaneously effects a state from itself—Kant defines practical freedom negatively. He does not fully separate the will from the sensible; instead, he excuses the will of practical freedom from the necessity of the sensible. The sensible affects the will but does not determine it. In contrast to an *arbitrium brutum* (a sensibly determined will), the human will is an *arbitrium sensitivium* (a sensibly affected will), which is certainly influenced, yet not completely determined, by the mechanism of nature.[49] For Kant, human beings are different from animals precisely because they can decide which sensual impulses to follow—they are affected but not determined by their inclinations.

But what does the pure transcendental idea of freedom have to do with practical freedom and, ultimately, the solution to the original antinomy—namely, the supposed reconcilability of the mechanistic causality of nature with freedom in the moral sense?[50] As I noted briefly, Kant immediately and tellingly alludes to the complex (if not confused) relationship between these two senses of freedom: "It is interesting that the practical concept of freedom grounds itself on the transcendental idea of freedom."[51] This statement has been ambiguously translated in most editions along the following lines: "the practical concept of freedom is grounded on the transcendental idea of freedom."[52] According to such a translation, the relationship between a transcendental and practical freedom is easily stated: Kant is claiming that the human being can only be practically free if he is also transcendentally free, that is to say, absolutely free.[53] Practical freedom is grounded on transcendental freedom. This is true in certain respects.

That does not, however, capture the entirety of what Kant claims here. He writes, "It is interesting that upon this idea of transcendental freedom, the practical concept of freedom grounds itself" (*Es ist überaus merkwürdig, daß auf diese transscendentale Idee der Freiheit sich der praktische Begriff derselben gründe*). The practical concept of freedom *grounds itself.* The precise transitivity of this sentence reflects the complex relationship of transcendental freedom to practical freedom, a complexity that comes to characterize Kant's entire ethical project. This is the question of the actuality of freedom—the manner in which freedom bears on existence. Kant reiterates his earlier suggestion that these two senses of freedom are distinct, even as the practical is grounded on the transcendental idea. The syntax of the sentence, however, complicates the grounding move. Whereas the prepositional phrase "on the transcendental idea of freedom" is the first element following the subordinating conjunction "that" (*daß*), "the practical concept of freedom" is the subject of the subordinate clause. While the transcendental idea of freedom serves as the ground, it is the practical concept of freedom that does the grounding. It "grounds itself" (*sich gründe*). Related in this manner—a point of some contention for Kant scholars who would do well to heed Kant here—these two senses of freedom are both associated and differentiated. At the very least, the complex transitivity of the sentence precludes any reading that suggests that a proof for transcendental spontaneity is necessarily a proof for practical freedom. The spontaneity of the mind cannot be transposed onto a spontaneity of the will.[54] Though a transcendental freedom might not prove a practical freedom, Kant claims that the transcendental idea of freedom has a grounding relationship relative to the practical concept of freedom. They are intimately related.

When Kant calls freedom a "need of reason,"[55] he is making a claim about reason's need of an absolute freedom, freedom as a transcendental idea.[56] Reason needs to be able to conceive of a causality other than that of nature. This need is especially evident with respect to moral agency. If human beings conceive of themselves as acting according to reason—that is, as having reasons for acting the way they do—Kant insists that they are then committing themselves to this alternate causality. It is in this sense that practical freedom "grounds" itself on the transcendental idea of freedom. The former "presupposes" the latter.[57] Without such a presupposition (or such a reflexive grounding on the part of practical freedom), the *ought* of the moral realm would be as inconceivable as it is in the physical realm. "Ought expresses a species of necessity and a connection with grounds that does not occur anywhere else in the whole of nature. In nature the understanding can cognize only what exists, or has been, or will be. It is impossible that something in it ought to be other than what, in all these time-relations, it in fact is; indeed, the ought, if one has merely the course of nature before one's eyes, has no significance whatsoever."[58] If human beings want to conceive of themselves as beings whose wills are determined not by natural laws alone, but by their own reason, then one needs a conception of causality other than natural causality. One needs a causality of reason, whereby one can pursue ends set by reason. The moral "ought"—the force of normativity—makes the distinction between causalities most sharply. If one denies the possibility of the transcendental idea of freedom, one risks eliminating the "ought" of morals. And this is something that Kant is unwilling to countenance. His conception of moral agency, and thus of the human, requires the presupposition of a radical freedom.

As we noted, however, the transcendental idea of freedom does not immediately prove practical freedom. The possibility that the human being might be able to conceive of an epistemic spontaneity does not require or even imply a spontaneity of the will. Transcendental freedom is a necessary but not a sufficient condition to establish the existence of practical freedom. What, then, is the function of a transcendental idea of freedom if it cannot prove practical freedom, or if practical freedom cannot necessarily be deduced from transcendental freedom? As intimated in the discussion of the possibility of a realm of *ought,* such an idea of freedom would have a regulative function with respect to practical freedom.[59] As a regulative idea—an idea that corresponds to nothing in experience—transcendental freedom serves as a model that, though not establishing the actuality of practical freedom, allows one to conceive of its possibility.[60] By ascribing a regulative status to transcendental freedom, Kant is not claiming that transcendental freedom must exist in actuality in order for one to conceive of the self as practically free. Instead, he is claiming that one needs the idea of freedom in order to conceive of the self as practically free. Transcendental ideas cannot be employed to constitute objects, only "to guide the understanding to a certain goal."[61] It is in this sense that Kant describes the function of the intelligible world, a world of radical freedom. Such a "concept of a world of understanding [is only] a standpoint that reason sees itself constrained to take in order to think of itself as practical."[62]

Although these might appear to be technical distinctions, they are in fact fundamental to the larger argument of this chapter concerning the subjective effectiveness of moral principles. As Kant continues to work out his ethical theory, he frames freedom in the transcendental sense in increasingly practical terms. By employing a regulative model of transcendental freedom, Kant affords the pupils of his ethical dietetics a radical alternative to the causality of nature. Such a model gives Kantian moral agents a radically different model of ethical being.

Whereas in the *Kritik der reinen Vernunft* Kant wrote that freedom must be assumed, in the *Grundlegung* he writes that "freedom must be presupposed as a property of the will of all rational beings"[63]—that is, from a practical standpoint we must presuppose our freedom.[64] Kant claims that if we do not presuppose our freedom, we would have to deny that a human being can act from a rational cause, that is to say, act in freedom. Kant says that he presupposes freedom so that he need not be forced "to prove freedom in its theoretical respect as well."[65] He presupposes freedom because he insists that it cannot be explained.[66] And elsewhere, he suggests that even if we can never bring this "practical presupposition" into harmony with speculative principles "not much is lost."[67] Even the most confirmed fatalist "must still, as soon as he has to do with wisdom and duty, always act as if he were free."[68] Presupposing our freedom, or our ability to judge according to morals, is equivalent to conceiving of ourselves as judging according to rational norms. The presupposition of freedom, then, is akin to a decision about how we conceive of ourselves. Kant refers us not to a speculative reason that would attempt to explain the origins of actions—their causality—but to a practical reason that is itself productive. In order to conceive of ourselves as spontaneous beings—that is, if we want to conceive of ourselves as more than mere physical beings tied to the mechanism of nature—Kant insists we must on practical grounds presuppose our freedom and thus our ability to act according to norms and not merely inclinations. Practical freedom grounds itself. Indeed, it must ground itself. In light of our inability to prove theoretically or deduce our freedom, we must practically presuppose it. Nor can we theorize or explain the metaphysical grounds of our freedom; again, we must practically presuppose them. And this presupposition involves a decision about how we are to conceive of ourselves. "Reason must regard itself as the author of its principles independently of any alien influences; consequently, as practical reason or as the will of a rational being it must be regarded of itself as free."[69]

It is evident that the relationship between the transcendental idea of freedom and practical freedom is complex. In the *Kritik der reinen Vernunft*, Kant calls the former "a problem for reason."[70] For the present purposes, suffice it to highlight Kant's emphatic imperative that we *must* either assume or presuppose freedom in this absolute sense in order to conceive of ourselves as free in the practical sense.[71] Freedom is the presupposition that Kant claims we *must* make. In both cases—with respect to the transcendental idea of freedom (of an unconditioned ground outside the causality of nature) and the practical idea of freedom (of a free moral agency)—Kant gives his readers a conditional statement that ultimately functions as an exhortation: if we want to conceive of ourselves as free and thus subject to rational norms, then we must presuppose our freedom. The distinction between the two senses of freedom may also, in another sense, be articulated as one of degree. While an absolute freedom is an absolute spontaneity, practical freedom is a spontaneity relative to the will, that is to say, practical freedom signifies a will that is not sensibly determined, not a will that is absolutely spontaneous. Practical freedom concerns the ability of reason to set its own ends.

At the same time, however, Kant is concerned that we not conceive of transcendental freedom as *merely* a presupposition. If we were to do so, would we not risk reducing freedom, as Kant puts it in the *Kritik der praktischen Vernunft*, to a "wretched subterfuge" that can only give us the "freedom of a turnspit"?[72] In an effort to address the actuality of freedom in this stronger sense, Kant formulates a different solution to the problem of freedom in the *Kritik der praktischen Vernunft*. He asks the more general question concerning how a causality from freedom and a natural causality are compatible:

> If, then, one wants to attribute freedom to a being whose existence is determined in time, one cannot, so far at least, except this being from the law of natural necessity as to all events in its existence and consequently as to its actions as well; for that would be tantamount to handing it over to blind chance. But since this law unavoidably concerns all causality of things in so far as their existence in time is determinable, if this were the way in which one had to represent also the existence of things in themselves, then freedom would have to be rejected as a null and impossible concept. Consequently, if one still wants to save it, no other path remains than to ascribe the existence of a thing so far as it is determinable in time, and so too its causality in accordance with the law of natural necessity, only to appearance, and to ascribe freedom to the same being as a thing in itself.[73]

In an effort to resolve the apparent contradiction inherent in the possibility of freedom for a sensible being, Kant claims not only that transcendental freedom must be seen as not contradicting natural causality but that causality according to nature and causality according to freedom must be united in one and the same subject. If Kant had insisted in the *Kritik der reinen Vernunft* and the *Grundlegung* that we must assume or presuppose our practical freedom, he makes an even stronger claim in the passage from the *Kritik der praktischen Vernunft* just quoted and argues not only for the necessity of the idea of freedom (as in the *Kritik der reinen Vernunft*) but for its actuality from a practical point of view. Our freedom is not only conceivable but is also exhibited in relationship to the moral law. In the second *Critique,* Kant is concerned to show how freedom is not only conceivable but real. And it is this concern that pushes his ethics from a formal project concerned merely with the conceptual necessity of freedom to an ethics concerned with an actualized freedom and thus with the character of embodied moral agents.

Kant argues for the actuality of freedom from a practical point of view through the causality of the moral law. But this argument involves a consideration of the human being from two perspectives. The presuppositions of the earlier texts concerned the transcendental idea of freedom; here in the *Kritik der praktischen Vernunft* they concern how the human being as such is to be understood—that is, Kant intensifies his claims by insisting that in order to save freedom from a natural causality, we must conceive of the human being in a radically different way.

Kant's Freedom and the Sensible, Intelligible Moral Agent

Kant's image of the moral subject in the *Kritik der praktischen Vernunft* is as follows. As the subject of freedom, the human being belongs to a world of pure reason, the noumenal. As the subject of experience and from the perspective of nature, the human being is bound to the phenomenal world.[74] Thus, concludes Kant, we must recognize that we belong to two worlds, the intelligible and the sensible. When we think of ourselves as sensible beings, we must regard ourselves as part of nature and its efficient causality.[75] When we think of ourselves as intelligible beings, we must regard ourselves as free and thus capable of self-legislation. To conceive of the possibility of freedom, though not to explain it, we must conceive of ourselves as capable of producing rational judgments that we can then perform under norms. Normativity is a function of this gap between the production of laws and the act of subordinating ourselves to them. Freedom emerges from this gap.

In the passage I quoted from *Kritik der praktischen Vernunft*, the conditional form of the first sentence is significant: "*If* one wants to attribute freedom." This is the language not of indicative claims but of conditional ascriptions. If we want to attribute freedom to the human being as a natural being, suggests Kant, then according to the formulations of causality we might think in the manner he outlines. Kant gives us not a metaphysical solution but a practical choice—that is, in the *Kritik der praktischen Vernunft*, Kant not only refuses to attempt a theoretical proof of freedom, he denies that one is possible in the first place. To presuppose our freedom is not to prove our freedom. Rather, if we want to conceive of the possibility of freedom, we must choose our freedom. And we must do so in a particular way. As the first sentence makes clear, freedom cannot be an object of theoretical knowledge, because we cannot know freedom as an object independent of us and given by sense perception. We cannot explain it according to natural laws. Any knowledge or conception of freedom is at the same time a determination to bring it about. A practical knowledge of freedom implies, even includes, a determination to be free. Regardless of whether one acts in accord with this potential or not, he still possesses the potential for autonomous action.[76] In the end, then, Kant's basic claim is that human beings have a desire to be free (or to ascribe freedom to themselves) though they are incapable of theorizing or thinking it.

We should not, however, confuse this practical presupposition of freedom with a completely self-determined will, for such an absolutely free will is, according to Kant, empirically impossible. Such a will could only be achieved in an infinite amount of time and would thus require an infinite existence, or immortality; therefore, Kant concludes that no sensible being is capable of such moral perfection. He insists, however, that the argument about our "moral destiny"—our capacity for infinite moral progress—is of "the greatest use."[77] The infinite deferral of a completely self-determined will (absolute freedom) leaves open the possibility of a more radically human freedom—that is, an attitude toward our freedom that can be developed and cultivated over time. It is this attitude, this presupposition that we are free—and not freedom itself in some noumenal sense—that Kant attempts to cultivate. Kant's ethics is less about making arguments about freedom than it is about cultivating a particular relationship to these arguments. Because freedom remains theoretically inscrutable, Kantian ethics exhorts us to adopt a particular disposition toward freedom. It exhorts us to adopt what Kant calls a moral disposition or an orientation toward our capacity to be free. In short, it exhorts us to act according to reason.

The presupposition of freedom, then, concerns not just the provision of rules but the formation or development of the individual human being. It is in this sense that Kant's division between a sensible self and an intelligible self (or what he sometimes refers to as an empirical and intelligible character)[78] organizes his broader ethical theory. If, writes Kant, "God and eternity with their awful majesty would stand unceasingly before our eyes," the motivation to act would be external.

> Reason would have no need to work itself up so as to gather strength to resist inclinations. . . . As long as human nature remains as it is, human conduct would thus be changed into mere mechanism in which, as in a marionette show, everything would be made to gesticulate well but there would be no life in the figures. Now, when it is quite otherwise with us; when with all the effort of our reason we have only a very obscure and ambiguous view into the future; when the governor of the world allows us only to conjecture his existence and his grandeur, not to behold them or prove them clearly; when on the other hand, the moral law within us, without promising or threatening anything with certainty, demands of us disinterested respect; and when finally, this respect alone, becomes active and ruling, first allows us a view into the realm of the supersensible, though only with weak glances; then there can be a truly moral disposition, devoted immediately to the moral law, and a rational creature can become worthy of the highest good in conformity with the moral worth of his person and not merely his actions.[79]

Our "obscure and ambiguous" view of that which we cannot theorize, the supersensible, incites reason to "work" and "gather strength," to become what it is not. Kant equates "life" not with *being* free or with the conformity of our actions to the highest good but with a disposition toward freedom and the moral law. Freedom concerns not a perfected will but a well-crafted comportment toward freedom. The entire dual structure of sensible and intelligible necessitates becoming. If freedom or the supersensible were immediately available to us, our incentive to act would be external to us, and therein lies Kant's anthropological claim: the dignity of the human being, its particularity, lies in this constant striving to become free, a striving that is motivated by a presupposition of freedom. The Kantian normative claim concerns not a moral status but a moral becoming. With its "obscure" view of the future, the human cannot be assured of knowing, much less experiencing, freedom in the transcendental sense. We are sensible beings and have no real hope that we might live forever. Kant's claims about freedom are not to be conflated with a discovery of reason as an object of knowledge; instead, they point to freedom in a more qualified, more radically human instantiation. So conceived, freedom is not a metaphysical claim or a matter of epistemology. The finite human being asserts its freedom and makes claims about itself from this presupposition.

It bears repeating that Kant equates this assertion of freedom with life itself. The marionettes are determined according to a "mere mechanism" because they are directly connected to the puppeteer through strings. Kant's metaphor suggests that were human beings to "behold clearly" the grandeur of a God and eternity, then we would be determined by divine laws. Life and freedom itself are a function of our finitude, of our decidedly phenomenal existence. For Kant, the mechanism metaphor concerns, then, not an absolute freedom, for no human will is perfectly good, but rather the relationship of moral agents to themselves. The marionette metaphor, ironically enough, points to the mixing of causalities in Kantian ethics. This irony is what we miss if we insist on interpreting the "form" of Kant's ethics, overly influenced by Kant's own insistence upon their "formality." This is the truth of Heine's satire of Kant's "mechanical, regular, almost abstract" lifestyle. The irony is lost on us when we fail to give due attention to Kant's writings on the role of freedom and ethics as "formative." The form of Kant's ethics is not only formal, but formative—its very form cultivates an ethical subject. It forms an ethical subject by subjecting it to an ethical dietetics.

This insight provides another way to read Kant's claim that freedom is the "keystone" of his critical system. He grounds reason in its own assertions, its own self-grounding. As Robert Pippin puts it, Kant's arguments about freedom are "assertions not matters of facts, or substantial metaphysical claims."[80] We have discussed Kant's distinction between a transcendental freedom and a practical freedom and can describe one final sense of freedom, freedom as the timeless decision to adopt what we have referred to as a moral disposition. By insisting that freedom be presupposed and that it is theoretically inscrutable, Kant brackets the theoretical problem of natural causality and freedom. This bracketing gesture resonates with late eighteenth-century proto-anthropology: we cannot explain what freedom is or how it is theoretically possible just as we cannot explain how the mind and body are related. We must simply proceed from a presupposition and act *as if* we could explain it. The *as if* of the presupposition of freedom, however, concerns not the reality of practical freedom but our ability to theoretically explain it. Kant is not exhorting us to act as though we are free even if we lack the grounds to do so. He is simply proceeding in a perhaps surprisingly non-metaphysical manner and claiming that once we take the practical standpoint, we must presuppose our freedom. The presupposition of freedom is a consequence of "saving," as Kant put it, our freedom from natural causality.

If we read Kant's theory of freedom in this fundamentally practical manner and focus less on the articulation of moral principles and more on the individual moral agent's relationship to them, we can reframe Kant's ethics and shift its focus from the logic of formal principles to the cultivation of a moral disposition or character. In this sense, Kant's ethics concerns the moral agent in all its finite, human nature.

The Moral Law and Moral Incentive

Kant's discussion of the moral law and the feeling proper to it, namely, respect, exemplifies the cultivation of a moral disposition and Kant's more fundamental attempt to conceive of how freedom might be actualized with regard to the human being. It is also the most complex example of the place of feeling in Kant's broader ethical economy.[81] For Kant, the moral law is nothing other than the autonomy of pure practical reason, namely, freedom. Early in the *Kritik der praktischen Vernunft*, he claims that consciousness of the moral law is the "singular fact of reason," a fact that "forces itself upon us."[82] The law cannot be theoretically deduced from antecedent data or empirical or intellectual intuition; it cannot be worked out through reason; it can only be recognized in its unique facticity. The moral law announces itself, and the origins of this announcement remain unknown. Kant's insistence upon the sheer facticity of the moral law has struck many commentators as, to say the least, rather odd. Hegel mocks it and its apodictic character as a "cold duty, the last undigested log in our stomach, a revelation to reason,"[83] and Adorno mocks its "givenness" as "blinding and irrational."[84]

As Dieter Henrich has suggested, however, such dismissals often overlook the very problem that Kant was dealing with, namely, how a universal, formal law might have a subjective effect or motivating force. Does Kant envision a particular mode of subjectivity that corresponds to the law? Kant insists that "the essence of all moral worth" is a function of the unmediated determination of the will by the moral law,[85] but the question of a moral incentive greatly complicates this matter. What mode of receptivity—or what Kant terms *Empfänglichkeit*—can be subjectively effective and, at the same time, not undermine the immediacy of the law? So-called moral sense philosophies like those of Shaftesbury and Hutcheson presuppose a *sensus moralis* that make moral judgment possible. Whereas both Hutcheson and Kant doubt that ethics can, ultimately, be theoretically grounded, Kant insists that the moral law cannot be an object of the senses, thereby begging the question of how the moral law can be subjectively received. At what point does the objectivity of the moral law intersect with the subjectivity of a finite human being? At what point does the form of the law intersect with particular forms of life?[86]

Questions concerning the receptivity of the moral agent are especially important in light of the connotations of "fact." *Factum* is the Latin term for "deed" or "act." Consciousness of the moral law, as *factum*, is the singular *act* of reason.[87] It is given as an already completed act, not as a simple fact of knowledge. In this sense, consciousness of the moral law has—as an act—an aspect in the grammatical sense. It is always already completed. We can understand this "act" as the analogue of the presupposition of freedom in the earlier works, where the presupposition of freedom was the always already completed "act" of reason. Whereas in the *Grundlegung*, Kant wrote of the need to presuppose our freedom, in the *Kritik der praktischen Vernunft* Kant strengthens his language and invokes—without any theoretical grounding—"an alleged a priori fact of practical reason."[88]

Kant addresses these questions concerning the receptivity of the law and the "fact" of reason most explicitly in the *Kritik der praktischen Vernunft* in the infamously difficult section "Von den Triebfedern der reinen praktischen Vernunft" ("On the Incentives of Pure Practical Reason"). Here, Kant considers what can be said about moral incentives—a question that had occupied him since at least his reading of Rousseau and Hutcheson[89]—by considering a "ground of determination for the will" or what he terms a *Triebfeder* ("incentive," *elator animi*). Kant's incentive would be the subjective condition of any action. Kant's semantics are key in this case as well. In his eighteenth-century lexicon Johann Christoph Adelung defines *Triebfeder* as an "elastic spring that sets the parts of a machine to movement."[90] A driving-spring, then, would analogously set the finite human being into action. The moral engine of Kant's ethical economy is driven by a mechanism of sorts, an elastic spring.

The discussion of a moral incentive, however, only makes sense with respect to a finite being—that is, the very problem of an incentive reiterates the fact that Kant bases his ethics on the finite human individual, a being whose reason is not yet in accord with the objective necessity of the moral law. The subject of Kantian ethics is the finite human being whose sensible nature requires an incentive, a driving-spring, to make it receptive to the law. This clear distinction between the moral law and the finite human being is confirmed by a hypothetical comparison of the moral subject to a divine will. We could imagine an infinitely rational being that always acts out of the moral law and thus does not feel the moral law as an imperative. Such a being would need no incentive to act in accord with the moral law, because there would be no distinction between this being and the law in the first place. Divided between its intelligible and sensible aspects, as Kant claims it is, the finite human being, in contrast, needs an incentive. The moral law, while inconceivable, cannot remain absolutely formal. Because of Kant's insistence that the moral law must determine immediately in order for an action to be morally worthy, there is only one possible origin for such an incentive: the moral law itself. For Kant, the moral law must be both the objective and subjective ground of determination. The moral law cannot remain at the level of objective principles. Morality is not simply a question of establishing the grounds of actions; it also concerns their subjective effectiveness. To meet Kant's standards for genuine moral worth—"the essential of all moral worth"— the moral law must be both objectively binding—universal and necessary—and subjectively compelling.[91]

In order to establish the conceptual possibility of genuine moral worth, Kant conceives of a moral incentive that can mediate these two demands. It cannot be an empirical or intellectual intuition; it cannot be a feeling like Rousseau's pity or a faculty like Hutcheson and Shaftesbury's moral sense. So what is this incentive? How does the universal law effect a subjective response? Kant's formulation of these questions is in itself key. These questions already imply a subjective need of reason. They reiterate

Kant's own claim that the formal, universal moral law requires a subjective incentive in order to motivate actions that would be in accord with the moral law. This intersection, however, cannot be fully theorized. It is, writes Kant, an "unsolvable problem"; therefore, he continues, "We shall not have to show from where the moral law supplies an incentive, but rather . . . what it effects in the mind."[92] The theoretical impossibility of knowing the law means that we can only "indicate" its effects. This theoretical impossibility—an impossibility acknowledged already in the *Kritik der reinen Vernunft* and in the *Grundlegung zur Metaphysik der Sitten*—means that we should be on the lookout for an effect, for something that emanates from the singular act (*factum*) of reason. We can never know the origin of the moral law or how it is possible for pure reason to be practical, that is to say, free. The question about the intersection of the moral law and its subjective effect is indexical.

This implication frames the self's relationship to the moral law throughout the *Kritik der praktischen Vernunft*. We cannot know the moral law. We can only recognize its effects and the fact that we should subordinate ourselves to it.[93] But how is this recognition even possible? (In a sense, this is akin to asking how the presupposition of freedom is possible.) For moral sense philosophers like Shaftesbury and Hutcheson, such a recognition was grounded in a moral sense—a concept that was meant to address the failures of a purely rational concept of the good to relate to the will itself. What we might term the affective moment in Kant's ethics is in part an affirmation of this insight. Whereas the moral law determines completely independently of "sensible urges," there is a need for an incentive, a need precipitated by the impossibility to deduce the law.

Feelings, Sensibility, and Pathology in Kant's Ethical Economy

In his *Anthropologie in pragmatischer Hinsicht*, Kant associates feelings with "sensibility," whose relationship to the mind is "passive" and characterized by "receptivity." To sense, to feel, is to be affected.[94] In contrast, thought's relationship to the mind is "active."[95] In the *Kritik der praktischen Vernunft*, Kant writes that all feelings discharge their effect in the moment when they are most intense—that is, feelings are short-lived moments of stimulation. Initially, they stimulate (*reitzen*), but then they let the heart fall back into a "languor."⁹⁶ While warning against the dangers of Rousseau's "inner light," Kant insists that certain feelings are fleeting and contingent, not only within an individual but between moral subjects. The perceived contingency and passivity of feelings and inclinations ground Kant's argument that an ethical economy predicated on inclinations and feelings would be tantamount to mere mechanism: "As long as human nature remains as it now is, human behavior would also be transformed into mere mechanism, just as in a marionette show where everything moves well but no life can be found in the figures" (147). If our inclinations are allowed to determine our actions, then we would be mere puppets. We would be bound and thus determined by the ever-changing and contingent stimuli of our inclinations.

Kant's claim that feelings are contingent implies something else as well, something often overlooked that exposes the social and contextual character of his ethics. Feelings are not simply *natural* or fixed. They are socially and historically contingent. Limiting his critique of affect to inclinations and emotions as they are manifest "in our time," Kant suggests that he is concerned with particular, historically specific types of inclinations (157). "As long as human nature remains as it is now," the human being will be subordinate to the contingency of stimuli. His critique is not simply a dismissal of feelings and affect as such; it is a distrust based on what he assumes to be their contingency. At the center of his critique is what he sees as the contemporary tendency to appeal to "yielding, soft-hearted feelings" rather than a "more appropriate dry and serious representation of duty" in order to have an effect on the mind. Feelings and inclinations vary in their shape and type and are thus, for Kant, subject to corruption. It is important to note, again, that Kant's critique of inclinations is historically specific. He is criticizing historically specific forms of inclination, not inclinations or feelings as such. More precisely, he is criticizing what literary and cultural historians have come to call the Age of Sensibility, or what Kant might have called the Age of Soft-Hearted Feelings.⁹⁷

Precisely because feelings and inclinations are, at least in part, contingent, they are subject to the stimulation of reason. Feelings can be altered. They can be stimulated and produced. Kant's appeal to a self-wrought feeling, then, is not an appeal to an ontology or original psychology but rather to a technology of the production of sensation. His entire critique of the contingency of affection is simultaneously a recognition that feelings can be transformed. As Allen Wood has recently argued, Kant's infamous distrust of inclinations is a distrust of inclinations "insofar as our nature has been shaped by society."[98] There is nothing wrong or evil about inclinations in themselves. Only in society do they become evil. Drawing on Rousseau's "proper love" (*amour propre*), Kant called this social malformation of human nature "unsocial sociability" and, in the *Kritik der praktischen Vernunft,* self-conceit and pride. Like Rousseau, Kant attributes the development of pride and even the propensity to radical evil to our social condition. If the human being searches for the "causes and circumstances [for his] perilous" condition, "[he] can easily convince himself that they do not come his way from his own nature" but rather "from the human beings to whom he stands in relation and association": "It is not the instigation of nature that arouses what should properly be called the passions, which wreak such great devastation in his originally good predisposition. . . . Envy, addiction to power, avarice, and the malignant inclinations associated with these, assail his nature, which on its own is undemanding, as soon as he is among other human beings . . . and they will mutually corrupt each other's moral disposition and make one another evil."[99]

Here in *Die Religion innerhalb der Grenzen der blossen Vernunft* (*Religion Within the Boundaries of Mere Reason*), Kant reiterates his claim that feelings and inclinations are insufficient grounds for ethics because they are historically contingent and, thus, unpredictable. At one point in the *Kritik der praktischen Vernunft,* Kant defines life as that faculty by which a being "acts according to the laws of the faculty of desire."[100] In so doing he ties mechanism to contingency and life to a certain form of universal necessity. He couples life with freedom and mechanism with its opposite, heteronomy. As he says, consistency is the "highest obligation" of the philosopher (9). Herein lies the explicit distinction between inclinations and principle. Principles allow for a resolute mode of thought. In fact, Kant equates a moral disposition with consistency and resolution. Kant's moral feeling, namely, respect, originates from reason itself and is thus distinct from sensible inclinations.

For Kant, an ethical economy predicated on inclinations is not only heteronymous but pathological as well. Kant's normalization of a particular ethical economy suggests that certain forms of subjectivity—certain ways of relating to the self and rational principles—are pathological. An inclination to turn subjective grounds of determination into objective ones, for example, is pathological because it indicates what for Kant is an abnormal relationship between the self and the moral law (74). It indicates a deafness to the voice of the law and a numbness to its incentive. In the *Kritik der praktischen Vernunft*, Kant's use of "pathological" eclipses that of sick and connotes "subjective" (79). That which is simply subjectively effected, he writes parenthetically, is pathological. The merely subjective is a source of sickness that can lead to an abnormal ethical economy. In his eighteenth-century dictionary of Kant's critical philosophy, G. S. A. Mellin defines "pathological" as that which depends on sensibility (*Sinnlichkeit*). From the Greek *pathologikos*, meaning that which depends on suffering, the pathological tends to be conflated with the sensible, because both denote receptivity. From a practical perspective, then, the self is pathologically determined, for example, when it allows itself to be determined through fear or hope. Expanding on the relationship of the pathological to the moral law, Mellin helps highlight a peculiar element of Kant's ethical economy: "The effect of the moral law on our feeling is pathological, because it awakens in us the feeling of displeasure that we should subordinate our sensible wishes to the law. Every influence on our feeling awakens a suffering; we feel a pleasant or unpleasant feeling which is a suffering, as is every feeling, and thus pathological."[101] The irony of Kant's ethical economy is that it is based on interrupting a pathological subjectivity by means of something whose effect is itself pathological, namely the feeling of respect. In the collocation pathological-subjective-sensible, it is evident how the Kantian ethical discipline is concerned less with the extirpation of sensibility than with maintaining a proper economy of sensibility-reason. That is, pathology manifests itself not so much in the body as in an abnormal mind, a mind that subordinates ethical determination to subjective grounds. As Kant suggests in *Die Religion*, radical evil is not a corruption of the body or sensibility but a failure of reason itself, an adoption of the wrong maxims along with an abnormal relationship of the self to the law and thus to itself. Everything in the Kantian moral regime is done to solicit, create, and instill a disquiet that makes the moral subject aware of a pathological solipsism and then turn toward an ethical economy. This economy is the normalized relationship between the mind and body that Kant lays out, a relationship that requires the presupposition of freedom.

The Uniqueness of Respect as Moral Feeling

While Kant's ethical economy appears to be organized around the immediacy of the moral law, "Von den Triebfedern der reinen praktischen

Vernunft" shows just how complicated this assumed immediacy is. Here Kant explains in detail how the moral law effects its own recognition through a complex of subjective affects. The moral law motivates the finite human being by producing pain, humiliation, and finally, respect. It organizes the ethical economy by producing a subjectively effective complex of feelings. This complex of effects begins as and is initially felt by the self as pain that interrupts sensibility:

> The essence of all determination of the will through the moral law is this: as a free will, and thus without the cooperation of sensible drives but even rejecting all of them and breaking off all inclinations insofar as they could be against the law, it is determined simply by the law. So far, then, the effect of the moral law as an incentive is only negative and as such this incentive can be recognized a priori. For all inclination and every sensible drive is based on feeling, and the negative effect on feeling (through which the breaking off which happens to the inclinations) is itself feeling. Consequently, we can see a priori that the moral law as the determining ground of the will, by thwarting all our inclinations, must produce a feeling, which can be called pain, and here we have now the first, perhaps the only case wherein we can determine from a priori concepts the relation of a cognition (here a cognition of pure practical reason) to the feeling of pleasure or pain.[102]

Reason appears as that which it appears not to be: reason appears as a feeling. Kant calls this occasion a subreption (*vitium subreptionis*) or an "error of appearance" (*Fehler des Erschleichens*), an optical illusion in the self-consciousness. We take the moral incentive for a "sensible impulse as it always occurs in so-called illusions of the senses" (117). This transcendental illusion is a crossing where the self takes what is supersensible as an object of the senses. The moral law is taken as a feeling.

What does it mean, however, for reason to effect a feeling? On the one hand, Kant says that all feeling is sensual, and thus determined by natural causality, but on the other hand, he says that respect is a feeling effected through reason (76). Moral feeling, claims Kant, is singular and the only feeling that humans recognize a priori and of whose necessity we can conceive (73). In a footnote in the *Grundlegung*, Kant had already discussed the peculiar status of respect as feeling:

> It could be objected that behind the word respect I only seek refuge in an obscure feeling, instead of distinctly resolving the question by means of a concept of reason. But though respect is a feeling, it is not once received by means of influence; it is instead, a feeling self-wrought by means of a rational concept and therefore specifically different from all feelings of the first kind, which can be reduced to inclination or fear. What I cognize immediately as a law for me I cognize with respect, which signifies merely consciousness of the subordination of my will to a law without the mediation of other influences on my sense. Immediate determination of the will by means of the law and consciousness of this is called respect, so that this is regarded as the effect of the law on the subject, and not as the cause of the law.[103]

This passage highlights the double nature of respect as a feeling and the blurring of the lines between reason and sensation. Unlike other feelings, which are the products of external stimuli, respect is self-wrought or produced by reason as a by-product of reason's becoming practical. And it is here in the analogical relationship of reason to feeling that one can observe both the particularity and generic identity of respect as a feeling.

Although respect is an effect of the moral law and self-wrought, it functions like a feeling. This analogical relationship reiterates not only the fact that for Kant the human being "can never be altogether free from desires and inclinations," but also that feeling is a necessary element in his ethical economy.[104] Respect has a neither/nor place for Kant. In order to maintain the purity of the moral subject it must be a self-wrought product of reason, but in order to have an effect on a finite human being it must function as an analogue of sensibility. It must mimic the pathology of sensibility. Although it mimics the pathology of affect, respect is itself not a *pathos* or something that we suffer. Herein lies the peculiarity of Kant's notion of respect: it is an active self-affection. It is a self-effected affect. It is a receptivity, a passivity that is self-affected through reason. The moral law can neither extirpate nor transcend sensibility; it must work through it.

Mellin distinguishes respect from other feelings in three regards: (1) The origin of respect is a priori, while the origin of other feelings is a posteriori; we know a priori that the idea of the moral law will afford a feeling that will counter all inclinations. (2) All feelings are mediated through our inclinations; the objects of inclinations and other feelings are objects of our senses, while the object of respect is the moral law, which is not an object of our senses. And (3) all other feelings can be cognized, while respect for the moral law is "inconceivable." We cannot understand how the moral law can govern the faculty of desire, whereas we can conceive of an object of, for example, hunger.[105]

Two elements merge in the feeling of respect: the unintelligibility of the moral law and its worthiness of respect. Because the moral law is inconceivable, it can only be presented as an object of respect. We do not simply suffer respect as we do other types of feeling. Moreover, respect not only indicates or points to the moral law; it recognizes it as something worthy of attention, something worthy of our subordination. Both of these elements—respect's object orientation and its particular recognition—constitute a particular relationship of the subject to the moral law. Since feelings or inclinations are understood generally as relating to an external object, respect as a relation to the law is a different kind of feeling. It is a relation of the self to itself. As Peter Fenves points out, however, this is a necessary relationship between the object (the moral law) and its feeling (respect). It is a necessity grounded in reason itself.[106] Thus, any relation that is not predicated upon this necessary relation is struck down. Respect is a particular and, for Kant, necessary disposition toward the law, an attitude of recognition. "There is something so singular in the boundless esteem for the pure moral law stripped of all advantage—as practical reason, whose voice makes even the boldest evildoer tremble and forces him to hide from its sight, presents it to us for obedience—that one cannot wonder at finding this influence of a mere intellectual idea on feeling quite impenetrable for speculative reason."[107] In its grandeur the moral law effects a complex moral feeling that affords no conceptual insight into the moral law itself; it simply necessitates a moral disposition marked by esteem and respect for the moral law, that is to say, the always already accomplished presupposition of freedom.

Finite human beings need the moral law to take its apparent detour through feeling. And the effect of reason on this feeling, writes Kant, "is to be cultivated": "It is a very sublime thing in human nature to be determined to actions directly by a pure law of reason, and even the illusion wherein the subjective element of this intellectual determinability of the will is held to be sensuous and an effect of a particular sensuous feeling (for an intellectual feeling would be self-contradictory) partakes of this sublimity. It is of great importance to point out this property of our personality and to cultivate so far as possible the effect of reason on this feeling."[108]

This illusion, this error—the appearance of reason as feeling—is part of the sublimity that must be cultivated. Kant's suggestion that the appearance of reason as feeling must be cultivated puts Kant's more fundamental claim about the necessary relationship between the moral law and respect in a new light. How, exactly, is the moral law a necessary object of respect? And what would it mean to cultivate the effect of reason on this feeling? At what point does this necessary relation become a normative relation, a relation that ought to be developed according to a rational norm?

The Function of Respect in the Ethical Economy

In Kant's detailed discussion of the place of respect in his ethical economy, we can observe how this necessity takes on a normative force. Kant assumes a threefold psychological reaction to the law—that is, Kant assumes that the moral agent will react in a particular way: First, he assumes that we will resist the law and its demands for moral purity. Second, he assumes that we will experience this resistance as pain, because the moral law will strike down our pride. Finally, we will experience this striking down as humiliation or "intellectual contempt."[109] The initial effect of the law is negative—it rejects and breaks off all inclinations. And its interruption is itself feeling and thus sensibility. Kant claims that by limiting and prescribing sensibility, the negative feeling retards the inclinations. Kant calls this negative feeling "pain," because it thwarts sensible impulses and breaks them off. The violence of the moral law against our pride in our own self-sufficiency will denigrate the "animal" side of the human being. In striking down pride, the moral law will strike down a particular relationship of the self to the self. The pain inflicted by the moral law would interrupt an economy of the self driven by inclinations. It interrupts the "life force" of the human (23). Kant calls this economy of inclinations "solipsism" (73), because it is thoroughly self-referential. The moral law as feeling interrupts the circularity of inclinations and thus its self-referential tendencies. The subjective effect of the moral law modifies the ethical economy by inserting a gap into its circular structure.

Kant identifies two forms of solipsism or what we could call self-relation: self-love, also referred to as a benevolence toward oneself (*Philautia*), and self-conceit or pride (*Arrogantia*). While the moral law merely restricts self-love, Kant writes that it "strikes down" pride. The moral law regulates the economy between self and inclinations—that is, it regulates the relationship of the self to the self. Its regulation of pride is particularly violent because pride is self-conceit, which Kant defines as a self-esteem that precedes conformity to the moral law. Pride refers only to the self. The moral law interrupts this circularity by making the self receptive to something that is both radically distinct and identical to itself, the moral law. The incomprehensibility and sheer otherness of the moral law interrupts the self-referential character of inclinations. This ethical economy does not, however, simply strike down. It also makes possible a positive, moral disposition. This moral disposition signifies a relationship of the self toward the law produced by a "positive feeling." Kant insists that by striking down pride, the moral law itself becomes an object of the "greatest respect" (73). We respect that which pains and humiliates, because it provokes recognition of the moral law and thus our possible freedom. The painful and humiliating violence of the law, he claims, effects a feeling of respect. This affective complex—pain, humiliation, respect—is, for Kant, moral feeling.

By means of this complex moral feeling, the moral law sets the ethical economy aright. The recognition of the moral law, however, is not a cognition of the law but a recognition of our corrupt human nature and the adoption of a moral disposition. The moral law forces us to compare our sensual nature to the assumed purity of the moral law, a comparison that highlights a humiliating gap that weakens our pride. Kant's basic assumption and normative claim, then, is that we will in fact be humiliated by what he claims is the non-coincidence of our finite sensible self and the purity of the moral law: "The moral law inevitably humiliates every human being when he compares it [the law] to the sensible propensity of his nature" (74). This humiliating recognition is predicated upon a normalized image not just of moral purity but of human nature. The image of moral purity and its implicit counterimage of a finite human being give Kant's ethics a normative effect that is meant to be disquieting. "What is essential" or genuine in the moral law is defined against that which Kant views as the corruption of the human will, a will that needs the corrective work of reason in the form of a normative ethical economy.

For Kant, morality is "essentially a response to a human condition" that has been sundered from natural human goodness. Embedded in Kant's claims about moral goodness is a fundamental social critique.[110]

For Kant, only the universal reach of reason can correct the human being's ethical economy. This correction, however, is accomplished through a sensible effect that interrupts a morally corrupt solipsism. By modifying the human being's ethical economy, this sensible effect alters the self's relationship to the moral law and thus itself. And it does so with dramatic violence, dramatic in the sense that this alteration is achieved by means of an exemplary comparison in which the subject is confronted with his corrupt self and thus, insists Kant, humiliated. This humiliation and weakening of the self "awakens" respect for the moral law as the agent or cause of this humiliation. As incentive, then, the moral law has an influence on the sensibility of the subject by effecting a feeling. This feeling, however, cannot precede the law. The incentive has an effect on feeling, but is itself free from all sensible conditions.[111] It is not, insists Kant, pathological in origin. Kant terms this positive feeling "respect" (*Achtung*). As the nominal form of "giving attention to," the feeling effected by the law is an active "paying attention to" or esteeming of the law itself. The very word conjoins the two elements of respect: the negative pain of humiliation and the moral disposition that arises out of it.[112] Respect is a "tribute that we cannot refuse to pay to [moral] merit whether we want to or not";[113] it is absolutely necessary, or as suggested here, radically normative. For Kant, respect emerges out of our consciousness of the free subordination of the will to the law.[114] As a feeling, respect is a consciousness and thus, in part at least, cognitive. It is, we could say, a cognitive feeling. All that is pathological is effected by an object of the senses and thus something we could cognize. Respect, in contrast, originates from something that we cannot know as an object of knowledge, something that cannot be known through intuition and the categories of the understanding. It originates through a causality of reason.[115] It is consciousness of an activity, not a state. As I have noted, the *factum* of reason is always already accomplished.

The ethical economy does not extirpate feeling. In fact, one could read the effect of the moral law, its derogation of inclinations and subsequent production of respect, as an insertion of feeling into the moral economy, albeit the insertion of a very particular type of moral feeling. In fact, Kant implies that respect overwhelms mere inclination and feelings like happiness and fear.[116] It functions, rather, like a second-order feeling, a feeling about feeling that struggles to establish its authority over mere inclinations. The particularity of respect as a feeling is especially evident in the multivalent connotations of the word *Achtung*. It connotes not only respect but an imperative of warning and authority as *Achtung!* It conveys an imperative force. One can observe this in Kant's own comments on moral apathy, which he insists is not "a lack of feeling or a subjective indifference with respect to objects of choice." Rather, moral apathy is the condition in which "feelings arising from sensible impressions lose their influence on moral feelings only because the respect for the moral law is more powerful than all such feelings together."[117] Moral apathy is the absence of uncontrollable affects, not the absence of feeling generally.[118] Feeling, in this case respect, plays a central role in the moral economy, an economy that is, as Kant writes, concerned to maintain a "peaceful mind," which is the "state of health in moral life."[119] And Kant refers to this state as a moral disposition. Although Kant never states this explicitly, it is, ironically perhaps, a feeling that makes possible what he elsewhere calls the "inner resting" of his ethical economy.[120] A feeling makes an ethical equilibrium, a moral disposition, possible.

Cultivating a Moral Disposition: Kantian Virtue and Moral Exemplars

For Kant, the feeling of respect is not expressive—that is, it does not express something prior in an already self-assured subject. Whereas a perception represents a quality of the object, the feeling of respect, writes Kant, figures a "more radical and purely subjective relation," "a mutation within ourselves."[121] It is the subjective relation of the moral subject to the moral law. Respect does not express a preexisting relationship; instead, it marks the stimulation and mutation of a subjective relationship to the law by reason. Respect marks the apogee of a moral cultivation of the self by reason. The feeling of respect marks not only the fact that something other is affecting us but also the crossing point of inside and outside. Just as the felt need of reason orients us toward a purposiveness of nature, the feeling of respect orients the subject toward the moral law. It is a signpost or compass by means of which subjects can orient themselves toward the proper, or normalized, relationship with the law. And as a signpost it is a consciousness of the moral law.¹²² But signposts and compasses always point to something else. They indicate not only a direction but a distinction.

Kant assumes the non-coincidence between an individual's status as a finite human being with sensuous inclinations and a reasonable being who can determine its will. One can imagine an infinitely rational being who always acts out of the moral law and does not feel the moral law as an imperative. It is only the finite human being who as an agent feels the moral law as a burden that conflicts with sensuous inclinations, and it is this finite being that Kant takes as his ethical starting point. From the perspective of the finitude of the human being, Kant speaks of the "levels of the moral disposition." This language of "levels" suggests a developmental, disciplinary aspect of moral being.

For Kant, the terms "moral disposition" (*Gesinnung*), "mode of thought" (*Denkungsart*), and "character" are closely related. *Denkungsart* signifies a certain conduct of thought or activity, whereas *Gesinnung* signifies a particular disposition of mind, and a moral *Gesinnung* signifies a "responsiveness" to the incentives of the moral law or a pure moral interest.[123] A moral disposition is bound up with a consciousness of our moral state, which according to Kant, is a consciousness of our (presupposed) freedom. It signifies, then, a particular cast of mind according to which the presupposition of freedom has always already been made. It refers not to a characteristic or quality of an agent but to the incentive by which an agent acts. Unlike some conceptions of virtue as an "enduring property of the agent," a disposition refers to the agent's relationship to a principle.[124] It affords a fixed point of orientation in terms of which particular choices can be made. Kant likens the acquisition of a moral disposition to a revolution in the "disposition of the human being." It is like a "rebirth" (*Wiedergeburt*), except that the agent is active rather than passive. It is a rebirth that the moral agent itself enacts.[125] Unlike some Protestant Christian understandings of conversion, wherein the event depends entirely on an objective act of divine grace, the "rebirth" into a moral disposition is the subjective, resolute adoption of a particular, that is to say, responsive, relationship to the moral law.[126]

As Felicitas Munzel argues, Kant identifies a moral disposition with his unique conception of virtue. Instead of signifying a particular self-control over inclinations (as might be the case in some uses of virtue), Kant identifies a moral disposition with virtue insofar as it signifies a self-control characteristic of the process of thought itself, "specifically of choice making or the subjectively practical use of reason in human moral life."[127] A moral disposition is not just the grounds for a particular action but an "acquired mental posture."[128] And for Kant, such a moral disposition can be cultivated, if not actually produced (since ultimately the adoption of such a disposition is a subjective choice), through a moral culture (*Kultur*). A moral disposition therefore signifies moral development and progress.[129]

Kant ties this notion of moral development to virtue and even refers to virtue as the "disposition conformed with laws from respect for law."[130] But the language of Kant's "moral disposition" and virtue should underline the distinction between these concepts and Kant's understanding of ancient eudaimonism in its Stoic and Aristotelian forms. As Robert Louden argues, "What is most objectionable about a de-ontological approach [that is, ethical approaches that stress what we *ought* to do, not what kind of person we ought to be] . . . is not present in Kant's approach. The conceptual commitment to agency and long-term characteristic behavior rather than atomistic acts and decision procedures for moral quandaries is evident here as one would expect in virtue ethics."[131] Kant is not concerned with the extent to which particular actions accord with determinate rules; instead, he is concerned with a moral agent's ability to live a rational life—that is, he is concerned with the resolution with which one lives according to reason as presented in his ethical dietetics. Kant's notion of virtue is similar to Aristotle's notion that the fully virtuous agent acts for the sake of the noble, perceiving that virtuous acts are good in themselves and choosing them for this reason.[132] And both Kant and Aristotle are concerned about the harmonizing of inclinations and reason in moral character. For Kant, a moral disposition is a philosophical habit of mind; however, it is not a habit in the sense that it is developed through a mechanism of habituation. Kant defines such a mechanistic notion of virtue as the formation of a habit, which is merely "to establish a lasting inclination apart from any maxim, through frequently repeated gratifications of that inclination."[133] Whereas Aristotle's virtues are nurtured and perfected, Kant knows only of a singular virtue—the original orientation of the ethical subject toward the moral law. Kantian virtue is not the cultivation of virtuous traits, but rather a moral disposition marked above all by its resolute orientation to the moral law. As Kant puts it, it means "to be consistent" with respect to the *factum* of reason.

A moral disposition, then, is not a "holiness of morals," either in an actualistic or volitional sense. A moral disposition does not imply a will "completely conformed with the moral law."[134] Such a holy, perfected will is an "archetype" for the finite human being who must always be progressing from a position of virtue or a moral disposition. The human being is "a creature and thus always dependent with regard to what he requires for complete satisfaction with his condition, he can never be altogether free from desires and inclinations which, because they rest on physical causes, do not of themselves accord with the moral law, which has quite different sources" (84 [Gregor, 207]). Virtue is always "moral disposition in conflict, and not holiness in the supposed possession of a complete purity of dispositions of the will." The finitude and imperfection of a moral disposition, however resolute, reiterates its developmental and cultivated character. But what must be highlighted is how the concept of a moral disposition—with its seemingly paradoxical notions of rebirth, development, and conflict—is a fitting frame in which to read not only the purity but the impurity of Kantian ethics, the ethical communication bridging the gap between reason and sensibility.

Because of the assumed non-coincidence between our sensuous and rational selves—that is, because of what Kant claims is a moral disposition always in conflict—the finite human being must be disciplined or cultivated into the normalized ethical economy that I have laid out. Human beings require an ethical economy that "morally educates" them (85). Moral being or absolute accordance with the moral law is never an actual human condition. When Kant writes of "what is essential to moral worth," he writes of something that is impossible for a finite human being. At the same time, what he terms a "discipline of reason" can cultivate a moral disposition (71). Only at a certain level of this disciplinary regime and after a great deal of work is the feeling of respect possible, a feeling that allows us "to perceive" the "sublimity of our own intelligible existence" (88). Kant's claim that a certain disciplinary regime "allows" us to perceive our intelligible existence may seem to reintroduce the possibility of heteronomy and thus contradict his insistence on the immediacy and a priori nature of the law's effect. But Kant's claim is that we can "get a taste of"—but not completely and wholly conform to—an intelligible existence. The possibility of this sublime feeling, however, is predicated on a prior experience: the self-affected feeling of respect that is itself not a *Lebensgenuß*, that is, it is not simply a feeling of pleasure. We feel this self-affection as the loss of pleasure, the interruption of a certain form of life. "This consolation is therefore merely negative with respect to everything that can make life pleasant. For no one will wish to have this occasion, perhaps not even wish to live under such circumstances. But he lives and cannot bear to be unworthy in his own eyes. This inner resting is thus merely negative with respect to all that may make life joyful. . . . It is the effect of respect for something quite different than life, in comparison and contrast to which life and its enjoyments have absolutely no worth" (88 [Gregor, 211]).

The self-affection of respect sets up a comparison and contrast between two "lives"—one that is "something entirely different" and one that is temporal, finite, something that the finite human being still lives. And it is this respect for "something entirely different" that Kant insists must be cultivated. The normative force of the ethical economy is predicated upon this distinction between what is and what should or ought to be.

Interestingly, Kant elsewhere argues that our predisposition to the good is best cultivated by merely giving "the example of good people (as regards conformity to the law)" so that the predisposition "gradually becomes a way of thinking." To arouse this feeling of "sublimity of our moral vocation"—respect for the law—is, insists Kant, an especially praiseworthy means of awakening a moral disposition.[135] Exposure to the moral law—or as Kant puts it "being instructed in the holiness of duty"—arouses recognition of the moral law. Such instruction stimulates a feeling of sublimity for our moral vocation. Discipline and instruction cannot transform us into an end-in-itself or make us free in a noumenal sense. (This is impossible in any sense of the term and not even the goal of Kant's ethical dietetics.) This would make freedom heteronymous. In the *Kritik der Urteilskraft* Kant defines discipline as the second and primary element of *Kultur:* "the emancipation of the will from the despotism of desires."[136] Through its circumscription of sensuous desires, discipline transforms the human being's inner will and makes it receptive to higher purposes than nature itself can provide, that is to say, discipline prepares the human being for the recognition of the ends of reason.[137] In order to redress the non-coincidence of our status as moral subjects and our status as empirical, finite beings with sensuous inclinations, Kant prescribes a discipline of reason. The culture of discipline induces the human being to keep his sensuous desires within a normalized order so that he might set himself higher purposes. The disciplinary aspect of culture reworks the sensuous part of our being by disciplining our desires so that the gap between it and our reason might be closed.

This disciplinary culture can prepare us for an experience of freedom in a more qualified sense. It affords a moral worth that is less than "essential," a disposition toward freedom.[138] Such instruction cannot produce the feeling of respect, but it can produce its empirical analogue. It is the *Sittenähnliche* or simulacrum of freedom. It can prepare the ground for moral being. Like his transcendental doctrine of faculties, Kant's ethics is based on the finite human being, and Kant acknowledges this throughout the critical canon. His ethics addresses this finite human being and demands a revolution: a revolution in the "disposition of the human being," a rebirth that Kant implores us to consider as possible.[139]

As I alluded, the practice of Kant's ethical discipline is a function of the exemplarity of the law, or better, the exemplarity of attaining respect for the law. Whereas the moral law remains inconceivable, we can encounter its effect through another, whose example "holds before me a law": "Before a humble common man in whom I perceive an uprightness of character to a certain degree greater than what I am conscious of in myself, my soul bows, whether I want to or not . . . Why is this? His example holds before me a law, that strikes down my pride, when I compare it [his conduct] with my conduct, and whose standard, and possibility as well, I see proven in fact before me."[140]

Respect is always "directed toward people, never toward things."[141] The moral law can only be experienced, if at all, through the example of another person. The moral law outstrips our abilities to experience it directly, and our only access, however mediated, is via an other whom we respect as exemplary. We recognize in his or her particularity the universality of the law. To say that a person exemplifies the moral law is to single out a particular instance of the moral disposition, this presupposition that we are in fact free. What we respect, as Henry Allison puts it, is the "autonomy of pure practical reason" in all rational beings.[142]

Cultivating a Moral Disposition: Ethical Exercises

In the previous two sections I have noted key moments in Kant's text where he speaks of the cultivation of a moral disposition or even the cultivation of the effect of reason on feeling. In this section I will outline more explicitly how Kant codifies this ethical exemplarity into a moral discipline, a discipline to which he ascribes the task of bringing "a wild soul onto the track of the morally good." The finite human being, he suggests, needs the "preparatory instruction," the mechanisms and the leading string of moral discipline in order to be made receptive to the moral law. "As soon as" these mechanical disciplines have had their preparatory effect, the "pure moral ground of motivation" can give the mind the power to tear itself away from its "sensual dependence."[143] The complex effects of the moral law have been investigated, as well as the psychological reactions that Kant insists it will effect, but what is one to make of these mechanical disciplines that seem to contradict the supposed purity of the moral law? How do these finite technologies intersect with human autonomy? To return to the discussion of the feeling of respect: how are these moral disciplines related to respect for the moral law and, thus, to a moral disposition? To what extent—if any—can the feeling of respect be prepared, disciplined, or to be more Kantian, to what extent can the subject be disciplined into receiving the law? To what extent can a moral feeling be stimulated?

Kant's ethical program would prepare the subjective "receptivity" of the mind for a purely moral interest. In other words, it would discipline a receptivity, an openness to the ethical economy that Kant normalized in the section on moral incentives in the *Kritik der praktischen Vernunft*. Accordingly, Kant's ethical disciplines would prepare the subjective conditions for the moral law, since the moral law itself cannot be produced, disciplined, or otherwise subordinated to subjective conditions. It is at this point in these preparatory practices that the universal force of the moral law intersects with the subjective conditions of its possibility—where the universal, objective force of the law intersects with the technologies of the self and particular forms of life. Kant organizes his ethical economy so that the moral law might have "easier access" to the self. It is organized to reduce what he sees as the radical gap between the finite human being and the moral law. Even if we are noumenally free, as finite beings our sensible selves must be disciplined so that the gap between this freedom and reason is closed. The possibility of recognizing the fact that we are free, implies Kant, is increased through an exposure to examples of the moral law, and Kant does not leave this exposure to chance. We are disciplined not into freedom but into a simulacrum of freedom, into the possibility of freedom in a limited, qualified sense.

In the second half of the *Kritik der praktischen Vernunft*, Kant outlines a complex moral discipline that would expose a "student" to the law and ultimately make him more receptive to moral feelings. Kant refers to this second section as the "Doctrine of Method of the Pure Practical Reason." It is not the technique with which one pursues "scientific knowledge" of pure practical fundamental principles. It is not a metaphysics. Rather, it is the technique by which objective practical reason can be made subjectively practical—that is, the discipline of reason entailed in this section is concerned with how the laws of pure practical reason can be afforded "access" to the human mind (151). In this sense, one could understand moral discipline as a dietetic regime through which—to use the title of Kant's own essay—the power of the mind makes itself master over its morbid feelings through sheer resolution. This ethical dietetics is not only outlined in but is intentionally cultivated by the *Kritik der praktischen Vernunft*.

Kant calls this discipline the method of the "founding and culture of true moral dispositions" (153). It is the disciplining and production of a particular attitude toward the law. As a prescribed method to be laid out by a teacher and followed by a student, it is repeatable. In fact, its success lies in its iterative character. Only through the repetition of its mechanisms might the student be in a position to adopt for him- or herself a moral disposition. It is in this context that Kant refers to it as a "moral catechism" (154). Kant's ethical dietetics is a systematic initiation into his ethics. He also calls it an ethical testing (*Prüfung*). The teacher scours biographies old and new in search of good examples of moral duty. He then presents these examples so that the student might have them "close at hand." These "exemplary duties" ground the entire discipline, but these exemplary moments of moral purity are not, unlike Kant's claims about the moral law, of unknown origin. They have been collected, laid out, or presented by a teacher. Kant even goes on to detail the movements of this discipline. The first exercise in this ethical dietetics is meant to habituate judgment according to the moral law so as to make moral judgment repeatable. The teacher engages the student, ideally a "roughly ten year old boy," with these prescribed exercises in order to habituate him into what Kant calls a moral judgment. The student must (1) learn to judge if a certain act (as presented by the teacher from the trove of historical biographies) is in accord with the moral law, and then (2) learn to judge whether it happens (subjectively) on account of the moral law. This cultivation of moral judgment, however, only generates interest in moral deeds. And it does so through "repeated exercise" of judging actions for their moral content. All this is done in order to stimulate "attention" to moral deeds. This attention, this form of *Achtung* is, one might say, the empirical analogue to the feeling of respect produced by the law. But because it does not yet awaken an interest in the moral law itself, this first exercise is insufficient. It merely habituates attention to the moral law.

Kant, therefore, introduces a second exercise designed to draw attention to the "purity of the will" through the "lively presentation of moral dispositions in examples" (160). These examples stimulate and then hold the student's attention to his freedom, to the simple and given fact that he is free. Kant transposes his transcendental argument about moral incentives (the complex of pain, humiliation, and respect) onto this moral discipline. The exposure to the purity of the will through these examples initially stimulates a sensation of pain, and then "relieves" the student from the force of his needs and emancipates him from the "displeasure" of these needs, an emancipation that makes possible the sensation of pleasure "from other sources" (160). The student is made receptive to sensations from other sources, namely, moral feelings. We can observe the detranscendentalized structure of subjectivation here. This process, however, is orchestrated by an act of discipline: the student's "attention is held to the consciousness of his freedom." His susceptibility to moral feelings is made possible through this "holding of attention." The student's attention is held or directed to a consciousness of his freedom through a "lively presentation" of moral dispositions. These images and words promote an attitude toward his freedom that allows the law of duty "easier access" to the subjective will.

Kant offers an example of how one of these moral sessions might go: "One tells the story of an honest man, whom someone wants to move to join the slanders against an innocent but powerless person (like, for example, Anne Boleyn, accused by Henry VIII of England). He is offered advantages, great gifts, or high rank; he rejects them" (155). Such behavior, claims Kant, will meet with the student's approval. But then the narrative must continue. Relatives threaten to disinherit him. Powerful people threaten persecution. The teacher should push the narrative to its climax where the honest man, now so threatened, finally wishes that he had never lived to see the day that brought such "unutterable pain." Even in the face of such pain, insists the teacher, this honest man remains resolute.

The teacher's narrative act includes the constant checking and testing of the student's reactions: "Thus one can lead the young listener step by step from mere approval to admiration, and from admiration to amazement, and finally to the greatest veneration and a lively wish that he himself could be such a human being" (156 [Gregor, 265]). This discipline stimulates pain, humiliation, respect, and ultimately, a positive attitude or disposition. These exercises are a type of "self-testing" through which the students begin to see themselves as "abject" and "contemptible." At this point a moral disposition can be "grafted" onto them.[144] This testing prevents the "intrusion" of corrupting inclinations by juxtaposing images of a pathologically determined will, one with a propensity to turn subjective grounds of determination into principles, with images of a will determined by the law.

A Subjective Pathology

Kant's juxtaposition in his ethical dietetics of a normalized ethical economy with other, contemptible relationships to the law reiterates the suggestion that certain forms of subjectivity are pathological. A propensity to make subjective grounds of determination into objective ones is indicative of an abnormal relationship between the self and the moral law. It indicates a deafness to the voice of the law and a numbness to its incentive. Throughout his description of these exercises and earlier in his discussion of the moral incentive, the term "pathological" increasingly connotes subjective. That which is subjectively effected, Kant writes parenthetically, is pathological.[145] The merely subjective is a source of sickness and an abnormal ethical economy. The logic of Kant's ethical economy and the disciplines that cultivate it are based on interrupting such a pathological subjectivity by means of something whose effect is itself pathological, namely the feeling of respect. In the collocation pathological-subjective-sensible, it is evident how the Kantian moral discipline is concerned less with the extirpation of sensibility and more with maintaining the normalized economy of sensibility-reason that he lays out in the first part of the *Kritik der praktischen Vernunft*. Pathology is tied less to bodily inclinations and more to mental abnormalities, to a mind that subordinates ethical determination to subjective grounds and is thus prone to solipsism. As Kant suggests in *Die Religion,* radical evil is not a corruption of the body or of sensibility but a failure of reason itself, an adoption of the wrong maxims. For Kant, pathology manifests itself at the boundary of mind and body. Everything in Kant's ethical dietetics is undertaken to solicit, create, and instill a disquiet that confronts the finite human being with an image of his pathological solipsism. And this image, Kant expects, will stimulate respect for the law and thus a moral disposition. Given what Kant assumes to be the non-coincidence of our rational and sensible selves and the incomprehensibility of the law, Kant's ethical dietetics is meant above all to demonstrate to the student the "feasibility" (*Thunlichkeit*) of observing the law.[146] Examples of moral duty are intended to demonstrate that even in the face of such a rational normativity it is possible to follow the law. It is possible to be moral, to be free—that is, Kant wants to point to examples of real persons who have adopted a moral disposition and presupposed their own freedom.

In Kant's ethical dietetics, the desires, the needs, the longings, of reason are disciplined and not simply given a priori. This education into a consciousness of the gap between our finite, sensible selves and freedom cultivates the infinite desires of reason for an impossible experience, namely, the touch-feeling-experience of the law. The disciplinary regime of morality is meant to encourage and craft a "healthy reason," an embodied reason, all of which are tied to the finite human being, a being that has a historical, socially specific existence.[147] The pathology of rationality sickened by solipsism and pride is contrasted to a normative image of a healthy reason that cognizes a priori. And we have already encountered the picture of a truly healthy reason: it is one that not only calculates and rationalizes but one in which the desires and needs of reason are infinite yet constrained. A healthy reason in this sense assumes its autonomy but regulates its own economy of self-interest. It is the subordination of reason to reason, or what Kant calls the "self-maintenance of reason."[148] As Kant writes: reason "does not work instinctively but requires trials, practice and instruction to enable it to progress gradually from one level of insight to another."[149] Kantian ethics is not simply a formal project. It is more akin to a practice. Reason and its feelings need discipline, and, it seems, a moral pedagogue who would be able to clear the "path to wisdom."[150] Confronted with the radical negativity of the law, the young child is directed to the instructor who is practiced in an ethical "way of living," who has already assumed his or her own freedom, who has adopted a moral disposition.

Reasoning from Moral Humans to a Moral Humanity

The formation of a moral disposition through an ethical dietetics melds two realms of causality—that of nature and that of freedom. Kant's pedagogical techniques are mechanisms or technologies that in themselves cannot, for Kant at least, create a moral disposition, since a moral disposition is a self-effected rebirth. This discussion has detailed just how complex this melding of causalities is. It is made even more so by Kant's insistence that a moral disposition, although it is acquired, cannot be acquired in time.[151] The acquisition of a moral disposition is timeless. If we understand this claim in strictly theoretical terms—that is, if one understands Kant's account as appealing "to a metaphysical doctrine of pre- or nontemporal choice," then the temporal acquisition is impossible and thoroughly aporetic.[152] If, however, one understands it in its ethical context, as a matter of practical reason, one can understand Kant's claim that a moral disposition is acquired, but not in time, as a practical necessity and not a metaphysical explanation. In order to conceive of the development of moral agency, one must conceive of the self as having always already acquired a moral disposition, as always already having presupposed our freedom, because such an acquisition (such a presupposition) is necessary for moral development itself. A human being must think of itself as having always already made, what is for Kant, this rational choice.

Kant's ethical dietetics—marked as it is by a combination of pedagogical techniques and "leading strings" and the language of virtue as a rebirth—highlights the melding of causalities in Kant's ethics. Kant's most popular (and thus nontechnical) articulation of this can be found in his 1784 essay "Beantwortung der Frage: Was ist Aufklärung?" ("Answer to the Question: What Is Enlightenment?"). In that essay, as Robert Pippin suggests, a "revealing mix of natural and artificial images" structures Kant's arguments about freedom.[153] Kant's basic and most famous definition of Enlightenment is framed in paradoxical terms: "the human being's emergence from his self-incurred immaturity."[154] Adelung defines "mature" as someone who is "free from paternal power."[155] On the one hand, a human being is born into immaturity and naturally grows out of it as he grows older and, following the metaphor, establishes his own domestic sphere. On the other hand, however, Kant claims that immaturity is "self-incurred" if we "lack the resolution and courage" to use our own understanding without the guidance of another. Kant dares us to use our own understanding. Thus, the courageous use of our reason would, it seems, be somehow unnatural, since it would be much more "convenient" to remain immature. But on the other hand, Enlightenment is fundamentally natural: since the human being's "inclination and vocation" to think freely is the "germ" upon which nature has "lavished most care."[156] Enlightenment is natural and artificial at once. This paradoxical image is reiterated by the fate of a public enlightenment that falls in part to the "guardians" who will "disseminate the spirit of rational respect for the person of value and for the duty of all men to think for themselves." The process of Enlightenment is analogous to the process of the foundation of a moral disposition. The mixing of images and the melding of causalities points to the fact that morals are, and freedom is, something "brought about, by the human working on and with nature."[157]

This extended discussion of moral techniques is meant only to open up Kantian ethics to an account of human agency as temporal and capable of change. In the end Kant is concerned with the possibility of becoming moral. His ethics should not be reduced to an inquiry into the epistemological grounds or metaphysical claims of human freedom; instead, it performs its own sort of bracketing maneuver. It brackets theoretical questions concerning what freedom is, or how we might know it in order to prompt a moral disposition. It rests on an account of the human being as both a rational *and* a sensible being that has the potential to recognize its capacity for freedom. This assumption of "what the human is" guides the normative claims of what the human should become.

However individualistic Kant's dietetics might seem, the individual ethical economy is always cultivated with the help of a pedagogue, through examples and, ultimately, in reference to a historical and social context. A moral disposition and the respect for the moral law is, for example, cultivated in opposition to the "weak feelings" "of our times." The moral economy of the individual Kantian moral subject is not without its historical and social context. This fact also means that the cultivation through a culture of reason of a properly "healthy reason" or a moral disposition—not the "healthy understanding" or "common sense" of eighteenth-century German popular philosophers—is wrapped up not just with the ends of the individual human being but with the ends of reason itself.[158] As noted at the beginning of this chapter, reason itself has ends, desires, and needs, all of which extend beyond (though they do not necessarily contradict) the individual human being. Kant concludes the

Kritik der praktischen Vernunft with the claim that science "is the narrow gate that leads to the doctrine of wisdom, if by this is understood not merely what one ought to do but what ought to serve teachers as a guide to prepare well and clearly the path to wisdom which everyone should travel, and to secure others against taking the wrong way."[159] With a critique of practical reason, Kant intended not only to establish the grounds of what an individual ought to do but to create a universal pedagogical template according to which the "moral predispositions of our nature" could be developed.[160] At stake are not just the predispositions of the individual human being but the entire human race. Kant's ethics leads not only to the cultivation and care of the self but to the cultivation of the ends of reason and thus the human as such. The very possibility of freedom is a concern not just with the self but also with the entire human species and with what Kant insists is its destiny.

The question becomes, then, to what extent can such a moral disposition be cultivated not just in the individual but in the human as such, in the entire human race. Can Kant's account of progress and development of human agency and moral becoming on the individual level be transposed onto a collective humanity? The possibility of this transposition raises a host of questions, among the most fundamental of which concerns the relationship between the dignity of the individual human being (which Kant insists on) and the realization of the ends of reason through the progress of the human species. The individual becomes dependent on the whole of the human species, but the unity and end of the latter is always tenuous. Kant's account of human agency as capable of change in time, then, opens up a space for a historical-social, anthropological supplement. Kant's pragmatic anthropology provides this supplement, drawing from a fundamental claim established in Kant's ethics. The relationship of the individual human being to freedom is not given; it must not only be presupposed but this presupposition itself has to be cultivated. The Kantian moral disposition—the relationship of reason and sensibility—has to be cultivated.

3

Freedom, Between Nature and Reason

Kant's Pragmatic Anthropology

The previous chapter outlined how Kant framed his own ethical dietetics as a "moral culture." In his ethics, however, Kant proved to be interested in more than establishing the rational grounds of moral life and the logical forms of moral judgments. In addition, echoing Hufeland's call for a treatment of the "whole human being," he also cultivated a particular relationship to objective principles and, more generally, a proper ethical economy. For Kant, a "healthy" reason requires a moral disposition, which can be cultivated through a culture of reason and ethical practices. These ethical cultures, be it Hufeland's medical anthropology or Kant's ethical dietetics, return one to the normative-cultural concerns of late eighteenth-century proto-anthropology.

When Hufeland wrote to Kant about the art of prolonging one's life, he described his book as an "effort to treat the physical in the human being morally, to present the whole of the human being, as well as the physical, as a being striving toward morality and to show how moral culture is indispensable for the physical perfection of human nature."[1] Whereas the proto-anthropology of the 1770s and 1780s looked not to Kant but rather to figures like Platner, the philosophical doctors, and Herder for guidance, toward the end of the century proto-anthropology increasingly oriented itself between the poles of *physis* and norm. When Hufeland claimed that "true anthropology" owed a great deal to Kant, he was referring to this normative-cultural reorientation and the fact that Kant framed his own pragmatic anthropology in just these terms.[2] Whereas the qualifying adjective "true" reminds one, again, of the disciplinary tensions surrounding the term "anthropology," it also reiterates the historical significance of proto-anthropology's cultural-normative turn. For Hufeland and a range of figures writing on proto-anthropology, culture provided the answer to both the question "What is the human being?" and the more normative one "How does one become a human being?"

> Only through culture will the human being become perfect. The mental as well as the physical nature of the human being must possess a certain degree of development, refinement, and cultivation, if he is to enjoy the advantages of human nature. A raw, uncivilized human being is no human being at all. He is only a human animal, which has the potential to become human, but as long as this potential is not developed through culture, he cannot lift himself above the class of comparable animals either physically or morally. The essence of the human being is his potential for perfection. Everything in his organization is determined to be nothing but to become everything.[3]

Culture had become an anthropological treatment program. But while Hufeland's "medical" anthropology focused on the treatment of individual bodies,[4] Kant's pragmatic anthropology focused on the human species. Kant transposed his ethical dietetics from the individual human being onto the human as such. As the "true" anthropology, Kant's was concerned with the health not just of individual ethical economies but with the ethical economy of the species. It oriented itself toward "the destiny of the human being" (*Bestimmung des Menschen*) and, thus, toward the formation of its moral disposition as a historical, species being. "The human being is destined by his reason to be in a society with other human beings and in it to cultivate himself, to civilize himself and to moralize himself by means of the arts and sciences."[5] In this chapter I argue that whereas Kant's ethics focused on the formation of an individual moral character, his pragmatic anthropology focused on the formation of the moral character of the entire species. This shift in focus relied on the conjoining, or confusion even, of the transcendental and empirical[6]—that is, Kant's pragmatic anthropology made use of both transcendental arguments and claims and empirical observations.

I use the term 'transcendental' in this chapter in a Kantian sense. As Kant defines the term in the *Kritik der reinen Vernunft,* transcendental questions concern the conditions under which something in the world can become an object of knowledge. In order to answer such questions,

Kant inaugurated what he termed a "Copernican revolution." This so-called revolution might properly be described, in Kantian terms at least, as a transcendental turn. According to traditional modes of epistemological explanation, to explain how a subject knows an object is to explain how the object is in itself.[7] According to a transcendental account, however, to explain how a subject knows an object is to explain how the object appears to a subject. The conditions of knowledge are to be found not in the object but in the subject. Kant's *transcendental* claim, then, is that experience is possible through certain subjective conditions (namely, the forms of intuition and the categories of the understanding that Kant argued for in the *Kritik der reinen Vernunft*). Kant's transcendental arguments concern the limits or conditions of human knowledge given such subjective conditions. A transcendental philosophy argues that in all empirical experience there are spontaneously generated or self-legislated rules. When I claim, then, that Kant confuses the transcendental with the empirical in his pragmatic anthropology, I am claiming that his anthropology confuses transcendental methods—methods concerned with the subjective conditions of possibility of knowledge—with empirical methods.

There is, however, a second sense in which Kant uses "transcendental." He figures reason as not merely a formal or logical faculty but also as a transcendental faculty with a "real use"—reason itself produces "concepts and principles, which it derives neither from the senses nor from the understanding."[8] Kant calls these self-produced concepts and principles transcendental ideas. Such ideas correspond to nothing in experience. These are the ideas to which Kant assigns a regulative use. In the concluding sections of his *Anthropologie in pragmatischer Hinsicht*, Kant describes the idea of a "destiny of the human species" as a regulative principle.[9] In the following sections I outline how the *Anthropologie* attempts to conjoin but sometimes confuses these two realms—the transcendental and the empirical—in an effort to extend the reach of Kant's ethics from the formation of the individual to the formation of the human species.

In the first section of this chapter I argue that Kant uses character as the mediating term of this transposition—that is, in his *Anthropologie* Kant moves from the character of the individual to the character of the human species. In the second section I outline how the transcendental and empirical are conjoined in terms of both the questions and very form of the *Anthropologie*. In the following sections I demonstrate how Kant frames his anthropological project in terms of a series of distinctions:

pragmatic versus physiological and knowledge of the world versus theoretical knowledge. I conclude the chapter with a discussion of what Kant terms the cosmopolitan character of his pragmatic anthropology and consider how the confusion of the transcendental and the empirical becomes not only a theoretical but also an ethical problem for anthropological inquiry.

Character and Anthropology

The second part of Kant's *Anthropologie* is entitled "Anthropological Characteristic" and is divided into discussions of the characters of (1) the person, (2) of the sexes, (3) of peoples (*Völker*),[10] and (4) of the species (*Gattung*). Much work remains to be done on the intricacies and problems of these first three sections and their relationship to Kant's broader understanding of character—sections that include discussions of different temperaments, the physiognomy of individual persons, and crude generalizations about the sexes and different peoples. The fourth section considers how Kant uses character as the mediating term for the transposition of his ethical dietetics from the individual to the species. Some of the comments in these sections of Kant's *Anthropologie* are quite disturbing to the modern reader, and charges of sexism and racism are clearly warranted.[11] Rather than detail and repeat, much less explain away or defend, Kant's sometimes offensive generalizations, in this chapter I try to understand their conceptual necessity. Given Kant's basic assumptions about anthropological inquiry, do the organizing concepts of his pragmatic anthropology—concepts such as progress, destiny, species-being, history, and freedom—necessitate such comments? And also important, are these sometimes offensive generalizations a necessary manifestation of the mixing of transcendental and empirical methods and insights that characterize his pragmatic anthropology?

In general, Kant's discussion of character in his *Anthropologie* echoes similar, though scattered, discussions in the first, second, and third critiques. This similarity reiterates at least one isomorphism of anthropology and ethics in the Kantian corpus. In the *Kritik der reinen Vernunft*, for example, Kant distinguishes an empirical from an intelligible character[12] and in the *Anthropologie* a physical character from a moral character. In the latter text, Kant defines a physical character as a "symbol of the human being that distinguishes him as a sensible or natural being" and a moral character as a "symbol that distinguishes the human being as a reasonable being endowed with freedom."[13]

Kant describes the formation of a moral character in exactly the same terms as he did the adoption of a moral disposition: "The grounding of character is like a rebirth, a certain solemnity of making a vow to oneself; which makes the resolution and the moment when this transformation took place unforgettable to him, like the beginning of a new epoch.— Education, examples, and teaching generally cannot bring about this firmness and persistence in principles gradually, but only, as it were, by an explosion, which happens one time as a result of weariness at the unstable condition of instinct" (294 [Louden, 392]).

Kant describes both the formation of a moral character and the adoption of a moral disposition as a "rebirth." As in a moral disposition, to have a character, in the fullest sense of the word, is to act and relate to oneself from the will rather than from instinct. The primary concern of Kant's pragmatic anthropology is the cultivation of such a moral character. "Here [in Kant's pragmatic anthropology] it does not depend on what nature makes of the human being but on what the human being makes of himself" (292 [Louden, 390]). Character signifies the human being's ability to overcome its sensible nature through the development of reason. To have a character, then, signifies that property of the will "by which the subject binds himself to definite practical principles that he has prescribed to him irrevocably by his own reason" (292). In this sense, moral character can only be "acquired"; it cannot be given by nature (294). Speaking of the transformation from "an animal with the potential for reason (*animal rationabile*)" to "a rational animal (*animal rationale*)," Kant again compares the adoption of a character to a "rebirth" (321). To have character is to commit oneself to the rational activity of setting ends, and Kant refers to the adoption of such a character as a "conversion" (*Umwandlung*) in which the self experiences a "new epoch." The development of moral character and the realization of the moral potential of reason mark the individual's self-transformation.

Kant's description of the formation of moral character as a "rebirth" and even his claim that education cannot produce it "gradually" would seem to diminish the importance of education and the notion of ethical development in general. As I argued in the previous chapter, however, this is not at all the case. Education and a "culture of reason" play key roles in Kantian ethics, and when Kant transposes his ethical dietetics onto the human species in the *Anthropologie,* they play an even more fundamental role. The moral character of the individual or species cannot be produced, but it can be developed. But wherein lies the difference? In what sense can "character be acquired" but not produced? (307).

Because "the human being is from nature wild and raw, he must be disciplined. The human being wants from nature to follow his senses and inclinations."[14] And whoever does not already have a character "can still have a nature, which is capable of character, for character can be imitated and established."[15] Kant ties character to the process of containing sensual desires, a process that he claims only succeeds with age. "Character establishes itself very late, around forty years of age, because at that point one is most able to separate concepts from instincts, because the instincts and inclinations have lost their power and the concepts begin to take hold, and then one makes principles, which make up character."[16] The human being's ability to "perfect himself" through the adoption of a character distinguishes him or her from all other beings on earth. Animals "are unable to do this."[17] The adoption of a character, then, is fundamentally reflexive, that is to say, a human being adopts a character *for him- or herself.* It is in this sense that Kant insists that a character must be acquired and not produced. The adoption of character is a rational choice and not the immediate effect of something outside oneself, like pedagogical techniques.

When I discussed the formation of an individual moral subject, however, I pointed out how Kant's ethical dietetics blurs the line between moral and pedagogical techniques on the one hand and pure practical reason on the other. Similarly, one can consider the dual structure of Kant's concept of character—intelligible versus sensible, moral versus physical—as an ideal that incites ethical work in the present. More important than the propositional truth of the ideal of a pure moral character, then, is its functional force. The cultivation or development of a moral character signifies the "harmonizing work" of the two orders of causality, of nature and of reason, toward a single end, a final purpose.[18] Character concerns the unity of reason and sensibility in the world and requires, as Felicitas Munzel puts it, not only the exercise of objective principles (the transcendental work of the *Kritik der reinen Vernunft*) but also the exercise of the subjective conditions of the possibility of realizing these principles.[19]

Kant's pragmatic anthropology more generally is an elaboration of this "harmonizing work" of moral character with respect to the human species. Given what Kant sees as the failure of all previous philosophy to provide a complete conception of moral character, he suggests that his *Anthropologie* might offer a solution to an old problem. Philosophers have presented "virtue only in fragments but have never tried to present it whole, in its beautiful form, and to make it interesting for all human beings."[20] A full account of virtue, one that attends to its "beautiful form," can only be written against the horizon of the "destiny" of the human species. Whereas animals may achieve their "complete destiny" as individuals, in the case of the human being only the species does (324). Kant conceives of his pragmatic anthropology, then, as the articulation of virtue in its most complete form. It will present virtue "whole." And for Kant, that means the articulation of the moral character of the human species.

Kant claims that according to its sensible character, the human being must be judged evil (by nature). But according to the character of the species, "one can assume that its natural destiny consists in continual progress toward the better" (324 [Louden, 420]). For Kant, the human being's progression toward the better or goodness is only visible with respect to the species. Whereas in the next chapter I will consider how Kant employs the "destiny of the human being" as a solution to the problem of virtue, in this chapter I detail the more immediate problem of Kant's transposition of an ethical dietetics from the individual to the species, for it is unclear from what perspective the progress of the human species can be observed. The fact that Kant orients his pragmatic anthropology toward the development of the human species raises a basic question: how does the pragmatic anthropologist come upon the privileged position from which to make his observations and claims about the human species?

The very structure and form of Kant's *Anthropologie* repeat these more conceptual transpositions. It does not start out with an explicit discussion of the species; instead, it moves from situational observations to general claims about human destiny. In this sense, it should be noted that Kant is not interested in studying the particular individual per se but rather in the repeatable situations and possibilities that the individual encounters— that is, his pragmatic anthropology is concerned with the situations and possibilities within which an individual might become human. In the

Anthropologie, the category "human" is always only a possibility. And it is this logic of becoming—of the deferral of being human to a future human destiny—that requires the supplement of anthropology. Pragmatic anthropology cultivates the presupposition of freedom just as Kant's ethical dietetics does, but from a fundamentally historical perspective.

The question of the species character of the human being, then, is more fundamentally a question about the conjuncture of a transcendental idea, the idea of a human destiny, and the empirical, the conditions of becoming moral. This possible conjuncture organizes the *Anthropologie.* Kant places transcendental claims about what the human should become alongside empirical claims about what the human being is observed to be. Kant's own conception of character, which presumes this division, requires the historical teleology of the human as species, but this historical-social character of Kantian ethics is only implied in the so-called critical canon. (One could even read the post-Kantian division of Kant's philosophy into a critical canon and the other works as an architectonic formalization of *homo duplex.*) Kant gives his pragmatic anthropology the task of mediating and narrating the development of human beings through time.

The problem of anthropology as posed by Kant, then, is how to articulate a form of normativity without the assurance of an antecedent norm for the human. The irony, however, lies in the fact that it is a problem of Kant's own making. If the divide between the intelligible and the sensible were not Kant's operative assumption, then anthropology would have no conceptual task to resolve. As will become evident, however, Kant's *Anthropologie* risks undoing itself until it simply brackets more theoretical or methodological questions concerning the mind-body problem and, ultimately, the reduplication of anthropological observation. At a certain point Kant simply brackets the theoretical problems that burden anthropological inquiry in order to carry out the more practical interests of his pragmatic anthropology. And this bracketing of theoretical problems makes possible the articulation of what Kant terms, in the conclusion of the *Anthropologie,* the "destiny of the human."

The Questions and Form of Kant's Pragmatic Anthropology

We cannot refer to a single Kantian anthropology because there is no one basic text. Kant lectured on anthropology twenty-four times between 1772 and 1796. He finally published his organized lecture notes as *Anthropologie in pragmatischer Hinsicht* in 1798.[21] In *Kant, Herder, and the Birth of Anthropology* John H. Zammito argues that after his initial lectures Kant's anthropology became increasingly nonempirical and dogmatic. Zammito goes on to argue that whereas the "pre-critical Kant" played an important role in the emergent discourse of anthropology in the 1770s, the "critical Kant systematically subordinated anthropology to metaphysics in way that ran against the grain of anthropology's disciplinary ambitions."[22] As I already discussed in chapter 1, however, in eighteenth-century Germany there were multiple anthropologies, and toward the end of the century commentators referred to an anthropology in crisis—hence my term "proto-anthropology." To speak simply of "anthropology's disciplinary ambitions," then, elides the inchoate character of the proto-discipline. Zammito's more fundamental concern, however, is with the consequences of Kant's subordination of anthropology to metaphysics, a subordination that he contends results in a "preemptive, metaphysical prescription of human nature" that remains ignorant of human diversity.[23] Zammito offers Herder's particularism as a more appropriately "anthropological" corrective to Kant's abstractions. By pitting Herder against Kant and insisting that the former's concerns were more "anthropological," Zammito obscures the fact that the very status of "anthropology" had come into question. By the last third of the eighteenth century, proto-anthropology had become increasingly concerned with and confused about the distinctions between the empirical and the philosophical. In fact, by 1800 proto-anthropology had become a science of how the dichotomies empirical and transcendental, the physical and the normative, might be conjoined in the figure of the human.

Zammito correctly notes the differences between Kant's pragmatic anthropology and the broader, eighteenth-century discourse of proto-anthropology. And yet it is precisely these differences that illuminate the more fundamental problems of an eighteenth-century science of the human. Kant's was not the first anthropology to reflect on the paradoxes of anthropological inquiry, but it was the one that most forcefully posed the question of whether anthropological inquiry could ground itself at all. Kant's critique of anthropological inquiry is instructive because it arises out of the tensions between the transcendental and empirical that characterize his moral philosophy and had come to mark the broader discourse of proto-anthropology.

On the one hand, then, in this chapter I am concerned primarily with questions related to Kant: If, as Kant asserts in the *Kritik der praktischen Vernunft*, the "mechanism of nature" is the "direct opposite of freedom," can an empirical endeavor like anthropology contribute anything to a Kantian ethics?[24] Is a Kantian ethics concerned exclusively with *pure* reason? If so, how would a Kantian pragmatic anthropology even be possible? On the other hand, however, I also take up in this chapter more historical-theoretical questions about proto-anthropology's increasingly normative character. As proto-anthropology became a science of the conjuncture of the transcendental and empirical, it came to consider the human being as a being that exists at the limits of two realms, nature and reason. But what science could reflect on such limits? How might a science of the human account for both the conditions of its own possibility and inquire into the actual, observable conditions of human beings? While proto-anthropology may have begun as a discipline of the body, it increasingly saw this body as inextricably bound to moral and philosophical concerns. In this sense, Kant's *Anthropologie* is essential not just for reflections particular to Kant but to broader questions concerning culture, normativity, and the human that proto-anthropology takes up around 1800.

The relationship of Kant's pragmatic anthropology to an intimated, but not fully articulated (Kantian) *moral anthropology* has become a central issue in recent Kant scholarship. Even the two editors of Kant's anthropology lectures, however, cannot agree about how they are related. Whereas Reinhard Brandt argues that "pragmatic anthropology is not identical in any of its phases of development with the anthropology that Kant repeatedly designates as the complementary part of his moral theory after 1770,"[25] Werner Stark argues that "an internal, positive relationship" does exist between the lectures on anthropology and his moral philosophy.[26] For Stark, "Kant considered anthropology to be an integral part of his philosophy (including his critical philosophy)." Similarly, Robert B. Louden makes perhaps the most forceful and detailed argument for this troubled relationship.[27] In the vein of Stark and Louden, I understand the relationship between morals and anthropology as one of a supplementary tension.

The very form of Kant's 1798 text intimates the possible conjunction of transcendental and empirical concerns. Kant divides his 1798 *Anthropologie* into two sections: "Anthropological Didactic: On the Way of Cognizing the Interior as well as the Exterior of the Human Being" and

"Anthropological Characteristic: On the Way of Cognizing the Interior of the Human Being from the Exterior." In his marginalia, he refers to the Didactic as the doctrine and the Characteristic as the "Doctrine of Method of Ethnology."[28] Making a similar distinction in the *Kritik der praktischen Vernunft*, Kant describes a Didactic as the theoretical establishing of principles and a Characteristic as the application of these same principles. Similarly, in his *Metaphysics of Morals* Kant describes a Doctrine of Method (Characteristic) as an exercise of reason in both theory and practice (411). It is tempting to see Kant's division of his *Anthropologie* into Didactic and Characteristic as a simple theory-practice divide, but these relationships—between theory and practice, ethics and anthropology—are some of the most complex and fecund in the Kantian corpus. As we will see later, the Characteristic is more a series of reflections on the characters of individuals, sexes, peoples, races, and the human species and their relation to the broader ends of the human than an explicit program of action. The first and longest part, the Didactic, in contrast, is divided into three sections on the internal organization of the mind or the faculties: the cognitive faculty, the feelings of pleasure and displeasure, and the faculty of desire. It primarily repeats Kant's empirical psychology, itself derived from Baumgarten. Concerned with establishing principles for anthropological inquiry, the Didactic serves a transcendental function, whereas the Characteristic, concerned with the application of these principles, serves a more empirical function. What then connects the Didactic to the Characteristic? What binds the Didactic's comments on consciousness and representations to the Characteristic's comments on human temperaments and physiology? How does a concern with the inside of the human being relate to a concern with the outside?

In his marginal comments, Kant notes that the Didactic asks, "What is the human being?" whereas the Characteristic asks how the particularity of every individual human being is to be recognized (410). The Didactic addresses what the human being is by considering its "inside," whereas the Characteristic addresses the particularity of human beings by considering the "inside of the human being from the outside." Kant organizes his pragmatic anthropology, then, on an inner-outer division that in turn implies a temporal division: what is the human being and what can the human being become in its particularity? This division of anthropology into an inner, seemingly atemporal universality, and an outer, temporal transformation, is analogous to the divide between the two realms of causality—nature and reason—discussed in the previous chapter. The division of anthropology repeats this division in Kant's corpus and resurfaces in the preface to the *Anthropologie:* a pragmatic anthropology considers what the human being "can and should . . . make of himself" (119). Anthropology emerges at the modal conjunction of "can and should." What is the human being as a natural being and what can human beings become in their freedom? Whereas the Didactic articulates the fundamental elements of the human—it is basically a faculty psychology—the Characteristic discusses how these elements are arranged and constructed and develop historically. The possible conjuncture of these two sections, and thus the more fundamental conjuncture of transcendental and empirical, is analogous to the melding of the two realms of causality discussed in chapter 2 with respect to Kant's ethical dietetics. Both the ethical and anthropological conjuncture of transcendental and empirical, reason and nature, concern how the human being can become a free moral being. Ultimately, the second part provides a plan for the future of the human, a future that outlines the human being's moral becoming.

In order to understand the relationship of these two sections and the larger project of Kant's *Anthropologie,* it is necessary to consider how Kant organizes the means of anthropological inquiry into a hierarchy of sorts:

> Travel belongs to the means of enlarging the scope of anthropology, even if it is only the reading of travelogues. But if one wants to know what to look for abroad, in order to broaden the range of anthropology, one must, however, through the interaction with his fellow city and countrymen, have gained knowledge of human beings. Without such a program (which already assumes knowledge of human beings) the citizen of the world [*Weltbürger*] will remain very limited with respect to his anthropology. . . . Finally, though not sources but as aids to anthropology, are: world history, biographies, even plays and novels. (120 [Louden, 232, trans. modified])

A pragmatic anthropology draws from an array of forms and genres, all of which serve as aids to the anthropologist. It does not have sources but only means. It is a thoroughly mediated form of knowledge. It cannot ground itself. It is a "doctrine of the knowledge of the human being systematically formulated" (119). It is unclear, however, if Kant understands anthropology itself as a system. Its "means" are simply aids and not sources of knowledge in themselves. Travelogues, for example, simply expand on already established anthropological insights, because—and this is Kant's key claim—one must first have already "gained a knowledge of human beings" through social interaction. The quality of insights gained from social interaction, however, depends on where one happens to find oneself. In a telling footnote, Kant describes what could be considered an optimal location for anthropological inquiry:

> A big city, the center of a kingdom, in which one can find government offices, a university (concerning the culture of science), as well as access to sea trade, makes possible an exchange of different languages and mores through rivers from out of the inner parts of the country as well as bordering distant countries—such a city, like perhaps Königsberg on the Pregel River, can be considered a place for the expansion of the knowledge of man as well as knowledge of the world; here, such knowledge, without even having to travel, can be gained. (120 [Louden, 232, trans. modified])

Königsberg, Kant's home in eastern Germany, is a serendipitous place for anthropological inquiry. But even this early stage of anthropological inquiry, in which one studies others, is itself merely an elaboration of prior knowledge. Both travel and the local observation of the anthropologist's fellows "already assume knowledge of human beings." And therein one can observe the entire organization of Kantian anthropology. Empirical, concrete forms of knowledge are subordinated to already existing forms of knowledge. Kant does not elaborate on the form or source of this prior knowledge of human beings in the preface, but the organizational structure of the *Anthropologie* into a Didactic and a Characteristic is a formal elaboration of what just such a prior knowledge might be. Anthropology concerns empirical forms of knowledge that are somehow derivative of prior claims. The problem, then, is how an empirical science can reflect on these prior claims and, thus, on its own condition of possibility.

Kant concludes the preface with the insistence that a pragmatic anthropology is both "systematic" and "popular," for it allows "the reading public" to order particular observations about human beings according to the "unity" of a larger plan, which itself allows for the unity of the larger science (122). How can such a science, comprised as it is of a seemingly vast array of individual observations about human beings, articulate its own conditions? What is this "plan" that makes Kantian anthropology possible? To what extent can the conditions of this plan be exposed or revealed? To what extent can anthropological inquiry be transcendental?

The Problem of Anthropological Observation

Kant begins the Didactic with a discussion of self-consciousness in which he outlines the means of self-observation and claims that self-consciousness underlies all knowledge of the human being. As Foucault suggests in his unpublished commentary on the *Anthropologie*,[29] the temporalization of the human being in the Characteristic is predicated on a prior temporalization of the human being (as the subject of anthropology) in the Didactic. Through his becoming conscious of himself, the human being "lifts himself infinitely above all other living beings on earth."[30] As a child, the human being merely "feels . . . himself," but once the child speaks through the *Ich,* it ushers in its "development into humanity." Anthropology observes and narrates this becoming conscious of the self and not a consciousness of other objects in the world. This becoming human begins, argues Kant, with the "representation of the *Ich,*" but anthropology cannot explain this phenomenon. Already at the beginning of the anthropology, Kant approaches the limits of anthropological inquiry. The anthropologist is not in the position to articulate how human beings "think" themselves. Anthropology cannot theorize this becoming conscious; it can only register it.

This limitation, however, would seem to put the entire anthropological project at risk, since Kant has already emphasized the limitations of empirical knowledge. Anthropology's task is not to probe the limits or grounds of consciousness or discern the difference that this first utterance of the "I" marks, a difference between feeling oneself (*sich fühlen*) and thinking oneself (*sich denken*). Anthropological inquiry begins at that moment in time when the "light" of consciousness appears to dawn upon the human being (127). Anthropology operates in the light of speech and not in the supposed darkness of nonspeech or that which precedes speech.

A few pages later, in a discussion of "egoism" and the development of the self, Kant opposes egoism to a "pluralism," which he defines as a way of thinking in which one is "not concerned with oneself as the whole world, but rather how one regards and conducts oneself as a mere citizen of the world" (130 [Louden, 241]). For Kant, anthropological inquiry begins with this assumption—the human being exists in a world of other human beings. Questions about the nature of this assumption—whether, for example, one has reason to assume the existence of other beings in addition to oneself—are metaphysical and have no place in anthropology. Anthropology assumes that the human being exists in a world Kant refers to as a community of other human beings. As will become evident in this chapter's discussion of the cosmopolitan figure of anthropology, Kant repeatedly ties anthropology and knowledge of the human being to the question of speech, utterance, and exchange. The "development" (*Bildung*) of the human is bound up with the linguistic utterance and language as utterance. In his brief discussion of the aids of anthropology Kant suggests that anthropological knowledge emerges out of social exchange in the form of language. Circumstantial evidence for this claim can be found in the initial form of Kant's anthropology, that of the lecture. Kant's pragmatic anthropology did not find written form until the publication of the *Anthropologie* in 1798.

Although Kant insists that anthropological knowledge concerns the human being as a citizen of the world, it must begin with knowledge of the self gained through self-observation. But how is this knowledge of the self acquired and how can it ground, if it grounds at all, anthropological inquiry? The Didactic positions itself to ground self-observation, but can the Didactic, with its interest in cognizing the interior as well as the exterior of the human being, ground anthropological inquiry more broadly speaking? Whereas Kant defines self-observation as the "methodical compilation of perceptions formed in us," the "actual purpose" of his discussion of self-observation is to issue a "warning" (133 [Louden, 244]). Self-observation involves a "composition of inner history of the involuntary course of one's thoughts and feelings." This attention to the self required by such a composition, however, can lead to "illuminism or terrorism." It can lead to confusion about the sources of thoughts and feelings, and this can land one in the "madhouse" (133).

For Kant, self-observation involves a complex of problems because its objects are thoughts and feelings. The real danger of self-reflection lies, then, not just in observing one's own inner experiences but in observing them involuntarily. To observe the various acts of representations in myself, suggests Kant, is worthwhile but only when I "summon them." "Eavesdropping on oneself" is dangerous since it is not guided by the rules and principles of thought (133). Reason must protect itself from its own thoughts and feelings. An undisciplined self-observation threatens to interrupt the subject's disposition toward a self-legislating and hence autonomous reason. What if thoughts, feelings, or dreams elude the disciplined reach of reason?

Kant's warning about self-observation stems from a prior division of the senses into an "outer" sense and an "inner" one, the latter of which he ties to self-observation. In his *Anthropologie* he distinguishes two kinds of senses: the "inner sense" is where the body is affected by the mind, and the "outer sense" is where the body is affected by external or material things (153). In the *Kritik der Urteilskraft* Kant makes an even clearer distinction between "objective sensation" and "subjective sensation" and suggests that "feeling" should only by used in the latter case.[31]

Kant claims that the complexities of self-observation arise because the "inner sense" perceives determinate relationships "in time, consequently in flux, where the stability of observation necessary for experience does not occur."[32] Unlike external experiences of external objects in space, the inner sense perceives its determinations only in the flux of time. Hence, whoever begins this "journey of discovery" into the self might end up in "Anticyra" or nowhere (Anticyra was an ancient Greek city destroyed by Philip of Macedon). When we observe ourselves, we rely on an "inner sense" that functions within the flux of time. This "inner sense" is predicated upon an "I" that is the subject of observation, and because this "I" is within time, it cannot ground itself. This "I," however, is also an object of observation: "I, as a thinking being, am one and the same subject with myself as a sensing being. However, as the object of inner empirical intuition, that is in so far as I am affected inwardly from sensations in time, . . . I cognize myself only as I appear to myself, not as a thing-in-itself. For this cognition relies on the conditions of time. . . . Thus I always cognize myself through inner experience only as I appear to myself" (142 [Louden, 254, trans. modified]).

The "I" as the thinking or reflecting subject and the "I" as object of perception or "inner sense" are the same. The "I" that observes is also the "I" that is observed. This formal (Kant insists that this is formal, a question of representation, and not a question of substance) doubling of the I as both subject and object of empirical perception derives from Kant's distinction between the "I of apperception" and the "I of apprehension." The latter is empirical, while the former is purely logical. The former is the "I as a subject of thought" or pure apperception (the merely reflective I). The latter is the "I as the object of perception" and as an object of perception it contains a "multiplicity of determinations" that make inner experience possible and observation so difficult (142). Unlike the assumed purity of the "I of apperception," the "I of apprehension" is of the empirical realm. It is affected; it is sensible. And as such it changes. It is subject to the dynamics of the world.

The difficulties of anthropology arise, then, from a confusion of the purportedly pure I and the empirical I, the I of apperception and the I of apprehension. This confusion, notes Kant, is "quite common." In fact, as discussed in chapter 1, this is precisely the confusion that characterized proto-anthropology throughout the eighteenth century. Kant has simply framed this historical problem in the language of his so-called critical project. Whereas the subject of inner sense may "belong to anthropology," it cannot "sufficiently answer the question: what is the human?" (396). The subject of anthropology, the I of inner sense, is insufficient for the very task of anthropology because it cannot reflect on its own conditions of inquiry. In constant flux, the I of the inner sense cannot ground itself. There is no grounded position from which the human as observing subject can observe the human as object. The subject of anthropology is always implied in the object of observation.

This more fundamental problem of self-observation underlies the difficulties of anthropological inquiry that Kant outlines in the preface. For Kant, there are three primary obstacles to anthropological inquiry: (1) The object of study, the human being, when observed appears disconcerted and thus cannot show how he or she actually is, and when observed, even pretends to be that what he or she is not. (2) "Circumstances of place and time produce . . . habituations" (121 [Louden, 233, trans. modified]). (3) "When the incentives are in action, a human being cannot observe himself. And when he does not observe himself, the incentives subside." All of these problems concern the ability (or inability) of human beings to observe themselves *critically*. Throughout his *Anthropologie* Kant is concerned that the basic anthropological reduplication—the fact that the human being is both the subject and object of observation—will elide critical judgments.

In these reflective conundrums of anthropology, we can observe a basic problem of post-Kantian philosophy: self-reflection. Can reflection ground itself? This problem—the doubling of anthropological reflection—haunts Kant's entire anthropology, because the "I" of apprehension cannot ground its own reflections. The empirical I can never fully ground anthropological inquiry. Faced with the apparent impossibility of anthropology, Kant delimits the task of anthropology yet again by bracketing the entire problem. The entire investigation of self-observation

> does not actually belong to anthropology.... This inquiry belongs to metaphysics, which has to do with the possibility of knowledge a priori. But it was necessary to go so far back, in order to prevent the transgressions of the speculative man with respect to these questions. As for the rest, knowledge of the human being through inner experience, because to a large extent one also judges others according to it, is more important than correct judgment of others, but nevertheless at the same time perhaps more difficult. For he who investigates his interior easily carries many things into self-consciousness instead of merely observing. So it is advisable and even necessary to begin with observed appearances in oneself, and then to progress above all to the assertion of certain propositions that concern human nature; that is, to inner experience. (142–43 [Louden, 255, trans. modified])

Transcendental philosophy limits anthropology, but this transcendental work does not "actually" belong to anthropology.

The transcendental arguments of the section of the *Anthropologie* on self-observation reveal how Kant's pragmatic anthropology sometimes mixes the transcendental task of philosophy and the empirical task of anthropology. Two forms of finitude approach each other. On the one hand, there is a finitude analogous to the limits of the faculty of knowledge as laid out in the *Kritik der reinen Vernunft*. In that work, finitude is tied to the forms of intuition and the categories of the understanding, which afford the a priori conditions of knowledge. This is a finitude of the faculty of knowledge that operates in the timeless realm of the a priori. The finitude of anthropology, however, is attached to an I of apprehension that is later attached to a body in time. This finitude, rather than ensuring a unity of knowledge as does the I of apperception in the *Kritik der reinen Vernunft*, emerges again and again in the flux of time. The human being of anthropology is not the "omnipresent" being of the transcendental aesthetic but a particular, finite being bound to conditions of space and time and thus bound to a certain perspective.[33]

The hedging of this entire distinction between the empirical task of anthropology and the transcendental task of philosophy, however, is apparent in the adverb "actually." Whereas the transcendental arguments might not belong to anthropology, they are in the text of the 1798 *Anthropologie*. Kant limits anthropology to observing how human beings appear, but as we have just read, he also imbues it with a concern for "human nature," a concern that pushes the pragmatic anthropologist well beyond particular observations in time. The Kantian anthropological observer moves from observing how beings appear in time to hypothesizing about the human as such. This delimitation of both sciences places the question of the human squarely between the transcendental and empirical. The transcendental conditions of knowledge intrude on anthropology—that is, they blur the lines between philosophy and anthropology. Anthropology emerges at this conjuncture of the transcendental and empirical. It operates at the limits of a critical reason that attempts to reflect on what makes knowledge possible and of an empirical observation of phenomena in the world.

The asymptotic meeting of the transcendental and the empirical finds its analogue in the divisions of the *Anthropologie*, which itself is conjoined in the figure of the human being. As I noted, the Didactic considers what Kant refers to as the fundamental elements of the human, whereas the Characteristic offers a plan for the development of these elements. This plan extends from the individual human being to the entire species and thus to the future of the human. In his *Streit der Fakultäten* Kant writes that after the *Kritik der reinen Vernunft* he learned that philosophy is not a "science of representations, concepts and ideas, or a science of all sciences . . . but a science of the human being, of his representations, his thought and actions; it should depict the human being according to all of his constituent parts, how he is and should be—that is, according to what nature has determined him as well as his relationship to morality and freedom."[34] This "is" and this "should" lead to two different "destinies for the human being." The "is" refers to sensibility and understanding, while the "should" refers to reason and the free will.[35] A science of the human would have to operate between these two modalities.

But does the future-oriented task of the Characteristic, the second section of *Anthropologie*, ultimately overdetermine the entire anthropological project? Perhaps this is a formal necessity of an anthropology that conjoins the transcendental and the empirical in the figure of the human.

The reduplication of the anthropological subject attempts to avoid the mistakes of "mere empiricism" and afford the transcendental empirical density. The question of what the human being is and can become emerges in the tension between the empirical and the transcendental, between nature and freedom: as a natural, sensual being the human being belongs to the world, whereas as a subject of reason the human being makes its own world. In the process of doing so, however, it assumes, even relies on, a prior dualism of mind and body. Kant's pragmatic anthropology is a product of this prior assumption. If this dualism were not the guiding assumption, there would be no need to speak of a possible conjunction of the transcendental and the empirical in the first place.

This reduplication also manifests the analogous relationship of Kant's moral philosophy and the teleology of the human species that was broached at the beginning of this chapter. The question of an anthropological reduplication is a tacit acknowledgment of this analogy: the human being is both a subject of nature, endowed with reason, and an object of nature, endowed with a sensible body. Kantian anthropology anticipates a possible melding of these two subjects, but its transcendental grounding alerts us to the continued subordination of any anthropological project to a transcendental project. As will become evident later in this chapter, Kant's anthropology is a blueprint of such a possible historical melding of Kantian subjects—a reconciliation of the individual and species.[36] It imagines how this reconciliation might be realized in the future; and while it is marked by hope and anticipation, it is also marked by a subjunctive hedging. This reconciliation *might* be possible; it *could* happen; it is a projection into an unknown future. And the human, as imagined by Kant, becomes a projection into an unknown future as well.

The irony of Kantian anthropology lies in the fact that it is not completely stymied by its own conceptual impossibility; it goes on to study the human from a practical perspective. This was possible because the question "What is the human?" is addressed not at a metaphysical but at a pragmatic level. The conceptual problem of reduplication that threatens anthropological inquiry is bracketed. It haunts the *Anthropologie,* but it does not derail it. For Kant, different types of inquiry can have different interests. The interests of anthropology are not primarily epistemological or theoretical; instead, they are practical, or what Kant refers to in his *Anthropologie* as pragmatic. The theoretical conundrums of anthropological observation, then, may not pose as fundamental a threat to anthropological interests as originally thought. The meeting of the transcendental and the empirical remains incomplete. They are held in an unresolved tension.

Pragmatic Anthropology

Despite the fact that Kant's pragmatic anthropology shares the fundamental question of reduplication with proto-anthropology, Kant insists that his is unique. In a now famous letter to Marcus Herz in 1773, who had just reviewed Platner's *Anthropologie für Aerzte und Weltweise,* Kant discusses his plans for his first anthropology course:

> I read the review of Platner's *Anthropologie.* I would have not come across it myself but now the forward-looking progression of its skill pleases me. I am reading this winter for the second time a *collegium privatum* of anthropology that I am thinking of making into a proper academic discipline. My own plan is completely different. The goal that I have is through [anthropology] to disclose the sources of all sciences of morals, of cleverness, of the methods to educate and govern people, consequently of all that is practical. Because I am seeking then more phenomena and their laws than the first grounds of possibility of the modification of human nature as such. Therefore the subtle and in my eyes futile examination of the way in which the organs of the body stand in relation to the thoughts is omitted. . . . Meanwhile I am working, from what appear to me to be very pleasant observations, on conducting a preliminary exercise in cleverness, prudence and wisdom itself before the academic youth. [This exercise], along with physical geography, is distinct from all other instruction and can be called knowledge of the world.[37]

Instead of concerning itself with how the organs of the body are related to the mind, Kantian pragmatic anthropology would instruct the "academic youth." It would be a science of morals and methods of education, a science of the formation and governance of the human being.

Herein lies the paradox of Kant's pragmatic anthropology. On the one hand, instead of trying to ground human nature, it would study human beings as they appear at a particular time, in a particular situation. On the other hand, it would study *human* nature—that is, the character of the human species or the constant and universal in the human. Pragmatic anthropology would consider an immutable human nature. And yet, as previously discussed, for Kant, the only immutable characteristic of the human being, the only anthropological truth, is that the human being has a character that it creates itself, insofar as the human being "is capable of perfecting itself according to ends that he himself adopts."[38] For Kant, pragmatic anthropology would bracket mind-body problems and consider "what he [the human being] as a free acting being makes of himself, or what he can and should make of himself."[39]

Such an inquiry is possible only by delimiting the interests of reason. We cannot know or explain what the human being is; we can only observe what the human being makes of itself through its own rational activity. And yet, as evident in the letter to Herz, from the first announcement of the lecture courses, Kant conceived of his anthropology not only as a study of but as a contribution (as a form of instruction) to the transformation of the human being. Like the ethical exercises discussed in chapter 2, pragmatic anthropology is an exercise for the youth. The educative impulse that undergirds the entire anthropology project parallels Kant's claims about education: "The human can only become human through education. The human being is nothing but what education makes of him."[40] The transformative power of education crafts the finite human being.

In terms reminiscent of a categorical imperative, Kant writes that pragmatic anthropology considers the potential for the human being to set ends for itself: it concerns "what the human being can and should make of itself."[41] This "should" may not be synonymous with the "should" of the categorical imperative, but it does indicate a certain analogy between pragmatic anthropology and Kantian morals. Whereas the imperative of the *Kritik der praktischen Vernunft* or the *Grundlegung* addresses the individual as "you" (*du*),[42] the *Anthropologie* addresses the human being as an entire species. In the preface to the 1798 *Anthropologie*, Kant writes that "all cultural progress, by means of which the human being advances his education, has the goal of applying this acquired knowledge and skill for the world's use. But the most important object in the world to which he can apply them is the human being. Because the human being is his own final end."[43] Anthropology serves the investigation of what the human being is and can become. Anthropology discerns, organizes, and distributes knowledge of human predispositions and possibilities. Whereas the collection and distribution of particular insights are empirical, Kant suggests that they also exceed the realm of the empirical in their application to that one being who is an end in itself: the human being. Anthropological inquiry serves ends and purposes that exceed empirical observation. In this sense, anthropology is concerned with employing empirical insights for the ends of reason and, thus, with ends that cannot be reduced to the empirical. This concern with causality—how particular observations are related to a larger whole—occurs against the horizon of a plan for a future human and in terms of a more complete conception of virtue and moral character. In this sense, pragmatic anthropology includes what Kant terms the "faculty of foresight," a faculty of particular interest, since it, more than any other, is the "condition of all possible practice and of the ends to which the human being relates the use of his powers."[44] Anthropology looks into the future of the human.

Pragmatic Versus Physiological Anthropology

Throughout the lecture notes and the 1798 text, Kant refers to his anthropology as pragmatic, and his contemporaries followed suit by referring to it as "the pragmatic anthropology."[45] For Kant, "pragmatic" takes on a range of meanings. This discussion will highlight two of the most important.[46] In contrast to many participants in the contemporary discourse, Kant did not refer to anthropology as the study of the "whole of the human being."[47] He derided late eighteenth-century proto-anthropology's concern with the mind-body relationship and considered his own superior because of its relative silence on the issue. Whereas he never denied that the body and the mind were related, he argued that knowledge of their relation exceeded the limits of reason. Like Schleiermacher, Novalis, Goethe, and Humboldt, Kant effectively brackets the problem.

Kant divides proto-anthropology into two types: physiological and pragmatic. Physiological anthropology seeks to explain the human by considering only what nature makes of him. For Kant, Ernst Platner's exemplified a proto-anthropology that "gropes for the causes of nature."[48] In his review of Platner's *Anthropologie*, Marcus Herz, Kant's former student and a renowned Berlin doctor, praises Platner's work for its hypothesis about the relationship of the body and mind: "From a simple hypothesis, concerning the movement of the *Nervensaft,* he [Platner] derives with a great deal of acuteness, a number of changes in the state of the body, which follow different ideas or different expressions of the powers of the mind."[49] But for Kant, such "hypotheses" are nothing more than conjectures that exceed the limits of reason: "The transition from bodily to mental movement cannot be further explained, thus Bonnet and others are very mistaken when they believe with assurance that they can connect the mind to the soul."[50] Unable to give an account of the mind-body relationship, physiological anthropology, insists Kant, resorts to metaphysical speculation; therefore, anthropology should have "nothing to do" with such speculative efforts. The discussion of self-observation noted Kant's concern that idle speculation could land one in the "madhouse."[51] For Kant, speculation is idle when it is not guided by a prior setting of limits for reason by reason; his criticism of physical anthropology arises out of a concern for the proper attitude of reason itself. Idle speculation does not recognize the need of reason to maintain itself by setting its own limits.

Despite his rejection of what he calls physiological anthropology, Kant frames his pragmatic anthropology in terms of the relationship between the human being and nature. In a comment that anticipates the subordination of nature to the ends of the human in the *Kritik der Urteilskraft,* the Friedlander notes to Kant's anthropology lectures read: "We are interested in the human being more than nature, for nature exists for the sake of the human being. The human being is the purpose of nature."[52] As the only being who is an end in itself the human being subordinates nature to its needs. This subordination of nature to the human being is a logical consequence of Kant's division of the human into a sensible being and an intelligible one. For Kant, anthropology should consider what the human being can make of itself, not what nature has made of it. The human being's transformative potential lies primarily but not completely in reason, for the germs (*Keime*) and predispositions (*Anlagen*) of this transformative potential are given by nature itself. Anthropology as the study of the work of reason, claims Kant, has not yet been undertaken: "All anthropology, which we have at this time, has yet to have the idea that we have before us. Everything that has no relationship to the prudential behavior of human beings does not belong to anthropology. Only that belongs to anthropology of which a clever use in life can be made. Everything where ideas originate belongs to speculation and not to anthropology. This is what Platner has done."[53]

The distinction between pragmatic and physiological anthropology arises not only out of a concern with the limits of reason but also out of Kant's insistence that it be useful for life and not simply theoretical. As discussed in chapter 1, however, proto-anthropology in general framed itself in terms of its practicality and concern that it be "for life." The question becomes, then: Useful in what sense? Practical in what sense? For Kant, the practical character of his anthropology takes its meaning from the practical character of his moral program.

As Henrich Steffens observed in 1822, Kant's emphatic rejection of Platner's *Anthropologie* indicates a possible affinity. "But that he [Kant] is so compelled to oppose his pragmatic anthropology to such an impossible physiological anthropology attests to the power the idea of a real unity of the natural and the spirit had over him. For what could force him to mention the impossibility of such a doctrine of anthropology."[54] As already noted, these physiological anthropologies did not necessarily "grope" for the causes of nature; rather, they often assumed an as yet unspecified relationship between inner and outer, freedom and nature. Kant's insistent differentiation has another history in the institutional reception of his critical philosophy.[55]

The influence of Kant's critical philosophy in late eighteenth-century Germany should not be underestimated. In his second (1790) book on anthropology, *Neue Anthropologie für Aerzte und Weltweise: Mit besonderer Rücksicht auf Physiologie, Pathologie, Moralphilosophie und Aesthetik,* Platner succumbed to Kantian criticisms and refers to his 1772 volume as a "very flawed book."[56] He insists that his new *Neue Anthropologie* is not simply an updated version but an entirely different book in which nothing of "speculative metaphysics" is to be found. He went to great efforts to remove all that which had been found to contradict Kantian critical philosophy. Because of the influence of his critical philosophy, Kant's pragmatic anthropology was bound up in significant and sometimes imperceptible ways to this broader discourse on proto-anthropology.

Kant refers to his anthropology not only as pragmatic but also as prudential or practical. As such, his anthropology would consider how rational insight could be applied in and to life. In the discussion of the difference between a metaphysics of morals and a moral anthropology in the *Grundlegung,* Kant refers to practical anthropology, not pragmatic anthropology. Although these terms, "practical" and "pragmatic," should not be conflated, they point to a similar project. Practical anthropology would be the empirical part of a moral philosophy and, thus, concern more specifically the relation of morals and anthropology or the moral use of anthropological insight. Pragmatic anthropology, as Allen Wood writes, considers "knowledge of human nature in light of all the uses we may choose to make of this knowledge, and not only for its moral use."[57] The primary though certainly not the only use of pragmatic anthropology, however, is ultimately a moral use in that this anthropology relates to the ends of the human. It relates its observations to an idea of what the human being is to become.

It is in this sense that Kant's idea of freedom as ethical autonomy finds its more empirical analogue in anthropology: "Anthropology is pragmatic but serves the moral knowledge of the human being, for out of it one must create the grounds of motivation to morality and without it morality would be scholastic and not applicable to the world."[58] A number of Kant's philosophical allies saw his pragmatic anthropology as a clear attempt to connect his morals with an empirical science of the human. G. S. A. Mellin, for example, defines Kantian anthropology as a doctrine of "the empirical conditions of ideas and actions of the human being, or of his [the human being's] entire *effectiveness*. . . . [A practical anthropology concerns] the application of morals onto the particular condition and state of the human faculty of desire, on the drives, inclinations, desires and passions of the human and the hindrances to exercising the moral law. It is the empirical part of ethics."[59]

Similarly, Schmid, author of the eighteenth-century Kant encyclopedia, defines Kant's pragmatic anthropology as "the applied and empirical philosophy of morals, actually the doctrine of virtue . . . the consideration of the moral law in relationship to the human being's will, and its inclinations and drives, and in relationship to the hindrances that they pose in exercising the moral law."[60] The connection between Kant's ethics and his pragmatic anthropology can be found in the latter's concern with the subjective effectiveness of moral principles.

Without anthropological insight, moral knowledge would remain merely theoretical and, thus, not practical for a finite human being. It could not aid in the pursuit of the ends of reason. To facilitate the subjective effectiveness of morals, Kant recommends the study of an anthropology that "teaches us to know ourselves properly."[61] Such an anthropology affords practical helps and insights that make the formation of a moral disposition more effective. In this sense, it concerns the actualization of moral being, not just theorizing about the will. In the *Anthropologie in pragmatischer Hinsicht,* Kant writes that anthropology studies what human beings can and should make of themselves. The former modality, what human beings actually do as observed by the anthropologists, is ultimately subordinated to the latter modality, what they should do. As an ethical project Kantian anthropology induces and cultivates a certain way of life, one in keeping with his ethical dietetics. Not just concerned with the application of particular moral rules, pragmatic anthropology cultivates, develops, and promotes a particular moral disposition—that is, it is organized and guided by a specific moral pedagogy. It is more than merely propaedeutic. It aims to cultivate the presupposition of freedom.

The pragmatic-transformative task of Kant's *Anthropologie,* however, is threatened by the basic epistemological question of eighteenth-century German proto-anthropology: from what point of observation can anthropological inquiry distinguish, as Kant puts it, "what of the human being is natural, and what is artificial or acquired," or what is the result of "education and other influences?"[62] Despite Kant's consistent efforts to bracket such transcendental questions, the theoretical and transcendental difficulties of anthropological inquiry remain. Kant returns to them throughout his text and the lectures. From what position can one observe and make normatively compelling claims about a being whose only universal and constant characteristic is its ability to create its own character? How can claims about the human or what it is to become human be made compelling against the backdrop of such negativity that human beings are only what they can make of themselves and nothing more?

In his lectures on pedagogy, Kant elaborates on what makes anthropological inquiry so difficult: "Because education teaches the human being some things and develops others: one cannot know how far the natural predispositions extend."[63] The process of education so blurs the distinction between what nature gives the human being and what the human being acquires through its own work that definitive claims about human nature are almost impossible. The very task of Kant's pragmatic anthropology—the investigation of what a free-acting human being makes of itself—concerns the articulation of what is natural and what is acquired through human effort.

Weltkenntnis versus Scholasticism

Kant frames the meeting of normative and empirical modes of inquiry and the possibility of anthropological norms not just in terms of the pragmatic-physiological distinction but also in terms of the distinction between knowledge of the world (*Weltkenntnis*) and theoretical knowledge (*Schulkenntnis*). Knowledge of the world concerns how the human being can set its own ends and recognize itself as its "own final end." It is knowledge of the human being as an "earthly being endowed with reason." And as such, it is a knowledge cultivated against the horizon of the entire species, against the horizon of the purposes of the human. It is knowledge "according to his species."[64] Theoretical knowledge, in contrast, considers the human being and other objects as "things in the world" and, thus, as objects of reason's theoretical interests and not as ends of reason.[65] Knowledge of the world contributes to the setting of ends, whereas theoretical knowledge merely explains things.

Kant associates theoretical knowledge with a "scholastic knowledge that belongs to the learned profession":

> Now whoever wants to apply scholastic knowledge, which one needs only in the school and in learned texts, to use in the world without seeing whether they are interesting or not is a pedant. . . . The word pedant comes originally from the Latin, for in Italy the *Hausinformatoren* was called *magistripendanei*. From this comes the Italian word *Pedanto* since *magistrio* was dropped and *Pedanei* developed into *Pedanto,* and thus the German word *Pedant.* These people presumably never left their study and, thus, when they socialized brought only their school knowledge and thus gave one the occasion to name those who did not know how to deal with others properly. A pedant can make use of his knowledge only in the school.[66]

Pedants never find their way out of the school and can apply their knowledge only for scholastic or cognitive-organizational purposes—that is, their knowledge refers only to other objects of knowledge. While originating in the school from the lips of the pedagogue, anthropology, insists Kant, must extend itself into the world. By appealing to an audience to make use of knowledge acquired in school, Kant envisions an anthropology that would mediate between the school, as a space for theoretical reflection, and the world, as a public space in which the human being is always among other beings. As a knowledge of the world, anthropology would "prevent learnedness from becoming pedantry."[67] For Kant, pragmatic anthropology would be a scholarly sanctioned discipline—because it is always preceded by scholastic grounding—that would inform the world; in other words, it would be a form of the public use of reason.[68] Anthropology takes up the practical task of applying reason to the development of the human being. The question "What is human?" coalesces around the question concerning the ends of the human and its future possibilities.

Kant makes a similar distinction in his *Logik* between philosophy as a cosmopolitan concept (*Weltbegriff*) and philosophy as a scholastic concept (*Schulbegriff*). The former is the science "of the final ends of human reason," whereas the latter is the system of "philosophical knowledge or the knowledge of reason."[69] According to the theoretical concept, philosophy concerns "cleverness" and is the purview of the "artisan of reason" who, in his quest for speculative knowledge, gives "rules for the use of reason." Philosophy according to the cosmopolitan concept, in contrast, concerns "utility" and, as the doctrine of wisdom, is the purview of the "practical philosopher, the teacher of wisdom through his doctrines and example." This is the "actual" philosopher. Philosophy according to the cosmopolitan concept is the science of the relationship of all knowledge and the use of reason for the "final end of human reason."[70] It therefore "necessarily interests everyone," while philosophy according to the scholastic concept concerns only "arbitrary purposes."[71]

Philosophy becomes a knowledge of the world when the effectiveness of reason in the world becomes the primary concern for a philosopher, when the philosopher, in this case Kant, can write that the intelligible world "can and should have influence on the sensible world in order to make it measure up as much as possible to this ideal."[72] Kant's distinction points to two types of knowledge, one concerned with categorization and another with practical ends. The distinction between a scholastic philosophy and a cosmopolitan philosophy lies in their different interests or purposes. Kant does not frame the distinction in terms of a scholastic philosophy grounded in reason and rational inquiry versus a cosmopolitan philosophy based in experience and empirical methods; instead, he frames the distinction as one concerning the "interests people have in the two fields of philosophy."[73] Different forms of philosophical inquiry pursue different interests.

Kant explicitly refers to pragmatic anthropology as knowledge of the world or cosmopolitan knowledge. Pragmatic anthropology investigates the human being "in order to conclude what he can make of himself or [how he] can use others; not psychology, which is scholastic knowledge."[74] Underlying pragmatic anthropology as cosmopolitan knowledge is the idea that human beings as a collective can best set and pursue their own ends when "we know ourselves."[75] In this sense, Kant distinguishes the practical interests of pragmatic anthropology from the theoretical interests of psychology and also physiology. The former investigates whether the human being has a soul and the origins of thought and sensations, whereas the latter seeks to explain memory from simply analyzing the brain. Pragmatic anthropology, in contrast, brackets both types of questions. And it is this bracketing that makes pragmatic anthropology a form of cosmopolitan philosophy. It brackets theoretical interests in its pursuit of its practical interests.

The Cosmopolitan Character of Anthropology

In his anthropology lectures, Kant recasts the distinction between a philosophy for the school and a philosophy for the world as a distinction not just between scholastic and pragmatic knowledge but between "knowing the world" and "having a world."[76] To know a world is to understand "the game" of nature, while to have a world is to play in this "game." To have a world is to participate and play along. To know the world is simply to observe. The scholastic philosopher is a disengaged observer, whereas the cosmopolitan philosopher is always aware of his place within nature. To know the world is to have theoretical knowledge of the world garnered from observation. To have a world is to interact with the game of nature that he has observed. To have a world is to be part of a world in practice. As previously noted, anthropological inquiry always implicates its subject in the object of study. The subject of anthropology is always also the object of anthropology. The human is always playing the "game" of being or becoming human. There is no position outside this game. This discussion of the "game" returns one to the fundamental question of anthropological inquiry: from what perspective can the human being be observed if the human being as observer is always already "in the game"?

As a cosmopolitan philosophy, pragmatic anthropology addresses more practical interests that would not necessarily have to be subordinated to these more theoretical questions. The reduplication of anthropological observation is intractable only from a theoretical perspective of "knowing the world." From the perspective of a cosmopolitan concept of knowledge, however, the reduplication of anthropological observation does not have to be resolved. In fact, it cannot be resolved, for pragmatic anthropology is always already aware of the recursive nature of anthropological inquiry, of the fact that it will always be conducted from the perspective of "having a world."

It is in this sense that Kant refers to pragmatic anthropology as a popular science. It is relevant to and concerns the ends of the human. The popularity of philosophy, however, "does not consist in setting aside scholastic standards, but only in not letting the form [of scholastic philosophy] be seen as the framework (just like one draws a penciled line, on which one writes, and later erases it). Everything scientific must be according to rules; but the technical [quality] of popular philosophy should not be seen, rather [the cosmopolitan philosopher must] condescend to the power of comprehension [of common people] and the typical expression."[77]

Pragmatic anthropology, as popular philosophy, has an analogous relationship to transcendental philosophy, as scholastic philosophy. The *grounding* of anthropological observation in the "I" of apprehension—a grounding, however, that is not actually a grounding, as was noted in the discussion of apperception and apprehension—is the erased "framework" drawn out by transcendental methods. This erasure is what constitutes the bracketing of metaphysical problems and theoretical conundrums. The bracketing merely conceals these problems from view so that the practical interests of anthropological inquiry may be pursued. The theoretical problems and conundrums of anthropological inquiry remain as the erased or bracketed framework of the entire project. As a popular, cosmopolitan science, pragmatic anthropology rests upon these theoretical and scientific principles, principles that remain, to a certain extent, contradictory.

As popular philosophy, pragmatic anthropology "condescend[s]" to an audience that extends beyond the small circle of scholars to which scholastic philosophy limits itself.[78] Its reliance on examples accessible to "every reader" are meant to utilize particular situations in order to establish more general claims in a manner accessible to a broader audience.[79] Similar to his morals' reliance on examples (in the Characteristic, or Doctrine of Method), Kant's pragmatic anthropology employs examples to ensure the effectiveness of its insights and to endow its individual observations with a broader purview. Marked by a performative force, pragmatic anthropology's use of examples is not about making knowledge claims but about encouraging particular behaviors.

It is fitting, then, that the exemplary figure of Kant's pragmatic anthropology is not the detached philosopher but the "citizen of the world." Pragmatic anthropology conducts itself from such a cosmopolitan perspective (120). But what is one to make of Kant's use of the term? Kant does not describe the cosmopolitan figure as a citizen of a particular political body, so what kind of world *citizen* is this cosmopolitan figure? In the context of the *Anthropologie,* "cosmopolitan" denotes an individual who lives in a world with and among other human beings at a particular time and in a particular place. In the preface to his *Anthropologie,* as we have previously seen, Kant regards the experience of living in a trade city, "like perhaps Königsberg on the Pregel River," with its access to different languages and customs, as optimal for anthropological study (121). It is amidst the daily exchange of language(s) and in interactions with people that anthropology is possible, and it is here within this daily exchange that Kant's citizen of the world operates. This cosmopolitan anthropology is the social analogue of the "I" of apprehension, since both are bound to the finitude of the body. The cosmopolitan is not, primarily at least, a juridical figure, a figure with claims to certain rights or even particular political affiliations. The cosmopolitan of the *Anthropologie* avails himself of and, in the case of the anthropologist as cosmopolitan, redistributes popular claims and observations. Anthropology is an empirical science of popular examples and popular exchange. In some ways the political project of the anthropology with its concerns for *the human* and relative disregard of the state is nonpolitical, if political is conflated simply with the state. But it is profoundly political inasmuch as it figures the human as always within the *polis* of life. As a lecture course, Kantian anthropology was also an exchange of sorts. And it is here that the object of anthropology emerges: in the constant exchange of daily language and discussion, in the popular examples, the human emerges in concrete forms. Theoretical questions concerning the body-mind relationship or the transcendental impossibility of anthropology are bracketed and questions of how human beings live take precedence.

Kant's world citizen, then, is not the traveling cosmopolitan but the frequenter of the *Tischgesellschaft* (a good meal in good company), and it is in the figure of the dinner table that Kant's pragmatic anthropology—now that it has bracketed more intractable concerns—takes shape.[80] Kant transitions from the Didactic to the Characteristic in concluding the first section of his *Anthropologie* by laying out guidelines for social interaction. He describes humanity as a way of thinking associated with sociability. The question was previously posed whether the Didactic, with its concern for the fundamental building blocks of the human being, the faculties, could ground anthropology. Kant concludes this first section of his *Anthropologie* not with such transcendental questions but with this discussion of the *Tischgesellschaft*, a figure of social interaction and exchange. The question "What is the human?" is figured in the dinner table: "The good living that still seems to harmonize best with true humanity is a good meal in good company."[81] Here amidst the exchanges of this *Tischgesellschaft,* which Kant even refers to as a symposium, conversation abounds and allows "human beings to exchange their thoughts in social intercourse" (279). In line with the pedagogical force of the text, Kant outlines the guiding principles of social exchange at the dinner table, principles concerning hospitality and trust. He even outlines the stages of a proper dinner. Every dinner should begin with the telling of stories, then move on to a reasonable discussion of them, and conclude with a convivial recollection of them. These principles and guidelines would insure that no guest returns home feeling "alienated" from another guest (281). They are intended to invite virtuous behavior; they uphold virtue by being inviting (282).

The cosmopolitan subject of anthropology is not the subject of apperception of the *Kritik der reinen Vernunft* or the pure moral subject of the *Kritik der praktischen Vernunft*. Parallel to the cosmopolitan concept of philosophy, the cosmopolitan subject lives and observes the human being amidst the dense plurality of particular worlds. Much like proto-anthropology's bracketing of the mind-body problem, such a cosmopolitan perspective defers the metaphysical import of freedom and morals and the theoretical conundrums of anthropological observation in favor of a "cosmo-politics"—that is, a constant negotiation of and dealing with the exigencies of the world. The primary source for the anthropologist is not the transcendental grammar of the categories but a dynamic familiarity with a cosmopolitical world marked by the historical transformations of the human. Kant's pragmatic anthropology ultimately brackets theoretical questions for the practical ends of anthropology. It erases from sight the conjuncture of transcendental and empirical.

The Self-Contradiction of Pragmatic Anthropology

The bracketing gestures of Kant's pragmatic anthropology are primarily intended to address methodological concerns—that is, Kant brackets the theoretical problems of anthropological inquiry but not his anthropological claims. The claims of pragmatic anthropology are not provisional. For Kant, general knowledge of the human being always precedes local or particular knowledge of the human being.[82] Knowledge of a particular human being is always subordinated to transcendental claims of what human beings are and should become. This fundamental claim underlines how the conjoining of the transcendental and empirical might be better described, then, as the absorption of the empirical by the transcendental. Kant's general knowledge of the human being is oriented toward the transcendental idea of a human destiny—transcendental because it corresponds to nothing in empirical reality. Thus, the second part of the *Anthropologie* is filled with claims and empirical observations about the character of the sexes, peoples, and races. It is in these sections where the transcendental impulses of a pragmatic anthropology butt up against what Kant takes to be anthropological observations based on empirical facts, when, in fact, Kant's empirical observations and claims have scant empirical detail.[83] The transcendental destiny of the human being mixes with empirically based knowledge of human beings. The question becomes, then, to what extent a general knowledge of pragmatic anthropology is functionally equivalent to an a priori knowledge. The cosmopolitan character of pragmatic anthropology is not technically synonymous with the concept of universality in *Kritik der reinen Vernunft*, where necessity denotes the universality of a priori judgments. The mixing of transcendental and empirical raises the question of whether the strong universalist thrust of the *Anthropologie* conceals entrenched prejudices or assumptions. If pragmatic anthropology cannot fully reflect on its own theoretical ground, can it uncover its own blind spots?

For Kant, knowledge of the human being can be either a local knowledge of the coincidental behavior or conduct of human beings or a general knowledge of "the nature of humanity." He describes his pragmatic anthropology as a general not a local anthropology because it concerns not just the particular conditions of human beings but the nature of the human. "The local conditions of human beings are always changing," says Kant, but "the nature of humanity never does";[84] therefore, a pragmatic anthropology concerns pragmatic knowledge, what the human can make of itself, "what flows out of its nature." Physical and geographic knowledge only limit anthropological knowledge because they are "bound to time and place": "Whoever has traveled and met many people, one cannot say that he knows human beings, for he only became acquainted with their conditions, which vary. If I know humanity, however, it [knowledge of humanity] must apply to all kinds of human beings."[85]

Whereas the nature of the human being does not change, the conditions of human beings do. A pragmatic anthropology makes claims about the human as such; therefore, it cannot rely solely on travel reports, which only give an account of human beings as they are at particular places and times. It relies on a broader horizon. This orientation toward the destiny of the human species also implies that Kant's pragmatic anthropology concerns the "destiny of humanity in its entirety."[86] Kant suggests that the entire species will take part in this progression. But does the progression of the entire species necessarily imply that every individual human being will participate in this progression?

Kant orients his pragmatic anthropology toward the conception of a human species and its promise of what the human being can and should make of itself: "The education of the human race" and its moral progression can only be discerned in the species "taken as a whole, that is, collectively (*universorum*), not all of the individuals (*singularum*), where the multitude does not yield a system but only an aggregate gathered together."[87] Kant, however, claims that the "character" of such a human species is taken "from out of the experience of all times and from among all peoples."[88] Kant's species concept involves both the regulative idea of a human destiny and empirical facts gathered throughout time and place.

Kant organizes his pragmatic anthropology around a tension familiar from the discussion in chapter 1 of the cultural-normative turn taken by proto-anthropology. Whereas Herder was concerned that certain notions of human progress risk subordinating human individuals to abstract categories (like humanity or the human species), he insisted they were nonetheless necessary. On the one hand, Herder seems to dismiss such normative categories: "You human beings of all parts of the earth . . . you have not lived and fertilized the earth with your ashes, so that at the end of time your offspring could become happy through European culture."[89] For Herder, normative categories rely on a notion of progress that subordinates the happiness of the individual human being to the historical (and deferred) progress of the species through culture. Herder calls such a theoretical subordination an "offense" to the majesty of nature and claims that every individual carries "the form in himself" according to which his own happiness can be developed. On the other hand, however, Herder emphasizes the conceptual necessity of a unified historical progress and the inability of individual human beings to achieve their own happiness without it: "If the human being were to receive everything from within itself and develop apart from external objects, a history of the individual human being [*eine Geschichte des Menschen*] would be possible but not a history of the human [*eine Geschichte der Menschen*], of the entire race" (345). Only the "working together of individuals" makes us human (347).

Herder attempts to resolve this tension by insisting that category concepts such as humanity or the human species only make sense "insofar as they exist in individual beings" (345). And for Herder, these concepts can be embodied in the processes of education and tradition. Human beings become human through the imitation of, exercise, and distribution of examples and given forms—images and examples that are afforded by tradition. Whereas Herder mocks the philosopher's attempts to follow the "growth of the entire human race" by losing him- or herself in an "idealistic world" and dreams, he extols the power of tradition to produce happy and contented individuals. These mimetic traditions, however, are undergirded by a robust theodicy. "God's purpose for the entire human race"—however confused and indiscernible it might appear in history—remains "unmistakable" (350). As the work of God, every human being carries the "divine character of its destiny." The happiness of every human being is divinely guaranteed.

"But what if the genuine end of providence were not this shadowy image of happiness, which each makes for himself, but rather the always proceeding and growing activity and culture that is put in play by it."[90]

This is Kant's response to Herder's critique of the starry-eyed philosopher and his dream of an infinite progress of the human species in his review of Herder's *Ideen zur Philosophie der Geschichte der Menschheit*.[91] Kant understands historical progress not in terms of individual happiness but as the progression of the entire human species over time. He considers the skills and abilities "developed by individuals not in terms of their usefulness for the individuals as such, but in terms of the contribution they make to the cumulative power of the species over time."[92] For Herder, such a subordination conflicts with his image of a benevolent god, who promises happiness not just for the species but for every individual. Herder's criticism boils down to this basic issue: by focusing on the progress of the entire human race, does Kant not turn abstract categories into final ends and the happiness of individuals into mere means? Does he not sacrifice the happiness of individual human beings to the development of the human species?[93]

Hannah Arendt puts this criticism even more forcefully but elides Herder's appeal to theodicy:[94] "In Kant himself there is this contradiction: Infinite Progress is the law of the human species; at the same time, man's dignity demands that he be seen (every single one of us) in his particularity and, as such, be seen—but without any comparison and independent of time—as reflecting mankind in general. In other words, the very idea of progress—if it is more than a change in circumstances and an improvement in the world—contradicts Kant's notion of man's dignity. It is against human dignity to believe in progress."[95]

This apparent contradiction is nowhere more evident than in Kant's claim that his pragmatic anthropology is concerned with the "destiny of the human being," for how can an empirical science pose questions about destiny? And if it does, and Kant's does, would it not necessarily subordinate the actual individual human being to an idea of human moral progress or an idea of freedom?

Returning to Kant's review of Herder's *Ideen*, one can see how Kant's response revolves around his conception of the human species:

> But if the human species signifies the whole of a series of generations going (indeterminably) into the infinite (as this meaning is entirely customary), and it is assumed that this series ceaselessly approximates the line of its destiny running alongside it, then it is not to utter a contradiction to say that in all its parts it is asymptotic to

this line and yet on the whole that it will coincide with it, in other words, that no member of all the generations of humankind, but only the species will fully reach its destiny. . . . the philosopher would say: "The destiny of humankind is on the whole a ceaseless progress, and its completion is a mere idea, but very useful in all respects—the idea of a goal to which we have to direct our endeavors in accordance with the aim of providence."[96]

While both Herder and Kant appeal to purposes and ends (providential or practical), Kant emphasizes not the theoretical grounds but the practical use of his conception of the human species and progress. Although the "destiny" of the human species is a "mere idea," it is, insists Kant, "very useful." Echoing his emphasis on the practical effect and not the propositional *truth* of a holy will in his ethics, Kant claims that the idea of progress and destiny instills within human beings a discomfort with our present circumstances. For Kant, Herder's appeal to tradition as the dominant mode of education and human development was too conservative; it would never make possible that critical distance that Kant deemed essential for human progress.[97] Whereas for Kant the human species can only progress by endlessly comparing itself with an idea of human perfection, for Herder, this critical insistence merely masks Kant's refusal to value human diversity and individual happiness. For Kant, the idea of a perfected human species was the only way out of a localized parochialism. The question dividing Herder and Kant is whether human beings can ever extricate themselves from their own situatedness. Given the problems of anthropological observation, are compelling norms—norms that exceed particular traditions or social, historical contexts—even possible? Kant insists that reason does have the capacity to generate such normatively compelling ideas. Herder insists that it does not.

Kant's pragmatic anthropology is, then, a general, universal anthropology. But what is the content of a general claim about the nature of the human if, as Kant argues, the human is always changing? Kant's insistence on a general, pragmatic anthropology returns the observer again and again to the fundamental negativity of his anthropology. This is why it concerns what humans as freely acting beings make of themselves. Human are those beings who can use reason to make themselves. They are ciphers of reason, blanks for the ends of reason. The reduplication of anthropological inquiry leads to an acute awareness of just how constructed claims about the human are—that is, any account of the human is, ultimately, an account of the self-determination of reason. An account of the human can look nowhere—not to nature, not to theology—but to itself. This, it would seem, is the anthropological freedom of modernity.

But what underlies the promise of such an anthropological freedom—that is, are there any guarantees or promises that the free, rational beings that pragmatic anthropology intends to cultivate will one day inhabit the earth? For Kant there are. As I discussed in chapter 2, Kant relies on a particular teleology to imagine the human. The next chapter considers how the complex promises of anthropology—promises that human beings can become truly human—rest on the necessary connection between Kant's pragmatic anthropology and his teleology of history. Although Kant brackets metaphysical questions and theoretical conundrums in order to deal *merely* with the finite human being as a citizen of the world, he ties his pragmatic anthropology to a teleology of history and the promise of a human destiny. Anthropology is at once open and closed: on the one hand, a negativity underlies anthropology, but, on the other hand, a destiny guides it. Human beings make themselves against a particular horizon of expectation. There is, for Kant, an anthropological goal. It is in this imbrication of anthropology, history, and destiny—in the mixing of transcendental and empirical—that an impure ethics unfolds.

4

Testing the Human

Kant and Forster on the Differences of Race and the Possibilities of Culture

The Destinies of the Human

Shortly after his formulation of the categorical imperative in *Grundlegung zur Metaphysik der Sitten,* Kant, in a parenthetical aside and only for a moment, sounds like an eighteenth-century European ethnographer. "Although the human being (like the South Sea Islanders) is intent on letting his talent rust and devoting his life to idleness, amusement, procrastination, in a word, to enjoyment, only as a reasonable being will [he] want all his talents and abilities to be developed . . . [in order to make himself] a useful human being."[1] Kant's voracious reading of travelogues bleeds like an empirical stain right into the middle of the *Grundlegung's* universal claims for human dignity. Here, in one of his central texts on moral philosophy—not in one of the scattered notes or stray remarks from one of the anthropology or geography lectures—the exemplarity of Kant's pragmatic anthropology takes a different form. Instead of the empirical being decontextualized or projected into a more general claim, it stands in for the human as such. The "lethargic" South Sea Islanders stand in for the entire human race. Contemporary stereotypes find their way, however parenthetically, into the purity of moral philosophy.

Kant uses the example of "lethargic" South Sea Islanders, however, to address the individual human being—the singular you (*du*) of the categorical imperative—who, one presumes, is to take this ethnographic claim as an incitement to make him- or herself a more "useful" human being. The example of the South Sea Islanders should provoke the work of culture, the work of becoming human. It should incite recognition of the "destiny of the human being."

This brief passage gathers all of the problems dealt with in previous chapters on Kant's ethics and anthropology: moral development, the purity and impurity of ethics, ethnography, and destiny. It also introduces another element, one that has become, as we shall see, a flashpoint of sorts in recent Kant scholarship: race. Kant's parenthetical use of such a Eurocentric ethnography begs the question, as Robert Louden puts it, "Who is the 'we' that is progressing towards perfection?"[2]

In order to understand the place of race in Kant's pragmatic anthropology, however, one needs to consider the relationship between anthropology, history, and teleology. Near the end of his 1798 *Anthropologie in pragmatischer Hinsicht,* Kant makes the connection between anthropology and teleology explicit:

> The summary of what pragmatic anthropology is, with respect to the destiny of the human being and the character of his development, as follows: The human being is destined through his reason to be in a society with other human beings and in it through art and science, to cultivate, to civilize, and to moralize himself. No matter how great his animal instincts might be to give himself over in passivity to the enticements of leisureliness and comfort, which he calls happiness, he is still destined to make himself worthy of humanity by actively struggling with the obstacles that cling to him because of the crudity of his nature.[3]

It is here, with its concern for human destiny, that Kant's pragmatic anthropology becomes explicitly normative. In its invocation of a historical teleology, Kant's pragmatic anthropology intersects with his morals. The dual claim that anthropology is both cosmopolitan, in the practical sense outlined in the previous chapter, and somehow universal coalesces in the, for Kant, necessary relationship between anthropology and teleology. The human being is destined as a species, and this destiny entails the presupposition of moral autonomy or freedom. But what are the ethical consequences of this intersection of anthropology and destiny, of empirical claims with normative assertions? This destiny is addressed only to the species, to the historical human being that Kant imagines as the future human being. The form of address is an ironic comment on the purported sovereignty of the Kantian moral subject. Only as a human being, as part of a historically constituted species, is the individual human being destined to become free. The individual human being is bound up with an anthropological negativity that would seem to be at odds with the freedom as imagined in Kantian morals.

But what does it mean for the human being to be destined? What does it mean to speak of a vocation of the human from the perspective of pragmatic anthropology? The question of vocation, in the sense of calling or, as I have translated Kant's use of the term, destiny, of the human being was a central question in late eighteenth-century Germany.[4] Moses Mendelssohn and Thomas Abbt, for example, debated this issue in a series of letters after Abbt's review of Johann Joachim Spalding's *Die Bestimmung des Menschen*, which went through thirteen editions between 1748 and 1794.[5] For Mendelssohn, the question of the vocation of the human being was the "measure and goal of all our [human] efforts and ambitions, the point toward which we must direct our eyes if we do not want to lose ourselves."[6]

As Reinhard Brandt observes, Mendelssohn distinguishes between two senses of *Bestimmung*. "The word *Bestimmung* means not only the positing of a predicate, from among many that could be applied to the subject, *Determination;* but also the positing of a final end to which something as a means should be used, *Destination*. . . . The *Bestimmung* of the human being can mean either *Determination* or *Destination*."[7] The first sense of the word, determination, connotes determination *as* something. A predicate is determined through its subject to be something. In this sense, one can determine a distance between two points based on a prior definition, or a subject might give form to an object. The second sense of the word, destination, connotes a determination not only as something but toward something through an appeal to a teleological structure (here *Endzweck*). Something can be destined to become something that it not yet is. Responding to Abbt's doubts about Spalding's text, questions concerning what this vocation might be and how it might be ascertained, Mendelssohn begins his response with an appeal to the human being in the second person singular, "you, oh human being!" (*du, o Mensch!*). His appeal focuses on the vocation of the individual human being, who through "discipline and constant effort" can become "more perfect" (1:217). Whereas Mendelssohn ties vocation to the individual human being, he claims that this vocation is determined, in the destination sense of the word, through "divine" or "higher" ends: "The divine purposes only extend themselves not only to every individual but to the whole as well, and they will be fulfilled most perfectly in the whole, and in the individual only with respect to the whole" (256). Whereas Mendelssohn ties vocation to the ends of a whole, the entire world, as subordinated to divine ends, Kant ties vocation or destiny to the ends of the human species. For Kant, as Brandt emphasizes, the "relevant whole" is neither the cosmos of a divine creator nor the individual; it is, rather, the human species. Kant writes, "It must be noted that with all other animals left to themselves, each individual reaches its destiny; however, with the human being only the species reaches its destiny, so that the human race can work its way up to its destiny only through progress in a series of innumerably many generations."[8] Only the species is destined to a particular end, and for Kant, this end is moral autonomy.

The semantic tension inherent in *Bestimmung*, as determined or as destined, figures the tension of a Kantian teleological anthropology in which the individual human being is determined through its bodily finitude but as part of the human species is destined to freedom. Only as a member of a future humanity is the individual truly human. Kant's use of *Bestimmung* affords a new vocabulary to describe the conjunction of the transcendental and empirical in anthropology. As natural beings human individuals are determined by nature, and as intelligible beings they are destined to become human. The human is both determined and destined; but what does it mean for a species, as opposed to an individual, to be destined? The logic of *Bestimmung* is ultimately anthropological: the human becomes and can pursue the ends of reason only in the realm of nature, the realm of time. In the following sections, I argue that Kant embeds the very possibility of moral autonomy in nature itself through a teleological assumption of a human destiny, however imperceptible and impossible this destiny might seem. *Bestimmung* functions at the limits of nature and freedom for the individual and the human species.

The Germs of Human Destiny in Kant's Essays on Race

As I argued in the previous chapter, Kant's *Anthropologie* hinges on a discussion of character and the predispositions of the human species, but this discussion is preceded by a series of sections that might seem ill-suited to a Kantian pragmatic anthropology whose stated task is to consider "what the human being can and should make of himself." Kant includes sections, for example, on the character of the individual,[9] the sexes, and peoples[10] (*der Völker*) and concludes with a short, seemingly cursory section on the character of the races. All of these sections address the subtitle of the second part of the *Anthropologie:* "How to recognize the inside from the outside." They can be read as pragmatic insofar as better knowledge of various temperaments or national types helps human beings to know themselves better. Ultimately, knowledge, here speaking in particular of the character of peoples, is pragmatic in a very particular sense: using anthropological insights to "make judgments."[11] But what are these ends for which empirical insights can serve as aids and helps? And what kinds of aids and helps does Kant mean here?

The *Anthropologie*'s section on race consists of little more than a few paragraphs and refers the reader to another work "written in accordance with [Kant's] principles" of the concept of race.[12] In the preface, Kant calls knowledge of the human races "theoretical knowledge of the world" and opposes it to pragmatic knowledge of the world.[13] The former is a knowledge of "things in the world, like the animals, plants, and minerals in different lands and climates," whereas the latter is a knowledge of the human being as a citizen of the world. In the *Anthropologie,* Kant describes race as a mere typological knowledge—that is, race seems to facilitate the classification of human beings into theoretical categories, much as a Linnaean taxonomy facilitated the efficient classification of plants. Race, however, was a fundamental concern of Kant's, not only as one aspect of character, but also as a necessary concept for the "destiny of the human being." Kant's thinking on race in the 1770s and 1780s laid the groundwork for his fuller articulation of teleology in the 1790s. In the section on race in the *Anthropologie*, Kant argues that nature has made as its law not the "making similar" of a phylum (*Stamm*) but its "diversification into infinity."[14] The diversification of races was "intended" as a divergence from a common monogenetic origin. As will become evident, this assumption begs the question as to how open to diversification this prior unity is. The conceptual difficulty of Kant's anthropology, at least in terms of race, lies not just in a possible dehistorization of empirical particularity but in the possibility of an a priori closure, the transposition of a prior unity onto a particular form.

One of the driving questions here is just how flexible (or inflexible) Kant's anthropological unity is. This more fundamental question raises a host of complex issues: What is the relationship (if any) of Kant's monogenetic account of race to the assumed unity or destiny of the human species? How does Kant use the concept of race to figure a possible relationship between a natural teleology and a moral teleology? Kant works through these issues in a public debate on race with the German naturalist Georg Forster.

From 1775 to 1788 Kant published four essays dealing with race: "Von den verschiedenen Racen der Menschen" ("Of the Different Races of Human Beings," 1775), "Bestimmung des Begriffs einer Menschenrace" ("Determination of the Concept of a Human Race," 1785), "Muthmaßlicher Anfang der Menschengeschichte" ("Conjectural Beginning of Human History," 1786), and "Über den Gebrauch teleologischer Principien in der Philosophie" ("On the Use of Teleological Principles in Philosophy," 1788).[15] Kant's interest in race emerged in part from his voracious reading of travelogues, which afforded him and a European reading public a more detailed picture of the variety of the human species. These ethnographic accounts also began to complicate the notion of a unified, whole humanity. Kant wrote these essays at the time of what has been referred to as the "second age of discovery." In the second half of the eighteenth century, Louis Antoine de Bougainville and Captain James Cook, to name but two of the most important explorers of the day, sailed to the South Pacific with explicit scientific programs. Previous expeditions had of course noted the differences of lands and peoples from those found in Europe and made useful discoveries, concerning, for example, navigational techniques; but theoretical interests remained secondary to the primary expeditionary tasks.[16]

Urs Bitterli describes the character of expeditions in this "second age of discovery" as threefold: (1) A greater emphasis was placed on the peaceful and friendly interaction with native peoples so as not to make the study of foreign lands and peoples more difficult. (2) The resolution of outstanding questions in geographical and natural science was a clear goal of certain expeditions.[17] (3) Expeditions attempted in all branches of sciences but especially ethnography to avail themselves of new knowledge and experiences.[18] The royal instructions to Bougainville specified that because "knowledge of these islands and continents is still so incomplete," he must "study the trees and the actual products of nature" and bring back examples.[19] These explicit directives for scientific inquiry meant that the expeditions of Bougainville in 1767 were joined not just by astronomers and geographers, who had been necessary for oceanic navigation, but botanists, zoologists, and proto-ethnographers.[20] In his *Cook, der Entdecker* (*Cook, the Explorer*), Georg Forster notes that Cook conceived of the "business of discovery" in much broader terms. Whereas his predecessors stayed on the South Pacific islands no longer than the crew's rest and ship's repairs required, Cook "eagerly" collected detailed information and reports on the "inner form of the country" and familiarized himself with the "national character of the natives."[21] Like Bougainville, Cook brought a range of scientists with him as well, including the naturalist Johann Forster and his son Georg. One peculiar and telling characteristic of these late eighteenth-century expeditions was the development of detailed "ethnographic" questionnaires for scientific research on expeditions. Not simply a leisurely curiosity, these questionnaires were based on the most up-to-date scientific knowledge of the time. The French Académie de Medecin distributed a fifteen-page questionnaire, intended for use in the South Pacific, that sought specific knowledge always in relationship to previous information. Two of the questions, for example, were "Do the inhabitants suffer from leprosy?" and "Must one attribute the swelling in the arms and legs that Cook observed to this disease?"[22]

This second age of discovery brought to European cities an array of reports that attested to the variety and diversity of human beings. In certain respects, such reports were historically unique because of their breadth and scientific organization. For Kant, however, they were also a mass of unorganized empirical observations and, as such, invited speculation as to the variety of the human species. He complained that the knowledge that they spread about the "diversities in the human species" only served to "stimulate" the mind to exceed its own limits.[23] In part recirculating the generalizations and stereotypes of some of these travelogues and reports,[24] Kant's essays on race and his geography and his anthropology lectures from this period are peppered with statements and assertions about, for example, the lethargy and passivity of North American Indians, the uneducatability of "Negroes," and a tacit endorsement of slavery.

Most of his comments on racial hierarchies concern the educatability or the value of a particular people for a broader, intellectually conceived, cultural progress—that is, a sometimes implicit racial hierarchy orders races according to how much and to what degree they contribute as a group to the cultural progress of the human species. In unpublished notes on his anthropology lectures, Kant asserts that the "Negroes" (*Neger*) "are unable to govern themselves,"[25] that the natives of India are incapable of science and enlightenment (*Aufklärung*), and that the "Native Americans" are incapable of culture. The white race, in contrast, contains "all predispositions to culture and civilization and can obey as well as dominate." He even suggests that all of human history is the labor of the white race: "Egyptians. Persians. Thracians. Greeks. Celts. Scythians. (not Indians, Negroes)."

Kant wrote his first essay on race, "Von den verschiedenen Racen der Menschen," in 1775 (although it was not published until 1777, in a slightly revised form), as an advertisement for his physical geography lectures, but he addresses two conceptual issues. First, he considers how to organize the vast amount of information about the diversity of human beings collected in travelogues and reports. He uses the concept of race to organize an influx of ethnographic data. In this sense, race afforded a degree of typological efficiency. Second, and perhaps more important, Kant wrote this essay "to police polygeneticism and thus protect monogeneticism."[26] Against the backdrop of European exploration and the discovery of the Americas, Henry Home (Lord Kames) popularized the polygenetic argument—made by, among others, Voltaire and Hume—that humanity was actually constituted not by a single line of descent but by distinct groups that lacked a common origin.[27] Recognizing the threat that polygeneticism posed to his own theoretical assumptions, Kant claimed that it was nothing more than a thinly veiled materialism. It was a function of a broader eighteenth-century tendency—one discussed in relation to his criticism of Platner's proto-anthropology—"to naturalize the account of the human being."[28] It threatened to blur the distinction between the human being and organic life.[29] For Kant, then, the question of the unity and variety of humanity was a methodological one.

In this first essay on race, Kant outlines an initial response to polygeneticism and an organizational method for addressing the glut of empirical, ethnographic information by defining the "unity of the species" through an appeal to Buffon's rule—animals that produce fertile offspring with one another belong to the same species.[30] He argues that a clearer definition of *species* would enable Europeans to discern better the variety of the world:

> In the animal kingdom the division of nature into species and kinds [*Arten*] is grounded in the common law of propagation, and the unity of the species is nothing more than the unity of the generative power, which is generally good for a certain variety of animals. Thus, necessarily Buffon's rule: that animals that produce fertile offspring with one another (whatever the differences of form [*Gestalt*] might be) still belong to one and the same physical species. This is regarded as the only definition of a natural species of animals generally, in contrast to the school species [*Schulgattungen*] of the latter. The school division concerns classes [*Klassen*], which divide the animals according to resemblances, the natural division concerns phyla [*Stämme*], which divide the animals according to relationships in terms of generation.[31]

Kant's first step in outlining a natural history of the human being is to draw on Buffon's rejection of Linnaean categories as abstractions of real, physical relationships.[32] In place of Linnaean categories based on common morphological traits, Buffon proposes relationships of temporal filiation.[33] Kant takes seriously this claim that the real character of the species lies in its generative ability through time.[34] The unity of a species lies not in morphological similarities—immediately visible similarities—but in a temporal continuity guaranteed through reproduction. For Buffon, "the very reality of the species was a temporal reality, with each species governed by its own inherent and therefore specific force."[35] Similarly, Kant argues that the division of nature is based on common lines of descent or "phyla" (*Stämme*), not morphological similarities. Generic relationships between animals are based on their generative capacity.

The contrast Kant makes between a school distinction (*Schuleintheilung*) and a natural distinction (*Natureintheilung*) corresponds to a distinction that he develops in later essays between a description of nature (*Naturbeschreibung*) and a natural history (*Geschichte der Natur*). The former describes the state of nature as it appears in the present and thus is limited to unique observations bound to particular moments in time. The latter, in contrast, gives an account of nature's development through time. Here, one can note how Kant aligns his notion of a natural species not only with time but, through an opposition to "school species," with life or nature itself in an attempt to distinguish his natural history from the abstraction of Linnean categories. The injection of time into the species concept binds the species to the time of nature. There had been, however, previous genetic accounts of nature, even of the human being, throughout the eighteenth century. So what form of temporality does Kant inject into his account of race and, thus, into his account of the human being?

I noted Kant's use of the terms "germs" and "predispositions" previously, but have not yet discussed them in terms of race.[36] For Kant, germs are the preexistent, determinate structures that predispositions activate and harmonize with experience. Predispositions are functional principles that adapt to varying conditions and environments.[37] Germs preexist in the very structure of organisms; they are the "grounds of a particular development." In terms of race, Kant argues that the same germs have been in all human beings from the beginning of time. They then express themselves in response to environmental conditions. Different germs express themselves in different parts of the world. And over time, unused germs cease to be expressible and can even disappear. In this discussion of germs and predispositions, one can better understand the kind of temporality that Kant injects into his concept of natural history. On the one hand, these germs and potentials emerge or actualize themselves in time. In this sense organisms develop in time. They are temporal. On the other hand, however, these germs are "grounds" given by nature. The human being, therefore, possesses a prior, nontemporal ground for its development.

In these early essays on race, Kant argues that human beings are determined to inhabit the whole of the earth. Their destiny is geographical distribution. Because the human being "was destined for all climates" and for the entire earth, Kant reasons that human beings must have certain germs and natural predispositions that make them "suitable" to their particular place in the world.[38] The human being must have sufficient germs to allow him to adapt himself to any place on earth. According to Buffon's rule, then, all human beings belong to one species, because the human species contains not distinct kinds (*Arten*) but different variations or subspecies (*Abartungen*). It is in this sense of a unified humanity that Kant defines race.

A race is all these inherited differences that have emerged over time and become permanent. According to Kant, a race is a single common line of descent that carries on despite geographical displacement or mixing with other "subspecies" of the same line of descent. And more fully, "Among the subspecies, i.e., the hereditary differences of the animals which belong to a single phylum, those which persistently preserve themselves in all transplantings (transpositions to other regions) over prolonged generations among themselves and which also always beget half-bred young in the mixing with other variations of the same phylum are called races" (430 [*AHE*, 85]). Different races cannot revert back to their original unified form. "Once a race has taken root and has suffocated the other germs, it resists all transformation just because the character of the race has then become prevailing in the generative power" (442 [*AHE*, 96]). Different races emerge through this process of differentiation, a process that facilitates the human being's unique ability to adapt. And yet race was always there as a predisposition. Environmental influences merely activate a given potential. It is in this sense that Kant sees race a marker of the destiny of the human being.

Races are subsets of the human species through which nature ensures that human beings can flourish and inhabit the entire earth. With its atemporal typologies, Linnaean descriptions of nature cannot account for such change and adaptability. In the face of such a conceptual failure, Kant insists that one must "dare . . . a history of nature" (443). And this is precisely what his conception of race does. It entails not just a temporalization but a historical account of nature. Kant's first reflections on race do not offer a detailed explanation of what this history of nature might be, but they do mark the entrance of time, and more important, the promise of teleological time—a time with a discernable end and direction—into race and life itself.

The discussion of time in Kant's concept of race, however, should not obscure a basic question. If in his debate with polygeneticists Kant assumes a common origin, what might this original phylum, or what he terms this phyletic or stem species (*Stammgattung*), have been? Whereas Kant doubts whether one could ever "find the original human shape unchanged somewhere in the world now" because of its modifications over many generations, he does suggest that the "whites of brunette color" might at least be an "approximation" for such an original species (440).[39] He even speculates that it could possibly be found "in the thirty-first to the fifty-second degree of latitude in the ancient world . . . in which we find the most fortunate mixture of influences from colder and hotter regions. . . . Here indeed we find white but brunette inhabitants whose form we must assume to be the closest to the phyletic (or stem) species."[40] This racial hierarchy is repeated in other texts as well.[41] For example, Kant writes: "Humanity is in its greatest perfection in the white race. The yellow Indians already have a lesser talent. The Negroes are much lower, and the lowest of all is part of the American peoples."[42] Does race, then, become a marker for the destiny of particular groups of human beings?

In "Bestimmung des Begriffs einer Menschenrace," Kant clarifies his claim in "Von den verschiedenen Racen der Menschen" that "all people on the wide earth, whatever their differences with regard to form[,]" belong to the same natural species, that is, that all human beings belong to one singular common line of descent.[43] He also omits any suggestions of qualitative differences between the races.[44] All human beings are, historically speaking, part of a collective, unified whole. Skin color is the only essential racial difference: "No other characteristic is necessarily hereditary."[45] At this point, Kant claims that all other differences, either physical or in character, are contingent. Skin color is the differential quality of racial categorization because only it is "unfailingly hereditary" (*unausbleiblich erblich*).[46] Kant claims that skin color is the only marker of racial distinction and classification.

In this essay Kant dissociates physical (skin color) from moral characteristics, but this disarticulation of the physical from the moral is made possible by a fundamental abstraction of the human as such.[47] Physical differences between human beings are absorbed and apparently erased by a prior, monogenetic unity. But does this theoretical distinction, which affirms the common origin of all human beings, necessarily imply a common human destiny—that is, just because Kant argues for a common human origin, does he necessarily commit himself to a common human destiny? Does a natural or monogenetic unity necessarily imply a moral unity?

Reiterating the distinction between a description of nature and a natural history, Kant writes that those who wish to understand race by appealing only to "observation" are bound to fail. "It is important to have determined previously for oneself the concept that one wants to clarify through observation, before one consults experience on its account. For one finds in it [experience] what one needs only when one knows beforehand what one is looking for."[48] Denying the empirical observer any epistemological privilege, Kant suggests that observation can merely elaborate concepts already articulated by reason. Mocking the French missionary Abbé Demanet, Kant disparages any claims that the only ones able to make a judgment with regards to the "Neger" are those who "spent some time in Senegambi." Kant shifts the epistemological privilege of the travel writer or the observing scientist to the philosopher (92). An observer cannot discern what of a race results from climatic factors like the sun and the wind or what is to be "attributed to birth" by simply relying on empirical observation. The description of nature divides the human being into different varieties (*Arten*) based on hypostatized differences and morphological similarities. Physical differences only constitute class differences. Classes can be considered different races only under two strict conditions: first, they must have a common line of descent or phylum, and second, they must have inherited characteristics that differentiate classes of the same line of descent from one another (99). According to Kant, "There are no different varieties of people at all"; there is only one human species. These terminological distinctions between classes, species, races, and varieties are functions of Kant's distinction between a description of nature and a natural history. "In natural history, which only deals with generation and phyletic origination, kind and species are not distinguished as such. This distinction occurs only in the description of nature, since it merely depends on the comparison of marks. What is called a kind in the latter, must more often be called race in the former" (100n [*AHE*, 153]). There is not a single characteristic or marker within a human class that is "necessarily inherited" (95). What then makes characteristics that are not essential to the species still "unfailing"? It must be, argues Kant, that the germs and predispositions lie in the species itself (97). Their presence and process of development can only be discerned through a natural history based in the concept of race. As noted above, race is the only marker for the "unfailingly hereditary" traits in the classification of the human races. Thus, with respect to the historical development of these germs in human beings, it is the only marker for the "purposive character" of nature itself (102). Race is the only marker for nature's purposive distribution of human beings throughout the earth.

It is in this sense that Kant seems to dismiss his earlier suggestion in the 1775 essay that whites may have been the original phylum. "It is therefore impossible to guess the shape of the first human phylum (as far as the constitution of the skin is concerned); even the character of the whites is only the development of one of the original predispositions that together with the others were to be found in the phylum" (106 [*AHE*, 159]). The mixing and hybridization of different races over generations has so obscured such a first human phylum as to make such hypotheses mere conjectures. The concept of race, then, will not help us discern an original phylum, but it will allow us to give an account of the monogenetic unity of the human. And thus it will highlight a natural purposiveness. Only the historicization of nature and the human being can account for this unity. Only a history, a narrative of this development, can lend the human species unity. This narrative, however, does not remain merely conceptual; instead, Kant repeatedly mixes his conceptual account of this "purposiveness of the organization" of the races with the empirical. Despite his insistence that such a purposiveness cannot be inferred from skin color, he goes on to offer probable "explanatory grounds." He claims, for example, that nature's "wise arrangements" of the "Negro" skin color allow him to adapt better to an African environment (104). But Kant does not stop with this more general claim; instead, drawing on contemporary debates, he offers a medical explanation for skin color.[49] The empirical continues to insert itself into Kant's increasingly conceptual and teleological account of race.

In "Von den verschiedenen Racen der Menschen," Kant appealed to germs and predispositions as insurance against external influences. "Nothing foreign," he writes, comes into the animal and "distance[s]" it from its destiny. These original germs and predispositions are placed by nature itself and guarantee that only "true degenerations [*Ausartungen*] are brought forth [and] perpetuate themselves."[50] In "Bestimmung des Begriffs einer Menschenrace," Kant argues that these germs and predispositions are placed by nature in human beings in order to ensure the historical destiny of the human species to inhabit all the earth, because only through them can the human develop according to the specific needs of different geographical climates. Natural (or given) germs in concert with environmental factors determine characteristics. Race, then, marks a fundamentally different and historically necessary relationship to the world. Different races constitute different paths of human development. Kant's insistence that "nothing foreign" can enter the organism is, more fundamentally, a concern about ensuring not only the destiny of the human being but protecting the unity presumed to underlie the human species. For Kant, race is a functional and historical necessity. This assumption, however, begs the question not only of the dehistorization of the empirical object but of whether this assumed prior unity excludes a priori the particular itself. Is the Kantian dinner table—the *Tischgesellschaft*—of the *Anthropologie* that seemed so welcoming always already full? Can a surprise guest ever find a welcoming seat?

Recent scholarship has given a great deal of attention to Kant and race. On the one hand, some scholars seem, as they are want to put it, to regret the fact that Kant's writing exhibits racial stereotypes but insist that, as Robert B. Louden says, Kant's "theory is fortunately stronger than his prejudices, and his theory is what philosophers should focus on."[51] Race and racial hierarchies, by these lights, are peripheral to the universalizing thrust of his larger project.[52] On the other hand, scholars like Robert Bernasconi, E. C. Eze, and C. W. Mills have argued that Kant's "racist" comments irrevocably compromise any universal claims that his ethics might attempt.[53] Pauline Kleingeld aims for a middle ground and argues that Kant's views on race changed and by the 1790s he had let go of most of his racial prejudices.[54] Whereas we can only share these criticisms and acknowledge, as I have done, how troubling some of Kant's comments on race are, here I am less interested in determining whether Kant was "racist" (in the 1780s *or* the 1790s, either by the standards of his contemporaries or our own) or whether these statements may or may not invalidate his universal claims. Of primary importance for my reading of Kant's pragmatic anthropology is the question of how race functioned for Kant in the first place. Particularly interesting is Kant's claim that an empirical inquiry into race cannot, as he says in "Bestimmung des Begriffs einer Menschenrace," "satisfy" reason.[55] What is it precisely that a clearer concept of race could satisfy? Why race?

In "Bestimmung des Begriffs einer Menschenrace," Kant assumes that the existence of only four different races—red, black, yellow, and white—can be explained by these same germs: these races "must have been laid in the germs of the original line of descent of the human species as natural predispositions, which remain unknown to us."[56] And that is the crux of Kant's monogenetic account of the human species. The assumption of an original phylum of the human species to which all human beings belong leads Kant to assume the existence of germs and predispositions. While this original phylum can only remain unknown, we cannot explain the variety and adaptability of the human without thinking *as though* all human beings descend from such an original phylum. This also means that because "the human being was destined for all climates and every condition of the earth," all seeds and "natural predispositions" must have been present in all human beings at some point so that they could be "developed or restrained" according to the human being's "place in the world."[57] That is to say, the original human being had the potential for all races, and only a monogenetic account of human development over time can adequately explain the human being's adaptability.

Kant's racial hierarchy naturalizes common eighteenth-century organizations of race through an appeal to the natural givens of germs and predispositions. These racial divisions, implies Kant, are predicated upon the natural distributions of germs and predispositions. Kant's concept of race raises a host of issues. Not only does it appeal to racial stereotypes and hierarchies common to his age, but just as important for the argument here, it presents some fundamental problems to his own pragmatic anthropology. The second section of the *Anthropologie,* the Characteristic, considers the "physical character" of the human being as a natural being. Pragmatic anthropology, however, is concerned with what humans as free beings make of themselves. Physical anthropology seems to be an interloper within the field of pragmatic anthropology. Kant's philosophy of history and his naturalization of human diversity through race (grounding racial hierarchies in a racial biology) merge in the figure of the species and, more precisely, in an extension of natural history to human history. The destiny of the human species, it seems, can only be guaranteed in the melding of transcendental and empirical claims—that is, Kant ties the apparently transcendental claims of human destiny to nature itself. The unity of the human species and the naturalization of a particular racial hierarchy are grounded in the relationship of natural history to teleology, a relationship that Kant forcefully defends in his public debate with Georg Forster. Even in these essays on race prior to this debate, however, Kant injects time into thinking about the diversity of the human being. Without such a temporalization, ethnographic accounts of human diversity, suggests Kant, would be paltry, decontextualized observations. They would be precisely the type of anthropological minutiae that, as I demonstrate in the next chapter, Schleiermacher claims populate Kant's *Anthropologie.*

Teleological Anthropology: Kant and Forster's Exchange on Race

In 1786 Forster criticizes Kant's two essays on race in *Noch etwas über die Menschenrassen* (Something Else on the Human Races). Most immediately, this essay takes up the question of whether the "Negro" is a kind or a species of the human being, a question that goes straight to the heart of Kant's increasingly forceful claim that all human beings are part of a collective whole. Forster, however, directs his most poignant criticisms at what he sees as Kant's reliance on theory at the expense of the facts as observed and gathered by people like himself who had traveled and engaged non-Europeans not from a reading chair but from an ethnographic immediacy. The debate between Forster and Kant, then, concerns the broader dilemma of Kant's pragmatic anthropology: how to reconcile normative claims concerning the predispositions, potentials, and destinies of the human species with ethnographic evidence of human difference. Kant, however, conducts his side of the debate as a continued and pointed critique of ethnography as such. The Kant-Forster debate gained particular relevance given the increasing interest in questions of race in the 1780s subsequent to Christoph Meiner's *Grundriß der Geschichte der Menschheit* (1785) and Samuel Thomas von Soemmering's *Über die Körperliche Verschiedenheit des Negers zum Europäer* (1785), initially published as *Über die Körperliche Verschiedenheit des Mohren vom Europäer* (1784). To summarize their general orientation, one need only recall Soemmering's stated assumption of the "advantage of the white man over the Negro" (*Vorzug des Weissens vor dem Neger*).[58]

Forster criticizes not only Kant's monogenetic account of race but his approach to the entire problem of human diversity. Not only does Kant privilege theoretical inquiry over empirical observation, he subordinates ethical concerns to theoretical ones. Given what Forster sees as Kant's tendency to favor the "faculty of abstraction" over "perception," this is not surprising.[59] On the one hand, Forster's criticism of Kant is an exhortation to develop and employ all faculties, not just those associated with theoretical knowledge. But on the other hand, his criticism is a plea to focus on what he terms *Fakta*—simple facts that are immediately present to the senses, especially vision. These are "just suddenly there" (135). In response to Kant's speculation that there are only four races, Forster asks why we should believe that there are not, in fact, more. Facts, insists Forster, often challenge Kant's claim that "one finds in experience what one needs, if one knows before, for what one is looking" (133). While Kant's pithy dictum might well be true, it is also possible to delude oneself into believing that one has found something that isn't really there at all. An errant principle can lead us to lend objects the "color of his [the observer's] glasses." Whereas Kant argues that judgments derived from strictly empirical observation are limited, Forster suggests that a more

Kantian form of judgment imposes its concepts onto nature. Determinations based on limited knowledge are useful only within limited areas of study. If our field of view is expanded or if our point of view is displaced, if our conditions change, suggests Forster, then our prior determinations can prove limited and, still worse, limiting. If the ethnographer brings back different data, might our concept-driven determinations about race need alteration? Musing on the historical longevity of sciences, Forster anticipates a future, fifty years from the time of its publication perhaps, in which even the *Kritik der reinen Vernunft* might seem "out of date."

From this exchange, one can already discern what Forster sees as the danger of Kantian anthropology. Whereas it attends to the particular, to the empirical, it always judges the particular according to a rational idea that seems outside the flux of nature. Since mistakes can be made in the "business" of philosophy just as often as in the "moment of observation," any claim about race, writes Forster, must be "tested" against any new knowledge of the human species that might emerge from the observations of the new travelers. "With respect to the actual color of the South Sea Islanders," Forster, in a jocular aside to Kant, asks: "Why don't we just ask the honest seaman himself?" (134, 135). Just as Kant had wrested epistemological privilege from the writing traveler, Forster attempts to return it those wandering scientists. The work of Forster's close friend Soemmering proved a case in point of the dangers of a scientific program driven by theoretical assumptions. In a letter to Soemmering in 1785, Forster encourages him to revise his *Über die Körperliche Verschiedenheit des Negers zum Europäer* and make it clear that the Moor, because he can speak, is capable of reason and thus must be considered a human being and not an ape.[60] Forster is satirizing Soemmering's suggestion that black peoples are closer to apes than are Europeans, a claim he bases on the supposed similarity of facial profiles. He repeats his criticism of Soemmering's book in his 1786 essay on race, *Noch etwas über die Menschenrassen,* where, in a passing reference to the discussion of human diversity, he writes that the "ape had no part in the development [*Bildung*] of the Negro."

For Forster, Soemmering's conclusion concerning the developmental disparity of whites and blacks was a consequence of what one could find in nature if looking through a conceptual lens. While Forster doubted the theoretical basis for a monogenetic account, he maintained an ethical commitment to the unity of the human species—that is, he separated his theoretical claims from his ethical commitments. Forster's nature is a matter of nuances and slight differences: the "diversity" of nature is not more striking than the "eternal unity [of nature] that always shines through" these differences.[61] Forster defers questions of normative belonging to a separate sphere of inquiry. Scientific evidence (empirical data), he suggests, should not be marshaled to make normative claims. For Forster, Kant's most troubling move was to insert normative claims into what Forster considered the strictly scientific—and thus theoretical—debate about race.[62]

Later in *Noch etwas über die Menschenrassen*, in the context of the debate about whether blacks and whites are of the same species, Forster continues to privilege empirical evidence—morphological characteristics that can be ascertained only in the "moment of observation"—and proceeds to a more direct critique of Kant's description of the distinction between nature and the history of nature:[63]

> If one separates natural science into a description of nature and history of nature—a separation that I can hardly let stand, when both are only always united and treated as parts of a whole—so it might appear that the describer of nature can better come to terms with the question. It appears that Kant accepts that every difference of character would be sufficient for the describer of nature to constitute a species. I cannot satisfactorily answer, because the best author, who treated science systematically, Linnaeus, wrote in Latin. His divisions are called classes, orders, genera, species, and varieties. Now it appears to me that a variety is always defined through changeable arbitrary characteristics; it is thus accepted that a variety can pass over into another. If Kant would prefer to use *Art* as variety in this sense, then it is only a confusion of words, about which one can easily come to terms. *Gattung*, in contrast, if it should be translated as species, requires in the Linnaean sense unchangeable characteristics. In the history of nature, the situation is different if as Kant claims, it concerns only generation and descent [*Abstamm*]. In this sense however the history of nature can only be a science for the gods and not for men. Who is capable of demonstrating the ancestral line of even one variety up to its *Gattung*, if it does not emerge first from under our eyes?[64]

Where is that "fortunate place," continues Forster, "which alone held all of nature's resources, nature closed up within itself, the resources for every climate and every element?" (151). Forster is not defending polygenesis. In this essay at least, he is agnostic about the issue (153). He is simply arguing, as he puts it in the fragment "Menschen-Racen," that no one can know with "apodictic certainty" whether there are multiple human phyla (*Menschenstämme*) or not (157). Forster doubts the very possibility of natural history as Kant had defined it up to his 1786 essay "Muthmaßlicher Anfang der Menschengeschichte." Such claims, he suggests, are products not of nature but of speculative reason that engages in dubious ethical claims.

Forster is keenly aware of the moral uses or abuses that had been made of the polygenetic account of race. As is characteristic of his approach to such matters, however, he doubts whether ethical failures could be directly traced back to theoretical principles:

> By separating the Negro as an originally separate line of descent, do we not cut the last thread through which this mistreated people is connected to us, and found at least some defense and mercy from the European atrocity? Let me ask if the thought that the blacks are our brothers even once would have caused the whips of the slave drivers to fall? . . . How should we believe that an improvable statement of doctrine could be the only support of a system of our duties, because for the entire time that it was assumed to be certain, it prevented not one shameful act? (155)

A theoretical commitment to racial unity or universal belonging does not guarantee ethical practices, but as was the case with Soemmering, theoretical claims can embolden natural or biological determinisms, which can lead to troublesome ethical claims. And it is this confusion of ethical and scientific modes of inquiry that Forster tries to disentangle.[65] For him, the problem with Kant's concept of teleological judgment lies not with the theoretical potential or scientific utility of such claims but with their ethical ramifications. He wonders how much "harm" is engendered by such a reflective distance from the world. A scientist, just like any other human being, is inextricably connected to his or her "specific place."[66] The scientist can never be completely detached. The claims of a theoretically grounded racial categorization must be repeatedly "tested" against empirical realities. For Forster, Kant's temporalization of the human species through the concept of race exemplifies this type of abstraction.

Amid the back-and-forth of Kant and Forster's debate on race, however, I want to emphasize Forster's suggestion that the universal be "tested" against the particular. This testing of the universal rule or concept against a particular observation is immensely suggestive, since it implies a dynamic form of universality. In his typically practical manner, Forster intimates a form of universality that is open to difference and a form of revision that an anthropology of and for the citizen of the world might require.

In "Über den Gebrauch teleologischer Principien in der Philosophie" (1788), Kant argues that Forster had misunderstood his argument and proceeds to explain the *appropriate* use of teleological principles. He poses two basic questions: To what extent can teleological arguments be made about objects—in this case the unity of species—that exceed both theoretical and empirical forms of knowledge? And what are the limits of teleological claims? Kant implies that neither Forster's argument nor his own, at least as outlined to that point, can sufficiently account for race or the human species. Forster may not be completely wrong headed in his critique, since, as Kant himself admits, "not enough light" had been shed on how this teleological principle should be appropriately used.[67] Although he thanks the "mere empirical traveler" for his "stories," Kant says that without a "guiding principle" travelogues are "mere fumbling around." Without such principles, travelogues can never reveal anything "purposive." Kant sees this same level of empirical confusion in Linnaean taxonomy, which is defined by an atemporal morphology that encourages the endless categorization of empirical data under logical rubrics.

The proper use of teleological principles is a function of our need to think of nature as a unified whole. Even purported opponents of teleology ultimately fall back on such principles. Whereas Forster accuses Kant of smuggling his own ideas into ethnographic observations, Kant reminds Forster that he too follows a system with fundamental principles, namely Linnaeus's.[68] All scientific study assumes a certain unity of nature, otherwise all natural events would have to be assumed to be absolutely unique and a science of nature would be impossible. In "Über den Gebrauch teleologischer Principien in der Philosophie," Kant elaborates on the principle that would allow for research into the historical continuity of the human being through reproduction, and he better articulates the principle that makes a natural history possible.

To make his argument, he returns to a distinction he had made in "Von den verschiedenen Racen der Menschen" between a description of nature and a natural history. A description of nature only makes use of immediate perceptual data and, as a consequence, defines nature in terms of efficient causality. In contrast, natural history is predicated upon a conception of nature from "a synthesizing perspective grounded in the ideas of reason."[69] According to a possible natural history, the observer of nature thinks a cause that lies originally in the phylum of the species itself."[70] Only a principle of reason, one that conceptualizes the historical unity of nature can guide observation and make sense of the variety of human beings. In order to observe, the observer must "pay attention . . . to descent, not merely the characteristic similarities." A teleological principle of nature affords us a way of thinking of nature as a systematic whole; it guides our reason where theoretical sources of knowledge "can't reach." Reason's appeal to teleology derives not from the nature of an object but from "our own intentions and needs."[71]

Kant's formulation of a natural history presages a distinction that he makes in the *Kritik der Urteilskraft* between a determining (*bestimmende*) power of judgment and a reflecting (*reflektierende*) power of judgment. In a determining judgment, the universal (the rule, the concept, the law) subsumes the particular. The concept is given, and we judge whether the given particular is an instance of that concept. In a reflecting judgment, the particular is given for which a universal or concept must be found. The former is constitutive, while the latter is reflective—that is, whereas the former makes claims about how the world actually is, the latter makes only heuristic claims. Natural history is a reflecting judgment.

Natural history meets a need of reason, and the teleological principle that underlies it guides this needy reason into realms where our sources of knowledge are limited. As conceived of by Kant, then, race has no proper place in a so-called description of nature, because it is a concept grounded in the reason of each observer. Empirical description has nothing to say about an underlying purposiveness of nature. Empiricism's silence with respect to questions of purpose pushes reason beyond the immediacy of mere observation. The distinction between natural history and a description of nature is motivated by what Kant refers to here as the "needs" of reason.

Written as a commentary on the Mendelssohn and Jacobi pantheism controversy,[72] Kant's 1786 "Was heißt: Sich im Denken orientiren?" ("What Does It Mean to Orient Oneself in Thinking?") expounds on these needs. Interested in what he calls the "self-preservation of reason," Kant distinguishes between rational "wanderings" in the field of the suprasensual and "empty dreaming."[73] Whereas the latter is labeled "impertinent inquisitiveness," the former is guided by a subjective distinction, namely a feeling of need. Through a series of conceptual analogies, Kant compares this subjective feeling of need to the subjective distinction that we feel between left and right, a distinction that allows us to orient ourselves spatially. Similarly, suggests Kant, the subjective feeling of the needs of reason orients us logically. Because "reason wants to be satisfied," it often pushes us to the limits of experience and thus toward frontiers of experience where we no longer encounter objects of intuition but "mere space."

In this absence of any known objects, reason cannot rely on objective criteria and must, instead, be guided by a subjective distinction, which is the felt need of reason. This need is not a feeling, insists Kant, because reason does not feel; instead, reason sees its lack and effects through the cognitive drive a feeling of need. Reason creates the feeling of its own need. Faced with this need and the absence of any objective intuition, we have no other option, insists Kant, but to test the concept with which we "intend to venture out beyond all possible experience" to see if it is free of all contradictions. Then we are free to relate that object to objects of experience without, of course, making it sensible. This act of relating a supersensible object to objects of experience is done to serve the "experiential use of our reason"—that is, the object does not become an object of knowledge but rather an object of use. Were we to mistake it as an object of knowledge, we would, writes Kant, be "day-dreaming" not "thinking" (137). The feeling of reason's need motivates us to protect reason by replacing a subjective need with a principled concept. To orient oneself in thinking, then, is to tend to reason with reason, to preserve reason itself and protect it from superstition, enthusiasm, and all other forms that might impose themselves upon reason (145–46).

For Kant, the most immediate "use" of such an orientation concerns the judgment of the "contingent existence of things in the world" (138).[74] Without the assumption of a first cause or intelligent creator, argues Kant, we cannot explain the purposiveness (*Zweckmässigkeit*) and order of the world. These have to be assumed in order to pass judgment about the world. They have no theoretical value in and of themselves but they serve the uses of theoretical inquiry. With respect to theory, the need of reason is a "compass" and a "signpost" into the supersensible realm; it guides reason itself by distinguishing between what can be known and what can be useful.

Returning to Kant's essay "Über den Gebrauch teleologischer Principien in der Philosophie," one can understand natural history not as the discovery of a *real* history of nature but as a useful assertion of a way of thinking. It is the "narration [*Erzählung*] of natural events where no means of reason can reach."[75] In response to Forster's mocking questions about just where on earth one might find the original monogenetic pair, Kant says that while the existence of such a pair might be an implied consequence of his theory, its actual existence "lies completely beyond" the bounds of human understanding (179). A Kantian natural history does not, as Forster suggests, posit the existence of an original pair as a fact. "A true metaphysics knows the limits of reason" (179). Kant's response to Forster places the entire discussion of historical continuity in theoretical brackets—that is, it insists that teleological thinking makes no metaphysical claims about nature itself. A teleological history of nature is merely a reflective or heuristic judgment. As we saw in our discussion of the needs of reason, such heuristic claims are, for Kant at least, practically useful but not epistemologically certain. And in this distinction lies the critical potential of such claims. Whereas Forster doubts the ethical utility of such heuristics, Kant's reliance on them suggests that they are an essential element of his broader, anthropologically inflected ethics. We must assume the unity of the human species if we want to work now to achieve it.

Kant's teleological history has forged an odd alliance—a compatibility even—between the teleological and the empirical. For the reader, the "possibility" of uniting a natural teleology with a pure, practical teleology or morals (in the form of a human destiny) is the most important ramification of Kant's essays on race (183). For Kant, only such a unity could "secure the objective reality to the doctrine of practically pure ends." The possible melding of the two orders of causality, the two forms of purposiveness, is the only promise for the embodiment of moral autonomy and freedom. Whereas teleological principles only help us think *as though* nature operated according to an underlying principle unity, a pure practical teleology will have to be allied with an empirically determined nature if we are to imagine a possible future in which the ends of reason might be realized. Kant is suggesting that if a pure practical teleology, namely, morals, "is destined to realize its ends in the world," then this very possibility would have to be embodied in nature itself. The "objective reality" of such an end would have to be "effectuated in the world." The ends of morals would have to be real and indicated by nature itself. Kant holds out the possibility that the ends of the moral and physical worlds might overlap.

Kant considers this latter principle of purposiveness—the melding of a natural teleology as natural science with a teleology of freedom as morals—in the second section of the *Kritik der Urteilskraft* (*Critique of the Power of Judgment*). In his 1788 essay "Über den Gebrauch teleologischer Principien in der Philosophie," Kant had already suggested that skin color is "the sure sign" of hereditary difference (165). Such hereditary peculiarities are a function of nature's organization and design, which ensure that human beings inhabit the entire earth. At this point in Kant's thinking about teleology, race is the only "sure sign" of the purposiveness of nature. It is the only marker of nature's purposiveness that the observer of nature can see. The decoupling of the moral and the physical that was evident in Kant's more specific attempt to disentangle racial types and moral characteristics is, in the end then, reversed yet again. Skin color and race indicate nature's purpose. Skin color points to the underlying purposiveness of nature itself, because it shows how nature itself ensures the human being's adaptability. If race is a marker of such purposiveness and thus of historical progress, does Kant's racial typology imply a certain racial teleology? The question still remains as to what role nonwhite races play in Kant's idea of human destiny.[76]

In the first part of "Über den Gebrauch teleologischer Principien in der Philosophie," Kant sharpens the distinction between a description of nature and a natural history. In the second part, he offers his first clear definition of an organism:[77] "Because the concept of an organized being already implies that it is material, in which everything stands in a reciprocal relationship as cause and effect, and this can only be thought as a system of final causes, and thus leaves human reason as the only possible method of explanation a teleological one and in no case a physical-mechanical one: and thus in physics one cannot ask whence all organization comes from."[78]

The causality of history and natural organisms are both teleological. This notion of organization, the reciprocal relationship of causes and effects, is an analogue of Kant's notion of history in the *Anthropologie*. In order to explain the variety and differentiated hierarchy of human beings and races, Kant appeals to a teleology of history whose analogue in nature is to be found in the organism. The species history of the human being requires the prior assumption of natural germs and predispositions. Kant conceives of the differences among races, for example, in terms of natural predispositions, which allow different human beings to adapt to different environments. Difference is a function of nature's more fundamental purpose for human beings to populate the entire earth. One could read all of Kant's anthropological categorizations—from temperaments to national types—as functions of such a natural purposiveness. Nature requires and thus cultivates difference in order to fulfill the common destiny of the human. In the end, difference itself is subordinated to a prior, though conceptual, unity.

Moral Teleology Through Cultural History

The preceding discussion has followed Kant's gradual articulation of teleology and the historical progression of the human species in terms of race. In the texts most often associated with Kant's philosophy of history, however, there is little to no mention of race. In fact, the purposiveness of nature takes on entirely different contours. "Nature's highest purpose is not the mere spread of human beings throughout the world, but the freedom which (may) arise from human cultivation."[79] In his "Idee zu einer allgemeinen Geschichte in weltbürgerlicher Absicht" ("Idea for a Universal History from a Cosmopolitan Perspective"), for example, Kant makes no mention of race and clearly posits freedom as the end of the human. Published in a popular journal in 1784, this essay relies on the melding of a philosophy of history and a natural teleology to tell the story of the human, a story that might answer the question "What is the human being?" The title of the essay condenses the two intentions of Kant's pragmatic anthropology; on the one hand, it anticipates a universal history, but on the other, it ascribes a cosmopolitan perspective to this history. It is not a universal history told from nowhere but a history from the perspective of a citizen of the world, from the perspective of a human being living in the world and among other human beings.

As Kant points out in an introductory footnote, this essay was in part a response to a journal report by an anonymous scholar, who, after visiting Kant, reported the following: "A favorite idea of Professor Kant is that the final purpose of the human race is the achievement of the most perfect civil constitution, and he wishes that a philosophical historian would endeavor to provide us in this respect with a history of humanity and to show to what extent humanity at various points in time has approached or drawn away from this final purpose, and what remains to be done in order to achieve it."[80] An idea, according to the *Kritik der reinen Vernunft*, is a "spontaneous projection of reason" to which nothing in experience is adequate, "and yet which is for all that no mere chimera or fantasy."[81] Kant's idea for a universal history, then, would be a project for the future, something toward which a future, philosophically inclined historian could work. Such a world history would be a story (*Geschichte*) concerned with the "narration" (*Erzählung*) of the "appearances . . . of the freedom of the will."[82] As a retelling of what the human being does out of freedom (as a free being), this world history would narrate; it would relate these actions by bringing them into a larger whole in the hope of discovering a "regular pattern." Recalling the formulation in his *Anthropologie* that pragmatic anthropology concerns what humans as free beings make of themselves, Kant's cosmopolitan history concerns not the metaphysical grounds or the transcendental conditions of human beings but what human beings do. And just as in the pragmatic anthropology, this history should organize these disparate actions into a meaningful whole. This universal history would be a story of the human, its past, present, and future, because it would narrate the development of the "original predispositions" not only of the individual but of the entire species. Kant then explains why the transition from individual to species is necessary. "If nature has set the terms of [the human being's] life so short (as has really occurred), then nature perhaps needs an immeasurable series of generations, which passes its enlightenment one to the other, in order to drive the germs in our species to that level of development which is commensurate to its purpose" (19). In the face of death, a universal history concerns itself only with the species, because only when figured through the species, not the individual, can the development of the human being's potential for reason be told. The human being can develop according to the ends of reason only through the human species—that is, only through the species can the natural human being develop into a moral being. Nature gives reason as a potential (not a complete) gift with the expectation that the human being *qua* species will use it to develop itself. This potential reason is nature's only acceptable gift, because everything else results from the human being's own energies and activities: "The human being should . . . be led not through his instinct . . . ; he should rather produce everything out of himself" (20).

This insistence on autonomy is evident in Kant's essay "Von den verschiedenen Racen der Menschen," in which he claimed that germs ensure that "foreign" influences will not interfere with the development of human beings. In this essay, history is the domain of the human being's self-transformation, but this transformation is only possible through the assumption of a "plan of nature" or "final purpose of nature." Only by thinking of nature as working according to a final purpose, can individuals conceive of themselves as moral beings who can realize their own purposes. To conceive of the human being as purposive is to tell the story not of the individual human being but of the human species. For Kant, moral being is tied to the categorical unity of the human being. But is Kant suggesting that the human being is a natural, historical being, in a Hegelian sense, who develops in accord with the *natural* development of reason?

In the ninth and final thesis of "Idee zu einer allgemeinen Geschichte in weltbürgerlicher Absicht" Kant suggests that the plan for a cosmopolitan history is itself part of the ends of nature. (Kant made a similar move in the essays on race, where his philosophy of history is melded to his teleology of nature.) Kant's idea for a human history—to represent human actions not as an unplanned aggregate but as a system—is not "absurd," he suggests, because, as Susan Meld-Shell puts it, this plan is "inseparable from its own physical embodiment."[83] The idea for a universal history is embodied in nature itself, and the hope for a future history of the human being is predicated upon this "guiding thread" that Kant hopes might one day be found:

> I believe that a guiding thread will be found, a guiding thread that can serve not merely to explain the confused play of human things, or for political prophesying of future political changes . . . ; but a consoling view into the future (what we have no reason to hope for

without assuming a plan of nature) will be opened up, a view in which can be shown at a great distance how the human species does work itself up to that state in which all germs, which nature placed in it, can fully develop and its destiny here on earth can be fulfilled.[84]

This purposiveness of nature is the propadeutic of freedom, because it affords human beings the "comforting view" that they can realize their potential to become moral. Through its consoling effect, the idea of a universal history motivates human beings to overcome their natural instinct by containing it. The idea of a universal history from a cosmopolitan point of view is not just philosophical speculation: it posits purposiveness in order to make possible a certain way of life in the present. It is not a necessary claim about the ontological or epistemological status of this purposiveness; it is an ethical claim. It is a claim that is "useful," even "consoling."

Only with the reassurance and consolation of purposiveness, suggests Kant, might human beings be able to free themselves from the constraint of natural desires and become moral. The hard work of ethical being requires encouragement, an encouragement in the form of a nontheological account of what the human being can become. The reflective idea of a plan of nature, of a teleology of nature, encourages moral becoming and thus ethical autonomy. In this popular essay, then, we can observe the less-than-metaphysical tone of a Kantian ethics that is driven more by an attitude toward freedom than a metaphysical claim about it. The consoling gesture of Kantian ethics in general and of his philosophy of history in particular also marks the imbrication of the human being and nature.

In order to conceive of human action systematically—and thus encourage ethical being—Kant narrates or, more accurately, anticipates a narration of the human being that assumes natural purposiveness. Without the consoling promise of the possible embodiment or actuality of freedom, there would be no incentive to become moral. One can observe in this instance how Kant deploys the incentives and supplements of an impure ethics as discussed in Chapter 2 but on a grander, historical scale. He deploys them for a philosophy of history. This conjuncture also points to the intimate connection of Kant's pragmatic anthropology and history. The future historian of this universal history, suggests Kant, will find the guiding thread of his own history in nature itself. Yet again the possibility of transcendence is mired in the impurity of being in the world—the very idea of a universal history is indexed by nature itself. Nature gives, points human beings toward, a "guiding thread" so that they might imagine their own history.

Kant readily concedes that to want to write such a history, one would have to assume that not only nature but also history functions according to a "final end." The author of such a history would have to assume that "the course of the world" conforms to certain rational ends.[85] Kant admits that this is a "strange" and "absurd" desire. So "strange," in fact, that such an undertaking would most likely result in a novel (*Roman*). What is one to make of this comparison of a future, universal history and the novel? And why does the comparison strike Kant as "strange" and "absurd"?[86]

This comparison relies presumably on a prior distinction between history and illusion. To conceive of such a history on the basis of an illusion-reality dualism, however, would be to ignore the functional analogy of history and the novel. As Kant writes, history is narrated; it is written; and above all, it is a story, a *Geschichte*—that is, like a novel it is aware of its own made-ness. History is conscious of its own fictionality, in the sense that it, like the novel, is something that has been crafted by human beings. To cite Kant's definition of an idea in the *Kritik der reinen Vernunft* again, there is nothing in experience that is "adequate" to the idea of a universal history just as there is nothing "adequate" to the world made by the novel. Both create possible worlds: Kant's history creates a possible future for the human being, and novels create possible worlds for their characters.

In his *Anthropologie*, however, Kant insists on the limits and dangers of novels. Whereas the novel is in a certain respect always "systematic" in that it portrays characters and events as operating within a larger whole, it always "represents the untrue as true."[87] Novels merely entertain (247n). The "reading of a novel" causes "habitual distraction," because the mind is allowed and even encouraged to insert digressions and imagine other possibilities (208). Kant's distinction between a cosmopolitan history and the novel arises, then, out of a fear that his philosophy of history and anthropology might be susceptible to such distractions and digressions—that is, he is concerned that such novel distractions might dislocate the "destiny of the human being."

Despite Kant's distinction there is a functional analogy between the novel and a cosmopolitan history, and this analogy has to do with their formal construction. It can be understood in terms of a broader temporalization of history in the second half of the eighteenth century, a temporalization that might shed light on the relationship of Kantian history to anthropology. As Reinhart Koselleck argues, the second half of the eighteenth century saw a lexical displacement of "the adopted foreign word *Historie*," which primarily denoted the recounting of events, by "Geschichte," which referred not only to the event but also to the reporting of the event.[88] This lexical shift was accompanied by a semantic shift as well when *Geschichte* became, as Koselleck writes, "collective-singular," which underscores the shift away from *Geschichte* as plural (plural events) to *Geschichte* as a unified whole. This singularization of history allows history to be conceived of as a system with an "inner organization" that is constituted in the very act of its making.

Kant alludes to this semantic shift in "Über den Gebrauch teleologischer Principien in der Philosophie" when he complains that natural history is easily confused with the description of nature because of the long and common use of history as the Greek *historía*. History can only speak of itself—that is, history becomes a reflective act of its own telling. It becomes subject and object simultaneously. This shift to a collective singular also involves, as Bianca Theisen puts it, a fusion of the "two levels of history as an interrelation of events and history as history writing, as narrative or as philosophy of history which is conceived of as generating the historical process."[89] As Novalis writes, "History produces itself. Only through the combining of the past and the future does it emerge."[90] *Geschichte* also involves an apparent contradiction. As a temporalization of the present in the form of narrative, history is not simply determined by the past. It is not the result of an accumulation of events; instead, it is constituted in the present and is thus open. Even though history is a human product, its future remains unknown. The future is unknown because it can be made. Kant's philosophy of history and anthropology exemplify this. "Counsel can no longer be obtained from the past but must be obtained from a future that is itself to be created."[91]

One finds this singularization of history in Kant's plan for a cosmopolitan history, which is to tell a story of the past, the present, and a future that it cannot know, one that must be imagined or, in Kant's case, projected through an idea of reason. Since we are "too near-sighted to ascertain the secret mechanism of [nature's] organization," writes Kant, we can only rely on the "idea" of a universal history to provide us with a guiding thread that will allow us to "present" human actions as a system.[92] And this history is written for and by a "learned public," who can "authenticate" it. This history only exists insofar as it is told, as it is written and authenticated by a learned public. "The first page of Thucydides," writes Kant, is the "beginning of all true history."[93] Only with Thucydides and other Greek historians, he suggests, do human beings become conscious of their own telling of the history of the human being. And this self-awareness takes the form of a narrative identity that affords a meaningful unity or, to use a Kantian phrase, moral purposiveness to the human and thus makes the human possible. The self-consciousness of historical narrativity makes the co-belonging—the transhistorical unity—of the human possible. Kant's future history would find its possible fulfillment in the human of the future, for, as previously demonstrated, it is only in the human species that "all the germs that nature has placed in it" can be developed. Humanity as species would become the figure for the destiny of nature. The human species indexes the convergence of nature and reason, because it is the point of recursion in which subject and object overlap. This recursive point where the human being becomes human is history, or better, the act of telling the history or story of the human being becoming human. The reflective telling of the history of the human being is the beginning of the human. As Kant intimates throughout his essay, however, the future of the human, its categorical unity in a universal history, is not at all certain. His idea is "only a thought of what a philosophical head ... could attempt from another standpoint."

Kant's essay on a universal history anticipates his argument in the *Kritik der Urteilskraft* that culture not history is the space in which the human progresses toward the ends of reason. Whereas Kant had attempted to formulate a "natural history" in his essays on race, by 1790 he was referring to culture as the ultimate end of nature that absorbs both nature and the human being. Culture can do the conceptual work of unifying the species that race did for a natural history and that history did for the human species in "Idee zu einer allgemeinen Geschichte in weltbürgerlicher Absicht." Both the *Kritik der Urteilskraft* and the *Anthropologie* turn what had been a "natural history" and a cosmopolitan history into a "cultural history" that accounts for the possible merging of nature and the human being. The *Kritik der Urteilskraft* makes clear what was only intimated in "Idee zu einer allgemeinen Geschichte" and the *Grundlegung*. "Teleology considers nature as a kingdom of ends, morals considers a possible kingdom of ends as a kingdom of nature. In the former the kingdom of ends is a theoretical idea for explaining what exists. In the latter, it is a practical idea for the sake of bringing about, in conformity with this very idea, that which does not exist but which can become real by means of our conduct."[94] Here, Kant points to the analogous functions of purposiveness, or here teleology, in nature and in morals. Both concern the setting of ends. Whereas the teleology of nature has a theoretical function (explaining what is), the teleology of morals has a practical function (to effect a particular idea).[95]

In the *Kritik der Urteilskraft* Kant argues that a physical teleology affords us enough proof to assume "the existence of an intelligent cause of the world," whereas a moral teleology concerns "us as beings in the world and thus as connected to other things in the world."[96] But because it is *moral*, a moral teleology concerns the relationship of our own human causality to purposes and even as a "final purpose that must be sought by us in the world." Thus, moral teleology ultimately raises the question of whether reason requires us to "go beyond the world" to think of nature as purposive. As evident in the discussion of the needs of reason, physical teleology arises out of a need of reason to explain the apparent contingency of the natural world. Moral teleology, however, tasks reason to pursue its ends and satisfy its needs in this world. It emerges from the needs of reason to account for the human, to answer the question "What is the human being?" not in terms of "Who is God?" or "Where does the human being fit into the cosmos?" but in terms of the human being itself, in terms that human beings have laid out for themselves. In the face of the phenomenal character of all human knowledge—the recognition that we are severely limited in our knowledge of things-in-themselves—we human beings must give our own accounts of ourselves. The distinction between a natural and moral teleology makes explicit the ethical implications of the idea of a universal history. From a moral or practical perspective, teleology concerns bringing about or making real the development of the ends of the human being, whereas a natural teleology aids the explanation of nature. This distinction was present in nascent form when Kant suggested that the idea of a universal history was "consoling." Kant's teleology of history is not an epistemological claim; it is pragmatic and practical. Thus, whereas the essays on race (in the 1770s and 1780s) worked out the form of a physical teleology, the *Kritik der Urteilskraft* and the *Anthropologie* are concerned with transforming this form of teleology into a moral one.

The Culture of Moral Character

In the *Kritik der Urteilskraft* Kant offers a cursory account of what a universal history might look like. According to Kant, culture, as the "ultimate end" of nature, is "the cultivation of the ability of a reasonable being to set its own ends through freedom" (431). The first aspect of culture is "skill" or "advancement" of subjective purposes, which nature achieves through the "inequality among men." The natural inequality of human beings is connected to the "development of the natural predispositions of the human species" (442). One encounters this first aspect of culture in Kant's "Idee zu einer allgemeinen Geschichte in weltbürgerlicher Absicht," where he argues that the efficiency of nature has made antagonism the "most natural means for developing predispositions." Without the strife of our unsocial sociability, the human being's talents would "remain rotten in their germs" and their natural predispositions would remain "eternally undeveloped." The human being wants "peace but nature knows better what is good for the species. It wants strife."[97] As I noted in the discussion of the differences between Herder and Kant's philosophy of history in chapter 3, for Kant, conflict, not individual happiness, affords individual human beings a critical distance from which to evaluate the traditions and culture that form them.

The second and primary aspect of *Kultur* is discipline (*Disziplin*): "the emancipation of the will from the despotism of desires."[98] Through its negation of the domination of sensuous desires, discipline transforms one's inner will and makes it receptive to higher purposes than "nature itself can provide," that is to say, discipline prepares the human being for the recognition of the ends of reason (433). In order to redress the noncoincidence of our status as moral subjects and our status as empirical, finite beings with sensuous inclinations, Kant prescribes a discipline of reason. The culture of discipline induces human beings to keep their sensuous desires in check in order to set themselves higher purposes and thus preserve the only means of their own account giving, reason itself. The disciplinary aspect of culture reworks the sensuous part of our being by disciplining our desires so that the gap between it and our reason might be closed. As the *Sittenähnliche* or simulacrum of freedom, culture prepares the human being to be an end-in-itself. It is the ultimate end of nature. Through its work on behalf of reason, the world becomes, for Kant, almost synonymous with culture. The world is what human beings have made of it. The disciplinary aspect of culture is a second preparatory step that cultivates the desire of human beings to make themselves moral. The discipline of reason, culture, incites recognition of one's own purposiveness as a moral being who can set his or her own ends.

For the Kantian subject, the struggle to discipline the body is compounded by the human being's inherent finitude or death, which marks the limits of an individual's reason. Herein lies the need for a universal history. The transformation of a sensible human being into a moral subject is only possible through culture, the process through which rational insights are transferred from generation to generation. Culture has become the ultimate end of this world, because in it the ends of reason and the materiality of the world might merge and become embodied. Culture is the means of pursuit, the means of satisfying the needs of reason. Its task is the embodiment of reason and thus freedom. Culture figures the shift of Kant's notion of cultivation from an ethics of self-cultivation (a cultivation of the individual as discussed in chapter 2) to a cultivation of a supra-individual, the species. But this second notion of culture—the one that replaces a natural history—must, like the germs of Kant's concept of race, which have seemingly dropped out of Kant's philosophy of history, have a material substrate through which knowledge or the "trials of reason" can be transmitted from one generation to the next. Just as Kant's theory of race relied on the transference of inheritable traits through given germs, so too does his notion of culture assume a materialization of cultural knowledge. The teleological orientation of both natural history and culture also means that, for Kant, culture is the material element of the normative project of becoming human. As he writes in the *Kritik der Urteilskraft,* "art and the sciences" prepare human beings for a "dominion" in which only reason rules and allows them to "feel a suitability for higher purposes" (433).

In "Idee zu einer allgemeinen Geschichte in weltbürgerlicher Absicht" Kant frames the discussion of the actualization of reason less in terms of culture and more in terms of the historical narration of human becoming. "Our species [develops] from the lowest level of animality gradually to the highest level of humanity." This historical development of human moral predispositions is "very artificial," because reason itself relies on techniques and exercises. In the three distinct moments of the human being's historical becoming, the species is civilized, cultivated, and moralized.[99] As in the similar account in the *Kritik der Urteilskraft,* however, culture is merely a "simulacrum" of the moral, which is available to us only as an approximation of the idea. In the final pages of the *Anthropologie,* in a section on the character of the human species, Kant details the historical transformation of *animal rationabile* into *animal rationale:* the merging of a plan of nature and a plan of anthropology.

He organizes human predispositions into three types: technical, pragmatic, and moral, thereby outlining the subjective conditions of reason. The development of technical potential consists of the application of reason to fulfill the immediate needs of the human being's animalistic nature, such as food and shelter. The technical use of reason, according to Kant, is the management of things through a mechanical exercise of reason. The pragmatic potential of reason consists of the human being's ability "to make skillful use of other humans for his own purposes."[100] The self-centered character of reason is, paradoxically, what drives individuals beyond themselves. To better realize their own ends and out of a "natural compulsion" to social relations, individuals emerge from the "brute force of sheer self-violence." Through education and discipline, the advances of one generation are passed on to the next. With the pragmatic use of reason, human beings become conscious of their species character, a consciousness that distinguishes the human from the nonhuman: "With all other animals who are left to themselves, every individual achieves his entire destiny, with man however, only the species."[101] But what is the role of the *Anthropologie,* the text itself? How does it fit into this historical account?

The Unifying Promise of Kant's *Anthropologie*

In the preface to his *Anthropologie,*[102] Kant claims that his pragmatic anthropology is both systematic and popular. Its "completeness of headings" gives the reading public both an opportunity and an imperative to contribute to the science of anthropology themselves. Whereas its "headings" might be complete, the anthropology as such is not; instead, it is a provocation to contribute to the knowledge of the human being not simply as a theoretical object but as a citizen of the world. As Susan Meld Shell puts it, it is an outline, a "rubric" for the work of culture.[103] The *Anthropologie* is organized by a plan through which the "lovers of this study" can distribute the work among themselves and "become a unified whole through the unity of the plan."[104] Kant imagines his *Anthropologie* as a textual means of unifying human beings not only by making the human species the object of knowledge but by turning his pragmatic anthropology itself into a project that unifies. Kant's anthropology is simply a rubric for a collaborative project, and only as a rubric, as a collection of headings, is it complete.

Kant's rubric, however, has a clear orientation to what Kant terms the "character of the species" (321). As I noted in chapter 3, character, for Kant, harmonizes the two distinct realms of causality—the intelligibility of freedom and the sensibility of nature. But in terms of nature at least, any definition of the character of the human species is impossible. Such a definition would require the comparison of two difference species of rational beings. Experience, however, affords us only one (321). The only species of rational beings that we know of is the human species. We cannot fully define the character of the human species because there is no point of comparison.

To order the human being within the system of nature, one is left with a statement of performative force: the human being "creates" its character itself, and develops and perfects it by pursuing the ends that it has adopted. The human being as species creates its own place in the order of nature. According to the "idea of all possible rational beings on earth," however—that is, thinking not only of what is given but what is reasonably possible—Kant claims that the human species does have a character: unsocial sociability. Although nature has sown the "germ of discord" in the human species, it has intended that the human being's own reason will bring it out of such discord, or at least, allow its reason a "constant approach" to harmony (322). Such discord is the means for achieving the end of nature, namely the "perfection of the human being through a constantly progressing culture." Hence, the human being creates its own character but only under the guidance of nature's "inscrutable wisdom," a wisdom that is embodied in a "progressive culture" through which the perfection of the human being is possible. Culture, for Kant, is the realm of becoming human; it is the realm where the facticity of human sensibility and the normativity of its intelligibility might harmonize.[105] As the ultimate end of nature, culture is the realm in which the human being can transform itself from a sensible creature into a moral human being. Culture, for Kant, makes the presupposition of our freedom possible.

The formative power of culture and, thus, the human being's ability to create its own character is figured in the human hand. Human fingers and fingertips, Kant claimed, have been formed by nature to be undetermined for everything—that is, suited for the infinite uses of reason.[106] The human being manipulates things through technical uses of reason and organizes things into the social sphere of culture through reason's pragmatic uses. Such formative power creates human beings through the production of cultural objects through which they can cultivate, civilize, and thus, ultimately perhaps, moralize themselves. This transformative power of culture is linked to a cosmopolitan society toward which the human species "feels" itself destined to progress.[107] The entire anthropological project is folded back into the destiny of the human being and the plan of nature: unsocial sociability is part of nature's plan to ensure progress, and the movement toward a cosmopolitan society is compelled through a feeling that nature has planted within us. But this recursive path back into nature is a source not of knowledge but of consolation. It should give us hope that we might pursue freedom "not without [a] well-grounded surmise."

Kant's *Anthropologie* becomes, then, a privileged repository for the insights and artifacts of culture that make the human possible. Kant gives his audiences a plan that, he suggests, is *natural*. The contingency of nature, while not overcome, can be approached with an attitude of freedom: an attitude that contingency, strife, and nature itself can be managed. The irony is that all of this is natural. It is as though nature's wisdom promises its own overcoming. Kant's pragmatic anthropology is impossible without a teleological account of human becoming, because without it anthropology would simply be the occasional observations of a systematic philosopher on daily life. In the Friedlander notes on Kant's anthropology lectures, this systemic need is identified and used to criticize the deficiencies of all previous histories. They have simply chronicled empires. With the exception of Hume's history of England, no one, claims Kant, has written a history of humanity. Bemoaning this lack but anticipating his own history, Kant suggests that a true history, a history of humanity, would not only observe the human being but "bring his conduct and his phenomena under rules."[108] For Kant, pragmatic anthropology and history are inextricable, because the human being's finitude requires a history.

For Kant, pragmatic anthropology concerns the proper relationship of the empirical and transcendental, a relationship that, he argues, finds its unity in the human as the subject and object of anthropology. The human being is the author of a cosmopolitical history that stitches past, present, and future into a unified humanity. The author of a cosmopolitan anthropology is tasked with a universal synthesis. This postulation—Kant writes that such a history "could" be written by a "philosophical mind"[109]—of a unified history, the unity of transcendental and empirical, however, does not resolve the apparent impossibility of anthropological inquiry. Kant's pragmatic anthropology leaves in its wake two fields of influence: on the one hand, its often opaque relationship to the Kantian transcendental project of the critical canon, and on the other hand, a strained and sometimes illegible relation to the range of eighteenth-century German proto-anthropologies. It is strained because Kant's pragmatic anthropology pushes the possibility of anthropology to the breaking point by forcing it to confront its own limits. It is illegible because, despite obvious but scattered evidence of influence in both directions (between Kant's own *Anthropologie* and other proto-anthropologies), it is difficult to discern the exact relation of Kant's anthropology to those other proto-anthropologies.

Forster's Alternative Anthropology?

Returning to Forster and the pressure that he puts on Kant's theoretical project (initially tied to race), we might better understand the tensions between the transcendental and empirical tendencies that characterize late eighteenth-century proto-anthropology. One could also see Forster as offering an alternative to Kant's own proto-anthropology. In a comment that resonates with Kant's explanation of teleology as a "leading principle," Forster argues that although the order of nature does not follow "our classifications," a system should be our "guiding thread" (*Leitfaden*).[110] Kant admitted that his distinction between natural history and a description of nature was unclear, and his "Über den Gebrauch teleologischer Principien in der Philosophie" is an attempt to redress this fact. In a letter to Friedrich Jacobi in November 1788, Forster confesses his own confusion and blames Kant's philosophical jargon and "technical language," which had the "most impenetrable and prickliest shape of a provoked hedgehog."[111] Forster's evident frustrations with the language of Kantian philosophy, however, did not deter him from engaging Kant as his next study.

On the one hand, Forster relied on a Linnaean taxonomy predicated on morphological differences and similarities. He writes of the "physical difference of the *Neger*" and describes his evidence for racial differences as "physiological and anatomical."[112] Evidence of racial difference can be seen. It is available to immediate visual perception. On the other hand, however, Forster relies on Buffon. Forster's essay "Ein Blick in das Ganze der Natur" (A Gaze into the Whole of Nature) was written as an introduction to his lecture course on Buffon's "histoire naturelle" that Forster held at the University of Kassel in the fall of 1781. Large sections of this essay are simply translations of Buffon's text.[113] In "On Buffon's Hand," Forster argues that the compartmentalization, the "innumerable divisions and subjects" of science, has produced human observers who neglect the whole and commit themselves only to the parts. Such a division of knowledge, insists Forster, "represses the Enlightenment" and thus the distribution of knowledge."[114] Such a division of knowledge is inadequate for a nature and a world that is oriented to "movement [and] change not consistency and indestructibility" (87).

At the center of this flux of "forces and drives" is the human being, who by observing nature "lifts himself up step by step to the internal place of the all present and all powerful" (81). The human being as observer, as the locus of this observing gaze, is the center of a "great and magnificent" theater, whose "agent" we never see but whose effects we constantly glimpse. Since "creation and destruction" are characteristics of an omnipotent being, all the human being can do is observe nature's unity. Limited as it is to observing isolated moments in time, the human being cannot explain the constant emergence and transformation of nature. Forster, therefore, predicates his anthropocentric conception of nature not on the individual but the species. For Forster, like Kant, a view of nature as a meaningful whole is only possible with respect to the species:

> An individual . . . counts for almost nothing in the universe. A hundred such singular creatures, even a thousand, are still nothing.

> The species themselves (collective) are the only beings of nature. . . . In order to judge them properly, we must regard each and every species no longer as a collection or a row of singular similar things that follow each other in a consecutive order, but as a whole, independent of number and time, always living and never the same. . . . Time only has a relationship to individual creatures. (89)

The individual being is limited to isolated observations in time, but a "being that could represent the entire species" as just described would be capable of a more "complete judgment" (90). In the place of the species, this being could unite experiences and distinct moments of time. Human beings are unique in their ability to exceed their individuality by collecting, extending, and connecting their observations. The human being, "especially an educated human being," is "no longer a mere individual." The ability of human beings to transmit their thoughts and experiences from generation to generation allows the individual to become a species-being, who "reads the past, sees the present, and judges the future" (91). Here, Forster exudes optimism in the teleological judgment of a wise and educated observer and the power of culture (or education) (*Bildung*) to unify human beings.

Up to this point, Forster's account of the human being as an observer of nature, especially its emphasis on the species, resonates with Kant's teleological account of nature. But Forster describes this hypothetical individual as having a "commanding gaze" and as someone who "sees" flowers grow and bloom and "hears" the nightingale come to song (89, 90). This person perceives nature come into being as already unified. Both Forster and Kant recognize the epistemological limits imposed upon the individual observer through the certainty of death and temporal and spatial limitations. Unlike Kant, however, whose teleological thinker would impart a systematic unity on nature through his or her own reason, Forster inserts his observer into an already unified nature. For Kant the human being as subject of reason unifies nature through a regulative idea, whereas for Forster the human being, even as an imagined species being, perceives nature's prior unity. Instead of unifying the phenomena of nature through an act of reflecting judgment, Forster's observer receives nature's prior unity, a unity that exceeds the individual's own cognitive and sensual faculties. This unity cannot be thought but only perceived. He concludes his essay by asking, "Who can order an infinite number of objects? . . . Who is capable of casting a gaze into the universe? . . . Where is the beginning, where is the end of such a gaze?" Forster's concluding question could be extended to Kant's insistence on the necessity of a teleological judgment: from what position can such a judgment ever be made? Forster's insistence that any observer is already bound to the world that is the object of observation—apparently without his or her recognition—radicalizes, rather than overcomes, the problems of Kantian anthropology. As subjects of anthropology we are also the objects of anthropology. And if we are always bound to ourselves as objects of observation, how can we ever reflect on ourselves and our own limits?

A little over a month after Forster wrote to Jacobi that he planned to study Kantian philosophy, he challenged, in another letter to Jacobi, Kant's conception of God as a postulate of reason. Forster had evidently read Kant's *Kritik der reinen Vernunft* and was thus able to respond to the philosophical "jargon" that had frustrated him only a month earlier. In a comment analogous to the critique of a one-sided employment of the faculties in his essay on race, Forster again challenges Kant's singular reliance on reason as a source of knowledge: "But sensibility is so much more exquisite than representation, it is the peace, higher than all reason."[115] Forster's challenge to Kant presages Wilhelm von Humboldt's and Friedrich Schleiermacher's own challenges to Kant's pragmatic anthropology. At the very least, Forster points to the apparent contradiction of anthropological inquiry: as a science of the human, anthropology conceptualizes—that is, makes rational—that which is not simply reason, the human.

According to Alexander von Humboldt, Forster began "a new era of scientific travel, whose purpose is comparative ethnology and regional geography [*Völker- und Länderkunde*]."[116] In his other work, especially his *Reise um die Welt* (*Journey Around the World*) and *Cook, der Entdecker,* we can see why Forster became such an exemplary figure for later anthropology. Forster opens his own translation of the *Reise um die Welt* with the promise of a "philosophical history of travel" characterized by two basic traits. First, it would be self-reflective. "Two reports from one and the same trip might seem excessive," writes Forster, but with Captain Cook, he had a captain concerned with the economy of the ship, whereas Forster himself was concerned with the "variety of objects that nature had strewn about the land." The differences in their "sciences, heads and hearts necessarily brought about differences in [their] sensations, observations and expressions."[117] Two travelers have rarely "seen the same object in the same manner," and consequently each gives, "according to his own . . . sensations and way of thinking" a particular report (13). Philosophers, claims Forster, have tended to criticize travelers for their apparently contradictory accounts, while at the same time appropriating particular aspects and even particular sentences of these same accounts. Kant's own use of travelogues in his essays on race was proof of this tendency. Forster insists that philosophers like Kant have constructed systems that upon closer observation "deceive us with false appearances" (12). Their conceptual accounts do not match up with observed reality.

In order to avoid such pitfalls, suggests Forster, we must know our observer before we make use of his observations. Readers of travel reports must be aware of "how the glass is always colored" (13). The second aspect of Forster's philosophical history of travel is a criticism of the simple empiricism of most travel reports, which, he claims, are often little more than "a mass of loose individual parts, out of which no art could bring forth a whole." Kant's influence upon Forster's method and categories could hardly be more apparent, simplified though they may be.

Forster's essay "Über lokale und allgemeine Bildung" ("On Local and Universal Culture," 1791) develops this philosophical history of travel by suggesting a form of observation grounded in a dialectic of local and universal. "What the human being has been able to become," writes Forster, "he has everywhere become according to the local relationships. Climate, position of the towns, height of the hills, direction of the rivers, condition of the earth, particularity and variety of the plants and animals have, on the one hand, benefited him and, on the other hand, have limited him. They have influenced his bodily form and his moral behavior."[118] Similar to his account of the human being's relationship to nature in "Ein Blick in das Ganze der Natur," Forster considers the human being's development, in part at least, as a function of his relationship to the natural world. Nature affects the human being not just physically but morally as well. And because nature is characterized by "particularity and variety," it affects the human being in a variety of manners. The differences between human beings are a correlate of nature's own difference. Thus, "the human being is nowhere everything, but becomes something different everywhere." The "dispersion of peoples" across the earth, writes Forster, preceded their "moral education." This original geographical difference of peoples allows the multiplicity of natural predispositions, which are sometimes, claims Forster, very contradictory, to be perfected according to their own particular conditions. The various potentials of the human being could only be perfected and developed through a prior, perhaps more original, diversity. Without attention to the particularity and multiplicity of the human being's natural potentials and "powers," broader, more holistic accounts of the human being measure and compare "our fellow human beings" to an "abstract norm of perfection" that will always find them morally and physically "misformed."

As previously noted in reference to race, Forster's attention to particularity is complemented by a concomitant commitment to a form of universality. The "local, the special, the particular must disappear into the universal, if prejudices of one-sidedness are to be overcome" (48). Forster grounds the universality of European knowledge in an exchange with local knowledges throughout the world; European knowledge is a "philosophical booty of an explored globe." All peoples of the world "receive out of Europe their own ideas back with the stamp of universality newly minted" (49). Forster's dialectic privileges Europe as a center for the exchange and redistribution of a universal knowledge, not as the center for the production of universal knowledge.

Forster's notion of exchange resonates with Kant's cosmopolitan anthropology, an anthropology that emerged in the exchange of language and ideas. Forster, however, is concerned that the redistribution of "European universal knowledge" might transform humanity into Europeans, thus "the beautiful appearance of multiplicity" would be "lost" (49). The "fortunate light of the true Enlightenment" is a product of a dialectic of local and universal knowledge, but Forster connects the dialectic of local and universal knowledge, and one might say even grounds it, in a dialectic of forms of knowledge. Forster grounds the "problem of humanity," the possible unity of local and universal, in the dialectic of reason and sense, of philosophical and empirical. The goal of a "true Enlightenment" is "an unrestricted dominance of reason with the unreduced excitability of feeling." The problem of local and universal knowledge, of the claims of universal norms and the plurality of humankind, is ultimately the problem of a new form of knowledge: "reason, feeling and fantasy unified in the most beautiful dance" (55). For Forster, this dance, this play of faculties, can be achieved, or at least it requires, an "aesthetic education." Art gives us in its works "the unified richness of human and universal nature, understood purely and harmoniously reunited" (55). As the "representation of a beautiful individuality," art attends to the particular of "all nations." A universal literature, in which we read the "flowers . . . that the genius of literature has scattered over the entire earth" is a fundamental part of the "education of our aesthetic sense" (56). A universal literature and art—that is, one that is composed of European and non-European works—is essential to the education of the human being. In a move that anticipates Schleiermacher's appeal to *Poesie*, Forster appeals to aesthetics to solve the contradictions of anthropological inquiry.

Although Forster's debate with Kant on race may have suggested that Forster had an ahistorical view of the human being, his own anthropological work reduces such expectations. Whereas Forster rejects Kant's radically teleological notion of natural history, he conceives of the temporality of the human being as a function of his transformability: "A *Neger* is actually only in his fatherland a true *Neger*. Each and every being of nature is, what it should be, only in the place, for which it allows it to originate. . . . The *Neger* born in Europe . . . is a modified creation."[119] Like Kant, Forster suggests that the human being can change in time, but he admits that he still does not understand Kant's notion of natural history. He remains committed, in part at least, to a Linnaean taxonomy that conceives of categories in terms of characteristics and similarities and continues to doubt a Kantian natural history that conceives of taxonomy in terms of what Kant would refer to as a teleological history, but only, it seems, because we lack "historical reports and monuments."[120] We lack the "evidence" to make historical claims about the origins of lines of descent. Recognizing the consequences of Kant's claim that the observer can "think" a "unified cause" into nature, Forster, in his "Versuch einer Naturgeschichte des Menschen" ("An Essay on the Natural History of the Human"), asks if one actually gains anything through the "generalization of concepts, when one, for example, orders many peoples under a common concept."[121] Continuing, he writes that natural appearances differ from "that which we add, from our way of representation" and, "when applied to the particular," our representations "correspond to nothing real."[122] In the end, Forster never accepted the consequences of the limits Kant placed on reason, but his proto-anthropology is similar to Kant's and a host of other proto-anthropologies in that it brackets more metaphysical concerns regarding mind-body dualisms and the conundrums of anthropological inquiry in favor of going about the work of anthropology.

Forster's own work affords us a perhaps not fully articulated alternative to the abstract taxonomies of nature and the dialectic of local and universal, an alternative exemplified in his planned but never fully published collection of essays on ethnology and regional geography. In the preface to *Kleine Schriften. Ein Beytrag zur Völker- und Länderkunde, Naturgeschichte und Philosophie des Lebens* (1789), Forster says that these texts all consider "the natural sciences in the broadest sense."[123] In this work one sees the dialectic that characterizes his entire work in formation. It becomes evident why Forster claims that all of his work was "especially concerned with anthropology," which considered the "lively impressions" that are the products of an "unmediated perception" (345). This anthropological perception—anthropological in the sense that it is always tied to the human being as the singular observer of nature—is the source of a "future, fuller knowledge of our earth and all that is within it" (345). Forster does not reduce comparison to morphological characteristics. He appeals to what one could refer to as cultural comparisons as well, such as between morals and languages, but he does not subordinate these characteristics to a teleology of culture. Knowledge of the diversity of the human being requires not simply a physical comparison but a comparison of the way in which different peoples interact with one another and the world and their particular environment.

The inhabitants of the South Sea Islands "reveal their relatedness at first sight through the similarity of their morals and their language."[124] This "study of the human," argues Forster in his *Geschichte der Reisen seit Cook: Ankündigung* (*History of Travel Since Cook*), is quickly becoming a "new organ" that will allow the human to understand better the "influence of local relationships on the activities, the organization and the way of thinking of the human being."[125] Forster's own proto-anthropology brings together two aspects of the broader discourse. As I discussed in chapter 1, proto-anthropology was intent on accounting for the "whole human being." In this sense, proto-anthropology considered both the mind-body problem and the variety of humankind. Forster's proto-anthropology conjoins an anthropology of the faculties with an anthropology of difference. As previously demonstrated, Forster imagines a unity of human faculties. This dispersion of human potentials, however, has spread the fullness of the human being beyond the individual and throughout the various peoples of the globe. Characterized by a multiplicity of "predispositions" that are found nowhere in full but everywhere in part, the whole of humankind exists only in determinate and particular forms. The whole is spread across the earth. The human being's potentials, the range of human capacities, have been dispersed both temporally and geographically; therefore, only a comparative study of the human being as manifest in a plurality of forms and peoples can successfully address the possible unity of the human species. The division of the individual's predispositions finds its physical analogue in the difference of peoples. Thus, natural scientists become anthropologists when they address these two forms of difference together. This is the moment of comparative anthropology. The "philosopher of humankind" considers the contrast between the physical and the moral character of the human being as an "abstraction that does not lie in the realm of reality but in our way of representation."[126] The mind-body problem is an "apparent" problem that one must bracket. To answer the question "What is human?" one must bracket or defer more metaphysical questions and undertake the practical work of a comparative ethnography.

As I suggested in the discussion of Forster's "Über lokale und allgemeine Bildung," the center of this comparative anthropological work is Europe in the form of the European scientist, be it Cook on his journeys to the South Seas or one of the various scientists who joined him. Forster highlights the perspective of this anthropology. The anthropological gaze is isolated within not just any human individual but within the European scientist as the organizer and dispenser of a world knowledge. Forster anticipates a time when the entire earth will be available to the "European spirit of discovery" through which humanity will be able to see the "relationship of things."[127] This point of view is made possible through the comparative work of the European anthropologist and traveler, who amalgamates the knowledge of those lands and peoples made available to a European scientific and reading community through the work of the second epoch of discovery.[128]

Friedrich Schlegel eulogizes Forster in "Georg Forster: Fragment einer Charakteristik der deutschen Klassiker" (1797). In what he terms a "Characteristic," Schlegel promotes Forster as a unique personality and an exemplary public figure. Although Forster died in Paris in 1794, the publication of his *Kleine Schriften: Ein Beitrag zur Völker- und Landeskunde*) (1789–93) kept him in the public imagination. Citing Forster's complaint that in Germany there is "no public opinion," Schlegel celebrates Forster as the only author whose "cosmopolitan" works have "developed, nourished . . . and disseminated" a public *Bildung* and follow the "traces of a final end in the world . . . and humanity."[129] Forster, according to Schlegel, fulfilled two aspects of Kant's pragmatic anthropology: that it be cosmopolitan and that it function against the horizon of a teleological history of the human. Forster's commitment to a public form of reason was born, suggests Schlegel, from his travels:

> For his mind the journey around the world was perhaps the most important event in his life. If his trip with Cook really was the original germ out of which that free striving, that broad wide gaze perhaps first later fully developed itself: one might then wish that young friends of truth, instead of the school, could more often choose a trip around the world; not just to enrich the catalogues of plants but to educate themselves to true life wisdom.
>
> Such an experience with such original predispositions, with an open receptivity, with a not too common level of analytical reason and a constant striving for the infinite must have laid in the soul of the young body the ground for that mixture and constant web of intuitions, concepts, and ideas which so oddly characterize the intellectual mood of the man. He always paid attention to the value of a universal receptivity and lively impressions from intuition of the objects as fully as it deserved. (194)

Schlegel focuses on the particular dynamic that characterizes both Forster's and Kant's anthropologies: the convergence of a concern for "life" with a striving for the "infinite." Forster's cultivation of a mode of perception that is both passive and active, or as he says, "lively," is precisely the dynamic between local and universal knowledge that I discussed earlier. Forster sees the possibility (or impossibility) of such a form of knowledge as tied up in problems of narration as a form of account-giving or justification. For Forster, this narrative of the human being ascribes to both sensual perception and reason a spontaneity and productivity that Kant denies to the former. As Schlegel describes it, only through the complementary work of perception and reason can Forster's goal of bringing together the particular and universal be realized. This dialectic between particular and universal is a dialectic and dynamic of human faculties and potentials. "[Forster] proceeds from the particular but knows to play it quickly over into the universal and relates it everywhere to the infinite. He never employs the imagination, feeling or reason alone. He is interested in the whole of the human being" (194–95). Forster aims "to excite" and "to reunite" what he terms the "essential predispositions" of the human being (201).

Forster takes up the proto-anthropological task of cultivating the whole of the human being, both in terms of individual faculties and in terms of human difference, of the diversity of human beings. This is the task of a comparative anthropology. In Schlegel's terms, it "plays" the particular over into the universal. This idea returns one to Forster's insistence that the universal be "tested" against the particular. The play between particular and universal implies a double movement, not just from particular to universal or from the universal to the particular, but from universal to particular and from particular to universal in one continuous reciprocal movement. Whereas Kant conceives of his pragmatic anthropology more in terms of the conjuncture or possible meeting point of the empirical and transcendental, Forster appeals, in his perhaps unphilosophical (less than systematic) but very readable way, not necessarily to a singular point but to multiple points of conjuncture. Schlegel describes this more dynamic interplay of universal and particular, infinite and finite, as "the webbing and connection of the most different knowledges" (206). The human being becomes human not in a regulative projection of reason, as it does with Kant, but in a dynamic, complex web of interactions between universal and particular, philosophical and empirical. This dynamism is Forster's legacy to proto-anthropology.

Anthropological Normativity After Kant

For both Forster and Kant, a science of the *anthropos* concerns the possibility of narrating how the human being becomes human. In the preface to *Cook, der Entdecker,* however, Forster doubts whether a single, individual life, much less an entire species, can be narrated:

> Who is in the position to see through the relations of our species with a sure, all encompassing gaze, plan, and purpose, a development according to a particular goal, and to discern an assured movement to perfection out of the confused chaos of its destinies: he would outline that perfect representation of Cook's achievements that would relate them all and would teach us, how far he led his

century in knowledge and enlightenment. . . . But it would be a miscalculation to dare such steep heights with mere eyes, where such an overview is possible. Without wanting to delve at this moment so deep in the destiny of humankind, let us state nevertheless the connections that lie closer to the light of day so that this appears to our own point of view.[130]

Both Forster and Kant's proto-anthropologies tarry "closer to the light of day." Both attempt to bracket out metaphysical and theoretical problems.

For Forster, Kant's teleological account of race—and by extension his historical and cultural teleologies—undermined the more fundamental task of anthropological inquiry—temporal and geographical comparisons. For Kant, however, such an anthropological particularity undermined the critical potential of reason. The Forster-Kant debate about race and anthropology leaves us with two basic questions: How can comparisons extend beyond particular instances of observation without erasing the particularity of life? And in the face of ethnographic particularity, how is the narration of the human being possible (or even desirable)? Kant's solution was a teleology that reflectively inserted a purposiveness into nature. But for Forster, Kant's regulative insertion of a human destiny inappropriately injected normative claims into scientific debates. The reception of Kant's essays on race by figures such as Soemmering had convinced Forster of the ethical dangers and speculative errors of such mixings. At the beginning of this chapter, it was noted how Kant equated a knowledge of race with "knowledge of things in the world, like, for example, animals, plants and minerals."[131] Throughout this chapter, however, it has been evident how Kant's concept of race served other kinds of knowledge as well. Racial typologies found their way into practical and moral claims, claims about the progress of the human species. At times, race proved to be more than theoretical knowledge. Racial typologies became "sure signs" of nature's purposiveness. Theories of racial difference sometimes masked moral prejudices and assumptions.

Whereas Forster claims that the natural scientist and philosopher must assume a prior unity of nature, Kant finds that they can only narrate such a unity through a regulative account. Whereas Kant turns the narrative strategy into a heuristic *as if,* Forster, like Herder, ultimately appeals to a metaphysical God who is a first cause outside and separate from nature. And herein lies the fundamental difference between Kant and Forster.

Kant's insistence that anthropology project a human destiny is his most radical anthropological claim, for it emerges, like the assertion of a thread of history, as a consoling gesture. It emerges out of what Kant considers a *human* need, a need of reason to posit moral ends. Whereas Kant may mark the finitude of understanding in the *Kritik der reinen Vernunft*, he just as vigorously marks the infinite desire of reason in the *Kritik der praktischen Vernunft*. His *Anthropologie* operates at the limits of both projects. It is bound up with the ends of the human being and thus imbricated with the infinite desires of reason. The paradox of Kant's pragmatic anthropology is that the ends of reason are melded into nature itself. Pragmatic anthropology is humanity's account-giving of itself, but it is also a strictly limiting gesture on Kant's part. Kant's pragmatic anthropology limits anthropological inquiry to what human beings can make of themselves and thus frames itself as a counter to the desires of other proto-anthropologies to explain metaphysical problems. These other proto-anthropologies have been seduced by the promise of explaining the relationship of the body and the mind, nature and freedom. Pragmatic anthropology, in contrast, attends to the needs of reason through a reflective teleology that consoles. It is dietetic. It would prevent sicknesses brought on by exceeding the limits of reason. In the absence of a theological account of the human—where God justifies the human—the human must justify itself. Pragmatic anthropology offers just such a justification by providing a complete account of the historical progress of the human species. It affords the individual human being a "consoling" account of his or her own failure to attain perfection, a consolation that is to be found only in the human species and its collective historical destiny. This consolation, although it is not verifiable, is necessary. Kant's pragmatic anthropology ends, then, with one anthropological claim: human beings must conceive of themselves as beings who can make of themselves what they desire. The task of a pragmatic anthropology is to make this claim compelling and give the individual human being the hope that it is realizable.

However regulative Kant's anthropological telos might be and however consoling the promise of a human destiny might seem, Forster's criticisms continue to haunt Kant's pragmatic anthropology. Kant sends future anthropologists and future historians out to look for consoling signs that the two realms of causality (rational and moral) are compatible. This is the mixture of normative and empirical that Forster warned about. The transcendental idea of the historical progress of the human species reaches down into the empirical, and the empirical comes to stand in for the transcendental. Kant's seemingly incidental comments on race exemplify this movement, this melding of the two realms of inquiry. This mixing of transcendental and empirical is also apparent in Kant's hierarchy of races and his notion of historical progress. Despite his attempts to disentangle race and moral characteristics, skin color remains a "sure sign" of purposiveness, a consoling gesture of nature.

There remains, then, the danger that Kant's pragmatic or teleological anthropology will subordinate the particular to the historical march of the universal. And yet, Kant's insistence that a natural purposiveness is a regulative principle should not be dismissed out of hand. Understood in a more dynamic way, the critical force of Kant's regulative ideas—the ideas that organize his pragmatic anthropology, such as the human, the human species, destiny—might serve as a catalyst for historical progress. The idea of the human might allow for critical reflection on the current conditions of human beings. The next chapter will consider three different responses to Kant's mixing of the normative and empirical. But before moving on, it is useful to recall a brief section in the *Kritik der reinen Vernunft* that anticipates a form of normativity that might well have afforded Kant and Forster another point of conjuncture. Kant distinguishes a "comparative universality" (*komparative Allgemeinheit*) from a "strict universality" (*strenge Allgemeinheit*).[132] A universal judgment of the latter type is a priori true and no exception is at all possible. A judgment of comparative universality, in contrast, is taken from experience and means that "as far as we have noticed, there is no exception to this or that rule." Kant does not mention this "comparative universality" in the *Anthropologie,* but I would suggest that this is precisely the form of normativity intimated in his and Forster's proto-anthropologies—a universality open to difference and characterized by dynamism: a universality that is constantly *tested* by the particular, a universality that must give an account of itself, must narrate itself in the face of particularity. Schleiermacher, Novalis, Goethe, and Wilhelm von Humboldt, each in his own way, articulate anthropologies that demonstrate just this sort of comparative universality Kant had promised.

PART THREE

Three Responses to Kant

5

Poesie as Anthropology

Schleiermacher, Colonial History, and the Ethics of Ethnography

In 1796, Friedrich D. E. Schleiermacher (1768–1834) accepted a position as chaplain at the Charité Hospital in Berlin, where on December 30 he received a dinner invitation to the house of "Kant's favorite student," the renowned medical doctor Markus Herz.[1] At the dinner party, Schleiermacher began his friendship with Henriette Herz, Dr. Herz's much younger wife. Henriette introduced Schleiermacher to the "Berlin society," which by July would include the young Friedrich Schlegel, who had moved from Jena to Berlin.[2] In a letter to his sister, Schleiermacher describes his friendship with Schlegel as marking a "new period" of his intellectual and social life.[3] Six months after their first meeting, Schlegel moved in with Schleiermacher.[4]

Soon after meeting Schleiermacher, both Friedrich and his brother August Wilhelm Schlegel exhorted Schleiermacher to "convert" soon to *Poesie* and even to write a novel.[5] After returning to Jena in 1800, Friedrich Schlegel wrote how pleased he was to learn that his former roommate had finally begun to reflect "so seriously and in such detail on *Poesie*."[6] Schlegel's comment, especially his use of "Poesie," is curious because Schleiermacher's work from his early Berlin period concerns not poetry but travelogues, anthropology, and religion.[7] Of course, the semantic range of *Poesie* extended beyond poetry itself to include what may be termed an "aesthetic sense." Schleiermacher's explicit references to *Poesie* are few but suggestive; the term appears most prominently in his terse and biting review of Immanuel Kant's *Anthropologie in pragmatischer Hinsicht,* a review that concludes with the unelaborated assertion that the *Anthropologie* fails because of Kant's "ignorance about art, especially *Poesie*."[8] Marked by a poetic insensitivity, Kant's *Anthropologie,* or as Schleiermacher calls it, his "collection of trivialities," is the "negation of all anthropology"—a claim to which we shall return.[9] While writing this review, Schleiermacher was also engaged in what he alternately refers to as "a study for myself" or that "damned calendar," a project that would occupy him for over three years.[10] This "damned calendar," which he could never finish, was a history of the English colonies on the east coast of New South Wales, or what Schleiermacher refers to as New Holland (present-day Australia).

Schleiermacher's Critique of Kant's Recursive Anthropology

In this chapter I will consider Schleiermacher's first response to Kant's pragmatic anthropology and its relationship to Schleiermacher's early work. This early work—his colonial history of New Holland, his review of Kant's *Anthropologie,* and his *Über die Religion: Reden an die Gebildeten unter ihren Verächtern* (*On Religion: Speeches to Its Cultured Despisers*)—exemplify an early challenge to Kant's pragmatic anthropology and late eighteenth-century ethnography. Functioning at the intersection of proto-anthropology and aesthetics, these early texts question the categorical stability of proto-anthropology's most basic category: the human being. In a move that lends his early corpus a distinctly early romantic character, Schleiermacher appeals to *Poesie* as a model for using "humanity" or the concept of "the human" in a dynamic and historically dense way. I will outline the arguments of Schleiermacher's review of Kant's *Anthropologie,* discuss his incomplete historical-ethnographic study of the colonies in New Holland in terms of his critique of Kant's *Anthropologie,* and finally, highlight traces of his work on anthropology and ethnography in *On Religion.* Ultimately, I argue that Schleiermacher's early oeuvre is marked by a decidedly anthropological character that relies on an analogical relationship between a self-reflexive proto-anthropology and *Poesie.*

Schleiermacher's review of Kant's *Anthropologie* and his colonial history of New Holland[11] should be read within the frame of the proto-anthropology discussed in chapter 1. As I argued there, proto-anthropology was considered a "practical philosophy" that demanded that philosophy be conducted "for life: the attention to natural history, philosophy of history, history of humanity, aesthetics and pedagogy was part fruit, part impetus of a practical spirit in philosophy," a practical spirit that emboldened philosophers to make philosophy "useful for life."[12] Proto-anthropology integrated various sources and forms of knowledge in order to produce a knowledge "for life"—that is, it was interested primarily not in the metaphysical possibilities of human beings but in their worldly exigencies. It implied, then, a particular attitude toward scientific inquiry. Unlike the atemporal efforts of metaphysics to address questions of the human being, anthropological knowledge emerged within particular moments of experience and through language. Anthropological knowledge emerges within time, because we, as both the subject and object of this science, always appear to ourselves within time. As a "philosophy of life," proto-anthropology is a philosophy of temporal, lived truths. The temporal particularity of these truths makes them more practical for individual human beings.

While proto-anthropology may have sought to attend more carefully to the empirical and to make philosophy more "practical," Schleiermacher questions whether it could assume the unity, on either a normative or pragmatic level as does Kant, of its most basic category: the human. Considering the consequences of assuming the transhistorical unity of the human as such, Schleiermacher questions the anthropological imperative to study the human being from an empirical proximity. If anthropology is to emphasize temporal and spatial particularities, how can it assume a unified and universal, transtemporal category of the human? "The human," says Schleiermacher, is still "the great puzzle."[13] A science of the human being was therefore replete with problems and contradictions. As I argued in detail in the previous chapters, Kant was acutely aware of these problems. Schleiermacher makes clear, however, in a way that Kant only intimates, that these questions are not simply epistemological. They are ethical as well: how do the various modes of anthropological inquiry— its forms of perceiving and knowing—affect relations (normatively or practically) with ourselves, others, and the world?

Kant's approach to anthropology was particularly suggestive, if not troubling, for Schleiermacher because it both reflects on and illustrates the contradictions of anthropological inquiry. For Kant, all attempts to establish anthropology as a "science with thoroughness" encounter "great difficulties," because anthropology requires a mode of observation in which the subject and the object are of the same type.[14] Similar to his attempts to establish the limits of reason in his critical philosophy, Kant's pragmatic anthropology tries to delimit the possibilities of being human. Yet any efforts to ground anthropological inquiry as a science are frustrated by human limitations in space and time. As Schleiermacher argues as well, this problem of anthropological inquiry is intractable, because these acts of delimitation begin and end with a figure that is both the subject and object of inquiry.

Although Schleiermacher never wrote a programmatic anthropology, he did offer a promise of such a program, as well as an example of anthropological practice. His review of Kant's *Anthropologie* could be read as a critique of what proto-anthropology risked becoming, just as his colonial literary project could be read as a reflection on the possibility of ethnography. The discussion below outlines the perils of anthropological inquiry, according to Schleiermacher, and the fragments of his alternative.

Whereas Kant suggests that his *Anthropologie* is scientific, if not systematic, Schleiermacher calls it a "collection of trivialities." In his opinion, it exemplifies how easily anthropology can deteriorate into the accumulation of isolated observations and, sometimes, pernicious generalizations and stereotypes when it lacks a synthesizing form. Schleiermacher's critique of the organization of Kant's text, however, reveals a more fundamental incongruity between Kant's critical philosophy and his pragmatic anthropology. As Kant makes clear in the preface to his *Anthropologie*, pragmatic anthropology is to have an effect on the human being's moral transformation. But how, asks Schleiermacher, can a pragmatic anthropology be produced by someone who has spent his life mostly in "self-reflection"?[15] Self-reflection might be a necessary starting point for anthropological inquiry, yet the anthropological observer cannot remain the primary object of perception. Never moving beyond this initial phase of self-reflection, Kant's anthropology, argues Schleiermacher, is merely a manifestation of inner experience.[16]

Kant's reliance on inner experience and self-observation, continues Schleiermacher, derives from his division of proto-anthropology into two forms: a physiological one that considers what nature makes of the human being and a pragmatic one that considers what human beings make of themselves. For Schleiermacher, these two forms correspond to two more fundamental claims: "all choice in the human being is nature" and "all nature in the human being is choice."[17] Schleiermacher argues that the Kantian image of the human as divided between a sensible being and an intelligible one must reject the first claim, because, according to Kant's own critical philosophy, nature is precisely what "the I" must overcome if the human being is to bridge the gap between sensuous being and reason. Kant's abnegation of nature is nothing more than a "deification of choice" that Schleiermacher sees best expressed in Kant's basic claim, namely that all nature "in the human being is choice" (367). Here, the contradiction of Kant's pragmatic anthropology unfolds. Kant argues that pragmatic anthropology relies on empirical insights that can either help or hinder the human being's moral development; but according to what Schleiermacher sees as Kant's denial of the human's sensual being and his deification of the will, empirical insights could be neither a help nor a hindrance to the human being: "If there are no physical means of observing or treating" the mental faculties, Schleiermacher asks, where then do the observations about that which helps or hinders these faculties come from? (366). How, asks Schleiermacher, is Kant's pragmatic anthropology possible?

Kant's two-perspective solution, his division of the human being into an intelligible being and a sensible one, is undermined by his pragmatic anthropology. As Jacqueline Marina explains, Schleiermacher suggests that we can assume transcendental freedom in the Kantian sense (the ability to realize a certain goal through reason alone), yet to achieve such a state requires impure work, namely reacting to particular desires and undergoing very practical exercises to care for the self. We must assume our finitude—our sensuous self—in order to become free.[18] The contradictions of Kant's *Anthropologie*, suggests Schleiermacher, manifest themselves in the structural confusion of the text, in which individual observations stand completely "alone and needy," lacking a context in which they could prove helpful or pragmatic.[19] In his critique, Schleiermacher goes even one step further and declares Kant's *Anthropologie* the "negation of all anthropology." In his opinion, anthropology according to Kant's "way of thinking is not at all possible" (366).

Schleiermacher's argument about the incompatibility of Kant's ethics with his anthropology—that is, that Kant's formal, individualistic ethics necessarily excludes empirical insights and, thus, anthropology in general—has been repeated in various forms ever since Schleiermacher's review. As I argued in chapter 2, however, this criticism misapprehends certain elements of Kant's "way of thinking." And yet Schleiermacher's critique in particular accentuates a more fundamental problem, one that appeared in Kant's essays on race in particular. For Schleiermacher, the problems and perils of Kant's pragmatic anthropology are not merely epistemological or theoretical; they are ethical—Kant's pragmatic anthropology, with its blurring of transcendental and empirical questions and its focus on the "destiny" of the human species, encourages a particular "way of thinking." It cultivates certain types of relationships with the self and with others.

Schleiermacher cites what he considers to be an exemplary instance of this problem: Kant's "treatment of women as some sort of degenerates [. . . and his] characterization of peoples [*Völker*], resemble the joys of food on the table [*schmeckt nach den Freuden der Tafel*]" (369–70). For Schleiermacher, Kant's pragmatic anthropology is like a buffet where one can pick and choose from an array of ethnological types. The isolation of individual observations and lack of context that Schleiermacher criticizes on a formal level emerge now as both an ethical and a theoretical problem. Kant's pragmatic anthropology produces relationships between the observer and the objects of anthropological inquiry in which the object of observation is just another natural object to be classified according to theoretical categories. These problems are already familiar from the previous discussion of Kant's essays on race. In the subsequent discussion of *Über die Religion*, one finds a similar critique of a metaphysics that "classifies and divides."[20] In his review Schleiermacher claims that Kant's dismissal of women and his disparaging treatment of various peoples reflect his conceptual division and ultimate subordination of a sensible self to an intelligible self. For Schleiermacher, Kant's pragmatic anthropology demonstrates the pragmatic consequences of a Kantian image of humanity and the notion of freedom that undergirds it. Schleiermacher concludes his review with a seemingly cursory remark: Kant's anthropology fails in part because of his complete "ignorance about art, especially *Poesie*."[21] But the question comes full circle, back to what is *Poesie* for Schleiermacher and what does it have to do with proto-anthropology?

Upon learning about Schleiermacher's reflections on *Poesie* in 1800, Schlegel tells Schleiermacher that he expects not just a novel but elegies.[22] Although Schleiermacher's colonial history of New Holland may not have been the novel that Schlegel was hoping for, it exemplifies the analogical relationship between *Poesie* and anthropology, a relationship that functions as an implicit critique of Kant's pragmatic anthropology. From 1799 to 1802 Schleiermacher worked on the New Holland material for publication in Johann Karl Philipp Spener's *Historisch-genealogischer Calender oder Jahrbuch der merkwürdigsten neuen Welt-Begebenheiten*.[23] The fragments, notes, and letters that remain of this project reveal Schleiermacher's extensive knowledge of the materials available at the time on the colony in New Holland. The variety of materials also indicates that what began as a translation of David Collins's *An Account of the English Colony in New South Wales* (1798) became something much more complex. The extant material includes a lengthy extract from *The Gentleman's Magazine and History Chronicle* and translations and summaries of English travel literature. In the critical edition of Schleiermacher's works, there are also two passages from Schleiermacher's own unpublished manuscript "Zur Siedlungsgeschichte Neuhollands (Australiens)" (On the Settlement History of New Holland [Australia]). In a letter dated February 22, 1799, Schleiermacher tells Spener that the Collins travelogue must not only "be assembled but also expanded through other materials, and preferably transformed rather than simply excerpted."[24] The Collins project, suggests Schleiermacher, should be something more than "a simple understanding." He envisions a project that would resignify the history of the English colonial undertaking from numerous perspectives, not just that of one travelogue. On September 8, 1799, he laments the dearth of information concerning what occurred in the "motherland" in relationship to New Holland and news about the visits of a few New Hollanders in England.[25] Unsatisfied with a translation that would simply recount the colonial experience from Collins's perspective, which was that of the individual colonial agent, Schleiermacher requests all available information on the colony's relationship to its metropole, including transcripts of parliamentary debates and information on the English constitution.[26] The transformative, creative character of the project lends it a literary nature; it functions more like a metanarrative of the entire colonial undertaking in New Holland than a simple repetition of Collins's individual experiences. Schleiermacher's expanded project challenges the narrative authority of Collins's ethnography by observing and commenting on its context of production.

Investigating New Holland as an undertaking driven by a manifold of colonial desires, Schleiermacher articulates the possibility of a more reflexive model of anthropological perception. He refers to his New Holland project as a "study for myself" from which it would be very difficult to part.[27] Schleiermacher never did fully part from this study, and it became part of his larger philosophical project and lent his later work a fundamentally anthropological character. His later work became increasingly concerned with the reduplication of the human being as both observer and observed that had come to characterize proto-anthropology.

The Privilege of the Non-eyewitness Ethnographer

Although much of what Schleiermacher wrote about New Holland has been lost, there remains, among other fragments, a section of Schleiermacher's own "Zur Siedlungsgeschichte Neuhollands," which is a rewriting of the history of New South Holland based on the source material that he had borrowed from Spener. Synthesizing the various accounts of the natives by the Dutch explorer Francois Pelsaert and the English sailor William Dampier, Schleiermacher writes as follows: "The inhabitants, the most miserable type of people . . . , completely without clothes, and what is more without shelter, much worse off than the ants, whose own shelters, the immensity of which had never before been seen, filled the plain; without the beginnings of agriculture or horticulture, even without tools . . . and so miserably tormented by flying bugs that they could barely dare to open their eyes: Thus did Pelsaert and Dampier find them."[28]

These earliest European travelers found what appeared to them to be a completely other "type of people" on the west coast of New Holland. Schleiermacher asks, "How should such a New Holland be of any use to the Dutch?" The only conceivable response, suggests Schleiermacher, must be to prevent other nations from pursuing their own interests by establishing colonies. After recounting James Cook's 1770 landing, Schleiermacher compares accounts of the inhabitants on the east coast to those of the west coast. "The inhabitants were at first seen in general with few and insignificant differences [from the inhabitants of the other coast] . . . a people spread very sparsely across the land—never did you see even fifty at one time—without any hint of laws or a civil constitution, of religion or superstition, of agriculture or arts, in every respect on the lowest level of human culture [*Bildung*]."[29] This description of the New Holland native peoples recounts a European encounter with more than sheer foreignness. From the perspective of the European traveler-ethnographer, the profound distance between themselves and the natives of New Holland is one not only of geographical space but also historical time. The natives of New South Holland are on the "lowest level of human culture [*Bildung*]." The European travelers consider synchronic differences among peoples to represent the diachronic development of humanity's reason. Europeans, or so these travelogues seem to suggest, can observe their past by observing the presents of non-European peoples.

The second section of Schleiermacher's own "Zur Siedlungsgeschichte Neuhollands" is based on a summary of *The Voyage of Governor Phillip to Botany Bay* by Arthur Phillip and John Stockdale (which was translated into German in 1791). Throughout the travelogue, Phillip and Stockdale catalogue and celebrate the governor's efforts to befriend the natives. They describe the success of the first meeting with the natives as a function of Phillip's professional knowledge and friendliness."[30] In his own rewriting of Phillip's text, however, Schleiermacher argues that Phillip's affability arose neither from a "feeling of original equality," nor from a desire to establish himself as a model of "morality." It was rather, argues Schleiermacher, a "level of cleverness, for there was nothing that the new inhabitants could have won from the old. For what purpose could we have used these people?"[31] Phillip's friendly demeanor is a function not of a belief in a common humanity but of successful colonial practice. A tolerant relationship between the colonized and colonizers, observes Schleiermacher, advances the colonial project. Schleiermacher's own text breaks off here, yet even in its incomplete state there is little doubt that he, like Kant, considers the spatially and temporally removed ethnographer to possess a privileged perspective on these distant events.

Schleiermacher's fragmentary text can be read as an extension of his critique of Kant's *Anthropologie*. Weaving together an array of ethnographic and historical details on the colony in New Holland, Schleiermacher transforms the poverty of individual accounts into a self-reflexive, critical treatment of colonial and ethnographic practice. In his review of Kant's *Anthropologie*, Schleiermacher writes that it is impossible to reflect "on the particular . . . if one doesn't begin the process at a higher starting point."[32] His account of New Holland exemplifies such a "higher point" at which the practices of ethnographers, proto-anthropologists, and colonialists are the object of inquiry just as much as the non-Europeans, who are the more traditional objects of anthropological inquiry. Schleiermacher offers an anthropology of anthropological and ethnographic practice—that is, his fragmented text reflects on the very premises of reason and knowledge.

A brief consideration of the various travelogues and ethnographic texts that Schleiermacher cites in his own project will clarify the ramifications of Schleiermacher's incipient anthropology. The Phillip and Tench accounts report little interaction between the Europeans and the native population. Tench says that his knowledge of the natives was limited, because of their "unwillingness" to interact with the Europeans.[33] In contrast to the Phillip and Tench accounts, Collins's text of 1798, the original impetus for Schleiermacher's interest in New Holland, offers a more complex account of the natives. With an appendix devoted to detailed accounts of the natives, Collins's text is more systematic and explicitly ethnographic: he includes chapters on the natives' government and religion, appearance, courtship and marriage, customs and manners, diseases, funeral ceremonies, and language. While the natives of the Phillip and Tench texts remain nameless and external to the narrative of colonial activities—they make only occasional appearances in chance and often precarious encounters—the natives of Collins's text are a constant presence. Collins refers to particular members and leaders by name and follows them throughout the text. Whereas Phillip and Tench make little or no attempt to compare the natives with the Europeans—thereby portraying the natives as absolutely other to the Europeans—Collins makes deliberate attempts to establish such relationships. He refers to the "good understanding between us and them" and praises the desire to "establish harmony" and the shared "knowledge of our humanity."[34]

Despite his efforts to emphasize the Europeans' and natives' common humanity, some differences, suggests Collins, exceed rational analysis. Collins details what he describes as the violence of the natives' courting rituals, in which a woman is stolen from one tribe and forcibly dragged to another. For Collins, there remains a seemingly unalterable foreignness and that serves as the basis for his ultimate conclusions that the natives are "children of ignorance" (137). His own befuddlement, suggests Collins, is only exacerbated by problems of communication. "It was observed," he writes, that the natives "conversed with us in a mutilated and incorrect language formed entirely on our imperfect knowledge and improper application of their words" (209). The object of ethnographic inquiry, namely the natives' attempts to make themselves intelligible to the colonizing Europeans, disturbed the ethnographer's efforts at objectivity. There were no uninterrupted bridges between the Europeans and the natives. The natives, despite Collins's narratives of common humanity and mutual understanding, remain foreign.

Schleiermacher's colonial history attempts to foreground the differences that Kant's pragmatic anthropology absorbs into a general narrative of humanity's historical progress. Schleiermacher lets the foreign remain foreign, to a certain degree, by commenting on the means and goals of colonial practice. Schleiermacher seems to ask whether or not there is something beyond the anthropological gaze through which we are bound to see only ourselves. How, if at all, asks Schleiermacher, can peoples separated by oceans and what seems like historical epochs relate to each other? This is precisely the problem of Schleiermacher's proto-anthropology: how can anthropological inquiry assume a common humanity without relegating some peoples to past moments of a European humanity's historical becoming? Can anthropological and ethnographic inquiry acknowledge or even advance difference and a universal recognition of humanity without reifying the category "human"?

Religion's Double Moment: Historical Intuition of the Infinite

The discussion thus far has shown how Schleiermacher connects the ethical and theoretical problems of Kant's *Anthropologie* to the latter's "ignorance about *Poesie*" and transforms his colonial history into an alternative ethnography. The implied relationship between anthropology and *Poesie* and Schleiermacher's reformulated ethnography finds a surprising resonance in Schleiermacher's best known text of 1799: *Über die Religion: Reden an die Gebildeten unter ihren Verächtern*.[35] In *Über die Religion* Schleiermacher establishes a relationship between religion and history, a link that highlights the analogical relationship of *Poesie*, anthropology, and religion. Schleiermacher appeals to the dynamism of *Poesie*, an oscillation between historical particularity and a universal wholeness, to reconcile the tensions common to religion and anthropology. In his classic study on romanticism, Rudolph Haym argues that with the dialogical form of *Über die Religion* (Schleiermacher addresses an audience of cultural religious critics in the first person throughout the text) Schleiermacher "joins the poets and poetic critiques" of German romanticism and echoes their "polemic against the Enlightenment."[36] More strictly theological treatments have argued that *Über die Religion* is a plea either for the revitalization (Seifert) or rejection (Brunner) of Christianity. Historians of religion and philosophers have read *Über die Religion* in terms of their complex religious-philosophical heritage, which includes Schleiermacher's work on Kant from 1788 to 1794 and his work on Spinoza in the winter of 1793–94.[37]

Although Karl Barth refers to Schleiermacher's "anthropologicalization of theology,"[38] there has been no explicit discussion of the link between Schleiermacher's *Über die Religion* and his own reflections on proto-anthropology. And more important, scholarship that has referred to the "anthropological" character of *Über die Religion* has made almost no effort to consider what Schleiermacher understood "anthropology" to be. In an effort to apply Schleiermacher's insights to contemporary debates in religious studies on the relation of history and religion, Thomas E. Reynolds has recently argued that *Über die Religion* balances "religion and history . . . in an ongoing dialectical tension" in which a "generically religious disposition arises and . . . is from the beginning woven substantially into historical life."[39] Expanding on Reynolds's argument, I argue in the following section that this "dialectical tension" of history and religion is analogous to the "anthropological" tensions encountered in the New Holland materials. Schleiermacher appeals to an aesthetic sense, a *Poesie*, to reconcile this "dialectical tension" common to religion and proto-anthropology.

In defending religion before its "cultured" despisers, namely, students of the Enlightenment and his own romantic circle, Schleiermacher identifies the unique character of religion, and he contrasts it with metaphysics and with morals.[40] In order for religion to claim its "own domain," it "renounces" whatever is not its own: "It does not want to determine and explain the universe like metaphysics, it does not want to develop further and complete the universe out of the power of freedom and the divine power of choice of a human being like morals. Its essence is neither thinking or action but intuition [*Anschauung*] and feeling. It wants to intuit the universe, wants to devoutly listen in on its own representations and actions, it wants to be seized and filled from its immediate influences in a childlike passivity."[41]

Like religion, both metaphysics and morals concern the universe: metaphysics leads into the totality of things in its attempts to explain nature, while morals leads into the infinite in its attempts to expand the realm of freedom. But unlike religion, metaphysics and morals both begin with the finite, whether the human being or the human species. In contrast, religion begins from above with the infinite, the universe, which religion "wants to intuit." As the "necessary and indispensable" counterpoint to metaphysics and morals, religion is "the highest in philosophy" of which both metaphysics and morals are "subordinate sections" (212, 209). Schleiermacher characterizes religion as this overarching "intuition of the universe" (213).

As the "hinge" of his argument, intuition specifies an openness or radical receptivity to a universe that "reveals itself to us in every moment" prior to our own knowledge or action (214). In intuition we perceive relations and unity within the universe; this unity makes both metaphysics and morals possible. Everything must proceed from intuition, claims Schleiermacher. Neither a mode of knowledge (metaphysics) nor a form of praxis (morals), religion relies on the influence of the "intuited on that which intuits [*Angeschauten auf den Anschauenden*]" (213). The object of intuition takes priority over the subject of intuition. Schleiermacher's distinction between the intuited and that which intuits, however, should not be taken as an inverted rehabilitation of a Kantian dualism, because the intuited and that which intuits inhere within each other. Underlying Schleiermacher's characterization of religion is an insistence on the immanence of the infinite in the finite. To say that religion begins with the infinite means that it begins within the infinite in the finite.[42] This emphasis on wholeness permeates *Über die Religion*, where the subject of religion intuits a universe that is a united, living whole of which that same subject is part.

Schleiermacher's notion of "intuition" must be read in terms of Kant and post-Kantian philosophers like Fichte and Schelling. In his *Kritik der reinen Vernunft* (1781), Kant defines intuition as that through which knowledge is "immediately" related to objects.[43] For Kant, intuition is an immediate relationship to objects in the world, a relationship that is possible only when an object is given to us; but just as "thoughts without content are empty," so too are "intuitions without concepts blind."[44] Schleiermacher, in contrast, distinguishes intuition from any other form of reflection, because intuition is receptive, an ability to be affected by an object. Whereas Kant insists that concepts are the necessary counterpart to intuition, Schleiermacher insists that intuition precedes concepts. For Schleiermacher, religion designates an immediate relationship afforded by an intuition or nonreflective receptivity of the universe: intuition emerges "from an original and independent action of the first, which is then taken up, condensed and understood by the latter."[45] Religion does not posit or categorize the universe; it recognizes it.

For Schleiermacher, religion, as the "sense and taste for the infinite" (213), is an experience common to humanity: "And when we have intuited the universe, and then look back on our I, as it disappears into that which is infinitely small in comparison, what can be closer to the mortal than true and authentic humility? When in intuition of the world we perceive our brothers, and it is clear, how each of them without difference in this sense is what we are, its own representation of humanity . . . , what is more natural than to embrace them all without respect to opinions and mental strength, with inner love and dedication?" (236 [Crouter, 45; trans. modified]).

Schleiermacher locates a common humanity not in a feeling of positive belonging or the universality of reason but in a universal capacity to intuit or experience the infinite. If we as human beings share a common humanity, it is in large part marked by this capacity for radical receptivity and openness. But this common experience is, at the same time, radically particular. Unlike a Kantian understanding, religion does not have any transhistorical structures or transcendental categories. To intuit the universe (to *be* religious) is to be affected in a radically particular way. There are as many forms of intuition as there are persons to intuit. While religion is a universal capacity, "only the particular [is] true and necessary" (215). To be human is to be religious (or capable of religion) and to be religious is to experience something singular. We could describe this tension between the universal and particular character of religion as the dual moment of religion. Religion is both a universal capacity and a particular experience. For Schleiermacher, the dual moment of religion addresses the question of how religion can be a human universal whose "truth" lies in the particularity of experience. What conception of the universal can be so bound up with the particularity of experience?

These questions prompted by the dual moment of religion are analogous to those prompted by Schleiermacher's review of Kant's *Anthropologie* and Schleiermacher's colonial history. Schleiermacher's review asked how a science of the human can heed difference, while his ethnographic encounter with otherness and absolute particularity in the New Holland narratives asked how the category of the "human," with its universalizing connotations, could be used in a historically dense sense. What types of belonging, what images of a common humanity or "the human" are possible in the face of such particularity? What would it mean to study an *anthropos* whose universality is its very particularity?

Kant's pragmatic anthropology and philosophy of history were characterized by a similar tension. For Kant, however, the tension was between, on the one hand, the universality of the idea of a human destiny and the progress of the species and the dignity of the individual human being, on the other. In our discussion of Kant's essays on race and his *Anthropologie*, we saw how his teleological history threatened to subsume the integrity of the particular. And yet we also saw how, for Kant at least, transcendental ideas might make it possible to critique the influence of traditions and the formative processes of a mimetic culture that defined Herder's particularism. Despite their differences, however, Kant, Herder, and Schleiermacher concur that the universal—humanity for Herder, the human species for Kant, and religion for Schleiermacher—has no ontological existence. The kind or type has no being. The difference, then, lies in how they propose to employ these universal categories. The more productive question concerns not whether such universals exist (of course they do not—as Herder would put it, no one is suggesting that stone-ness exists somewhere) but how we relate them to each other and whether they can be useful and compelling. Kant argued that such universal ideas were, in fact, in their regulative use quite practical. The idea of a human destiny, for example, could incite critical reflection and dietetic work in the present. However ambivalent (or confused) Herder was about such ideas, he did acknowledge that they were useful in making clear the "connection" of all human beings.

Schleiermacher takes up this problem not only in *Über die Religion* and his revisions of ethnographic texts but also in his later work on interpretation, hermeneutics, dialectics, and ethics. In fact, it becomes the task of a philosophy committed not so much to establishing permanent bridges between cultures as to reflecting on the very possibility of engaging the foreign across oceans, intersubjectively, and within ourselves. It is also, in part at least, the task of Schleiermacher's reflections on religion. The remaining sections outline Schleiermacher's alternative to Kant's use of universal categories.

The Aesthetic Form of Religion and Anthropology

In the fifth speech of *Über die Religion*, Schleiermacher conjoins the universality and particularity of the human being through an account of religion. Schleiermacher's theoretical account of the double moment of religion—its historical and generic character—intimates the analogical relationship of religion and proto-anthropology, since both are forms of engagement with the world (or universe) in a mode of dialectical tension. With this double moment in mind, *Über die Religion* can be read in relation to Schleiermacher's critique of the accounts of the foreign in Phillip's, Tench's, and Collins's travelogues and ethnographies, and as a rebuke to Kant's *Anthropologie*. These texts fail as models for anthropology and ethnography, because they make everything conform to their own image. Their own notion of humanity is their "everything" (243).

The fifth speech also lays out the concept of plurality: Schleiermacher assumes that the plurality of religions is "necessary and unavoidable" (294). If we want to understand religion as more than a universal predisposition devoid of content and grasp it in its "appearances," we must accept its plurality (295). According to its essence, religion is infinite and irreducible, but in order to exist it must be perceptible; therefore, claims Schleiermacher, "it must have in itself a principle to individualize itself" (296). The plurality of religions corresponds to the manifold and finite ways that particular persons or particular communities intuit the universe. Correlative to religion's plurality is its historicity. Religion never remains purely potential; it reveals itself in an infinite number of finite and specific forms, in the density of languages, cultures, and history. Similar to an anthropology that emerges within temporal exchanges and the density of life, religion, claims Schleiermacher, can be found among neither the "rigid systematizers" nor the "shallow indifferentists," but among those who live in it as their "element" (314). If one wants to study religion, says Schleiermacher, one must observe it in its "determinate forms" in which everything appears "real, powerful and determined" (310).

Religion must be observed in the historically particular forms of positive religions, which have "strong characteristics" and a "marked physiognomy" (297). Schleiermacher urges his audience to pay attention to how religion bears the "traces of the culture of every age and the history of every human type" (312 [Crouter, 111]). While the essence of religion consists of individual intuitions, individual religious experiences do not necessarily on their own constitute a religion. A religion emerges when a single intuition becomes the gravitational center around which other experiences coalesce and acquire a referential significance. A religion emerges when "a particular intuition of the universe" becomes "out of free choice" the "central point" of the whole religion to which everything within it is referred (303). As finite, historical beings, we are born into communities of meaning that are characterized by particular, unique experiences. Religious intuitions are experienced and lived within a horizon of history. In his notebooks from his early Berlin period, Schleiermacher writes: "History is always religion and religion must always be according to its nature historical."[46] Religion and history are bound together, because history signifies that referential "totality" within which a single intuition can emerge as the center of an individual religion. In the second speech, Schleiermacher historicizes religious experience into three levels of "culture" (*Bildung*). In the first, the universe is experienced as an undifferentiated unity and God as a being without characteristics. In the second, the universe is experienced as a multiplicity without unity, or as the necessity of elements and forces (natural causality). In the third level, the universe is experienced as a "unity in difference."[47]

Schleiermacher's proto-anthropology of religion intimates an alternative mode of anthropology that would make what he terms in *Über die Religion* the "recognition of the foreign" possible.[48] In order to come to terms with the plurality of religions and their often foreign character, suggests Schleiermacher, we require alternative modes of perception. We have seen this anthropology in inchoate form in his New Holland ethnography. As Schleiermacher suggests, some of the characteristics of various religions can seem "grotesque" and utterly foreign (312). The particularity and plurality of religions are jarring and even disconcerting, especially for those despisers of religion, whose "philosophical and moral manners" and insistent "politeness" demand tolerance but suppress the unique character of religion (296). In such language, one hears the echo of Schleiermacher's struggle with Collins's attempts to narrate a common humanity and his criticism of Kant's ethically problematic ethnography. Similar to Schleiermacher's ethnographic imperative to let the foreign remain foreign, religious experiences, too, must remain on some level foreign, or else religion will devolve into an empty and polite universality. As I have discussed, religion as intuition "is and will always remain something particular, distinct, the unmediated perception, nothing more" (215); it can only appear "in an infinite number of thoroughly determinate forms" (299). Religion emerges and lives within the historical density of particular experiences and forms. While there may be no determined inner "relationship" between specific religious experiences, every individual intuition can lead to another one through a "thousand random combinations" (300). But how are these relationships between specific religious experiences discerned? How can an array of seemingly disparate and determinate experiences be related to one another? Schleiermacher's anthropology raised similar questions, and their possible resolution in *Über die Religion* points to the affinities of proto-anthropology and religion.

Although one cannot conflate religion and proto-anthropology, I do want to highlight their analogous structure. As we have seen, there is no specific or necessary content of religion; religion is rather a mode of experiencing or relating to the universe. Proto-anthropology and religion share this mode of relating to the world, a mode that reveals the imbrication of the human and the universe. Because both recognize the complex relationships between the universe and the human, they demand an openness to a world that precedes knowledge or action. Recalling his criticism of Kant's *Anthropologie* as betraying an ignorance of art, especially *Poesie*, Schleiermacher appeals to the figure of *Poesie* to reconcile the often competing claims of historical particularity and a universal wholeness, a problem common to both anthropology and religion. Schleiermacher turns to another faculty, an aesthetic sense, to address this tension.

In the third speech "On *Bildung* to Religion," Schleiermacher argues that the "religious predisposition" of contemporary youth has been "violently repressed" (252). The imperative to understand everything has robbed them of their faculty of sense. Whereas the understanding orders the world according to categories of reason, sensibility "wants to find and be found; it wants to perceive what and how something is for itself and recognize everything in its unique character" (254). Schleiermacher's contrast of sensibility with understanding resonates with his critique of Kant's pragmatic anthropology, which classified peoples according to theoretical categories. Schleiermacher also criticizes Kant for lacking a higher point from which to transform individual observations into something more than "needy" observations lacking a context.[49] This criticism takes up Schleiermacher's insistence upon the second element of this sensibility: an imperative to perceive or, to be more accurate, intuit everything as part of the whole. Schleiermacher describes this second element as follows: "But may they realize that in order to intuit every thing as an element of the whole, one must necessarily have observed it in its particular nature and in its highest perfection. For in the universe it can only be something through the totality of its effects and connections; everything depends on this. To know only one point of view for everything is just the opposite of having all points of view for everything."[50]

The particular must be perceived in terms of the whole, while the whole must be perceived in terms of its manifestations in the particular. This dialectic of perception strives to maintain the dignity of the particular and the universal and underlies both religion and art, which, Schleiermacher writes, stand beside each other like "befriended souls" (263). Both religion and aesthetics depend upon a sense that "strives to grasp the undivided impression of something whole" (254).

Expanding on this dialectic of perception, Schleiermacher argues that everyone has three different "directions of the senses," or forms of perception (261). One is directed toward one's self, while a second is directed outward toward the "undetermined in the intuition of the world." A third combines the two in a constant "back and forth oscillation" (*hin und her Schweben*) between both. This third form of sensibility manifests itself in art and works of art and oscillates between perception of the self and the outside world. Its oscillation is manifest in a double imperative: "Look outside of yourselves to any part, to any element of the world" (261 [Crouter, 68]). Only through the oscillation between the finite and the infinite can "the infinitely big" be related to "the infinitely small" (262).

For Schleiermacher, this third element, the aesthetic mode of perception, demands both receptivity and constant movement. It is a dialectic of receptivity and spontaneity. Intimating the affinity of this form of perception to *Poesie*, Schleiermacher concludes his third speech with a play on Friedrich Schlegel's definition of *Poesie* in the 116th *Athenaeum* fragment: "Let us intertwine the past, present and future in an endless gallery of the most sublime works of art, eternally multiplied through a thousand mirrors" (265). Although Schleiermacher never uses the term *Poesie* in *Über die Religion,* his citation of Schlegel makes clear that the "hin und her" of art recalls the "hin und her" of *Poesie*. Schleiermacher appeals to an early romantic notion of *Poesie* as a figure of an alternate mode of perception that ceaselessly reflects between the objects and subjects of inquiry; it oscillates between particular and universal, a mode of perception that constantly renegotiates the relationships between particular experiences and categories of reason. While the aesthetic sense, or what I am suggesting as its romantic equivalent, *Poesie,* is the only thing that can bring religion to "perfection," it is also, writes Schleiermacher, the "sanctuary of true science" (263). Not simply a mode of experience particular to religion or a literary genre, *Poesie* is a model for a science, a *Wissenschaft*, that alerts the human to its "reciprocal relationship with the world and acquaints the human with himself not only as creature but creator" (264). This recalls Schlegel's 115th *Athenaeum* Fragment: "All art should become science and all science should become art."[51] *Poesie* functions at the conjunction of the empirical and philosophical. The double imperative of *Poesie* and religion in *Über die Religion* is the analogue of the double imperative of the proto-anthropology that we saw in Schleiermacher's New Holland history, where the human being is reduplicated as both subject and object, creator and created, observer and observed—that which intuits and that which is intuited. The recognition of this doubling is the product of eighteenth-century proto-anthropology.

The imbrication of religion and proto-anthropology emerges in the mutual concern with the category of the "human." Schleiermacher tasks both with providing alternate ways of appealing to and employing a category that, as Schleiermacher's criticism of Kant's *Anthropologie* and his rewriting of the colonial ethnographies show, is all too often emptied of its particularity and density. At the same time, however, Schleiermacher appeals to proto-anthropology and religion to provide an account of a common human experience, a co-belonging of humanity. Both proto-anthropology and religion struggle with the question of how to appeal to concepts like "humanity" and the "human" without reifying them and thus stripping them of their normative force. Schleiermacher's intimated solution is an appeal to *Poesie,* whose central characteristic, as a model for both religion and anthropology, is a dynamism that becomes the mark of Schleiermacher's later work on hermeneutics, ethics, and dialectics.[52] What makes Kant's pragmatic anthropology such a "collection of trivialities" is an ignorance of *Poesie* not simply as a literary genre but as a particular way of engaging the world. For Schleiermacher, *Poesie* is an analogue of an anthropological method that transforms the ethnographic observer into an artist who is both object and subject of inquiry. In the oscillation of Schleiermacher's *poetic* proto-anthropology, the "human" emerges and recedes between empirical necessities and normative promises. In this sense, then, Schleiermacher, like Kant, recognizes the usefulness of transcendental ideas, but whereas Kant's ideas are one-time projections of reason, Schleiermacher, like Forster before him, suggests that such ideas can be revised. Universal forms and ideas must always be tested against the particular exigencies of life. Humanity is only a "transient form."[53]

6

Lyrical Feeling

Novalis's Anthropology of the Senses

Kant's philosophical project, and the Enlightenment project for which it often serves as a synecdoche, is "one of bridging, not just sounding the abyss of dualism between reason and nature."[1] In his *Logik* Kant writes that to consider the unity of the human is to ask "What is a human being?" a question he assigns to anthropology.[2] Karl Heinrich Ludwig Pölitz claimed in his *Populäre Anthropologie* that by 1800 this emergent science of the human had entered a "state of crisis."[3] In his *Anthropologie in pragmatischer Hinsicht,* Kant describes this crisis in anthropology as a decision between a physiological anthropology that considers what nature "makes" of the human being and a pragmatic anthropology that considers what humans as free agents can and should make of themselves.[4] The very modality of Kant's formulation—the facticity of "makes" versus the normativity of "should"—condenses the crisis of proto-anthropology.

In a crossing of the empirical and normative forms of proto-anthropology, the early German romantic Friedrich von Hardenberg, better known as Novalis, adds a third question to anthropological inquiry: what does the human as a natural being make of the human? This chiasmic reformulation of Kant's distinction between nature and rational norm radicalizes what was already the fundamental problem of proto-anthropology: the implication of the human being as his or her own object of study. With the rise of the life sciences and the subsequent naturalization of the human body during the eighteenth century, the rational human being becomes part of and in part nature. At the juncture of a Kantian critical philosophy and the emergent life sciences, Novalis reformulates Kant's dualistic division of proto-anthropology by turning anthropological inquiry back on itself in a recursive act that poses a question: If nature determines the human being and human beings form themselves as natural beings, thereby forming nature, how might an anthropology account for these processes of mutual formation that always fold back upon themselves? How can an anthropological inquiry account for both the distinctions and nondistinctions of the human and nature?[5] In this sense, Novalis is concerned less with the topics often associated with the history of anthropology—racial difference, comparative ethnology, and travel—and more with the structural problem of the human being's relating to itself as human, a problem that, as will become evident, has perhaps surprising ethical implications. While devoting the occasional entry in his encyclopedic *Das Allgemeine Brouillon* to "Anthropo[logie],"[6] alluding to Kant's *Anthropologie*[7] and Platner's *Anthropologie für Aerzte und Weltweise*,[8] Novalis does not explicitly discuss proto-anthropology; instead, he intimates an anthropological form of knowledge that acknowledges both the human being's material character (the body of the human being as a material given) and its rational character (the productive potential of reason). This double acknowledgment suggests a form of anthropological inquiry that wavers between the normative anticipation of a pragmatic anthropology and the physiological gaze of a medical or more empirical anthropology. Like Schleiermacher's embrace of the contingency of the category human, Novalis frames his normative concepts in dynamic terms. While the reduplication of the human being as both the subject and object of observation threatened to undo Kant's pragmatic anthropology until he bracketed it, Novalis, like Schleiermacher, embraces this reduplication and considers it the only way to make normative claims more flexible.

The double character of such an anthropological mode of thought is nowhere more evident than in Novalis's conceptualization of sensibility. In this chapter I consider how Novalis develops these questions concerning the relationship of the senses, reason, and the body in terms of a broader theory of modernity. Novalis redefines sensibility in order to undo oppositions of nature and culture, physis and norm. This rethinking allows Novalis to frame his own proto-anthropology as an ethical response to modernity's purported fragmentation of sensibility and the human being in general. I begin by considering the perplexing formulations of sensual experience in Novalis's most famous poem, *Hymnen an die Nacht* (*Hymns to the Night*). From these stylistic observations, one can see how these odd formulations respond to two main problems related to the fragmenting effect of modernity: the *commercium mentis et corporis* or mind-body problem and the famous question posed to John Locke by the Irish physician William Molyneux concerning the relationship of the senses to each other and reason, a question that Michel Foucault has termed one of the great "mythical experiences on which the philosophy of the eighteenth-century had wished to base its beginning."[9] That leads to a discussion of how the poem's response to these broader problems of modernity crystallizes around Novalis's concept of attention and its corollary, imagination, which figures sensibility and reason as fundamentally intertwined.

Sensibility in Novalis's *Hymnen an die Nacht*

Novalis's *Hymnen an die Nacht* is often read as a lustful hymn to death, an abnegation of the body, or a *Weltflucht*.[10] In reading the poem as a wish for transcendence of the body, many critiques have failed to account for the very bodily figures and images found in it. It is, however, important to attend to the poem's odd and somewhat perplexing figurations of sensual experience, figurations that cannot be easily explained by modern or Enlightenment paradigms of perception. The first hymn opens by suggesting an equivalence between life and sensibility: "What living, sentient thing loves not above all wondrous appearances of the widespread space around him, the most joyful light—with its colors, rays and waves; its gentle presence, as waking day? As life's most inner soul it is breathed by the giant-world of the restless stars, and swims dancing in its blue flood—the glittering, ever resting stone, the sensuous sucking plant, and the wild, burning and many formed animal—but above all the splendid stranger with sense-filled eyes, with gliding gait, and the tenderly closed, rich-toned lips."[11]

What is this sensibility equated here with life? The reference to light seems to tie light with vision and, perhaps, reduce sensibility as such to an ocular faculty. But this sensibility has a much broader semantic field. The giant-world, the stone, the plant, and the beast all "breath" the light. And the "stranger," with "sense-filled eyes" and "tenderly closed tone-filled lips," senses the light in its "gentle presence." Everything from stones to stars to "splendid" strangers engage the light with organs of not just sight but touch. The "stranger" breathes the light, inhales the light; consumes it; takes it into its body. The tactility of the experience is reiterated as the eyes of the stranger, those traditional organs of vision, are complemented by "tender lips." The light passes over and upon the body of the stranger. The descriptions of synesthesia complicate expected sensual pairs like light and vision, expectations based on a traditional Enlightenment paradigm of the senses that associates light with vision and knowledge. The differentiation of the senses within this paradigm also suggests a hierarchy of the senses that tends to privilege vision.[12] Sensual experiences are fused so that the oppositions presumed to guide the poem—light and night, vision and nonvision—are disrupted. In this first hymn, light as a metaphor exceeds the Enlightenment imbrication of knowledge and vision. Registered through an array of senses, light marks the confusion of traditional sense hierarchies and intimates a total sensual experience.

The second paragraph turns to the night. "Away I turn to the holy, the unspeakable, the secretive Night. Down over there, far, lies the world—sunken in a deep vault—its place wasted and lonely. In the heart's strings, deep sadness blows. In dewdrops I'll sink and mix with the ashes.—Memory's distances, youth's wishes, childhood's dreams, the short joys of a whole long life and hopeless hopes come greyclad, like evening mist after the sun has set. In other places Light's pitched happy tents. Should it never come back to Its children, who are waiting for it with simple faith?"[13]

An array of spatial deictics (*Abwärts, Fernab, hinunter-, Fernen*) shifts the focus away from the thing-ly objects and the stranger illuminated by the light and toward a night that is addressed from a distance. Its apparent distance, however, is immediately undercut by the familiarity of address: "you . . . dark night." The doubtless familiarity of the light is contrasted to a peculiar, distanced familiarity of the night, whose modes of perception are "unspeakable" and "secretive" and whose objects of knowledge are hidden under its coat. The organs and functions of vision appear here again but in a new, confusing constellation: "More heavenly than those flashing stars, appear to us the eternal eyes, which opened the night within us." These "infinite eyes" give access to the night: "Darkly, unspeakably we feel ourselves moved—I see a serious face startled with joy." Here, the transitive force of a nonvisible subject that cannot be uttered is felt, a perceptual experience that is juxtaposed with an experience of vision in a way that leaves the causal relationship between this "feeling" and the moment of vision ambiguous. It is not simply juxtaposed to other senses but imbricated with them on a level anterior to the functioning of different organs. In the night organs function differently. And here in the night, the night "sends me you—tender beloved." The night offers up a beloved that makes the lyrical I "human" ("mich zum Menschen gemacht"). Anthropological particularity is figured in terms of a specific form of perception that erases distinctions among organs of perception.

The radicalization of perception in the first hymn closes with a vision of consumption, a vision of total unity: "consume with spiritual ardor my body, so that I spectrally may mix myself with you more closely and then our bridal night may last forever."[14] The experience of the beloved night, of the beloved, culminates in a wish for a touch without mediation, without the organs of hands or lips but a touch or contact that would completely dissolve any distinction between inside and outside. The experience of unity, however, is spectral, or as Novalis writes, *luftig*. According to Grimm's dictionary, the word *luftig* describes a spectral being (*geisterhaftes Wesen*), something that fluctuates between body and soul, matter and ideas. The poem figures this desired unity, this erasure of distinction as spectral or between worlds. But what is this sensibility, this spectral sense that "mixes" body and soul and various forms of sensual experience? What sensibility can account for this seemingly impossible experience of unity?

Mapping Senses from World-Mind to Body-Soul

In order to answer these questions, one must turn to Novalis's notebooks and prose works. In a fragment from 1800, Novalis refers to the debates surrounding the question of the *commercium mentis et corporis,* or the mind-body problem as discussed in detail in chapter 1. There he describes the presumed opposition of the body and soul as one of the "strangest and most dangerous" of oppositions, one with a "great historical role."[15] Unlike the philosophical doctors of eighteenth-century Germany or the *médecins-philosophes* of the Montpellier school of medicine, Novalis neither denies nor affirms this opposition. Whereas Ernst Platner speculated about the existence of a fluid (*Nervensaft*) that would resolve this opposition, Novalis reflects on its historical and ethical role. He describes the opposition not as true or false—as a question of scientific fact—but as "dangerous and strange," two adjectives deviating from a strictly scientific register. Anthropological concerns about the naturalization of the body and the rehabilitation of sensibility, suggests Novalis, have an ethical as well an epistemological value.

In the middle of the *Fichte-Studien* (1795/96), a series of notes and fragments based on his studies of Fichte's Wissenschaftslehre,[16] Novalis reflects on the *commercium* problem[17] and its implications for the category of the senses:

> It is generally known that one distinguishes soul and body. Everyone who knows this distinction will thus establish an association between the two, in terms of which they are able to affect each other reciprocally. In this reciprocal relationship [*Wechselwirkung*] each one assumes a double role. Either they themselves affect one another or a third something affects one through the other. The body serves simultaneously also by means of the senses a communication of outside objects with the soul, and in so far as it is an outside object, it itself affects, as object, the senses by means of the senses.[18]

Novalis suggests that the contemporary discourse of proto-anthropology deduces a relationship of reciprocal effect from a prior distinction of the soul and the body.[19] Whereas Platner and much of eighteenth-century proto-anthropology speculated about an actual ontological ground of identity, Novalis appeals to a common deduction that the mind-body relationship manifests itself in a reciprocal functionality that is not necessarily a relationship of identity. Ascribing to both soul and body a double role, he suggests that each affects the other: the body affects the soul, the soul affects the body. Novalis's own evaluation of this "generally accepted" claim, however, remains obscured by the passive tone of his diction. The text reads more like a report based upon generally held opinions than the convincing defense of a scientific position. In fact, Novalis offers no clear resolution to the *commercium* problem, nor does he identify another model that could.

The reciprocal functionality of soul and body, continues Novalis, is made possible through the senses, which are themselves "not self-acting": "They receive and give what they obtain—they are the medium of the *Wechselwirkung*."[20] They are the "possession" of mind and body. As he notes in the *Fichte-Studien,* sense (*Sinn*) is "a tool—a medium" (550). The senses are heteronymous organs subordinate to outside purposes. And as organs or media they not only make possible the relationship between soul and body, they also make it perceptible. The unity of body and soul is discernable only as a mutual effect through the senses. Throughout his notebooks, Novalis uses both designations "the senses" (*die Sinne*) and "sense" (*der Sinn*). In this passage from the *Fichte-Studien,* he intimates a unified or singular sense that is anterior to the pluralization of sense into individual senses. He thus raises the question about the nature of a sensibility or total sense that might ground the senses. This total sense, he suggests, would be the "substrate of particular, individuated" senses. Thus, vision, taste, or sound, suggests Novalis, would be "modifications, individuations of the category sense." The "ground of the senses," he continues, is the (singular) sense (*Sinn*). This total sense, however, is a "negative material." It cannot be known or distinguished beyond its negativity. Thus, Novalis imbues sense and sensibility with both a formal (or ideational) and material (or physiological) character. Taken as a formal category, total sense is a "product of the imagination," but taken as the differentiated senses, sense is a physiological function (273). To think of the unity of sense requires a detour through its plurality of forms. Because of its ultimate groundlessness, all sensual perception, writes Novalis, is "second-hand" (550). Lacking a positive ground, the senses can only refer to their own activity. They have no determinate ground; they are fully self-referential.

Novalis organizes these second-hand forms of sense into two general categories:

> We have two systems of senses that, however different they may appear, are intimately intertwined. One system is called the body, one the soul. The former depends on outer stimuli whose essence we call nature or the world. The latter originally depends on the essence of an inner stimuli that we call the mind, or mental world. Normally this latter system stands in an association or nexus with the other system and is affected by it. Yet there are traces to be found of an inverse relationship and one soon notices that both systems should stand in a perfect reciprocal relationship in which each is affected by its world, forms a harmony but not a monotony. Simply put, both worlds, just as both systems, should form a free harmony, not a disharmony or monotony. (546)

The body depends on "outer stimuli" (*äußere Reitze*) from the outer world, while the soul depends on "inner stimuli" (*innere Reitze*) from the mind. These inner and outer forms of sense recall two eighteenth-century physiological terms: irritability (*Reitzbarkeit*) and sensibility (*Sensibilität*).[21] Novalis associates sensibility with mental or nervous stimulation that originates from within the individual, and he associates irritability with bodily stimulation that originates from outside the individual. The outer senses (vision, hearing, touch, taste, and smell) mediate outer stimuli. The inner senses mediate inner stimuli and processes. They are thus inherently self-reflexive, because they make available the very processes of perception and mental reflection. World and mind or body and soul are interrelated but nonidentical sense systems. (For Novalis, world-and-mind stands in an analogical relation to body-and-soul.) These two systems, writes Novalis, "should" be in a "perfect reciprocal relationship," but even in these normative terms the relationship is not one of identity. They are not the same but can enter into an almost infinite array of harmonious relationships.

The modal reformulation of the *commercium* problem imbues Novalis's proto-anthropology of the senses with a normative character; indeed, it shifts his discussion onto a historical register that imagines a different perceptual past and anticipates a future organization of perception in which the senses are media not just of outer but inner stimulation. As historical arrangements, the senses are open to future transformation. He imagines a future in which inner and the outer senses are inverted and the distinction between sensual systems is blurred. Future senses would mediate not just from world to mind but from mind to world. This perceptual future is the chiasmic crossing of Novalis's romantic anthropology.

A Normative History of Sensibility and the Reclamation of Feeling

With this synoptic overview of Novalis's conception of sensibility in terms of the *commercium* problem, one can better understand the broader significance of his proto-anthropology of the senses for his more general anthropological mode of thought. By suggesting that the soul "originally" depended on the irritation of the mind, Novalis temporalizes the mind-body relationship and sense systems, thereby suggesting that the relationship between outer and inner sense or irritability and sensibility emerges in historical processes and is not simply an atemporal anthropological truth.²² "Long ago," he writes in his *Allgemeine Brouillon* (1798/99), "a change of opposition occurred—and outer and inner stimulation—sensibility and irritability . . . canceled each other so that with the increase of outer stimuli the inner decreased and with it sensibility and irritability as well."²³ Novalis's temporalization of the senses (and sense in general) implies some historically past point at which irritability eclipsed sensibility after a longer period during which they had effectively neutralized each other. This eclipse, continues Novalis, resulted in a "disproportion" of the senses in which there was an "excessive stimulation of the senses."²⁴ Novalis's lament over the excess of outer stimulation is a critical account of modernity. Like Friedrich Schlegel's efforts to distinguish modernity from a classical past with regard to poetics, Novalis's theory of modernity distinguishes modernity as that epoch in which the outer senses dominate the inner senses, irritability dominates sensibility. This imbalance, he claims, has led to an "inadequately" observed and "spiritlessly" cared-for "inside" of the human being.²⁵ His temporalization of sensibility allows for the historical categorization of epochs according to how they organize perception. Modernity's instrumentalization of the senses (senses as mere organs or tools) is but one example of the historical organization of perception. Thus, the normative and ethical character of Novalis's project is tied to his historicization of the senses. Novalis reiterates this normativity when he speaks of a total sense that would be "means and purpose simultaneously."²⁶ This temporalization of sensibility entails an imperative for modern human beings to reinvent the relationship of sense systems through a rehabilitation of inner sense or sensibility.

For Novalis, the normative account of a total sense emerges in opposition to the isolation of the senses from one another and the body in modernity, a historical distinction that is itself a function of the reorganization of perception: "Seeing-hearing, tasting-touching, smelling are only fragmentations of a general perception-effect of a foreign body on us."²⁷ For Novalis, this historical differentiation of sensibility into individual senses makes possible certain Enlightenment conceptions of the senses as passive organs or tools. In his *Anthropologie,* for example, Immanuel Kant refers to the "undeniable passivity of sensibility," which simply delivers sense data to the "law-giving understanding."²⁸ In contrast, Novalis's normative account of sensibility imagines perception as an active process and offers an etymological argument: "*Wahr*—derivation from to continue—

perception [*Wahrnehmen*]—to grasp insistently / To take—is active reception" [Wahr—derivation von Währen—Wahrnehmen—beharrlich ergreifen/Nehmen—ist active Reception].[29] Working with the roots of the German *Wahrnehmen*, he points to a dynamic perception that actively seizes and thus selects its objects. Drawing on this etymological account of perception in general, Novalis further develops it such that sensibility does not simply transmit raw data but selects and sorts it and thus produces knowledge itself. Sensibility itself gives meaning, or has the potential to give meaning through combining and selecting sensual data.

For Novalis, modernity's reorganization of perception into an outer sensibility divided into five distinct and isolated senses is another manifestation of modern humanity's estrangement from nature. As Max Horkheimer and Theodor Adorno's allegory of Odysseus in *Dialectic of the Enlightenment* suggests, the division of the senses is a function of the division of labor, or in perhaps more romantic terms, the diremption of the process of *Bildung* from the creative power of nature. Odysseus stops the ears of the sailors and has his hands bound in order to separate himself from and thus maintain control over the sensual experience of sailing past the Sirens. The progress of the Enlightenment vessel is guaranteed through the logic of rational organization, which not only divides rational and sensual labor but sensibility itself. Sensibility becomes susceptible to rational organization once it is relegated to the body—that is, once it becomes nature. To paraphrase Horkheimer and Adorno, human beings know their senses and can distinguish them in so far as they can manipulate them.[30]

The broader Enlightenment debate about the organization of the senses finds an early articulation in a thought experiment posed by the Irish doctor William Molyneux in a letter of 1693 to John Locke, who then popularized it in the second edition of his *Essay Concerning Human Understanding*: Suppose a man were born blind and were taught by touch to distinguish between a cube and a sphere. Then suppose he were made to see, would he be able to distinguish by sight what before he was only allowed to touch—that is, would he be able to name what he saw?[31] Repeated and circulated throughout Enlightenment Europe in various forms, this thought experiment equates the blind man with the savage whose *Bildung* becomes the paradigmatic story of an enlightened education of perception. While some of the conclusions drawn from Molyneux's experiment may differ—be it in Condillac's *Traité des Sensations*

(1754), Diderot's *Lettre sur les aveugles* (1749), or Berkeley's *Essay Towards a New Theory of Vision* (1709)—almost all considerations were framed in terms of a few basic, though admittedly complex, questions: How are individual senses related to each other? Is there a form of perception anterior to the differentiation of individual senses? Is there a form perception anterior to discursive thought?[32]

These speculative musings about the possibilities of the senses and perception in general[33] underline as well the hierarchy of senses that emerges alongside their differentiation. As has been argued by a number of scholars, the Enlightenment was undergirded by the assumption that vision was the primary sense.[34] Within this Enlightenment tradition, however, there was also a growing suspicion of the primacy of vision. In Germany at least, Johann Gottfried Herder offered one of the most consistent and articulate critiques of the dominance of vision, though he did not begin to question the differentiation of the senses as such until much later in his work.[35] The debates surrounding the organization of perception took on a metonymic quality as the very organs of perception, the eye and the hand, became objects of debate, and Herder tended to speak on the side of the hand. In his early hymns to touch, Herder, too, emphasizes the warm immediacy of touch as contrasted to the cold distance of vision. In *Viertes kritisches Wäldchen* (*The Fourth Critical Forest*), Herder speaks of a "bodily truth" emerging once the "sense of touch"[36] is no longer "amputated and suppressed" by the dominance of vision.[37] Its immediacy, he suggests, makes touch particularly "anthropological," because those who can see and thus rely too much on their vision are "too distracted" to reflect on themselves. Those with sight do not study themselves, writes Herder in his short essay "Sinn des Gefühls" ("Sense of Feeling"), because "it is not necessary for us to engage ourselves. We only see and study appearances."[38] In contrast, those given over to touch, the famous blind man of Molyneux, for example, are always referred back upon themselves, because to touch is always in part to touch oneself.

In a note from a collection of fragments, Novalis cites Herder's essay *Plastik* and its reformulation of the Molyneux question: "Herder's Plastic. Pag. 7. The blind man or the man who can now see was taught to recognize his feelings visually. He often forgot the meaning of the symbols of the feeling—until his eye attained the skill to see figures of space and color images as letters of previously bodily feelings, to pull quickly together and to read the objects around him."³⁹ Whereas Herder insists on differentiating the senses, Novalis intimates an interdependence of the senses by appealing to the structural analogy of perception and language. The healed blind man recognizes his feelings by learning to see objects as "letters of previous bodily feelings" (*Buchstaben voriger Körpergefühle*), which he then learns to "read." Sensations are figured as letters, and perception as such is figured as an act of reading. The senses, suggests Novalis, are always interwoven with the figurations of language and the materiality of the letter, the text. Sensual perception is not simply the passive reception of external data transmitted through the senses; instead, like the reading of letters, it acts transitively upon sensual data. The senses select and combine a world of sensual data, in analogy with linguistic acts of reading. But this is not to assert that sense or feeling is simply the effect of language or that perception is a rhetorical effect; rather, this passage confirms just how interwoven physiological and mental processes are for Novalis. As evident in *Hymnen an die Nacht*, language highlights not the totalization but the differentiation of the senses. One of the speakers in Novalis's *Dialogue* even laments modernity's "fatal familiarity with the printed nature."⁴⁰ Modernity's compulsive reliance on print, he suggests, will leave us only with books, and we will no longer see things and "our five bodily senses will be as good as gone." The imbrication of physiological and mental processes undoes the question of priority with respect to feeling and reflection in general and underscores the spectral character of feeling. Feeling wavers between reason and sensibility.

The spectral character of feeling makes the historical resignification of sensibility and perception as such all the more possible. Having no positive ground, the senses and sense in general have an open future, according to Novalis: "The multiplication of the senses and the training of the senses is one of the main tasks for the improvement of the human race, the advancement of humanity. We saw already that the formation and multiplication of the soul is the most important undertaking. Outer stimuli we already have under control—and with them irritability—it depends on the multiplication and formation of sensibility and what is more, on the way that irritability and the outer stimuli do not suffer under this, that they are not neglected."⁴¹

The multiplication of the senses would involve an infinite increase in the receptive and active capacity of both inner and outer systems of sense to a point where passive and active become so intertwined as to be inextricable. To imagine the totalization of perception is to imagine the nondistinction of passive and active perception. The intensification of dualities, suggests Novalis, leads to the fusion of distinction into unity—that is, by increasing the capabilities of the individual senses, a totalized perception might emerge.[42] As a normative "task for humanity," however, this totalization of perception exceeds the individual body and is subsequently transposed to the imagined body of humanity and thus becomes a cultural task that relies on a genetic account of humanity. This transposition eclipses concerns of a physiological anthropology bound to the individual body and anticipates a normative anthropology that would undergird any possible totalization of perception.

Reformulating the eighteenth-century Molyneux myth, Novalis asks his reader to consider another thought experiment:

> If we were blind, mute and without feeling, our soul in contrast completely open, our mind the present outer world, the inner world would stand in relation to us, like the outer world now, and who knows whether we would notice a difference—if we could compare both states. We would feel such things for which our sense was lacking, for example, light, noise/sound etc. . . . We could only produce changes—the thoughts would be similar, and we would feel an effort, to obtain for ourselves the sense that we now call the outer sense. Who knows whether we could not shortly thereafter through various efforts produce eyes, ears etc., because then our body would stand so much in our power, would make up such a part of our inner world, as our soul does now. Our body may then not be so senseless, just as little, as our soul now. Who knows whether it would only appear senseless, because it made up a part of our self and the inner self-distinction, through which the body would first see, hear and feel for our self-consciousness. . . . We would in such a state already appear therefore senseless, because the soul would be the overwhelming power that attracts all attention in excitement to itself—just as we already often do not see, hear, feel when our soul is lively occupied—and our attention has directed itself only to it and vice versa.[43]

Imagining an inversion of inside and outside, soul and body, Novalis suggests a functional inversion of inner sense and outer sense and thus the nondistinction of the two. This imagined moment of nondistinction, however, would not be a collapse into total inwardness. Driven by an "effort" to produce "that sense that we now call outer sense," we might grow those organs that the soul lacks: eyes to see and ears to hear. Driven by a "feeling" for worldly effects, the body could produce organs of perception. Novalis distinguishes "feeling" (*Gefühl*) from "sense" (*Sinn*): "We would feel that for which our senses were lacking." "Feeling" exemplifies, on a level anterior to the differentiation of the senses, the senses or perception as such. Here, feeling is metonymic for sensual perception as such, while sense is associated with contingent sensations.[44] Even without the individual senses we would "feel" "light, noise etc." In this respect the senses and feeling indicate not different types but different degrees of differentiation. Feeling is the metonymic figure for individual senses. Oscillating between the material, physiological effects of the senses and the universalizable forms of a sense anterior to differentiation, feeling figures mediation as such, because it marks the confusion of inside and outside, self and world. "Sense," writes Novalis in the *Allgemeine Brouillon*, "indicates mediating knowledge, touch, mixing."[45] Feeling is always figured and articulated as the temporal unfolding of the senses. It only appears in the differentiation of the senses. To feel is to see, to hear, to taste, to touch.

In this thought experiment, the body as distinct from consciousness emerges as other in a distinction: the body emerges through what Novalis terms an "inner self-distinction." We become conscious of the mind-body pair through the figurative work of sense, the particular articulations of sensation and affect through reflection. The conditional form of the entire section ("Wenn wir . . . wären"; the repetition of *würde*) underlines the impermanent nature of the senses. Novalis's entire project here is conjectural. He imagines alternatives to the historical specificity of the senses. The process of distinction makes it impossible to distinguish between inner and outer states outside a historical-material framework. How could this "feeling" anterior to the differentiation of the senses be distinguished? For Novalis, the degree-zero of feeling is an impossibility or a negative ground that can only be imagined. In his *Allgemeine Brouillon* Novalis names the reflection on the impossibility of distinction "criticism," a teaching that

> refers us by the study of nature to ourselves, to inner observation and experimentation, and by the study of ourselves to the outer

world, to outer observations and experiments. . . . We understand of course everything other only through the making-foreign-to-the-self—self-change—self-observation. Now we see the true bonds of connection between subject and object—that there is an outer world within us which is with our inner in an analogical connection as the outer world outside of us is with our outside and that they are both connected like our inner and outer.

Now the so-called transcendental philosophy—the reference to the subject—the Idealism and the categories—the relationship between object and representation in a completely new light. Demonstrations of why something belongs to outer and inner nature . . . instead of not-I, Thou.[46]

Nature or the outer world is not simply what is other to the self-projection of the I, as detailed in Fichte's Wissenschaftslehre. The I, claims Novalis, relates to nature as Thou. This passage presents the broader chiasmus of a romantic anthropology of the senses: the formation of ourselves as nature is the formation of nature as ourselves. Through the mediation of the senses, the body becomes the axis for the crossing of humanity and nature. If the outside world is in us, and we are in the outside world, if nature becomes a familiar, dialogical Thou, then the distinction between observer-subject and object-nature is blurred. The same would be true for the distinction of inner and outer senses. If the human being is always already nature, then there would be no absolute distinction between inner and outer senses, because to reflect on the operations of the mind would be to reflect on nature. Or, in other words, the mental operations traditionally thought to be the object of the inner senses are so intertwined with the physiological operations of the body that the inner-outer distinction cannot hold. As is evident in the foregoing discussion of the mind-body relationship, this does not necessarily imply a relationship of identity. It simply means that the point of distinction is invisible or indeterminable. There is no outside position from which to ascertain this point of distinction. By stressing active reception, Novalis does not collapse the soul into the world but imagines a perception not determined by outside stimulation. As mediators between inside and outside, soul and world, the senses are historical products of this interaction of spheres. Novalis's notion of criticism is also a response to the questions inspired by Molyneux's thought experiment. Sense is not anterior to thought, but neither is thought anterior to sense; they are coemergent. And feeling figures this coextensive relationship that cannot be discursively grounded but only figured in tropes of the senses. Feeling marks the oscillation between the formal and transcendental, on the one hand, and the material and affective, on the other.

Attention to Feeling

Novalis emphasizes the reciprocal emergence of feeling and thought most clearly in his discussion of attention, which he suggests is a technique to direct and develop the senses in freedom or, as he puts it, to train them. In his *Anekdoten* (1798) Novalis suggests that one should be able simultaneously to "determine" and to "tune" irritability "at will" ["die Reizbarkeit beliebig zu stimmen . . . zu dirigiren"] and thus counter the dominance of outside stimuli over sensibility. Through attention, he writes, "We are in a position to allow an object to affect us: strongly or weakly, long or short, this or that object of the inner sense. Attention increases or decreases, determines the irritability of these organs. Through reduction, distribution, concentration, it reduces irritability—through unification, concentration of the same, it increases irritability."[47] Attention is the arbitrary manipulation of stimuli. In *Die Lehrlinge zu Sais* (*The Novices of Sais*) one of the voices discussing nature indicates attention's specifically anthropological character:

> Upon whatever the human being takes before him he must direct his undivided attention or I upon it . . . and when he has done this, soon thoughts or a new kind of perception emerges, which appears to be nothing but tender movement of a tinting or rattling pen, or wonderful contractions and figurations of an elastic fluid.
>
> They spread themselves from the point where the first impression stuck to all sides with a lively movement and take his I away with it. He can often immediately end this game by dividing his attention or by chance let it wander about, for they appear to be nothing other than rays and effects which that I excites to all sides to that elastic medium or his refractions in the same or in general an odd game of the waves of this sea with the rigid attention. It is most

strange that the human being first in this game becomes truly aware of his uniqueness his specific freedom.[48]

Here attention is equated with the inner processes of the I. An "undivided attention" makes the perception of the very processes of thought and cognition possible.[49] It is a form of self-observation in which the subject observes perceptions and thoughts that it itself "pulls together." By giving form to the various objects of the inner sense, like emotions and thoughts, it observes the very figuration of the I by availing the processes of thought to observation. Through its acts of distinction, it can stop, start, and interrupt these processes. In the "game" of attention, the subject can observe and even affect the interaction of the two systems of sense we have considered: "The outer world becomes transparent and the inner world becomes manifold and meaningful and so that the human being finds himself in an inner lively state between the two worlds in the most perfect freedom and in the most joyful feeling of power."[50] Attention observes the interrelationship of world and mind, body and soul. Attention creates new relationships and figures by distinguishing the I from itself, thereby allowing the individual to perceive its own "unique freedom": its own ability simultaneously to observe and be the object of observation. Attention, we could say, is the exemplary form of inner sense and even the exemplary anthropological sense, because it marks the susceptibility of sensibility to reflection, the radical interrelation of the two faculties. Capable of "localiz[ing] stimulation in an organ," attention underscores how pregnable sensibility is to the formal powers of reflection.[51] Attention then is precisely the technique that could realize Novalis's normative account of sensibility: it could concentrate and channel stimulation and thus counter the predominance of outer stimulation. The radicalization of the senses and ultimately the restitution of the inner senses are made possible by that very process of differentiation that marks modernity: the senses' individualization and functionalization into different organs. This is the paradox of feeling as well; the attempts to ground feeling repeatedly fall back on the differentiation of the senses in figurations and tropes of reflection.

Imagination as the Source of Ethical Norms

The oscillation of sense between reflection and physiological sensation is further developed in the second hymn of *Hymnen an die Nacht*: "They [the fools] do not feel you in the golden flood of the grapes—in the miraculous oil of the almond tree and in the brown juice of the poppy. They do not know that it is you who hovers around the bosom [*Busen*] of a tender girl, and makes a heaven of her embrace [*Schoß*]."[52] Returning to a differentiated sensibility, the lyrical I ascribes the fools' ignorance not to the limits of reason but to a failure to recognize the diversity of sensual media available to human beings. They misrecognize the night because of an insistent conflation of all knowledge and experience with the light of reason. They are fools because they do not "feel" the night in all its sensual forms: the taste of grapes, the touch of oil, the juice of a poppy, the pressure of the embrace. The variety of sensual experiences of the beloved finds its formal analogue in the variety of linguistic imagery of the poem. No singular linguistic utterance can arrest the proliferation of perception. The desire for a sensibility of nondistinction that concluded the first hymn—a desire, however, that was itself complicated by its spectrality, by the *Luftigkeit* of its form—is undone. The totalized perception, the feeling for the beloved, takes form in the stylized language that refers to itself. This is not a language of nondistinction or totality but a language of particular sensuality that revels in linguistic form. Amid the abstract conceptual desire for nondistinction emerges a poetic language that gives density to all those distinctions made available by taste and touch by objectifying a felt or sensed experience in an imagined reality. In this respect, we can reread the distinctions of the light from the first hymn and its figurative language—the glittering, ever-resting stone; the sensuous sucking plant; the golden flood of grapes (*der funkelnde ewig ruhende Stein; die sinnige, saugende Pflanze; der goldenen Flut der Trauben*)—not as an abnegation of the light but as performing the tensions inherent in the desire for nondistinction, for a feeling without organs and media.[53] These figurations of sense do not represent an abstract sense—vision or taste—but draw attention to the medium of language itself. The very language of the poem is a particular sensual experience. Thus, the poem exceeds a strictly mimetic relation to feeling and is itself bound up with and even performs feeling.

In the second hymn, the night is experienced through a range of senses, none of which is vision. The differentiated language of the poem undermines the "timelessness and spacelessness" of the night and interrupts any totalization of perception. The formal unity of feeling is undone by its own figuration in the poem. The insistent mixing of inside and outside makes *Hymnen an die Nacht* a poem of embodied sensation. Once reflected on, once put into language, the "feeling" of the night of nondistinction is differentiated into an array of sensual experiences that themselves take linguistic form, a linguistic form marked by its own materiality: the repetition of "s" and "z" in *sinnige, saugende Pflanze,* for example, draws attention to the material, sensual character of poetic language. Thus, the "feeling" for nondistinction once put into the language of reflection is a "feeling" for the absence of nondistinction, or its impossibility. For Novalis, the absence of this nondistinction, of an absolute, is registered through the senses, which are always already embodied in language. Concerning the lyric in general, Thomas Pfau writes that feeling is communicated "not through but as textual form."[54] We do not "feel" the absolute; we taste, feel, and touch its absence, its differentiation in linguistic form. Whereas the night is tied to a desire for the fusion of all forms and systems of sense, the light of "morning," the light of reflection always comes and transforms these feelings into objects of reflection. This, writes Novalis, is the "earthly violence" that never seems to end.[55] The possible totalization of perception is always, suggests the poem, interrupted by the differentiation of perception that comes in language as sure as the morning light. The more theoretical speculations of the Molyneux thought experiment, of which Novalis was well aware, find a practical answer in a poetic attempt to figure a perception anterior to sensual differentiation. As Novalis notes in his *Fichte-Studien* with respect to another ultimate unity, being (*Seyn*): "Reflection becomes here what feeling is—feeling what reflection is—they trade their roles."[56]

As the closing stanza of the fifth hymn tells us, this "eternal night" of "no distinction" is an "eternal poem." The attempt to figure a total sense repeatedly fails but this recursive movement always returns to the figurations of sense in language. This recursive movement is the "eternal poem." This moment of nondistinction is poetic—that is, it is an effect of that "wonderful sense that can replace all others": imagination.[57] As the highest modulation of sensibility, suggests Novalis, imagination affords us a sensual experience of the "timeless and spaceless" night of nondistinction. The totalization of perception, its radicalization into a sense that does not simply receive but produces, is figured as imagination. This imagination is one whose particularity lies in its ability to make available objects and experiences beyond those spatially and temporally immediate: "If the outer senses seem to stand under completely mechanical laws—the imagination is obviously not tied to the present and the continuity of outer stimuli."⁵⁸ Because imagination is not determined by outer stimuli, it is a normative counter to the excesses of stimulation. Its creative ability and reflective power free it from the rules of understanding. Characterized by its ability to increase the "irritability for the mind" (*Reitzbarkeit für den Geist*), imagination is a more complex and sustained level of attention.⁵⁹ As a "productive" force not bound to the present like the other senses and the understanding, imagination generates relationships limited neither by temporal or spatial proximity.⁶⁰

In Novalis's notes on Herder's *Plastik*⁶¹ there is a table that rearranges Herder's organization of perceptual fields, artistic forms, senses, and aesthetic media.⁶² Herder's hypothetical table, based on his discussion in *Plastik*, might look something like this:

space	painting	vision	surface
time	music	hearing	tone
force	sculpture	feeling	body

Compare this to the table in Novalis's notes on Herder's *Plastik*:

space	sculpture	vision	surface (*Fläche*)
time	music	hearing	tone
force	*Poësie*	feeling (*Gefühl*)	body

The most interesting aspect of the table, as Nicholas Saul notes, are two amendments that Novalis makes to Herder's organization. Novalis associates sculpture with vision and *Poesie* with feeling; Herder associates painting with vision and sculpture with touch and feeling.⁶³ Novalis's amendments tie *Poesie* (and not, like Herder, sculpture) to touch and feeling, and thus associate *Poesie* with what Herder saw as the "immediacy" of touch. If one reads Novalis's table as analogous to Herder's, then *Poesie* replaces sculpture as the ultimate art form. But Novalis's rearrangement of Herder's table exceeds the complex arrangement of the senses and feeling I have discussed. Novalis's arrangement of *Poesie* with "feeling" figures the oscillation between material sensations and universalizable forms. Elsewhere Novalis writes of *Poesie* as an "active sense of feeling." No longer merely a literary genre, *Poesie* is tied to an active sense. *Hymnen an die Nacht* performs what Novalis describes in *Die Lehrlinge zu Sais* as "a new mode of perception," a perception that allows Sais to hear, see, taste, and think "simultaneously."[64] For Sais, this radicalized perception opens up previously imperceptible relationships: "Now he found everywhere familiar things again, only wonderfully mixed, paired. . . . He noticed soon the connections in everything." Novalis figures total perception as not just the merging of different senses but the inevitable mixing of reflection and feeling. And imagination, as the sense that "can replace all others," drives this mixing through textual forms. Imagination, suggests Novalis, is a protracted application of attention, whose "inverted use of the senses" makes it an "active sense of feeling," where feeling is metonymic for all senses. Thus, imagination is a recursive function that figures its own actions and movements back into itself. It is a sense that organizes senses. Novalis's reconceptualization of the senses as imagination—the collective, single, active sense (*thaetiger Sinn*)—is precisely the normative dimension of Novalis's anthropology.

In the wake of Kant's so-called Copernican revolution that refigured not just the knowing but also the ethical subject, Novalis rethinks the ethical person. In his *Über die ästhetische Erziehung des Menschen* (*Letters on the Aesthetic Education of Man*), Friedrich Schiller had hoped to redress Kant's division of the intelligible being from the sensible being through an aesthetic education that would cultivate reason and sensibility. Both Novalis and Schiller envision an anthropological recuperation of the whole of the human being, a whole that historically speaking had been fragmented by modernity. Novalis's anthropology of the senses, however, reveals the persistence of a specifically Kantian dualism in Schiller's project, which ultimately maintains the Kantian distinction between an active, form-giving reason and a passive sensibility that is merely a conduit for data. Novalis argues not just for the unity of body and soul, reason and sensibility, a project common to a range of eighteenth-century figures, including Schiller in his early work as a medical student,[65] but for the more radical susceptibility of these faculties to each other. An active sense would be a paradox for Kant or Schiller. With his alternate anthropology, Novalis intimates an embodied ethics based on the original susceptibility of reason to feeling and feeling to reason. In contrast to the caricatures of romantic notions of sensibility, Novalis does not privilege one over the other. Reason and sensibility function in an interdependency (*Wechselwirkung*). The specificity of Novalis's project, however, lies in the surprising form of normativity that his anthropology of the senses intimates, a normativity that in the face of the limits of discursive thought relies on imagination.

As I noted earlier, the ground of the senses, sense as a total sense, is negative. Novalis writes in reference to the ground of being and Fichte's absolute I, that all grounds, origins, and transcendental unities are a "product of the imagination," "something freely made, something poeticized, something created."[66] As the traveling merchants in Novalis's *Heinrich von Ofterdingen* put it, imagination "gives us through words an unknown, wonderful world to perceive. Like out of deep caves rise up within us ancient and future times, innumerable people, wonderful lands and the most odd events, and tear us from our familiar present."[67] Not bound to the present and the immediate determination of outer stimuli, imagination makes possible new perceptual relationships. It creates other worlds not determined by present conditions or fixed, formal, ethical laws. And, as the merchants say, imagination makes these alternate worlds and inner experiences available through words and thus produces common, material forms through which persons might relate to each other. As the continual reorganization of relationships, imagination is a dynamic, ever changing process that hovers between cognition and perception. Faced with the failures of reason to objectively ground itself or morals, Novalis turns to aesthetics to mediate this failure and to imagination in particular to carry out a dynamic ethics, an ethics whose normative claims emerge reflectively in time and are always open to revision and reformulation.

For Novalis, norms, or common criteria, are regulative ideas in the Kantian sense—as products of a reflective judgment, they make no claims about what really is; instead, they function with an "as if"[68]—but by tying them to the imagination and thus intimating their proximity to fiction, Novalis ensures that every normative claim reflects on its own groundlessness. In contrast to Kant, for whom norms are products of reason and thus timeless and pure of the exigencies of history and experience, Novalis ties norms to the imagination, which operates within time. It produces norms that are not immutable but are open to constant revision. The difference is between a norm born of finitude and a norm born of reason's spontaneity. For Novalis, the significance of norms rests not in their epistemological but in their ethical value—that is, they are practically necessary. Speaking of norms as regulative ideas in his *Fichte-Studien*,

Novalis writes: "Every regulative idea is of unending use—but it contains no independent relationship to something real . . . for it is completely outside the sphere of the real. It is a law of the imagination—a schematic concept."[69]

Hymnen an die Nacht performs this dynamic normativity with respect to the unity of the senses. Instead of arguing for the epistemological truth of an absolute sense, the poem imagines an alternate organization of perception that functions as a critique of modernity. The poem, however, makes a strong claim for the particularity of lyric in performing this imagined, dynamic normativity. As Hegel writes, lyric is the poetic form whose task is "to free the spirit not from feeling but through it."[70] The lyric formalizes the reflective character of feeling, because, as Thomas Pfau writes, it "gives words and language to this enriched inner life so that as inner life it may find expression." The formal elements of lyric embody feeling in a "language that always reflects on its own medial character as language."[71] Novalis's lyric is not merely expressive—understood as putting into linguistic form a prior psychological state—rather it registers the inevitability of feelings' imbrication with reflection and language. The complexity and highly stylized character of the poem demand our attention. The poem demands reflection on the figurations of feeling, thus a reader is called to perform attention or the mixing of sensation and language in feeling upon reading. The normativity of the entire project is performed in the lyrical utterance, which gives linguistic and thus common, normative form to feeling. With a normative force, the lyric compels or incites its reader to attend to its formalization of feeling and sensibility and thus to experience a different type of ethical personhood: a normative ethics but normative in the sense of being dynamic and revisable. By compelling its reader to pay attention and read with the poem, the lyric creates precisely this dynamic relationship of revision. The reader can participate in the revision of the poem's claims about modernity's organization of the senses. The poem does not spell out the types of organs, senses, or forms of perception that will be possible in the future; instead, it encourages the reader to imagine them. Novalis's lyric performs a normativity marked by universal claims and an openness to future possibilities. Novalis's turn to language as the privileged medium of such a dynamic normativity—that is, as the medium wherein normative claims interact with contingencies in time—echoes Schleiermacher's appeal to aesthetics and *Poesie* and anticipates Wilhelm von Humboldt's appeal to an anthropology of language.

7

The Body of Language

Goethe, Humboldt, and the "Lively Gaze"

Bodies and Vision: Humboldt and Goethe in Jena

While most students in Jena had been captivated by Fichte's public lectures and Wissenschaftslehre, Wilhelm von Humboldt, along with his brother Alexander, as well as Goethe, had been drawn to something else—Justus Christian Loder's anatomy lectures.[1] In a letter to F. A. Wolf on December 22, 1794, Wilhelm von Humboldt writes that these lectures took up his "entire morning from nine o'clock on. As much trouble as these hours cause me, so much the more does the study interest me. And for the path that I had chosen, it was indispensable."[2] Wilhelm, writes his brother Alexander, "lives and practices anatomy with a cannibalistic fury." He "lives and spins in cadavers" and even "bought himself a whole beggar and . . . devours human brains."[3]

Wilhelm von Humboldt's voracious study of beggars' bodies in the labs and lecture halls of Justus Loder coincide, both historically and conceptually, with his work on two fragments between 1795 and 1797: "Plan einer vergleichenden Anthropologie" (Plan for a Comparative Anthropology) and "Das achtzehnte Jahrhundert" (The Eighteenth Century).[4] The first addresses the possibility that anthropology might unify what Humboldt terms the philosophical and the empirical. For Humboldt, a comparative anthropology would treat the empirical "speculatively [and] historical objects philosophically."[5] Acknowledging the plurality of anthropologies that had emerged by 1800, Humboldt terms his a "comparative" anthropology, not pragmatic and not medical. But why were his anatomical studies "indispensable" for the path that Humboldt had chosen, an intellectual path that included substantial plans for the study of anthropology? His essay written in 1795 begins with an analogy that offers a clue: "Like comparative anatomy, where one explains the structure of the human body through the study of animals, so too in a comparative anthropology can the particularities of moral character of the different human species be set beside each other and comparatively judged."[6]

Equating his comparative anthropology with a comparative anatomy, Humboldt appeals to a form of knowledge bound up with a certain form of observation. He also connects his anthropology, however tangentially, to the material or physiological character of eighteenth-century proto-anthropology. Whereas Kant's pragmatic anthropology had threatened to elide this connection, Humboldt reformulates it for his own purposes. But how did the study of death, in the form of anatomy, become a model for the study of life? Moreover, what types of observing and knowing underlie Humboldt's plan for a comparative anthropology, a proto-anthropology that would compare not only the diversity of humankind but the particularities of individual human beings to a normative notion of the human?

The goal of this chapter is not only to highlight the relationship of Humboldt's early work to eighteenth-century proto-anthropology (especially its later normative-cultural turn) but to continue the attempt to outline various alternatives to Kant's pragmatic anthropology. Humboldt's plan for what he terms a comparative anthropology cultivates a different form of observing the human. Humboldt's plan also picks up on Novalis's turn to language. This chapter considers the relationship between Humboldt's philosophy of language and his proto-anthropology. Instead of focusing on Humboldt's later, more canonical writings on language of the 1820s and 1830s—like his *Kawi Language on the Island of Java* (*Kawi-Werk*) or *Über das vergleichende Sprachstudium in Beziehung auf die verschiedenen Epochen der Sprachentwicklung* (*On the Diversity of Human Language Structure and Its Influence on the Mental Development of Humankind*)—the discussion will focus on his two early essays on anthropology and the travelogue of his trip to the Basque country around 1800. These early texts laid the groundwork for his more widely recognized work on comparative linguistics.

Before turning full attention to Humboldt, however, one needs to consider the efforts of Humboldt's lab partner in Jena, Goethe, to imagine a new scientific method and, more precisely, a new form of observation that might adequately account for the dynamism of nature. Whereas Goethe's work in the natural sciences does not explicitly address the proto-anthropology of his day, it takes up the fundamental problems of anthropological inquiry previously discussed and imagines a form of observation that unifies the transcendental and empirical.⁷ It becomes evident that Humboldt's cultural proto-anthropology transposes the formal elements of Goethe's comparative anatomy onto a comparative study of the human being.

Goethe's Comparative Anatomy

In the fall of 1784 Friedrich Jacobi visited Goethe in Weimar and later sent him a copy of his *Über die Lehre des Spinoza in Briefen an den Herrn Moses Mendelssohn* (*On the Teachings of Spinoza in Letters to Moses Mendelssohn*), which Goethe read and supplemented with a reading of Spinoza's *Ethics*. In a letter Goethe calls Jacobi's book a "polemic" and bemoans its "aversion to the literary," but he goes on to address Jacobi's criticism of Spinoza and subsequent call to faith:

> When you say one can only believe in God, I say to you that I think a lot of seeing itself, and when Spinoza speaks of a *Scientia intuitive*, and says: this kind of knowledge proceeds from an adequate idea of the formal essence of some of the attributes of God to an adequate knowledge of the essence of things [*Hoc cognoscendi genus procedit ab adaequata idea essentia formalis quorundam Dei attributorum ad adaequatam cognitionem essentiae rerum*]. These few words encourage me to devote my entire life to the observation of things that I can reach and from whose *essentia formali* I can hope to form an adequate idea, without worrying how far I will come or what is fitting for me.⁸

Goethe devotes his work on natural science to "observing things" and outlines a mode of observation that would be adequate to the dynamism of natural things. The following section briefly considers what this "observation of things" might have meant for Goethe and thus for Humboldt's anthropology. How are these endeavors, as Humboldt suggests, analogous?

In his "Erster Entwurf einer allgemeinen Einleitung in die vergleichenden Anatomie, ausgehend von der Osteologie" ("First Attempt for a General Introduction to Comparative Anatomy," 1795), Goethe recalls how the time spent with the Humboldt brothers studying cadavers prompted him to organize his thoughts about anatomical study.[9] Goethe writes that while anatomy and natural history are based on comparison, these comparisons are in turn based on individual observations. Traditional methods of anatomical observation rely on "outer signs," which, although meaningful, are insufficient.[10] They never lead to "something whole," because they are simply isolated instances of observation. By relying only on these "outer signs"—discrete visual data—no observer can discern how what now appears as a distinct part develops in relationship with other parts. Such isolated instances of vision can never "reconstitute" the organic bodies that the comparative efforts of anatomical dissection have sundered.

For Goethe, this form of vision undergirds an empirical method, in which the observations of various observers are often times in conflict. Different observers see different things. The anatomical similarities of animals, for example, are difficult to observe and are thus often "mistakenly recognized."[11] The claims that then arise out of these isolated observations are difficult to unify, because there is no "norm against which different parts could be tested." Goethe refers to this confused scientific method as "merely empirical." Without a norm to orient scientific practice, scientific observers can never discern the constant transformations of nature.

Goethe's critique of this "merely empirical" mode of observation is motivated, in part, by a practical concern. The scientist who operates according to such a "merely" empirical method has "no boundaries." An infinite number of individual observations are possible. Such a method can lead the scientist to exhaust himself in data gathering and analysis (228). Goethe insists that in order for observations to be valuable, scientists must be able to reintegrate what they have sundered. Observation requires a perception of both the singular and the whole; it requires that "point of unification," for without it observations remain singular and isolated just "as they were made" (227).

The desire to put things back together again, however, is just as troublesome. It can lead to speculation and a reliance on final causes. It is in this sense that modern science has limited itself to two "ways of conceiving of things." "Either one takes the thing too trivially and clings to the mere appearance, or one tries to find help through final causes, through which one always distances oneself from the idea of a living being. . . .

One loses oneself in empty speculation" (228). For Goethe, modern science had become stuck between a crude empiricism and a speculative metaphysics. If individual scientists simply observe, they run the risk of getting stuck on individual, isolated appearances, or singular data points. If, however, individual scientists try to free themselves from this visual localism, they risk subordinating the particular to a speculative final cause. The problem with this more speculative method lies not so much in final causes themselves but in the fact that the search for them tends to lead the scientific observer away from the object at hand, away from the living being. The irony of modern science, however, as Goethe points out, is that this is ultimately true for a "mere empiricism" as well, for it vivisects what was a living being into an aggregate of singularities. Both mere empiricism and metaphysical speculation cleave the observer and the living thing.

Goethe makes clear, though, that this methodological split characterizes not just modern anatomy. The problem of anatomical observation is the problem of "scientific" observation as such. In anatomy "as in other sciences," a mediating point is needed between mere empiricism and speculation. Goethe's discussion of anatomical observation is an implicit critique of a Baconian scientific tradition that at its base not only assumes but cultivates as a methodological necessity the strict division between object and subject.

In an essay published in 1792, "Der Versuch als Vermittler von Objekt und Subjekt" ("The Experiment as Mediator Between Object and Subject"), Goethe had already addressed these issues of scientific method. There he argued that the proper resolution to the failures of both mere empiricism and speculation about final ends required a complete rethinking and reaffirmation of experimentation. As the title suggests, the experiment should be the mediator between object and subject. Such a mediating role is opposed to a modern, Baconian science that, in Goethe's criticism, is the locus of a division between the scientific observer and nature. For modern science the experiment only engages its own artificial mechanisms. The modern experiment is isolated from nature itself. Experiments universalize one particular way of conducting an experiment. They produce their own objects of inquiry. In this sense, they are fundamentally artificial. They take their technically produced phenomena, not nature, as *physis*, as their objects of study.[12]

Goethe's appeal to nature as *physis* is not a call for naïve empiricism. For Goethe, all human experience is in some sense mediated. He is suggesting that objects of observation ontologically precede the act of observation. The human being already stands in relation to objects (not just opposed to as in *gegen-stand*) and thus nature itself. The title of the essay gives priority to the object before the subject, and the series of transitive verbs that follow throughout the essay reinforce nature's active character: natural objects "attract or repel," "please or displease," and "make use of or harm." Goethe is not suggesting that science forgo the experiment; instead, he is arguing for a reinvigorated commitment to experimentation that would take nature itself and not simply science's own artificial mechanisms as its object of observation.

Such a rethinking of experimentation would involve first of all the recursive observation of nature:

> The value of an experiment lies primarily in the fact that it, be it simple or compound, can be reproduced at all times under certain circumstances with a familiar apparatus and the requisite skill. . . . As valuable as each individual experiment might be when considered individually, it attains its value when combined or united with others. However, to unite and connect two experiments that have some similarity with each other requires more rigor and attention than even the sharpest observer usually demands of himself. Two phenomena may be related with each other but not nearly so closely as we think. . . . Thus one can never be too careful not to draw hasty conclusions, in order to prove something immediately or confirm some theory through an experiment.[13]

The repeated observation of and experimentation with nature, insists Goethe, should be the basis for the transition from empirical evidence to judgment.

In subsequent decades Goethe pursued these questions about observation in the context of his botanical studies and the continued refinement of a science that he termed morphology. Following the publication of his *Versuch die Metamorphose der Pflanzen zu erklären* (*Essay to Explain the Metamorphosis of Plants*) in 1790, Goethe eventually abandoned an attempt to publish his morphological writings in 1806–07. But in 1817 he began to gather all of these writings in a collection as *Zur Morphologie,* which he continued to revise and edit for years to come.[14] In two of the essays in this collection, "Bildungstrieb" ("Formative Impulse") and "Bedenken und Ergebung" ("Doubt and Resignation"), Goethe frames his search for a "unifying point" between empiricism and speculation—or the "difficulty in uniting idea and experience"[15]—in terms of eighteenth-century debates about preformationism, epigenesis, and the concept of the organism, all of which he ties to the demise of a traditional natural history.[16] The following section frames Goethe's reflections on scientific observation in the terms of these debates, for these historical debates about the concepts of life and generation, just like the debates of proto-anthropology, ultimately concerned questions of observation.

Goethe's Comparative Approach and Kant's Teleology

One of the central figures in these debates and in the development of Goethe's own work in natural science was the Göttingen physiologist Johann Blumenbach.[17] Until his own theoretical breakthrough in 1781, Blumenbach had defended Albrecht von Haller's version of preformationism, which argued that the generation of living beings is a gradual development of structures already in the egg. The preformationist model of Haller and the young Blumenbach implied that all offspring "ought to go on forever like their first parents."[18] It could not, however, account for the variety of species without appealing to theories of racial degeneration. In the case of humans, this was often taken to imply that various races are degenerate forms of a Caucasian race. While not rejecting or excluding mechanist or more vitalist explanations, Blumenbach argued that living bodies were organized by a *Bildungstrieb,* a formative drive that generates and adapts: "In all living creatures . . . there is a particular, innate lifelong active effective force [*Trieb*] that at first confers a certain form, then preserves it, and if it is destroyed, when possible, restores it."[19] Blumenbach's theory located purposive causality within the organism itself, whereas Haller's preformationism withheld purposiveness from nature by imputing generation to preformed genes, which were thought to have been implanted by an external source, presumably a divine creator. Blumenbach radically distinguished the living organism and its self-generating and adaptive ability from the artificial machine and its slavish dependence on an external source.

One of the most influential receptions of Blumenbach's work was Kant's conception of the organism, which he lays out in the second section of the *Kritik der Urteilskraft*—the "Critique of the Power of Teleological Judgment."[20] Here, Kant considers the possibility of an objective, material causality, a causality that would undo the distinction not only between the two realms of causality but between the different forms of scientific observation. Considering the possibility of such a natural purpose, Kant asks if an object in nature could have the "causality of its origin not in the mechanism of nature" but in a cause whose possibility lies in concepts. The idea of such a natural purpose assumes a fundamental distinction between a causality grounded in the determinacy of natural laws, which implies an infinite series of causes in time, and a causality grounded in presupposed concepts of reason. According to the idea of such a natural purposiveness, the various parts of a natural product, according to Kant, are only possible through their relationship to the whole. This means that no part can exist independent of the other parts and ultimately of the whole itself.

Distinguishing a natural product from an artificial product, Kant refers to the former as an "organized being" and the latter as a "mere machine."[21] For Kant, the paradigmatic organized being is a tree, which produces itself out of itself according to its own species. It produces itself as an individual tree through "growth" and the interaction of its constituent parts. Kant contrasts the tree with a clock as the paradigmatic machine. No part of a clock is the "cause of the production" of any other. The gears of a clock are present because of the other gears but not through the other gears; one gear does not bring about another gear, just as one clock does not bring about another clock. A clock relies on an outside entity for its movement, whereas a tree brings about its own movement. (A tree does incorporate outside material into itself, but only after making such outside material its own product by reworking the material within itself.) Describing the difference between a machine and an organism, Kant writes, "An organized being is not merely a machine: for it [a machine] has merely moving force. [An organized being in contrast] possesses within itself a productive force, and such a one, that it shares with other matter, which does not have it (it organizes); thus it has a reproductive, productive force, which cannot be explained through the capacity of movement (the mechanism) alone" (374 [Guyer and Matthews, 246; trans. modified]).

Organisms, then, are the only natural objects that are in and of themselves "purposive." The organism organizes material, thereby imbuing it with a constitutive power that machines lack. Machines acquire "productive force" (*bildende Kraft*) from outside themselves. This necessity points to the boundaries inherent in a natural product, for to distinguish a whole from the mechanism of nature as such requires boundaries and demarcations of inside (the *Naturprodukt*) and outside (nature).

Kant insists that such a natural purpose, however, "is only possible through reason" (370). To be a natural cause, an object must be its own cause and effect. Such a unity of cause and effect, the idea of such a whole, insists Kant, is possible only as an idea and thus only as a "ground of knowledge" (373). This is the point at which Kant elaborates on a distinction that he had only intimated in his discussions of race and purposiveness (see chapter 4). Such a natural purposiveness is a regulative, not a constitutive or determinative principle—that is, it is merely a heuristic that guides or suggests what we ought to look for in nature. It suggests that we look at natural objects *as if* they were organized according to such a purposiveness. Kant writes that "the organization of nature has nothing analogical with any causality that we know" (375). All we can say about the organism is that it is an "analogue of life." Kant draws an analogy between life and the organism on the one hand and between determination and the machine on the other. He associates the organism with self-perpetuating life and the machine with death.

Goethe, who was always influenced by Blumenbach, echoes Kant's claim that the organism is a unified, self-organizing being, but also stresses its internal diversity:

> When we become aware of natural objects, but especially living ones, and wish to obtain a view into the relationship of their being and effect, we believe that the best way to such knowledge is through the separation of their parts.... But these efforts at separation, continuously carried on, bring about certain disadvantages. The living thing is cut up into elements, but one cannot put it back together again and resuscitate it out of these elements.... Every living thing is not a particular but a plurality; even as far as it appears to us as an individual, it still remains a collection of living independent beings, which according to the idea, the plan are the same. But in appearance the same or similar could become different and

dissimilar. . . . The more imperfect a creature is, that much more are its parts the same or similar, and that much more do they resemble the whole. The more perfect a creature becomes, that much more do the parts become dissimilar to each other. . . . The more similar the parts are, that much less will they be subordinated to each other. The subordination of the parts points to a perfect creature.[22]

For Goethe, the "organism" was both an epistemological and ontological figure for unity in diversity.[23]

These debates about organic causality revolved around the question of observation. How could the organic development of natural objects be observed? These questions about unity in diversity and the relationship between the universal and particular are the same ones discusses throughout this book in relation to proto-anthropology. The reduplication of anthropological inquiry finds its analogue in these debates about natural causality and the possibility of observing it. What forms of observation could discern such complexity? As already seen above, the "formative drive" (*Bildungstrieb*) is, like the complex organic relationships that it was meant to elucidate, not immediately available to observation. Blumenbach writes, "The term *Bildungstrieb* just like all other life forces such as sensibility and irritability explains nothing itself, rather it is intended to designate a particular force whose constant effect is to be recognized from the phenomena of experience, but whose cause, just like the causes of all other universally recognized natural forces remains for us an occult quality. That does not hinder us in any way whatsoever, however, from attempting to investigate the effects of this force through empirical observations and to bring them under general laws."[24]

The *Bildungstrieb* is merely a concept that names particular effects; it is not an a priori principle that explains creation as such. Because one can only observe its effects and not its cause, the *Bildungstrieb* has an "occult quality." It remains unknowable even if, as Blumenbach suggests, empirical analysis suggests its existence.

Both Goethe and Blumenbach argue that the immediately visible merely indexes more fundamental though less perceptible relationships and complexities. Life itself resides, if anywhere, in the density of the body, in the depths of visually imperceptible relationships. For Goethe, previous attempts to articulate a vital force—like Caspar Friedrich Wolff's theory of epigenesis, which proposed a *vis essentialis* (essential force)—proved untenable. Even if organic material is ascribed a formative drive, as Blumenbach claims, there is always a remainder of matter. There always remains "something material-like that clings."[25] There is always a material excess that is prior to that life force. Such a force can only organize what is prior to it. As Goethe points out, the mechanical connotations of the term "force" belie this; otherwise, it would have to create something out of nothing.

Blumenbach's response to this problem of material excess, writes Goethe, is to "anthropomorphiz[e] the wording of the puzzle and name the object of discussion a *nisus formativus*, an impulse or a surge of action, which was to have caused the formation" (451). Blumenbach elides the entire problem by calling the secret of life a drive, an impulse that motivates the formation of organized beings. Blumenbach's solution to the problem of life, and more important for the present purposes, the observation of life, is to project a human faculty, desire as *Trieb,* onto nature. One looks into nature and finds only the self: the dynamism of nature, its *Bildungstrieb*, writes Goethe, is an "enormity" that "confronts" us like a "God" that we are obliged to worship, honor and praise (452). In this ironic rereading of Blumenbach's scientific hypothesis, Goethe undoes the distinction between natural and scientific creation. A posited theory of epigenesis is pushed into nature itself and thus demands appropriate recognition for its own creative powers. Goethe insists, however, that these scientific terms merely "stall us." Ultimately, the unity and freedom of the *Bildungstrieb* cannot be grasped without a concept of metamorphosis—that is, life itself cannot be observed and accounted for without an account of how life itself changes and transforms. But how can metamorphosis be observed or thought?

In his retrospective account of his philosophical studies "Einwirkung der neueren Philosphie" ("The Influence of Modern Philosophy"), Goethe writes that his reading of Kant was an "analogue of the Kantian way of thinking but a peculiar one" (445). Whereas Goethe was a peculiar, profoundly ironic reader of Kant, he also found a great deal to praise in *Kritik der Urteilskraft*. He claims that Kant's book put his own "disparate activities with both artistic and natural objects" right beside each other and "treated them as one; aesthetic and teleological powers of judgment enlighten each other." Goethe admired how Kant pushed aesthetics and scientific inquiry closer and closer until they were actually "related" under one faculty of judgment. In the *Kritik der Urteilskraft*, the "inner life of art and of nature" were no longer seen as "two infinitely separate worlds" but existed "for each other but not purposively for each other" (444). For Goethe, Kant had pointed to, if not explicitly outlined, the intimate relationship of art and science as grounded in the unity of nature.

The difference between Kant's and Goethe's understanding of organicism lies in the latter's underlying concern with how to account for a living thing in its development. According to a Kantian discursive epistemology, such an account was impossible. For Kant, human cognition operates through concepts. Limited to a discursive form of reason, human beings conceive of objects through static, universal concepts. For Goethe, this means that the dynamism of nature is always lost in the necessary abstraction of discursive thought. In his *Kritik der Urteilskraft*, however, Kant identifies two types of judgment: a determining (*bestimmende*) power of judgment and a reflecting (*reflektierende*) power of judgment. A determining judgment operates from a prior given law and subsumes particulars of nature under the universal. It moves from the general to the particular. A reflecting judgment, in contrast, moves from the particular, which is given first, to a universal. A reflecting judgment "gives itself . . . , and not nature, a law," according to which the particulars of nature can be subsumed.[26] A determining judgment is constitutive, in that it makes a necessary judgment about nature. A reflecting judgment is regulative, thus we must always think of reflecting judgments "according to an analogy." For Kant, the organism is only an analogue of life because it is only a regulative judgment with no claim on the ontological reality of life.

Claiming only to make "use" of Kant's theory of natural causality in the *Kritik der Urteilskraft*, Goethe, in his short essay "Anschauende Urteilskraft" ("Judgment Through Intuitive Perception"), says that he could not help but notice that Kant, "that entertaining man, proceeds in a cunningly ironic manner." Whereas Kant seems intent to limit dramatically the faculty of judgment, he suddenly, "with a knowing nod to the side, points beyond those limits that he had [just] drawn."[27] Reflecting on how Kant goes about arguing for the limits of judgment, Goethe pushes the entire Kantian way of thinking to its limits. For Goethe, when Kant introduces a reflecting power of judgment, Kant limits the human being to regulative principles about nature—such as the regulative principle of nature's systematicity. Kant claims to limit the human being's ability to know. Such regulative principles circumscribe human knowledge.

Kant does this no doubt, says Goethe, because he had observed how the human being so "arrogantly proceeds" on the basis of only one or two facts to make "hurried" and "thoughtless" claims.

And yet, as soon as Kant limits the power of judgment, he transgresses the limits that he just set. For Goethe, Kant's intimation of an *intellectus archetypus*—in the *Kritik der Urteilskraft*—points to a "divine understanding" that, in contrast to our discursive understanding, needs no images to cognize an object. If we are able to lift ourselves into the "upper region" through a belief in "God, virtue, and eternal life," surely, writes Goethe, we can do the same in the intellectual arena (448). If we can accomplish so much in the moral realm—think here of the Kantian teleology of the human species and the ends of reason—might we not be able, through the "intuition" (*Anschauung*) of a constantly creative nature, to become part of this natural process as well? With this nondiscursive form of knowledge we would be able to move from the whole to the parts without the use of concepts, or mediating images. It would grasp the particular in its own lawfulness without subordinating it to determinate judgment. This form of judgment, this intuitive judgment, would be adequate to nature; it would be a "presentation appropriate to nature."

A human "understanding cannot unite through thought what sensibility delivers to him disconnected" (449–50). Both "mere empiricism" and discursive thought are inadequate to the dynamism of nature. For Goethe, Kant's attempt to solve this dilemma by anchoring perception in a subject of reason that subordinates nature to a regulating judgment only cements the gap. Goethe resists, especially later in 1798–98, when armed with Schelling's philosophical insights, Kant's reflecting power of judgment.[28] Although he does not deny the necessity of a subject-oriented mode of perception, he suggests that a different, nondiscursive form of observation might be possible.

Goethe does not deny that the subject-centered mode of thought is necessary for scientific observation. Still, he insists that it be subordinated to a patient pragmatism—that is, scientific observers must submit themselves to the deliberate and repeated observation of nature as he outlined in "Der Versuch als Vermittler von Objekt und Subjekt." Such a mode of observation requires that "my thinking not separate itself from the objects, that the elements of the object, the perceptions of the object, flow into my thinking and are fully permeated by it; my perception itself becomes a thinking, my thinking becomes a perception."[29] Such a mode of observation acknowledges that the very act of observation is always already bound up with the natural objects. And this recognition entails an imperative to make our concepts as dynamic as nature itself. Nature as a unity is given or rather gives itself to us; therefore, our own thinking must become adequate to nature.[30] Our own modes of observation and cognition must become as dynamic as nature itself.

Goethe's "comparative method" addresses precisely this imperative for dynamic concepts.[31] "Two needs arise in us," claims Goethe, "when we observe nature." First, we must attain complete knowledge of the phenomena, and second we must "make them our own through reflection [*Nachdenken*]." "If we can survey an object in all of its parts, grasp it correctly and bring it forth in our mind, then we may say that we have perceived it in an actual and higher sense. And thus the particular always leads to the universal and the universal always to the particular."[32] The first step in this comparative method involves repeated observation of the empirical phenomena, and as I have noted, exhaustive observation involves recursive experimentation. A complete observation is only possible through the repetition of individual observations. In his essay on the experiment, Goethe speaks of a "higher order" empirical evidence born of a "series of contiguous experiments." Second, this higher form of empirical evidence would be made our own through reflection. Goethe's notion of a *Typus* carries out this reflective work. Unlike a Platonic form or Kantian idea, both of which are free of all empirical input, a *Typus* is grounded in physical objects but no one particular object: "No particular can be the model of the whole."[33] The *Typus* is not a taxonomic category but an image (*Bild*) that emerges and reemerges from the interaction of experience and ideas: "Experience must first teach us the parts, which all animals share, and how these parts differ. The idea must preside over the whole and in a genetic fashion draw out the universal *Bild.*" The *Typus* is an image that assumes the formative power of nature. We must reflect on the formative powers of nature and how they develop the individual parts of an organism. Observers must think the developmental processes that remain imperceptible to the eye. And they can only do that by reflecting on their own processes of observation. They must observe their own processes of reflective thinking.[34] In an ironic gesture to Kant's teleological judgment, Goethe calls it an "intuitive power of judgment" (*anschauende Urteilskraft*) through which the observer perceives particular objects in the world not as they are fixed at one moment in time but as they become and transform in time. The *Typus* is in constant flux. Unlike a purely intellectual category or a teleological judgment that is the product of thought, both of which remain fixed, the *Typus* is always becoming in the oscillation between experience and idea. The observer's "comparisons are always happening" and the *Typus* itself must always be "tested."

The *Typus* emerges in the oscillation between the particularity of experience and the universality of understanding. Summarizing the oscillation between the two modes as it occurs in the organic realm, Goethe writes, "If we observe all forms, especially the organic, we find nowhere something that is, nowhere something that rests, nowhere something that is closed in unto itself, but rather that everything fluctuates in a constant movement. Thus, our language is careful to use the word *Bildung* for that which is produced and for that which produces."[35] Observation necessarily relates to a subject and an object. Goethe's critique of Blumenbach and Kant's anthropomorphic projections does not suggest that scientific observation can do without such projections. More fundamentally, it is of a piece with Goethe's critique of a Baconian scientific tradition that ultimately severs the human being from the natural objects that it observes. Goethe's notion of a recursive observation that continually revises its given norms in hand leads to Humboldt's own proto-anthropology. Whereas Goethe uses his morphological observation to account for the development of plants, Humboldt adopts it in order to account for the development of human beings. Humboldt transforms Goethe's *Naturwissenschaft* into a form of *Kulturwissenschaft*.

Humboldt's Comparative Anthropology

In his essays on proto-anthropology and in his own travelogues, Humboldt transposes Goethe's morphology of plants onto human beings and ultimately onto culture. He writes that his proto-anthropology would observe the human being as though it were a "giant plant."[36] Whereas Goethe's morphology would measure the diversity of the plant realm, Humboldt's proto-anthropology would "measure the possible diversity of human nature in its ideal form."[37] Whereas Goethe's morphology would observe how the archetypal plant is manifest in particular plants, Humboldt's proto-anthropology would "investigate how the human ideal, to which an individual can never be adequate, can be represented through many [human beings]." Echoing Goethe's argument that a morphology of plants would alternate between particular observations and a more normative "point of unification," Humboldt argues that the science of the human being would hover between a universal idea and a particular through a "strict observation of reality" *and* a critical reason that posits the idea of the human being. Humboldt describes this idea as "nothing more" than nature that has been "expanded in all directions and freed from all hindrances" (351).

Humboldt's "human" operates like Goethe's archetypal plant. It is a critical idea that is subject to the constant revision and testing of empirical observations. Both Goethe's morphology and Humboldt's proto-anthropology are grounded on a form of normativity that is distinct from Kant's. For both, normative claims can be both universally compelling and open to revision. While the reduplication of the observer as the subject and object of inquiry was considered a threat to anthropological inquiry for Kant and the source of much contention for a broader proto-anthropology, Humboldt, like Goethe in his articulation of morphology, embraces it unapologetically. "That which observes and that which is observed here [in anthropological inquiry] is the human"; therefore, they will always refer back to the same being. Each side of the inquiry—the subjective and objective—can check and thus "advance" each other (347). Humboldt always assumes the functional—if not metaphysical—unity of the human as both subject and object of observation. There is no outside, no detached perspective from which to carry out the science of the human. Anthropology is the first science to recognize this fact. And Humboldt, following Goethe's lead, is the first to embrace it.

It is from this radically anthropological perspective that Humboldt's comparative proto-anthropology attempts to organize the "particularities" of human beings (337). For Humboldt, these "particularities" consist of various human "predispositions and abilities," which are organized differently in different human beings and different peoples (415). Humboldt terms these different forms of organization, the different ways in which predispositions and abilities are organized in different human beings, moral character. A comparative anthropology would be a second-order operation, for it would account for the organization of moral character, which is itself an organization of predispositions and abilities. Echoing Kant's pragmatic anthropology, it would account for differences in the moral realm, that is to say, not simply what predispositions and abilities are given by nature but how these are subsequently reworked and organized by human reason. What an organism, with its complex and barely discernable causality, is in the physical world, character is in the moral world. The causality of moral character—that is, reason's ability to effect change in the given or natural character of the human being—is the analogue of organic causality.

In Humboldt's transposition of the comparative method from morphology to anthropology, Goethe's plants become Humboldt's humans. Just as nature is characterized by a plurality of organisms and arrangements of its powers, so too is the human species characterized by different human beings and their particularity. Like Kant, Humboldt argues that the powers, predispositions, and abilities of the human being have been dispersed throughout the world among various peoples and cultures. As previously demonstrated, Kant tends to conflate the worth of the individual with the autonomy of reason, as the guarantee of the teleological progress of the human species. The value of the individual is a function of the historical possibility of freedom. For Humboldt, in contrast, the organization of powers of the human species is grounded in the "particularity of the individual," which we can "never hope to reveal" (478). For Humboldt, the individual human being is distinguished by an "inner self-sufficiency" that cannot be subordinated to vague notions of historical progress.

Does Humboldt's philosophy of history, then, simply restate Herder's criticisms of Kant's philosophy of history, criticisms that were concerned with the possibility of the individual being subordinated to abstract concepts? In his "Betrachtungen über die Weltgeschichte," for example, Humboldt argues that the teleological "perfection" of the human species, as laid out in Kant's philosophy of history is an abstraction. For Humboldt, such a "perfection" is only possible through the development of the diversity of individual forms. The "mistake" of Kant's cosmopolitan history is that it reduces human "races" to rational beings and neglects the fact that they are also "products of nature" (576). As a natural being, the human being is subject to the "power of the universe," and these powers are not necessarily compatible with the "ends of human destinies" (575). The ends of nature cannot, as Kant had hoped, be so easily melded with the ends of reason.

In the face of this detranscendentalized Kantian anthropology, Humboldt looks for an alternative mode of anthropological inquiry and finds a model in Goethe's critique of modern science, especially his critique of "mere empiricism." Humboldt envisions a comparative anthropology with both an empirical and a critical-normative dimension. Such an anthropological mode of thought would operate at the conjunction of the philosophical and empirical. "In order to know the human being with precision, what the human being is and to judge with freedom, toward what purpose he can develop himself, the practical sense of observation and the philosophical spirit must work together" (338). According to Humboldt, a radically anthropological mode of thought—one that embraced the possibilities of reduplication—could unify the divisions of proto-anthropology. It would unify empirical and philosophical modes of inquiry.

In order to recognize "what the human being is," anthropology would have to adopt natural scientific methods of observation. Just as the natural scientist "strives to determine the races and varieties of the animal world," so would the comparative anthropologist strive to discover the "constant characters of sexes, age, temperaments and nations" (352). In order to ascertain the diversity of humankind, the anthropologist would have to make use of empirical methods of research. A comparative proto-anthropology would require "a strict observation of reality." Humboldt writes, "Through physical means, through procreation and descent, the once acquired moral nature is carried forth and propagated. And through this, intellectual and moral progress, which otherwise would perhaps be temporary and transitory, participates to a certain degree in the stability and permanence of nature. The physical condition of the human being plays, in every respect, an important role in the *Bildung* of his character" (352).

The moral and intellectual development of the individual human being is transmitted physically. Any account of the historical development of the human being, then, would have to treat the human being in its relationship to the physical world. Anthropology is part natural science.

The empirical study of the human being according to natural scientific methods, however, can lead the anthropologist to assume that a particular characteristic is more "lasting" than it actually is (352). Natural scientific methods can lead to a "fatal" overdetermination of "the development of human nature," for the "nobility" of the human being rests on its "free individuality" (353). The dignity of the human being lies in the possibility that unlike other natural beings it is not determined by nature. In order for anthropology to recognize not only what human beings are, but also what they might become, it must be checked by a more normative form of inquiry, by an idea of what the human should become.

For Humboldt, *Bildung* signifies this melding of different forms of causality and different modes of inquiry. As a process *Bildung* unifies the formative powers of nature with those of reason. Often translated into English as "self-formation," "cultivation," or even "education," *Bildung* begins to acquire its modern meaning in mid- to late eighteenth-century Germany. Originally, *Bildung* was associated with an early modern iconographic tradition. Etymologically, *Bildung* is related to the German *Bild* (image) or the verb *bilden* (to form). In these iconographic traditions and well into the eighteenth century, *Bild* and *bilden* denoted production or formation through and in terms of examples. *Bildung* implied a mimetic formation. Throughout the eighteenth century, however, *Bildung* comes to mark not just the development or formation of an outer figure but the formation of an inner character or intellectual self. *Bildung* gradually becomes the privileged other of *Erziehung* (vocational or more practical education). The conceptual extrication of *Bildung* from *Erziehung* becomes possible when *Bildung* comes to signify an epigenetic process. In the second half of the eighteenth century, natural scientists such as Albrecht von Haller, Johann Caspar Lavater, and J. F. Blumenbach used *Bildung* to describe development in human embryos. Blumenbach argued that living bodies were organized by a *Bildungstrieb* (formative drive) that generates and adapts: "In all living creatures . . . there is a particular, innate lifelong active effective drive, that at first confers a certain form, then preserves it, and if it is destroyed, when possible, restores it."[38] Blumenbach's theory took advantage of and even radicalized the semantic expansion of *Bildung*. *Bildung* had come to mark an epigenetic force—that is, a force that places purposive causality within the organism itself. Blumenbach radically divides the living organism and its self-generating and adaptive ability from the artificial machine and its slavish dependence on an external source. In contrast to the mechanical, more practically oriented goals of *Erziehung*, *Bildung* came to connote an epigenetic, an organic creation of the self through its own efforts. The *Bildung-Erziehung* pair became the conceptual analogue of organism and machine, life and death.

In response to the *Berlinische Monatsschrift's* query "What Is Enlightenment?" Moses Mendelssohn made clear the new semantic force of *Bildung* and its expanding collocations: "The words Enlightenment, culture, and *Bildung* are still new arrivals to our language. They belong to a literary language [*Büchersprache*]. The masses hardly understand them."[39] Mendelssohn proceeded to define *Bildung* as a "modification of our social life; effects of hard work and the efforts of humans to improve their social condition."[40] *Bildung* became the activity of self-production and the imparting of purpose onto an individual life.

Humboldt, the figure most often associated with *Bildung*, however, stresses that *Bildung* as a process of self-organization always involves an engagement with the world beyond the self. For Humboldt, *Bildung* denotes a fundamental relationship between the self and the world: the subject and the world exist in a prior relation. This prior relationship assumes both the original receptivity and the spontaneity of the subject. The subject can only organize itself in and be organized through a world of which it is already a part. Thus for Humboldt, *Bildung* is not a narcissistic inwardness; rather, the very possibility of subjectivity rests, in part, on an outside: "Just as sheer power needs an object on which to exert itself, and sheer form, or pure thought, material in which it can express and maintain itself, so too does man need a world outside himself. From this springs his constant attempt to expand the sphere of his knowledge and his effectiveness."[41] The fundamental energies of an individual require interaction with something other, a not-I in order to take form. *Bildung* then "is the connection of our I with the world in the most general, most lively and freest interaction." In this sense, Humboldt's notion of *Bildung* is mimetic, not in the sense of pure imitation but in the sense of approximating the self to things, people, concepts, or images in the world. The self or a subject is constituted through a mimetic engagement with the plurality of the world.

Herein lies the paradox of *Bildung* that is so often forgotten. *Bildung* always puts the self at risk. It risks exposure to that which it is not, the world, an outside beyond its own rational efforts. It risks "alienation," in which it may lose itself in the world.[42] Self-organization as self-formation is a recursive process in which the self constantly engages that which it is not. For Humboldt, this exchange, this relational flow is not determined by a teleology of development—that is, *Bildung*'s only organizing principle is an engagement with the plurality of the world, an engagement that has no end. This is also the principle that underlies his comparative proto-anthropology.

For Humboldt, the problems of anthropological observation were also related to the more specific tasks of what one might refer to today as ethnography.[43] Like Kant, Humboldt insisted that the empirical work of observing other peoples—that is, ethnography—be guided by rational principles. For Humboldt, while the ethnographic detail afforded by travelogues is central to a comparative proto-anthropology, it cannot ground such an inquiry. In a letter to Schiller, Humboldt complains that all travelogues are "either concerned only with singular points of view or [are] merely a representation of what some traveler noticed during his stay, out of which always only comes something very one-sided."[44] They do not give us a view of "the whole." As an ethnographic project, proto-anthropology would seek out the "proper standpoint" from which to achieve such a view. In order to check the empirical overdetermination of the human being—the unwarranted conflation of particular observations about human beings with more general claims about the human or entire groups of humans—proto-anthropology must also make use of philosophical judgment. It must constantly compare the diversity of human beings as represented in the diversity of ethnographic accounts to an "ideal of humanity." Humboldt's comparative anthropology is not looking for an object of nature but something "undetermined," which cannot be reduced to a particular being. This undetermined something is better understood as a goal that one approaches.[45] Drawing on the dynamism of Goethe's morphology of plants, Humboldt imbues the category "human" with an empirical-critical force. The idea of the human emerges out of the constant interaction of the normative with the empirical.

Echoing Kant's pragmatic anthropology in certain aspects, Humboldt assumes what he terms "the species character of the human being" (*den Gattungs-Charakter des Menschen*) (340). At times, Kant's pragmatic anthropology subordinated human difference to the teleological unity of the human species. Humboldt, in contrast, is not bound by such a unity. His Goethe-inspired idea is more dynamic than Kant's teleological promise. Humboldt describes how it emerges in the "multiple forms" of individual human beings. This co-belonging of humanity in the form of an emergent idea allows for the critical work of comparative anthropology. Humboldt's use of the species concept functions as a deferred norm toward which an anthropology could work. He writes that the unity of the human being is "something undetermined," and as such the idea of such a unity must always refer back to empirical objects (350). The idea of the human being is a "sum of possibilities" that "reality . . . cannot exhaustively contain" (452). Such an idea inheres in the plurality of individuals and in the multiplicity of the world. It must always be checked against, always point back to the empirical.

Similarly, Humboldt is more open than Kant regarding the future possibilities of the human. Whereas Kant's pragmatic anthropology considers what the human being can and should become, Humboldt argues that anthropology considers what the human being is and could become. Humboldt would investigate the "individual differences" of an idea of the human being in order to "expand the concept of humanity" (355). That is, whereas Kant seems intent on delimiting the idea of the human being, Humboldt wants to expand it. He is concerned that "the freedom of the individual" not be limited by a concept of the species that is "too narrow or fixed."

At the same time, however, Humboldt warns that anthropology should not "fish around for a bunch of differences" (355). Humboldt echoes Herder's critique of Kant's historical abstraction, and he conversely echoes Kant's critique of Herder on this issue. Like Kant, Humboldt argues that anthropology should not emphasize the particular at the expense of the universal. Humboldt frames his proto-anthropology as a bridge between the demands of the particular and the universal. The goal, writes Humboldt, is to "find the causes, judge the worth and predict the development" of these differences among human beings (362). Comparative anthropology requires a new form of observation and a new type of anthropologist, a new observer of the human, one who is neither too empirical nor too speculative. Humboldt's comparative anthropology embraces the paradox of proto-anthropology's reduplication but also its commitment to *life*. The "best school" for the anthropologist "is life," in which the observer is called to weigh "freedom and lawfulness" against each other. He is called to "test" empirical against the speculative. The dual task of such an anthropology makes it "a branch of the philosophical-practical knowledge of the human" (364).

How is one to conceptualize the dynamics of such a future anthropology? How would it balance scientific observation with normative claims, the empirical with the philosophical? Kant's solution was to locate a teleology within nature itself. From the very beginning, Humboldt's anthropology reiterates the fact that the human being is and will remain part of "the chain of nature" (357). Because of the human being's "natural finitude," anthropological "ideals" (concepts such as the human species) must always be related "to empirical objects" (337). Humboldt compares anthropological inquiry to an "oscillation between world and idea," between what is and what ought to be. It would "treat empirical matters speculatively, historical objects philosophically, and the actual condition of the human being from the perspective of its possible development" (352). As a particular mode of inquiry, then, it would have to unify the "different intellectual predispositions" of the natural scientist, the historian, and the philosopher. Similar to the unifying disciplinary aspirations of proto-anthropology, Humboldt's comparative anthropology would be a metadiscipline.

Even within this future, unified anthropology, however, different modes of observation would still be operative. Like the natural scientist, the anthropologist would observe nature according to empirical methods; yet unlike the natural scientist, the anthropologist would assume the human being cannot adequately be accounted for by natural laws.[46] "The complex economy of the human body, its still inexplicable connection with the moral character, and the great difficulty of experimenting with the human being, ensures that those laws are still incomplete and unlikely that they will ever be completely known."[47] Like most other proto-anthropologies, Humboldt's comparative anthropology brackets the mind-body problem. It concerns itself less with the metaphysical conditions of the mind-body relationship and more with the practical consequences of their assumed unity. Recalling Kant's criticisms of Platner's anthropology, Humboldt writes that since we cannot know with certainty the "relationship" of the mind and body, we must concern ourselves with the interplay of our power of choice and nature. We can only observe how reason remakes nature.

Whereas a purely philosophical or speculative approach to the human being would lead to an impoverished notion of the "multiplicity of [human] forms" and the "determination of every individual," a natural-historical or merely empirical approach would lead to a material notion of the human being as not free to become something other (463–64). (In that case, Humboldt is referring to a natural science that reduces nature and the human being to mechanical laws of efficient causality or the comparison of organisms based solely on morphological similarities.) Echoing the aims of early proto-anthropology, Humboldt writes that a natural science grounded in mathematical methods "kill[s] the spirit" of that "philosophical doctor" whose attempt to study the physical morally and the moral physically constitutes the "art of knowledge of the human being."

Humboldt is acutely aware of the difficulties of his attempt to establish anthropology as a metadiscipline of the human being. Anthropological inquiry faces a "dangerous cliff." It is always in danger of treating "the human being as both a natural being but not too much of one" (353). For Humboldt, the human being is not only "part of the chain of nature," but also part of another realm. The human being exists not only within the realm of nature's lawfulness but also within the chaotic (*regellos*) realm of history (359). As a historian, the anthropologist must always be mindful of the fact that history is the "realm of fate and chance" (360). The whole of history cannot be observed as though one were observing a natural organism or a "pure product of the will." The historian, therefore, must proceed from particular appearances in order to observe a "regularity" that is "less strict and more difficult to observe" than that of nature itself (359). Unlike Kant, who increasingly melded the realms of history and nature, Humboldt continues to distinguish them.

The anthropologist must function not only as a natural scientist and historian but also as a philosopher, and for Humboldt this means that the anthropologist must never forget that the human being is a "free and independent being," and thus must be judged according an idea of reason (359). Whereas the historian seeks out the "individual" and the philosopher seeks the "universal," writes Humboldt, the anthropologist tries to maintain a "more middle direction" between the two extremes.[48] The future anthropologist, then, would study the human being from three different perspectives: as a natural scientist in order to study the human being as subordinate to natural laws; as a historian in order to study the human being as subject to the chance and chaos of history; and as a philosopher in order to study the human being as free and rational.

Unlike Kant, Humboldt does not subordinate his anthropology to a teleology of history or speak of a human destiny. He does write, however, of the "character of humanity" in particular epochs (in this essay, on the character of the eighteenth century) but doubts whether the "thread" that Kant hopes for will ever be found or could even be posited as an idea of reason. Not only because of the unpredictability of history but because of the power of choice itself will it be "hard to discover in the history of the human race a determinate order" (382). The particular "conditions" of the human and historical "chance" make a history of the entire human race in the Kantian, teleological sense doubtful. The variety and plurality of human forms and characters are "immeasurable." And yet the "thought" that this plurality and thus "all members of the human race in all times and nations" could be unified in "one great federation," writes Humboldt, is not in itself something impossible or even a "delusion." He insists only that the pursuit of such a "thought" must not subordinate individuals to a historical teleology of the species.

In fact, Humboldt suggests that the idea of a unified, transhistorical humanity be subordinated to the individual human being. The more normative category "human" should function as a "test" and "guide" to which individuals must constantly compare themselves and in terms of which they must 'think" (392). The concept itself, however, remains subordinate to the purposes of the individual as an end in itself: "Every effort toward the advancement of the human race, which does not proceed from the development of the individual, is simply fruitless and a chimera." Such universal categories are meant to help the individual "go about his own small and humble footpath but with firm and better understood steps" (389).

In this oscillation between the individual and the universal, we can observe the productive tension of Humboldt's comparative anthropology. Humboldt combines insights of eighteenth-century natural science, with its emphasis on empirical particularity, with a Kantian commitment to ethical autonomy—the natural with the moral. The empirical has a central place in Humboldt's anthropological inquiry. The ultimate goal of a comparative proto-anthropology is to compare simultaneously the multiplicity and differences of human beings and, recognizing this diversity, relate this matrix of difference to a critical idea of humanity. But what mode of observation can carry out such a project? I argue that Humboldt's early reflections on language and, especially, his studies of particular languages provided him with such a model. Similar appeals to language were evident in Schleiermacher's aesthetics of *Poesie* and Novalis's appeal to lyric. But it is Humboldt who makes the most compelling case for language as the most apposite analogy for anthropological inquiry.

From Philology to Linguistic Anthropology

In "Das achtzehnte Jahrhundert" Humboldt claims that only the poets have ever successfully studied character (434). In the fall of 1799, Humboldt published his *Ästhetische Versuche I. Über "Hermann und Dorothea"* ("Aesthetic Essays I: On *Hermann and Dorothea*") in the Paris journal *Magasin encyclopédique*. The article was intended to introduce his aesthetic ideas to a French audience; however, it was not just a translation or a rehearsal of previous arguments; instead, it is a concise statement of Humboldt's aesthetics and the role of the imagination in cognition.[49] This essay is particularly instructive for highlighting the relationship of aesthetics, especially imagination, with Humboldt's comparative anthropology.

Humboldt writes that because of their "imagination" poets have been more adept at the "art of observing the human being."[50] The observation of the human being requires that "understanding and fantasy" work in unison, since imagination is essential to anthropological inquiry. But why? Echoing Schleiermacher's claims about aesthetics, Humboldt argues that art allows us to observe nature with both our senses and our understanding.[51] Neither Schleiermacher nor Humboldt is suggesting merely that artists provide anthropological insights; instead, both are holding up aesthetics as a model for anthropological inquiry as such. The very form of aesthetic judgment models the type of dynamism—the movement between universal and particular—that underlies an expanded notion of the human being. Recalling Novalis's similar claims, Humboldt suggests that poets afford us alternate perceptual possibilities by creating "completely other organs than those that usually lead our life" (138). "Poetry connects the greatest reality with the most perfect ideal" (157). Unlike Kant, who assumes the disunity of understanding and sensibility and thus has as his task their unification, Humboldt assumes their prior unity. Imagination reveals this prior given unity: "The imagination is only a stronger memory."[52] It reveals the "original unity between world and the human being, upon which the possibility of all knowledge of the truth is based."[53]

The younger Wilhelm von Humboldt attributed much of imagination's potential to a related "aesthetic feeling" or "sense." In a letter to Georg Forster on October 28, 1789, Humboldt writes that the aesthetic sense can serve as "the true mediator between" the "deadly gaze and the immortal archetypal idea."[54] Throughout the early 1790s Humboldt was preoccupied with ancient philology, especially after meeting the famed professor of philology from Halle F. A. Wolf in 1792. Wolf and Humboldt exchanged letters for years on issues of translation and on Humboldt's own attempts to understand what he termed the moral character of the Greeks—the unique organization of their predispositions and abilities. Later in his life Humboldt cited these earlier attempts to understand the character of the Greeks as the precedent for his attempts to account for the character of the French and English in "Das achtzehnte Jahrhundert."[55] The relationship between his study of ancient philology and his study of contemporary cultures crystallizes only after his travels to Spain in 1799.

On September 8, 1799, just after Alexander von Humboldt had left for his famed journey to South America, Wilhelm, his wife, and three children left for Spain, where they traveled through the Pyrenees, then on to Madrid and south to Seville and then west to Malaga and Granada and then on to Barcelona and Valencia. Although Humboldt observed the dress, culture, and physiognomy of the local populations, it was their language that interested him most.[56] Upon his return to Paris in April 1800, Humboldt set down in a letter to Schiller praising his *Wallenstein* what would turn out to be one of the clearest articulations of his theory of language. This letter is key to understanding Humboldt's view of the relationship between language and anthropology, because it marks a turning point in Humboldt's interests and work. In this letter, dated September 1800, Humboldt praises Schiller for the way he "treats language" less as a means for "showing an object" and more as a "product of the human mind."[57] Schiller's literary work demonstrates the "sensible effect" that language, as a work of the human being, has on "thought and sensation." More than a medium for delivering ideas, language itself effects and creates. It "develops out of itself" a complex of "intuitions and sensations."

Humboldt emphasizes two elements of language. First, language is both representative and productive. It both "represents our entire mental activity subjectively" and produces mental objects. It is representative, in so far as it puts forth our subjective mental activity, and productive, in so far as it produces the very objects of this mental activity. It produces "sensible signs" within which our thoughts are unified and embodied (197). Language is the sensible medium in which the elements of our thought are unified in material form. It is the medium through which the human being "forms simultaneously himself and the world, or, what is more, becomes conscious that he separates a world from himself."

Second, language is organic in its form—that is, the form of language is characterized by the interrelationship of all its parts. This organic form "connects every individual part . . . with all others" (196). Humboldt writes that unlike painting which is organized through adjacent and immediate spatial relationships, language is organized temporally like music, in which "the past and the following tones only work together in the present ones." The very form of a language is predicated upon the interrelationship of past moments in the present. An utterance has meaning only if considered through a series of past utterances, but it is always a performance in the present. The present moment of language has meaning only against the backdrop of all previous moments of language. These two elements of language make it especially productive for the study of the human being, because they combine to reveal the human utterance not just in a present moment but in a broader referential context: "Because we gradually and only for ourselves and through our own thought have created language (a case in which everyone for whom words are more than empty sounds finds himself, because every true understanding is a newly coined expression), language returns to us the work of our mind, but only in so many and up to a certain point successful but always only partial attempts" (196)

And the work that language returns to us is a work that is both productive and receptive. Language "connect[s] more world with itself" and "develop[s] itself from within itself" (197).

Humboldt's account of Schiller's poetic language demonstrates not only his earlier conviction that language is an essential element to cognition but that language must be situated in reality. Propositions are not "abstract, objective combinations of words; they are utterances produced by intending subjects."[58] Humboldt had already argued this point in "Über Denken und Sprechen":

> The sensual signification of the unities, to which certain portions of thought are united in order to be opposed as . . . objects to the subject, is called in the broadest sense of the word: language.
>
> Language begins thus immediately and simultaneously with the first act of reflexion. Just as the human being awakes to self-consciousness out of the dullness of desire in which the subject devours

the object, so too is the word there—like the first impulse, which the human being gives itself . . . to look around and orient itself.⁵⁹

The linguistic utterance is an act that joins the speaker's subjectivity to the "world's materiality."⁶⁰ As a mental activity, language actively forms the world through fashioning an object in thought. But language also produces something other that confronts the speaker as a material object. Language, then, is the medium for the mental and material, the philosophical and empirical.⁶¹

Comparative Anthropology and Anthropological Norms

After a winter spent transposing Padre Marvel Larramendi's Spanish-Basque dictionary, Humboldt returned to the Basque country from April 19 to June 14, 1801. He explained his decision to Schiller in a letter:

> It [the Basque country] is at least the only European country that . . . has maintained its original language [*Ursprache*]. The grammar of this language is especially interesting and leads to many interesting observations about the development of languages in general. . . . All of this, however, can be studied and examined at home. Sometimes this seems to be the case for me, but don't you believe what the lively gaze affords? With my view of things I can hardly claim that I actually experience or learn much from traveling, that mere books could not give me. But the light that the actual presence sheds over the object, the mood that it itself gives to the observer, these make an incalculable difference. Not only particular nuances are lost with dead letters but above all the relationship of the individual, the unity of the whole. In order to understand a nation precisely, its authors, its customs, its works, one must, I believe, have been with it for some time.⁶²

Reflecting on Humboldt's pursuit of a mode of observation not limited to texts, Goethe goes on to note that only after his journey to Italy did Italian literature speak to him "through all of his senses." While on his own trip, Humboldt met with scholars on Basque language and culture like Don Pedro Pablo de Astarloa, a Durango priest who was preparing a manuscript on the Basque language (*Apológia de la lengua Bascongada*). His primary concern was with an ethnographic form of inquiry guided by what he termed a "lively gaze."[63] If Kant had denied the traveler any epistemological privilege, Humboldt returns it. He does so, however, only after transforming the traveler into an ethnographer. And he fashions himself as the exemplar of such a scientific ethnographer, who had moved beyond the mere descriptive activities of the travel writer. Throughout his diary, Humboldt attended to the sundry details of the Basque peoples and culture in order to conduct a study of a particular Basque character.

Upon his return to Paris and then finally to Berlin from the Basque country in 1801, Humboldt began work on *Die Vasken oder Bemerkungen auf einer Reise durch Biscaya und das französische Basquenland im Frühling des Jahrs 1801* (*The Basques or Notes on a Trip Through Bay of Biscaya and the French Basque Land in the Spring of 1801*). He continued to collect materials for the project but never published it.[64] Humboldt frames the project in terms of three historical questions: Where does the original language stem of the Basques come from? And to what other peoples are the Basques related?[65] And is their language related to any other languages? The first question concerns what Humboldt terms the "original particularities" of the Basques (13). Because they have been hidden and isolated from outside influences, the Basques have been able to maintain their "original" language, constitution, and customs. This geographical isolation has protected them from the "eye of the observer" and the "sword of the conqueror." Geographically speaking, the Basques stand "island-like" there—removed from the flow of external influences. And yet Humboldt writes that his efforts to distill these particularities ran into two fundamental problems. First, the Basques are not one, uniform people; instead, they are a complex of distinct, yet interrelated groups. Consequently, whatever character of the people (*Volkscharacter*) one might observe emerges only through a constant and "lively reciprocity" among the various groups. He cites as examples of this constant exchange, the lexical variations from village to village or town to town. Second, the idea of a "disconnected," isolated people, untouched by outside influences turns out to be only partially true. In the opening pages, Humboldt stresses the Basque land's geographical isolation from Europe through mountains and the ocean. He notes, however, a certain degree of interaction between the Basque peoples and other peoples and nations as evidenced by the slow degradation of native languages, degradation that Humboldt attributes to their involvement in trade.

Whereas their relative isolation has maintained their particularity, the increasing intermixture of cultures threatens to erase it. Humboldt writes that the pressures of the French and Spanish languages threaten to "eliminate" the Basque language over time (9). The "mutual contact" of almost all of Europe threatens to consume the Basque's particularity, suggests Humboldt, in less than a century. For Humboldt, this threatening form of contact is merely one effect of the developmental logic of culture: culture can erase differences that distinguish smaller "clusters of peoples." Humboldt suggests that the Basques have been able to maintain their particularity by remaining outside the monolith of European culture. They have not been swept up by and fully incorporated into European notions of cultural progress, notions that reduce culture to a "great mass" (10). The only vocabulary that Humboldt has to articulate this particularity, however, invokes the travelogue descriptions of many Europeans and even anticipates Alexander von Humboldt's description of South American natives as sensual and natural peoples. He writes that the Basques possess a "natural warmth and lively feeling"; their lively oral language will lose its "more sensual and diverse imprint" in the hands of writers (11). Considering his nascent philosophy of language, it is easy to understand his attraction to the Basque people. Their oral language exemplified for him a pure or nontextual language.

Whereas Humboldt tasks his proto-ethnography with locating this "lively" center of particularity, his actual ethnographic project relied not only on "eye witnesses" but on various "aids" (16). Dictionaries, news, histories, and grammars, or what he terms his "archival" sources, were essential supplements to his ethnography of the "lively gaze." They laid the groundwork for his work on the Basque nation. In an effort to rewrite the travelogue as an ethnography or a "scientific investigation," Humboldt prepared for his eyewitness work with conceptual and textual work in Paris between his first trip in the fall of 1799 and his second trip. While in Paris he read travelogues and met with Frenchmen, Spaniards, and Basque before beginning his travels. Humboldt expands the boundaries of observation to include supplementary techniques and preparatory work.

Humboldt, however, is careful to distinguish the "complete and careful" investigative work that he claims characterizes his ethnographic work from the "arbitrary" results that can result from a fully articulated, scientific system. Throughout his account, particular observations are placed alongside more general claims. His investigation assumes, as already suggested by the manifold aids of inquiry, a prior base of knowledge. Throughout the text, Humboldt appeals to this assumed knowledge by couching his observations and reporting in terms such as "as is well known," "every traveler will know," and "every observant traveler." This prior knowledge, however, does not overdetermine observed phenomena. The most important pool of assumed knowledge is linguistic, and he insists that all "foreigners" must proceed from a "sufficient" knowledge of the language. Drawing on his articulation of language as performance, as activity, he refers to language as the "living impression" of a people's "way of thinking and feeling." But this "living impression" is always supplemented by the study of what Humboldt refers to as "dead aids" (292). The conceptual and empirical, the systematic and particular, are both essential elements to Humboldt's re-imagined ethnography.

Humboldt grounds the "particularity" of the Basque in an organic vocabulary—it is a lively, living particularity with energy (*Energie*) and force (*Kraft*)—and, above all, in the organic connotations of *Bildung* itself. The vocabulary draws on the common eighteenth-century tendency to articulate the world in terms of energy or activity and not substance.[66] He makes a conscious attempt in his study of the Basques to distinguish it from the descriptive character of the travelogue genre, which fails to account for change. Humboldt's project aims to articulate both questions of genetic development and the contextual meanings of particular phenomena. The particularity of the Basque cannot be discerned through "external and arbitrary" causes; instead, it can only emerge through what he repeatedly calls the "lively gaze." For his Basque text, at least, this gaze is organized spatially. He organizes his text around geographical centers. Each section carries the title of a village or town that he visited and begins with a description of the geography of the particular place that folds out into a description and comments on the people themselves. The particularity of the Basque people is tied to geographic particularity.

In an exemplary section in the middle of his text, Humboldt reports on a dance. Attesting to his prior knowledge and thus expanding the context of the entire account, he writes that because he happened to be "in Durango on a Sunday, [he] didn't pass up the chance to visit the dancing square."[67] His authority as an educated and knowledgeable traveler is on display. And the deictic distance of the account's language that follows underlines this point: "the" dancer, "the" children, and so on.

The participants are objects of Humboldt's knowing, ethnographic descriptions. Repeated contextual comments about the general function of dances within Basque communities serve to solidify the authority of the text as not just an I-was-there-account but as one backed up by all the armature of an educated ethnographer: "One dances publicly on the square regardless of class." A temporalized narrative—*nachdem, gleich nach, sobald, folgen*—detailing every step establishes at the same time, however, the authority of the first-person report. Humboldt was there and can thus give a detailed accounting of what actually happened, but he can also situate this particular event into a broader context of meaning. These deictic shifts from first to third person and back serve to authorize the ethnographic narrative as both a *scientific, objective* account and a "first-person" narrative. This back-and-forth reaches its apogee, however, in Humboldt's own narration of the physicality of the dance, a narration that attests to his presence as ethnographer: "The violent movement of the arms, especially in the shoulders, the stamping of the feet, the endless stirring of the back and the hips, not to mention of movements that every eyewitness will recall, everything manifests the presence of the most intense desire. This makes the dance, considered objectively, neither noble nor gracious . . . but interesting in its authenticity because of its uniqueness. In this its fire always pulls the audience along with it" (131).

This account of the dance's energetic movement is given linguistic form in Humboldt's own breathless language. The repetition of particular movements invokes not just the dance itself but Humboldt's own physical proximity to the dancers. He tries, however, to contain the "desire" manifest in this wildly physical dance. "Observed objectively," he writes, the dance is "interesting" because of its authenticity and unique character. This grasp for epistemological grounding is reiterated in Humboldt's observation that the *fandango* dance follows the *culados* dance. The "particular character" of the latter dance, he claims, cannot be immediately grasped; instead, "one must know" that the *fandango* is being performed "in order to recognize it again" (130). The very citation of the dance in the local language only reiterates Humboldt's epistemological privilege. They are material traces or indices of his ethnographic knowledge, a knowledge not to be culled from the "exaggerated descriptions of the ethnographers [*Reisebeschreiber*]" (131). Distinguishing himself and his work from travelogues and even those travelers, Humboldt exfoliates this description into a discourse on Basque dance as such. No longer are we, as reader, experiencing a Sunday dance ritual; instead, we are taken on a discursive journey, a history of dance as it were, where Humboldt discusses the function of dance as such within the context of Basque culture without explicit reference to first-person accounts.

In 1812 Humboldt published "Ankündigung einer Schrift über die Vaskische Sprache und Nation" ("Announcement of a Work on the Basque Language and Nation"), in which he announces his intention to publish a monograph on the Basque. As a "unified language and history study,"[68] his text would overcome the "deficiencies" of previous attempts at world history that dealt with the "complex relationships of nations and races" (289). He emphasizes the necessarily comparative character of his project and claims that previous comparative projects have "satisfied" themselves with "fragmented comparisons" that lack multiple "points of comparison." Drawing on Goethe's morphology-based comparative method, his comparative project would observe the human being as though it were "an enormous plant." Like the organic development that Goethe's morphology was intent on observing, Humboldt's comparative anthropology is concerned with the human being, a race that "sprawls parasitically in changing directions, stretches itself across the face of the earth . . . creeps low and, while its roots are close to the earth, is refreshed and warmed by the thaw and sun of another higher world" (290). The organic character of the human being means that its development over time cannot be observed and accounted for by traditional scientific methods; instead, the careful, complete, and constant description of "individual stems" must ground the larger project of comparison of the various "forms of humanity." Humboldt's text, then, would only be an aid, since such a project must always be open to revision. The "inadequacy of printed matter," its very physicality, makes all aids, all texts contingent forms of knowledge (292). Humboldt's "Ankündigung" anticipates a future, more elaborate text with three sections: observations about his trip, an analysis of the language, and finally, a synthetic historical, philosophical investigation of the Basque and their language. The manuscript that Humboldt did write corresponds to the first section and the announcement's imperative to provide an "intuitive concept" of the land and its inhabitants. Such an "intuitive concept," claims Humboldt, would better convey how language, customs, and geographical locality are "interwoven." Humboldt is interested in a description that seizes on the complex of elements that constitute the particularity of the Basque.[69]

Humboldt's Basque studies are a prelude to what had become his primary object of study. As he says in a letter to Wolf in 1804: "For a few months now, I've been undertaking a very pleasurable study, and reveling in the ancient and modern poets. Ultimately, everything that I've been working on is language study.... I think I have discovered the art by which language can be used as a vehicle to traverse the highest and deepest, the multiplicity of the entire world. And I am becoming more and more convinced of this view."[70]

Humboldt explicitly connects his study of the ancients and the moderns through a more fundamental reflection on language. Humboldt continued with his interest in non-Greek languages when, as a Prussian diplomat in Rome, in 1805 he began to study the Aztec language Nahuatl. Lorenzo Hervás, an ex-Jesuit priest, allowed him to copy grammars of various American languages. After his travels in and around South America, Alexander von Humboldt contributed more materials. Humboldt's work on these American languages and the Basque languages initiated an empirical project considering the precise manner in which language serves as the medium through which we can experience the "multiplicity of the entire world." Humboldt thanked the Jesuits and other missionaries for what we know about the languages of the world. But "because they were primarily interested in converting the savages [*die Wilden*], their first concern was to eradicate all the old customs, everything to do with tradition and national memory, and in this way to transform the entire way of thinking and modes of perception of different peoples. Therefore they destroyed in part the object itself, which has been grounded, developed, and represented through them."[71]

Humboldt compares the American languages to the languages of the Basque or those other "uneducated oral languages of Europe." Their orality and the apparent absence of a traditional textual canon of literature make them, in Humboldt's view, "uneducated." This comparison demonstrates that linguistic characteristics are not necessarily transferred from one nation to another; the interrelation of languages is not spatially determined—that is, geographic proximities are not the primary factor for determining linguistic relations. The *Bildungsepoche* of languages, claims Humboldt, determines linguistic relations, and, for Humboldt, a *Bildungsepoche* denotes the complex historical relationships of certain groups of people and languages. In making this distinction, Humboldt is suggesting a more fundamental relationship between language and culture than geographic proximity could ever account for.

For Humboldt, languages manifest the synthetic dynamism that marked both Goethe's morphology and Schleiermacher's proto-ethnography. Languages oscillate between a universal form and a particular act. "The wonderful nature of languages consists in the fact that they can be understood by people who live in the greatest intervals of space or time. But on the other hand they allow each person to stamp his own particularity on it, and what is even more, to form it within himself."[72] Here, Humboldt anticipates in the broadest of strokes his more mature philosophy of language, but he also echoes Schleiermacher's philosophy of language. For both Humboldt and Schleiermacher, language was characterized by a part-whole dynamic. But whereas Schleiermacher tended to frame his hermeneutics in terms of "language," Humboldt always considered languages. He emphasized this synthesizing dynamic as manifested in particular *languages* and not in language as an abstraction.

In his early lectures on hermeneutics, Schleiermacher lays out this dynamic in the clearest of terms. Every utterance (*Rede*) or, as he also puts it, every speech act (*Sprechakt*) is marked by two aspects. First, every utterance manifests the totality of the language, which he terms its grammar. The grammar offers a potential of syntactic and semantic elements. Every individual is born into a language system that prescribes a linguistic grammar. This universal aspect of language conditions the individual speaker but also makes possible the communication of ideas. A new thought could not be realized or made comprehensible without being related to the already existing relationships found in language or between the already determined linguistic signs. Second, every utterance manifests language in the particularity of a speaker. Language is only realized through the act of speaking, which is always tied to an individual. Every utterance is a "life moment." Every individual speaker "produces something new in the language, for every connection of a subject with a predicate that has yet to be made is something new."[73] The second aspect, the hermeneutic, points to language as praxis, as always situated in a point in time and space.[74]

Humboldt describes a similar circularity in his "Ankündigung einer Schrift über die Vaskische Sprache und Nation":

> For language is everywhere a mediator, first between infinite and finite nature, then between one and another individual; simultaneously and through the same act it makes union possible, and originates from it; its whole nature never lies in a single individual, but must always simultaneously be guessed or intuited from an other;

yet it cannot be explained out of both of them either; rather it is (as that always wherein true mediation takes place) something unique, incomprehensible, simply given in the idea of the union of that which is (for us and our mode of thinking) thoroughly separated, and caught up only within this idea of union.[75]

Language always already exists as something external and prior to particular utterances. Every individual utterance presupposes language as other. And yet this aspect of language consists of nothing more than the totality of individual speech acts. These two aspects of language, what Schleiermacher referred to as the grammatical and the hermeneutic, are both produced by and united in language itself. Language unites the distinctions that it produces. No utterance has meaning simply on the basis of its grammar, likewise no utterance can be understood if reduced to its individual moment.

It is precisely this model of dynamic synthesis that Humboldt began to outline in his essays on a future comparative anthropology. Languages—always in the plural—offered Humboldt a ready medium through which to study the human, because they performed the very dynamic of universal-particular, transcendental-empirical, that marked his science of the human from the beginning. His canonical works on languages from the 1820s (like the introduction to the *Kawi-Werk*) should be read, then, in light of the essays on comparative anthropology, his work on the Basque language and culture, and his Nahuatl grammar. The particularity of the Basque language provides, historically at least, the background for one of his more general claims about the relationship of languages to culture, a claim that he summarized in *Über das Sprachstudium* (*On the Study of Language*, 1812): "Through the multiplicity of languages, the richness of the world grows [immediately] and the multiplicity of that which we recognize or know in it. It simultaneously expands for us the sphere of human existence, and it affords new ways of thinking and feeling. . . . The study of the languages of the earth is also the world history of the thoughts and impressions of humanity. This world history describes the human being in all zones and stages of his culture."[76]

By placing the study of languages in the center of a science of the human, Humboldt consolidates the conceptual framework and historical developments of eighteenth-century proto-anthropology. His plans for a comparative anthropology offer one of the most detailed responses to the conundrum of anthropological inquiry as laid out by Kant. Humboldt offers a model for relating questions of observation and normativity. If proto-anthropology had initially framed such questions in terms of the body's relationship to the mind or the relation of sensibility and reason, by the turn of the century Humboldt had traded these bodies for words.

Humboldt's turn to a linguistic anthropology—his claim that to study languages is to study the history of the human being—does two things. First, his incipient philosophy of language, as outlined in the discussion of his exchange with Schiller, situates language in reality, as discourse. By emphasizing the singular utterance and the act of speaking, Humboldt reiterates the broader, practical imperative of proto-anthropology to consider the human being in a particular pragmatic context. (Recall the previous discussion of proto-anthropology as a science of life.) Second, language as phenomenon gives the theoretical entanglements and reflexive form of proto-anthropology material reality. The circularity and self-reflective character of language—language as simultaneously grammar and utterance—repeats the reduplicative structures of proto-anthropology.

Before the hermeneutic circle there was the anthropological circle in which the human being was both subject and object of observation. As evident throughout this chapter, Humboldt embraces this anthropological circularity and reduplication. Languages are the medium through which the human being spontaneously "forms simultaneously himself and the world, or, what is more, becomes conscious that he separates a world from himself" (196–97).[77] Language has become a distinct, objective realm of its own. For Humboldt, languages supersede culture as the realm in which the entanglements of anthropological inquiry—the blurred distinctions between what is universal, given, constant in the human being and what is particular, local, and produced—are most discernable.

Conclusion

This book began with a historical question: why did Kant and a host of other German figures turn to a science of the human in the last third of the eighteenth century? How was it possible, for example, for Kant to reduce his questions in the *Logik* (what can I know? what can I do? what can I be permitted to hope for?) to one: what is the human? As evidenced throughout this book, the appeal to anthropology invoked less a fully formed discipline than a particular mode of thought, one marked by a reduplication of the human being as both the subject and object of observation. This chapter in the history of a nascent discipline proved to be an example of the modern imperative to be critical and reflective. The recursive structures of proto-anthropology echo those of a critical, late Enlightenment modernity. What is today referred to as the discipline of anthropology began as a confluence of questions around the problem of observation—questions concerning the mind-body relationship, the place of the senses within a reason-dominated Enlightenment, and the invention of culture and its attendant notions of historical progress and species being. The question of the *anthropos* was from its disciplinary beginnings as proto-anthropology burdened by a simple fact: the human being is "judge and party at the same time."[1] For a science of the human, the observer and the object of observation are the same thing.

Such a science offered a solution to the centrifugal character of knowledge in the modern age. Although it lacked clearly articulated disciplinary methods and assumptions, a science of the human, it was hoped, could unify both scientific knowledge and observation, each of which had been fragmented by the proliferation of scientific disciplines with their distinct modes of inquiry. The figure of the human could be the stabilizing center of all knowledge. But the doubling of the human being as both the subject and object of scientific inquiry raised a host of attendant theoretical problems, because such a radically anthropological perspective involves affirming the recursivity of all knowledge. It assumes that all knowledge is grounded in and thus refers back to the human being.

Like other proto-anthropologies of the late eighteenth century, Kant's pragmatic anthropology attempted to bracket the conundrums of reduplication by distinguishing transcendental and empirical questions and modes of inquiry. But these bracketing gestures merely erased, as Kant writes, the underlying theoretical structures. Anthropological inquiry mixed theoretical and practical questions and transcendental and empirical methods. Kant's pragmatic anthropology exemplifies the increasing confusion of transcendental and empirical, norm and physis, in the broader discourse of proto-anthropology.

The circularity of anthropological inquiry—the grounding of all knowledge of the human in human finitude—turned out, however, to be more than a theoretical problem. It was an ethical problem as well. The ethical ramifications were nowhere more evident than in Kant's attempt to reconcile the transcendental and empirical in his pragmatic anthropology—that is, he attempted to reconcile these two contrasting trajectories in a robust teleology of the human species. The two realms of causality—reason and nature—were to be melded through an appeal to the "destiny of the human." Such an appeal, however, was never fully able to answer the question of how open this human destiny was. Whether it was comments about the lethargy of the South Sea Islanders or appeals to contemporary medical accounts of skin tones, the empirical content of Kant's pragmatic anthropology, however sparse, cast the universality of this destiny into question. The bleeding of the empirical into the transcendental or the a priori exclusion of certain human beings or races from the progression of the species laid bare the more fundamental problems of a pragmatic anthropology.

Kant's pragmatic anthropology relies on a normative vision of human becoming. On the one hand, the regulative idea of a human species promises a critical lens through which human beings might repeatedly remake themselves in the present. On the other hand, such a normative idea can weigh like a theoretical imposition on the individual human being—overdetermining, extinguishing, and erasing human difference—excluding those human beings who, it turns out, had never belonged to this universal future of humanity. How can an account of the human be both normatively compelling and empirically open? The mixing of transcendental and empirical in proto-anthropology left open the possibility of an anthropological normativity, a thick universalism.

Part 3 of this book considered such a normativity as an alternative to Kant's teleological solution. The figures in chapters 5 through 7 did not simply reject Kant's normative anthropology; instead, they attempted to reconcile a robust normative image of what the human being should become with an equally dense account of what human beings are observed to be in their particularity. They pointed to ways in which a normative ethics might be less than pure, to ways in which human beings were always wrapped up in the particularity and contingency of life itself.

In his rewriting of a European ethnographic tradition, Schleiermacher exemplified an anthropology of reason and confronted the impossibility of observing human beings from a place outside the act of observation. In his lyrical anthropology of the senses, Novalis radicalized proto-anthropology's intimation that the mind-body problem was ultimately a question of observation. Novalis showed that any discussion of the senses or sense is always already tied up with language and the discourse of sensibility. Taking his lead from Goethe's morphology, Humboldt imagined a comparative anthropology that embraced the reduplication of the subject as the object of inquiry. Schleiermacher, Novalis, Forster, Goethe, and Humboldt offered suggestive alternatives to Kant. They all highlighted both the epistemological and ethical problems of the mixing of empirical and transcendental, even as they sought a more dynamic relationship between normative claims and empirical observations. Kant's pragmatic anthropology failed because it was not dynamic enough.

Forster was the first to suggest a normative category of the human that could be tested and revised. Schleiermacher, Novalis, Goethe, and Humboldt pushed this revisable, expandable norm even further. Novalis's revision of sensibility and the normativity of the lyric offer such a dynamism. Humboldt's comparative anthropology pursues an open and flexible universal. The category of the human had to become open to "testing"; it had to become dynamic. For all of these figures, aesthetics offered a model for such a dynamism. Schleiermacher turned to *Poesie*. Novalis and Humboldt turned to language itself. Even Kant and Forster appealed to narrative forms to imagine a more open and normatively compelling account of the human. In various and complex ways, aesthetics offered a model for the dynamism that came to characterize anthropological claims. All of these figures offer an alternative version of the normative category of human that is not posited as a timeless product of a pure reason. The category of the human came to take on a more contingent form. The category of the human became endlessly revisable.

These figures demonstrated how the contingency of *the human* was not an abandonment of normative claims. Schleiermacher, Novalis, Goethe, and Humboldt each offer an ambivalent embrace of Kant's normative anthropology. On the one hand, as Goethe says, they affirmed the need for a unified perspective through which to observe the human. On the other hand, they rejected the inflexibility of such norms. In the place of a singular, one-time postulation of the human, they offer up a revisable norm. They embrace the recursive, reduplicative force of an anthropological mode of inquiry and use it to imagine a radically anthropological normativity, a normativity born not of the atemporal or the transhistorical character of a pure reason but of the impurity of a radically anthropological reason. It is radically anthropological in the sense that it acknowledges Kant's claim that the human being has nowhere to look but to itself for its claims, its grounds, its future. The recursive form of anthropological reason is organized around and by the human being.

Kant concludes his *Anthropologie in pragmatischer Hinsicht* with the promise of a radically human destiny: the promise of the human lies in the "destiny of the human species" (*Bestimmung des Menschengeschlechts*).² Kant writes that given the history of the human race—a history marked by wickedness and strife—the tendency to misanthropy is understandable. In the face of this history, the "constant progression toward the good" is to be found in the idea of humanity, in the promise of a "progressive organization of the citizens of the earth into and toward the species as a system that is cosmopolitically connected."³ The promise of the human rests within the system of humanity. It lies in the hope that human beings can organize themselves into and as a system. True humanity is grounded within a system of human becoming, a system that would be closed off to the nonhuman. Kant writes that it "may well be the case that there are rational beings on other planets"—but human beings cannot know and, thus, cannot compare themselves with other beings. There remains only the human and its system of humanity.

While Humboldt, Schleiermacher, Novalis, and Goethe did not conjecture about the existence of rational beings on other planets, they recognized the consequences of a fundamentally anthropological mode of thought: anthropological reason could not deliver on all of its promises.

The pathos of this insight is registered in the longing language of Novalis's poetry for an absolute sense, a sense beyond distinction. "We search everywhere for the unconditional and always find only things."[4] We see it again in Schleiermacher's proto-ethnography, which acknowledges that other human beings will remain foreign. Difference cannot be erased through critical reflection. In the plan for a comparative anthropology, Humboldt embraces the contingency of anthropological inquiry and the endless oscillation between the normative and the empirical. But his rejection of an anthropological telos imbues anthropological inquiry with a restlessness. Goethe acknowledges that while such a dynamism "is a very worthy gift from above," it is also a "most dangerous one. It leads to formlessness, destroys knowledge, dissolves it. It is like a centrifugal force [*vis centrifuga*]."[5] They all suggest that Kant's system of humanity will remain forever incomplete.

This pathos, however, was already present in Kant's texts. For Kant, reason was not just a formal faculty. It has needs and desires. Reason does not rest content merely to create its own transcendental ideas and regulative principles; it goes looking for "sure signs" of them in nature. The human species "feels itself determined by nature" to progress toward a cosmopolitical system of humanity.[6] The pursuit of the destiny of the human species is based upon a "well-grounded assumption of a natural tendency."[7] All of these natural signs, these promises, "console" the human being. These moments mark the restless character of this anthropological mode of thought. They mark a desire that extends beyond the recursive and reflexive imperative of modernity. There is an intimated acknowledgment that the restlessness of the human cannot be fulfilled by the circularity of reflection, that this circularity cannot satisfy the desires of reason. The human cannot be reduced to its own reflections.

What happens once we become not only human but all too human? What remains after the human being has been reduced to itself? The result is the reflection of all questions back to that figure whence all knowledge is now presumed to originate and to which all knowledge now refers. Kant's anthropology keenly articulates how dynamic human beings are in their ceaseless re-creation of themselves and the world. Human beings are temporal beings hurtling into a future that Kant claims should always be of their own making. The human being is always becoming. The cost of becoming human is that we cannot be human.

Doch uns ist gegeben,
Auf keiner Stätte zu ruhn,
Es schwinden, es fallen
Die leidenden Menschen
Blindlings von einer
Stunde zur andern,
Wie Wasser von Klippe
Zu Klippe geworfen,
Jahr lang ins Ungewisse hinab.
        (Hölderlin, "Hyperions Schicksalslied")

[But to us is given,
To find no resting place,
They faint, they fall
The suffering human beings
Blindly from one
Hour to the next
Like water thrown
From cliff to cliff
Downward for years into the unknown.][8]

Notes

INTRODUCTION

1. Schlegel, *Ideen*, in *Kritische Schriften und Fragmente*, 2:226.
2. Geertz, *Interpretation of Cultures*, 36.
3. Ibid., 34.
4. Pippin, *Modernism as a Philosophical Problem*, xv.
5. Foucault, "What Is Enlightenment?" 46.
6. Kant, *Kritik der reinen Vernunft*, A849/B877. Translations of the *Kritik der reinen Vernunft* are either mine or are taken from Kant, *Critique of Pure Reason*, translated and edited by Paul Guyer and Allen W. Wood (hereafter "Guyer and Wood").
7. "Habe mut, dich deines eigenen Verstandes zu bedienen." Kant, "Beantwortung der Frage: Was ist Aufklärung?" in *Gesammelte Schriften* (hereafter "AA"), 8:33.
8. "Unser Zeitalter ist das eigentliche Zeitalter der Kritik, der sich alles unterwerfen muß." Kant, *Kritik der reinen Vernunft*, Axi.
9. See Schmidt and Wartenberg, "Foucault's Enlightenment," 283.
10. Habermas, "Taking Aim," 149.
11. Riedel, "Anthropologie und Literatur," 108.
12. Korsgaard, *Sources of Normativity*, 8.
13. One of the most important publications of eighteenth-century German anthropology, *Der ganze Mensch*, edited by Hans-Jürgen Schings, defines anthropology primarily as a physiological anthropology. Accordingly, anthropology is an eighteenth-century medical discourse of the body, the traces of which can be found in everything from politics to literature. For an excellent overview of this research program, see Riedel, "Anthropologie und Literatur."
14. Garber and Heinz, *Zwischen Empirisierung und Konstruktionsleistung*, vii.

CHAPTER 1

1. Concerning the debates on the generation of life and the organic and the more general collapse of the mechanist paradigm, see Roger, *Life Sciences*; Richards, *Romantic Conception of Life*, esp. 207–37; Larson, *Interpreting Nature*; and Roe, *Matter, Life, and Generation*. On the history of eighteenth-century psychology, see Hatfield, "Remaking the Science of Mind." On the phrase "schöne Wissenschaften," see Strube, "Die Geschichte des Begriffs 'schöne Wissenschaften.'"
2. Wenzel, *Menschenlehre*, ii.
3. Ibid., iii.
4. On the various uses of the term in eighteenth-century Germany, see Linden, *Untersuchungen zum Anthropologiebegriff*; see also Pfotenhauer, *Literarische Anthropologie*.
5. Ith, *Versuch einer Anthropologie*, 76.
6. See Käuser, "Anthropologie und Ästhetik im 18. Jahrhundert," 204; see also Proß, "Herder und die Anthropologie seiner Zeit."

7. I am indebted to Ben Bennett for this suggestion. I do not use "anthropology" or "protoanthropology" to mean "image of man," as it does in Descartes's or Hobbes's "anthropology of man." There have been various attempts to define anthropology, with often confusing results. In one classic study Wilhelm E. Mühlman simply asserts that "anthropological science originates out of the curiosity-interest in distant and far-off lands and their different types of people" (*Geschichte der Anthropologie*, 13). He then proceeds to summarize about two thousand years of "exotic curiosity," always from Europe out, from Thucydides to Malinowski, and their efforts to find "man's place in the world" (242). Various attempts to delimit anthropology etymologically offer interesting but less conclusive information. For a brief summary of such attempts, see Marquard, "Anthropology."

There are some studies on the background of early modern anthropology. See, for example, Hodgen, *Early Anthropology*; see also Dilthey, "Die Funktion der Anthropologie."

8. See Bell, *Goethe's Naturalistic Anthropology*, 24.
9. Fülleborn, "Abriss," 155.
10. Zammito, *Kant, Herder, and the Birth of Anthropology*, 221. There is a broad but very general literature on the history of eighteenth-century German anthropology. See, for example, Kondylis, *Die Aufklärung*, 119–47; Krauss, *Zur Anthropologie*; Linden *Untersuchungen zum Anthropologiebegriff*; Schings, "Der Philosophische Arzt," 11–40; Marquard, "Anthropologie"; and Schings, *Der ganze Mensch*.
11. Kondylis writes of the "primacy of anthropology." See Kondylis, *Die Aufklärung*, 119.
12. This slogan is captured well in the title of Schings's *Der ganze Mensch*.
13. Zammito, *Kant, Herder, and the Birth of Anthropology*, 221.
14. Here is a sample of titles from 1791 (the year of Platner's revised anthropology) to 1810. I have included only those texts with an explicit reference to anthropology in the title or subtitle: Platner, *Neue Anthropologie*; Paulus Usteri, *Grundlage der medizinischen-anthropologischen Vorlesungen* (1791); Justus Christian Loder, *Anfangsgründe der medizinischen Anthropologie und der Staatsarzneikunde* (1791); M. Wagner, *Beyträge zur philosophischen Anthropologie* (1794); Ith, *Versuch einer Anthropologie*; G. A. Flemming, *Über den Charakter des Menschen* (1794); Ludwig Heinrich Jakob, *Grundriß der Erfahrungs-Seelenlehre* (1795); Wilhelm von Humboldt, "Plan einer vergleichenden Anthropologie" (1795); J. D. Metzger, *Medizinisch-philosophische Anthropologie für Ärzte und Nichtärzte* (1798); Immanuel Kant, *Anthropologie in pragmatischer Hinsicht* (1798); Pölitz, *Populäre Anthropologie* (1800); Justus Christian Hennings, *Anthropologie und pneumatologische Aphorismen* (1800); Wenzel, *Menschenlehre*; J. Görres, *Aphorismen über die Kunst, als Einleitung zu Aphorismen über Organomie, Physik, Psychologie und Anthropologie* (1802); Gottfried Immanuel Wenzel, *Vollständiger Lehrbegriff der gesammten Philosophie Band II: Metaphysik der Natur und Anthropologie* (1804); Lorenz Heinrich Wagner, *Physiologisch-anthropologisches Lehrbuch* (1805); Jakob Friedrich Fries, *Neue (oder anthropologische) Kritik der Vernunft* (1808); and Franz von Paula Gruithuisen, *Anthropologie oder von der Natur des menschlichen Lebens und Denkens für angehende Philosophen und Aerzte* (1810).
15. Zedler, *Grosses Vollständiges Universallexicon*, 1:522.
16. Moravia, *Beobachtende Vernunft*, 20.
17. Sloan, "Gaze of Natural History."
18. For an in-depth study of the emergence of French anthropology, see Moravia, *Beobachtende Vernunft*.
19. I take this concept from Marquard, *Schwierigkeiten*, 124.
20. Ian Hunter argues, convincingly I think, that the publication of Wolff's *Vernünftige Gedanken von Gott, der Welt und der Seele des Menschen auch allen Dingen überhaupt* (*Rational Thoughts on God, the World and the Human Soul, and All Things in General*) signaled a return of the "full-blooded metaphysical scholasticism to the [German] Protestant University, especially to the University of Halle," where Thomasius had begun to establish a "rival enlightenment." See Hunter, *Rival Enlightenments*, 265.
21. On university metaphysics and Wolff's metaphysical system, see Beck, *Early German Philosophy*, 256–75.

22. Schneiders, "*Deus est philosophus absolute summus*," 13.

23. Hunter describes this image thus: "Through its fundamental positing of man as a being of pure reason temporarily mortgaged to the experiences and inclinations of his sensible nature, university metaphysics sought to program an ethos of intellectual self-purification and clarification. It is the normative lineaments of a *homo duplex* that show through in the dialectical historian's exemplary oppositions: between a pure intellectualism cut off from experience, and a brute empiricism lacking insight into its transcendental conditions; between a pure rationalism in cable of providing sensible man with motivating norms, and an impure voluntarism incapable of providing such norms with a rational basis." *Rival Enlightenments*, 20.

24. For an in-depth accounting of this shift, especially as it pertains to France, see Roger, *Life Science*, esp. 354–68.

25. Moravia, "Sciences of Man," 248.

26. On the German reception of Locke, see Beiser, *Fate of Reason*, 165–92.

27. Locke, *Essay Concerning Human Understanding*, 59.

28. See Bell, *Goethe's Naturalistic Anthropology*, 22.

29. Hissmann, *Psychologische Versuche*, 93.

30. Platner, *Anthropologie für Aerzte und Weltweise*, 57.

31. See Heintel, "Einleitung," xi.

32. He was doubtful about what he termed the "universalizability of particular statements of experience that were drawn from individual cases" [Verallgemeinerung der besonderen Erfahrungssätze die aus einzelnen Fällen gezogen sind]. Tetens, *Philosophische Versuche*, xix.

33. Ibid., xx.

34. For more on this, see Theisen, "Macroanthropos," 251. For a more general reading of Novalis's reformulation, especially in *Das Allgemeine Brouillon*, of the classificatory schemas of natural science, see G. Neumann, "Naturwissenschaft und Geschichte als Literatur."

35. The following discussion of analogy draws on the entry "Analogie," in Ritter, *Historisches Wörterbuch*, 1:226.

36. Novalis, *Das Allgemeine Brouillon*, in *Schriften*, 3:321.

37. Novalis refers to the "mathematicity of analogy" ("Über Goethe," in *Schriften*, 2:647). For more on his association of analogy and mathematics, see "Blüthenstaub," in *Schriften*, 3:425nn795–96. See also Daiber, "Experimentalphysik des Geistes," 31.

38. On anthropology's relationship to popular philosophy, see Zammito, *Kant, Herder and the Birth of Anthropology*, 15–42.

39. Wenzel, *Menschenlehre*, v.

40. Kant, *Anthropologie in pragmatischer Hinsicht*, AA, 7:120. Translations of *Anthropologie in pragmatischer Hinsicht* are either mine, or are taken from *Anthropology from a Pragmatic Point of View*, translated by Robert B. Louden (hereafter "Louden").

41. Wagner, *Beyträge*, xxii.

42. Platner, *Anthropologie für Aerzte und Weltweise*, xxvi–xxvii.

43. Garber, *Descartes Embodied*, 133. My brief summary of the Cartesian problem is indebted to Garber.

44. This brief outline draws on a range of sources. See Heinz, *Wissen vom Menschen*, 55–75; Th. Rentsch, "Leib-Seele-Verhältnis," in Ritter, *Historisches Wörterbuch*, 5:185–206; and especially, the various contributions in Nadler, *Causation in Early Modern Philosophy*, especially Eileen O'Neill, "*Influxus Physicus*," 9–26, and Mark A. Kulstad, "Causation and Preestablished Harmony in the Early Development of Leibniz's Philosophy," 93–118.

45. Platner, *Anthropologie für Aerzte und Weltweise*, xvii.

46. Linden, *Untersuchungen zum Anthropologiebegriff*, 53. Johann Gottlieb Fichte, for example, based part of his lecture series "Logik und Metaphysik Vorlesungen," which he held every semester in Jena from 1794 to 1799, on Platner's *Philosophische Aphorismen*. See Johann Gottlieb Fichte,

Nachgelassene Schriften zu Platners "Philosophischen Aphorismen," 1794–1812, in *Fichte-Gesamtausgabe*, vol. 2, pt. 4.

47. As Riedel notes, Platner's *Anthropologie für Aerzte und Weltweise* "follows Haller's neurological model in all its parts: brains and nerves are a 'system of canals' in which a 'fluid material' called 'nerve fluid' or 'spirit of life' moves." Quoted in Zammito, *Kant, Herder, and the Birth of Anthropology*, 251.

48. Heinz, *Wissen vom Menschen*, 63.

49. Ibid., 64–65.

50. This gap is evident again in Platner's claim that the soul is not immediately related to the "mechanical life of the human being." Platner, *Anthropologie für Aerzte und Weltweise*, 6.

51. Wezel, *Versuch über die Kenntniß des Menschen*, 8–10.

52. Wagner, *Beyträge*, xiii.

53. Klügel, *Encyklopädie*, 287.

54. On the history of Haller's lectures and the debates that they initiated, see Richards, *Romantic Conception of Life*, 307–24; see also Jantzen, "Physiologische Theorien."

55. For more on this as well as a more extensive treatment of the *philosophische Ärtzte*, see Schings, "Der Philosophische Arzt"; also see Riedel, *Die Anthropologie des jungen Schiller*, 11–39.

56. Hissmann, *Psychologische Versuche*, 251.

57. Johann Georg Zimmermann, *Von der Erfahrung in der Arzneykunst*; quoted in Zammito, *Kant, Herder, and the Birth of Anthropology*, 243.

58. Weikard, *Der philosophische Arzt*, iv.

59. Riedel, "Anthropologie und Literatur," 108–9.

60. Ith, *Versuch einer Anthropologie*, 81.

61. Platner, *Anthropologie für Aerzte und Weltweise*, 254.

62. I am indebted to Kondylis's explanation of this rehabilitation; see Kondylis, *Die Aufklärung*, 42–58.

63. Quoted in Heinz, *Wissen vom Menschen*, 62.

64. At this point I am using the term "sensibility" in the broadest possible terms. It was often used as a catchall term to signify sensations (*Empfindungen*) as understood by the Germans who adopted English empiricism. The term "sensibility" also included the "moral feelings" described by the moral philosophy of Shaftesbury, Hutcheson, and Rousseau. Eventually "sensibility" also came to include even the more medical and scientific discourses of Brown and Haller around irritability (*Reitzbarkeit*).

65. Pölitz, *Populäre Anthropologie*, 13.

66. See Heinz, *Wissen vom Menschen*, 25n1; see also Riedel, *Die Anthropologie des jungen Schiller*, 106.

67. For an overview of this shift from a rational to an empirical psychology, see Riedel, "Erster Psychologismus."

68. Sulzer, *Kurzer Begriff*, 159. On the history of these "obscure ideas," see Riedel, "Erkennen und Empfinden."

69. Moravia writes that in the work of La Mettrie, Buffon, d'Holbach, and others "not only nervous sensibilities but also the passions, emotions and higher psychic operations" became included in the "sphere of empirical knowledge" ("Sciences of Man," 251).

70. Sulzer, *Eine allgemeine Theorie der schönen Künste*, 408–9.

71. Quoted by Riedel in "Erkennen und Empfinden," 417.

72. J. G. Herder, *Vom Erkennen und Empfindung der menschlichen Seele. Erster Versuch*, in *Herders Sämtliche Werke*, 8:176–77. See also Ith, *Versuch einer Anthropologie*, 135.

73. Ith, *Versuch einer Anthropologie*, 141.

74. Wagner, *Beyträge*, ix.

75. Ibid., xiii.

76. Kant, *Anthropologie in pragmatischer Hinsicht*, AA, 7:161.

77. Wagner, *Beyträge*, viii.
78. Herder, *Erster Versuch*, in *Herders Sämtliche Werke*, 8:180.
79. John Zammito makes this point very well. See *Kant, Herder, and the Birth of Anthropology*, esp. 137–60.
80. The literature on Herder's anthropology and philosophy of history is extensive, and I do not need to repeat it here. For a thorough account of Herder's place in eighteenth-century anthropology in English, see Zammito, *Kant, Herder, and the Birth of Anthropology*; see also Proß, "Herder und die Anthropologie seiner Zeit."
81. Loder, *Anfangsgründe*, 593.
82. Gruithuisen, *Anthropologie*, 94.
83. Wenzel, *Versuch über die Kenntniß des Menschen*, v.
84. Pölitz, *Populäre Anthropologie*, 4.
85. This historical being that becomes the object of anthropology has various terms within the discourse of anthropology: *Mensch, Menschheit, Gattung*, species. These terms mark either a historical unity or continuity or, at the very least, a dynamic human "nature." The form and function of this temporalization of human being varies according to its context of use. As we will see throughout the following chapters, *Menschheit* for Kant and the romantics comes to mean not necessarily a phenomenally observable belonging but a regulative idea. *Menschheit* becomes a historical task. Just as important for the discourse of anthropology, however, is the collective function of these concepts. This more cultural-historical dimension of the terms abstracts from individual differences to a collective notion of the human that exceeds difference. The exact formulation of the collective term is just as much an object of debate as its temporality is. On the history of these terms, especially in terms of the political semantics of *Menschheit* as an oppositional pair with monarch or king, see Koselleck, *Vergangene Zukunft;* on the critical function of *Menschheit*, see *Geschichtliche Grundbegriffe*, s.v. "Menschheit."
86. Pölitz, *Populäre Anthropologie*, 211.
87. Ith, *Versuch einer Anthropologie*, 79.
88. Ibid., 289.
89. In what follows, I follow Gyorgy Markus's discussion of the eighteenth-century German culture concept in "Culture: The Making and the Make-Up of a Concept."
90. Ibid., 18.
91. Hufeland, *Makrobiotik*, 281.
92. Markus, "Culture," 22.
93. Heinz, *Wissen vom Menschen*, 104–6.
94. Herder, *Ideen*, in *Herders Sämtliche Werke*, 13:348.
95. A fuller discussion of *Bildung* can be found in chapter 4.
96. On the coincidence of anthropology and ethnography, see Zammito, *Kant, Herder, and the Birth of Anthropology*, 236; see also Wokler, "From *l'homme physique*."
97. Pölitz, *Populäre Anthropologie*, xxxvii–xxxviii.
98. Schmid, "Einleitung," xviii.
99. Pölitz, *Populäre Anthropologie*, 9.
100. Jakob, *Grundriß einer Erfahrungs-Seelenlehre*, xi–xiii.
101. Mellin, *Encyclopädisches Wörterbuch der kritischen Philosophie*, 1:279.
102. Wagner, *Beyträge*, xi.
103. Schmid, "Einleitung," xviii.
104. Ibid.
105. Ith, *Versuch einer Anthropologie*, 79.
106. Jutta Heinz and Daniel Purdy refer to an "anthropological Enlightenment." See Heinz, "Doppelrolle," and Purdy, "Immanuel Kant and the Anthropological Enlightenment."
107. Garber and Heinz, *Zwischen Empirisierung und Konstruktionsleistung*, vii.
108. Kant to Hertz, Letter 79, AA, 10:145.

109. See Kosenina, *Ernst Platners Anthropologie und Philosophie*, 18–25.
110. Pölitz, *Populäre Anthropologie*, xiv.
111. Kant, *Anthropologie in pragmatischer Hinsicht*, AA, 7:122.
112. Platner, *Neue Anthropologie*, 74.

CHAPTER 2

1. Hufeland to Kant, Letter 728, AA, 12:136.
2. Hufeland, *Makrobiotik*, v. By the time the third edition was published in 1805, Hufeland had changed the title to *Makrobiotik, oder die Kunst das menschliche Leben zu verlängern*.
3. Kant to Hufeland, Letter 746, AA, 12:157.
4. Kant, *Der Streit der Fakultäten*, AA, 7:98.
5. Ibid., 100–101.
6. In *Pädagogik* (AA, 9:486) Kant refers to this principle as a "moderation of affect" that commands one to "suffer and accustom yourself to enduring." *Pädagogik* consists of the lecture notes first published by D. Friedrich Theodor Rink. Paul Natorp reprinted Rink's text without alteration in the Akademie Ausgabe.
7. Kant, *Der Streit der Fakultäten*, AA, 7:98.
8. Kant, *Kritik der praktischen Vernunft*, AA, 5:152. Translations of the *Kritik der praktischen Vernunft*, *Grundlegung zur Metaphysik der Sitten* (hereafter "*Grundlegung*"), and *Die Metaphysik der Sitten* are either mine or are taken from Kant, *Practical Philosophy*, translated by Mary J. Gregor (hereafter "Gregor").
9. For a discussion of this ethics of cultivation in Kant to which I am greatly indebted, see Hunter, "Morals of Metaphysics." I extend Hunter's discussion of the *Grundlegung* to the *Kritik der praktischen Vernunft*; see also Hadot, *Philosophy as a Way of Life*, and Rabbow, *Seelenführung*.
10. Kant, "Was heißt: Sich im Denken orientieren?" AA, 8:140.
11. Although Rawls acknowledges Kant's "complex conception of the person," he is most interested in working through the "categorical imperative procedure" in order to establish how a moral judgment conforms to the requirements of practical reason. See Rawls, "Themes in Kant's Moral Philosophy," in *John Rawls: Collected Papers*, 510–15. I draw here on Hunter's characterization of some contemporary Kant scholarship. See Hunter, "Morals and Metaphysics," 909–10.
12. The dismissal of Kantian ethics as too formal and abstract continues to be the dominant reading outside a vanguard of Kant scholars. See, for example, Mahmood, *Politics of Piety*. Also see Connolly, *Why I Am Not a Secularist*, and Agamben, *Homo Sacer*. As Zammito notes, however, it is the "impure reason, embodied and contingent, that has become the most important focus of concern of some of the most exciting recent work in Kant studies." *Kant, Herder, and the Birth of Anthropology*, 348. See, for example, Wood, "Unsocial Sociability." For work emphasizing not only anthropological ideas but also questions of unity, purpose, and practical reason, see Neiman, *Unity of Reason*, and Gibbons, *Kant's Theory of Imagination*.
13. Hegel, *Werke*, vol. 7, sec. 194. For more on Hegel's reading, see Wood, *Hegel's Ethical Thought*, 154–73.
14. Zammito, *Kant, Herder, and the Birth of Anthropology*, 339.
15. Kant, *Der Streit der Fakultäten*, AA, 7:99.
16. Heine, *Zur Geschichte der Religion und Philosophie in Deutschland*, in *Sämtliche Werke: Historisch-kritische Gesamtausgabe der Werke*, 8:1, 81.
17. I am drawing here and in what follows on Mark Lilla's discussion in "Kant's Theological-Political Revolution."
18. Kant, *Kritik der reinen Vernunft*, B21–22.
19. Ibid., A314/B371. See also B611 and *Kritik der praktischen Vernunft*, AA, 5:144, where Kant speaks of a "need of reason" (*Vernunftbedürfniß*) that springs from the moral law.
20. See also Kant, "Was heißt: Sich im Denken orientieren?" AA, 8:138, 139, 141, 159.

21. Kant, *Grundlegung*, AA, 4:388 (Gregor, 44).
22. Kant, *Kritik der reinen Vernunft*, A28/B44.
23. Ibid., A680/B708.
24. Pippin, *Modernism as a Philosophical Problem*, 54.
25. Kant, *Grundlegung*, AA, 4:389.
26. Kant, *Kritik der reinen Vernunft*, B3.
27. Kant, *Grundlegung*, AA, 4:389 (Gregor, 44).
28. Ibid.
29. These are the types of questions that have pushed Kant scholars to challenge the more traditional readings of Kant as a strict ethical formalist. My work, then, follows in these paths. See Frierson, *Freedom and Anthropology*, and Shell, "Kant's True Economy of Human Nature." The relationship between Kant's moral theory and anthropology has become of great interest in Kant scholarship, and I will discuss it in chapter 3. Robert Louden has recently referred to Kant's interest in empirical human nature as an "impure ethics," which Kant variously refers to as moral anthropology, practical anthropology, or simply anthropology. See Louden, *Kant's Impure Ethics*.
30. Kant, *Grundlegung*, AA, 4:389 (Gregor, 45, trans. modified).
31. For more on the formulation of this problem, see Frierson, *Freedom and Anthropology*, 48–49.
32. Kant, *Logik*, AA, 9:24.
33. On this point and the importance of the telos of reason in general, see Velkley, *Freedom and the End of Reason*. See also Kleingeld, "Kant on the Unity of Theoretical and Practical Reason."
34. Kant, *Kritik der praktischen Vernunft*, AA, 5:157.
35. Kant, *Kritik der reinen Vernunft*, A549/B577 (Guyer and Wood, 541, trans. modified).
36. Munzel, *Kant's Conception of Moral Character*, 63.
37. Ibid., 64.
38. McCarthy, "On the Way to a World Republic?" 226.
39. Kant, *Kritik der praktischen Vernunft*, AA, 5:3.
40. Kant, *Kritik der reinen Vernunft*, A451/B479.
41. Ibid., A444/B472.
42. For an account of the development of the concept of freedom in Kant's critical system, see Allison, *Kant's Theory of Freedom*.
43. The problem of reinstating a form of freedom arises in the modern era in a manner unnecessary for Aristotle because of his notion of final and formal causality. Kant, in his own manner, is seeking to recover the telos of a final causality in a Newtonian world from which such possibilities had been stripped.
44. Kant, *Kritik der reinen Vernunft*, A533/B561.
45. Ibid.
46. For a discussion of spontaneity, see Pippin, *Idealism as Modernism*, 29–55.
47. Kant, *Kritik der reinen Vernunft*, A533/B561.
48. Ibid., A534/B562.
49. Ibid. Henry Allison makes a similar point in *Kant's Theory of Freedom*, 126.
50. Ibid., 25.
51. Kant, *Kritik der reinen Vernunft*, A533/B561.
52. See, for example, page 533 of the Guyer and Wood translation and page 465 of the Smith translation of *Kritik der reinen Vernunft*.
53. Such a reading is supported by ample textual evidence. See, for example, Kant's discussion on A801–2/B829–30. For an extended discussion of this problem and all of the related passages, see Allison, *Kant's Transcendental Idealism*, 316–20.
54. Pippin makes this same point. See *Idealism as Modernism*, 53.
55. Kant, *Kritik der reinen Vernunft*, A451/B479.

56. When Kant discusses the "need of reason" here, he is speaking of the need of reason "to appeal to a first beginning from freedom in the series of natural causes" (ibid., A451/B479).

57. Kant, *Kritik der reinen Vernunft*, A448/B476.

58. Ibid., A547/B575 (Guyer and Wood, 540).

59. For a more extended discussion of the regulative function of the transcendental idea of freedom, see Allison, *Kant's Transcendental Idealism*, 319–29.

60. In other places, however, Kant seems to suggest that he can discuss practical freedom without transcendental freedom. See *Kritik der reinen Vernunft*, A801–2/B829–30. Henry Allison summarizes and offers his own response to these difficulties. See Allison, *Kant's Theory of Freedom*, 54–70.

61. Kant, *Kritik der reinen Vernunft*, A644/B672.

62. Kant, *Grundlegung*, AA, 4:458 (Gregor, 104).

63. Ibid., 447. For a more detailed account of the presupposition of freedom from a practical standpoint, see Wood, *Kant's Ethical Thought*, 174–78.

64. Elsewhere in the *Grundlegung*, Kant writes, "But the rightful claim to freedom of the will made by common reason is based on the consciousness and the conceded presupposition of the independence of reason from merely subjectively determining causes . . . the consciousness of itself as intelligence, i.e., as independent of sensuous impressions." Kant, *Grundlegung*, AA, 4:457 (Gregor, 104).

65. Ibid.

66. Ibid., 459.

67. Kant, as cited in Ameriks, *Kant's Theory of Mind*, 200. See also Kant's 1783 review of Schulz's *Sittenlehre* in AA, 8:13–14.

68. Kant, review of Schulz's *Sittenlehre*, in AA, 8:13. For more on the presupposition of freedom in relation to arguments against fatalism, see Wood, *Kant's Ethical Thought*, 177–78.

69. Kant, *Grundlegung*, AA, 4:448 (Gregor, 96).

70. Kant, *Kritik der reinen Vernunft*, A802/B830.

71. Terry Pinkard also notes this presupposition. See his *German Philosophy*, 42–44.

72. Kant, *Kritik der praktischen Vernunft*, AA, 5:95–97 (Gregor, 218).

73. Ibid., 95 (Gregor, 216).

74. Ibid., 111.

75. For an overview of the various accounts and debates about such a two-perspective or two-aspect solution, see Nelkin, "Two Standpoints." This solution, of course, derives from a similar solution regarding speculative reason in the *Kritik der reinen Vernunft*, where the coexistence of freedom and nature is deemed possible, because appearances are not things-in-themselves. If phenomena are not things-in-themselves, "but merely representations," which relate according to empirical laws, they must have "grounds" that are not appearances. Nature cannot be the complete and sufficient cause of events. Phenomena, then, have two causal moments: one with respect to their intelligible causes as free and another with respect to their appearance as the result according to the necessity of nature (A537/B565). These causal moments are distinct but simultaneous (*zugleich*). Kant solves the dilemma of freedom—how freedom could exist together with the mechanism of nature—through a dualistic image of the world.

76. Allan Wood makes a similar point in "Kant's Compatibilism."

77. Kant, *Kritik der praktischen Vernunft*, AA, 5:122.

78. Kant, *Kritik der reinen Vernunft*, A539/B567.

79. Kant, *Kritik der praktischen Vernunft*, AA, 5:147 (Gregor, 258).

80. Pippin, *Modernism as a Philosophical Problem*, 49.

81. While there is a great deal of work dealing with Kant's discussion of moral incentives in general, there are, for the most part, only scattered discussions of moral feeling and respect. See, for example, Allison, *Kant's Theory of Freedom*, 120–28; Ameriks, "Kant und das Problem der moralischen Motivation"; Fenves, *Peculiar Fate*, 221–35; MacBeath, "Kant on Moral Feeling"; and Sokoloff, "Kant and the Paradox of Respect."

82. Kant, *Kritik der praktischen Vernunft*, AA, 5:31.
83. Quoted in Henrich, "Concept of Moral Insight," 69; see also Henrich, *Selbstverhältnisse*, 6–56.
84. Adorno, *Negative Dialektik*, 258.
85. Kant, *Kritik der praktischen Vernunft*, AA, 5:71.
86. Giorgio Agamben asks a similar question but insists that there is no such point of intersection for the Kantian moral law. See *Homo Sacer*, 51–54.
87. I owe this point to Munzel, *Kant's Conception of Moral Character*, 66.
88. Ameriks, *Kant's Theory of Mind*, 210.
89. On Kant and the so-called moral sense philosophers, see Henrich, "Hutcheson und Kant"; see also Goy, "Immanuel Kant."
90. Johann Christoph Adelung, *Grammatisch-kritisches Wörterbuch der Hochdeutschen Mundart*, http://mdz.bib-bvb.de:80/digbib/lexika/adelung/text/.
91. Kant, *Kritik der praktischen Vernunft*, AA, 5:71.
92. Ibid., 72 (Gregor, 198).
93. In the *Grundlegung* Kant writes that we must "recognize" (*erkennen*) that we are subject to such categorical imperatives (AA, 4:454).
94. In his *Anthropologie in pragmatischer Hinsicht* Kant distinguishes two kinds of senses (*Sinne*). The "inner" or subjective sensual experience is a feeling (*Gefühl*) of pleasure or displeasure through which the subject feels himself determined to the "maintenance of or resistance to the state of this representation" [zur Erhaltung oder Abwehrung des Zustandes dieser Vorstellung] (AA, 7:153). The "outer" or objective sensual experience is an *Empfindung* through which the subject is affected by "material objects" (*körperliche Dinge*). In the *Kritik der Urteilskraft* Kant makes an even clearer distinction between "objective sensation" and "subjective sensation" and suggests that "Gefühl" should only by used in the later case (AA, 5:206).
95. Kant, *Anthropologie in pragmatischer Hinsicht*, AA, 7:140.
96. Kant, *Kritik der praktischen Vernunft*, AA, 5:147.
97. See Barker-Benfield, *Culture of Sensibility*. In a German context, see Nowitzki, *Der wohltemperierte Mensch*.
98. Wood, *Kantian Ethics*, 5.
99. Kant, *Die Religion innerhalb der Grenzen der blossen Vernunft* (hereafter "*Die Religion*"), AA, 6:93–94; Kant, *Religion and Rational Theology*, 129.
100. Kant, *Kritik der praktischen Vernunft*, AA, 5:9.
101. Mellin, *Encyclopädisches Wörterbuch der kritischen Philosophie*, 4:515–16.
102. Kant, *Kritik der praktischen Vernunft*, AA, 5:72–73 (Gregor, 198, trans. modified).
103. Kant, *Grundlegung*, AA, 4:402n (Gregor, 56n).
104. Kant, *Kritik der praktischen Vernunft*, AA, 5:84.
105. Mellin, *Encyclopädisches Wörterbuch der kritischen Philosophie*, 1:52–53.
106. Fenves, *Peculiar Fate*, 226.
107. Kant, *Kritik der praktischen Vernunft*, AA, 5:80 (Gregor, 204).
108. Ibid., 117 (Gregor, 234).
109. Ibid., 75.
110. Wood, *Kantian Ethics*, 5–7.
111. Kant, *Kritik der praktischen Vernunft*, AA, 5:75.
112. For more on the relationship between respect and humiliation, see Saurette, *Kantian Imperative*, 122.
113. Kant, *Kritik der praktischen Vernunft*, AA, 5:77 (Gregor, 202).
114. Ibid., 80.
115. Ibid.
116. Henry Allison suggests something similar in *Kant's Theory of Freedom*, 126.

117. Kant, *Die Metaphysik der Sitten*, AA, 6:408 (Gregor, 536). I owe this insight to Saurette, *Kantian Imperative*, 96.
118. Wood, *Kantian Ethics*, 147.
119. Kant, *Die Metaphysik der Sitten*, AA, 6:409.
120. Kant, *Kritik der praktischen Vernunft*, AA, 5:88.
121. Ibid., 126.
122. See also Wood, *Kantian Ethics*, 36.
123. Kant, *Kritik der praktischen Vernunft*, AA, 5:152.
124. See Wood, *Kantian Ethics*, 130–31.
125. Kant, *Die Religion*, AA, 6:47.
126. On Kant's "rebirth" as a secular form of Christian conversion, see Pinkard, *German Philosophy*, 57.
127. Munzel, *Kant's Conception of Moral Character*, 165.
128. Ibid., 167.
129. For an extended argument on this point, see ibid.
130. Kant, *Kritik der praktischen Vernunft*, AA, 5:128.
131. Louden, "Kant's Virtue Ethics," 477.
132. Herdt, *Putting on Virtue*, 325.
133. Kant, *Die Metaphysik der Sitten*, AA, 6:479 (Gregor, 592).
134. Kant, *Kritik der praktischen Vernunft*, AA, 5:128.
135. Kant, *Die Religion*, AA, 6:50.
136. Kant, *Kritik der Urteilskraft*, AA, 5:431.
137. Ibid., 433.
138. Kant, *Kritik der praktischen Vernunft*, AA, 5:71.
139. Kant, *Die Religion*, AA, 6:47.
140. Kant, *Kritik der praktischen Vernunft*, AA, 5:77 (Gregor, 202).
141. Ibid., 5:76.
142. Allison, *Kant's Theory of Freedom*, 126.
143. Kant, *Kritik der praktischen Vernunft*, AA, 5:152.
144. This grafting metaphor captures the melding of causalities in Kant's ethics. For more on this, see Munzel, *Kant's Conception of Moral Character*, 335–45.
145. Kant, *Kritik der praktischen Vernunft*, AA, 5:79.
146. Ibid., 77.
147. Kant, "Was heißt: Sich im Denken orientiren?" AA, 8:142. Kant's "healthy reason," however, is not the same as the "healthy understanding" or "common sense" of Moses Mendelssohn and the popular philosophers like Christian Garve. For Kant, a truly healthy reason cognized everything a priori, whereas the latter cognized everything a posteriori.
148. Ibid.
149. Kant, "Idee zu einer allgemeinen Geschichte in weltbürgerlicher Absicht" (hereafter "Idee zu einer allgemeinen Geschichte"), AA, 8:19.
150. Kant, *Kritik der praktischen Vernunft*, AA, 5:163.
151. See Kant, *Die Religion*, AA, 6:35, 39–40, 44.
152. Allison, *Kant's Theory of Freedom*, 145.
153. Pippin, *Modernism as a Philosophical Problem*, 48.
154. Kant, "Beantwortung der Frage: Was ist Aufklärung?" AA, 8:35.
155. The term *mündig* derives from *munt*, a legal term that denotes the place of the father over his wife and children in the domestic sphere. In this sense, *mündig* would signify a son who has grown to become his own *Hausherr* and thus legally his own master. See Sommer, *Historisches Wörterbuch der Philosophie*, vol. 6, s.v. "Mündigkeit."
156. Kant, "Beantwortung der Frage: Was ist Aufklärung?" AA, 8:41.
157. Munzel, *Kant's Conception of Moral Character*, 344.

158. Kant, "Was heißt: Sich im Denken orientiren?" AA, 8:140.
159. Kant, *Kritik der praktischen Vernunft*, AA, 5:163 (Gregor, 271).
160. Ibid., 162.

CHAPTER 3

1. Hufeland to Kant, Letter 728, AA, 12:137.
2. Ibid.
3. Hufeland, *Makrobiotik*, 281.
4. Karl Philipp Moritz's *Magazin* could be read in this context as exemplary of cultivating the power of the mind over the body. On the relationship of these medical discourses, see Bezold, *Popularphilosophie und Erfahrungsseelenkunde*; see also Hess, *Reconstituting the Body Politic*.
5. Kant, *Anthropologie in pragmatischer Hinsicht*, AA, 7:325.
6. Foucault alludes—however cryptically—to this confusion as well. See Foucault, *Order of Things*, 340–43. On Foucault's discussion of this confusion, see Han, *Foucault's Critical Project*, 17–37.
7. This brief account is indebted to Gardner, *Kant and the Critique of Pure Reason*.
8. Kant, *Kritik der reinen Vernunft*, A299/B355.
9. See Kant, *Anthropologie in pragmatischer Hinsicht*, AA, 7:331.
10. Kant defines "a people" (*Volk*) as "the number of human beings united in a region, insofar as they constitute a whole" (ibid., 311).
11. For a more detailed outline of the content of these sections, see Louden, *Kant's Impure Ethics*, 74–100. I will take up the charges of racism in the following chapter. One place to begin a discussion of Kant and gender is Schott, "Gender of Enlightenment."
12. In the *Kritik der reinen Vernunft*, we have this discussion that parallels the discussion of character in the anthropology fairly well: "Even though it is reason, it must nonetheless exhibit an empirical character. . . . Thus every human being has an empirical character for his power of choice, which is nothing but a certain causality of his reason, so far as that causality exhibits, in its effects in the [field] of appearance, in accordance with which one may derive the rational grounds and the actions themselves according to their kind and degree, and estimate the subjective principles of his power of choice. Because so far, then, as regards this empirical character there is no freedom; and yet it is only in the light of this character that the human being can be studied solely by observing, and in the manner of anthropology seeking to institute a physiological investigation into the motive causes of his actions." Kant, *Kritik der reinen Vernunft*, A549/B577 (Guyer and Wood, 541).
13. Kant, *Anthropologie in pragmatischer Hinsicht*, AA, 7:285.
14. Kant, [*Anthropologie-*] *Vorlesung des Wintersemesters 1775/76* (Friedlander), AA, 25:654.
15. Kant, *Anthropologie in pragmatischer Hinsicht*, AA, 7:307.
16. Kant, [*Anthropologie-*] *Vorlesung des Wintersemesters 1775/76* (Friedlander), AA, 25:654.
17. Kant, [Anthropologie-] *Vorlesung des Wintersemesters 1781/82[?]* (Menschenkunde), AA, 25:1196.
18. Munzel, *Kant's Conception of Moral Character*, 52.
19. Ibid.
20. Kant, *Anthropologie in pragmatischer Hinsicht*, AA, 7:295 (Louden, 392).
21. There is a significant body of work that treats not only the historical periodization of Kant's anthropology lectures in relation to his other work but the evolution of the lectures themselves until the final publication of the *Anthropologie* in 1798. I will not discuss the differences among the lectures here. For a more historical treatment of the lectures and their development, see Zammito, *Kant, Herder, and the Birth of Anthropology*, 292–307; see also Wilson, *Kant's Pragmatic Anthropology*, 7–26, and Erdmann, "Zur Entwicklungsgeschichte." On the shift from an empirical psychology to a pragmatic anthropology, see Brandt, "Ausgewählte Probleme der Kantischen Anthropologie." For a comprehensive overview of the lectures, see Brandt and Stark, "Einleitung."

22. Zammito, *Kant, Herder, and the Birth of Anthropology*, 3.
23. Ibid., 299.
24. Kant, *Kritik der praktischen Vernunft*, AA, 5:29.
25. Brandt and Stark, "Einleitung," xlvi.
26. Stark, "Historical Notes," 21.
27. See Louden, *Kant's Impure Ethics*.
28. Kant, *Anthropologie in pragmatischer Hinsicht*, AA, 7:410.
29. See Foucault, "Introduction." My reading of Kant's *Anthropologie* in this section is indebted to Foucault. For more on Foucault's commentary, see Allen, "Foucault and Enlightenment," and Han, *Foucault's Critical Project*. For a fuller account of Foucault and Enlightenment anthropology, see Foucault, *Order of Things*, 303–41.
30. Kant, *Anthropologie in pragmatischer Hinsicht*, AA, 7:127–28.
31. Kant, *Kritik der Urteilskraft*, AA, 5:206.
32. Kant, *Anthropologie in pragmatischer Hinsicht*, AA, 7:134.
33. Brandt, "Guiding Idea." For more on this, see Frietsch, "Michel Foucaults Einführung."
34. Kant, *Der Streit der Fakultäten*, AA, 7:69.
35. Ibid.
36. Manfred Kuehn uses this term "blueprint" as well; see his introduction to Kant, *Anthropology from a Pragmatic Point of View*.
37. Kant to Herz, Letter 79, AA, 10:145–46.
38. Kant, *Anthropologie in pragmatischer Hinsicht*, AA, 7:321 (Louden, 417).
39. Ibid., 120 (Louden, 231).
40. Kant, *Pädagogik*, AA, 9:443. I cite Natorp's text from the Akademie Ausgabe. Kant lectured on pedagogy four times: during the winter semester of 1776–77, the summer semester of 1780, the winter semester of 1783–84, and the winter semester of 1786–87.
41. Kant, *Anthropologie in pragmatischer Hinsicht*, AA, 7:119.
42. "Handle nur nach derjenigen Maxime, durch die du zugleich wollen kannst, dass sie ein allgemeines Gesetz werde." Kant, *Grundlegung*, AA, 4:421.
43. Kant, *Anthropologie in pragmatischer Hinsicht*, AA, 7:119 (Louden, 231).
44. Ibid., 187.
45. See, for example, Pölitz, *Populäre Anthropologie*.
46. For other accounts of the variations of pragmatic, see Wood, "Unsocial Sociability."
47. Brandt notes this as well and adds an argumentative tone to boot: "Kant's anthropology does not set out from the 'whole of man' as a unity of body." See Brandt, "Ausgewählte Probleme," 19.
48. Kant, *Anthropologie in pragmatischer Hinsicht*, AA, 7:119.
49. Herz, "D. Ernst Platner," 37.
50. Kant, [*Anthropologie-*] *Vorlesung des Wintersemesters 1772/73* (Collins), AA, 25:9.
51. For an especially provocative reading of Kant and Platner, see Brown, *Gothic Text*, especially the chapters "At the Limits of Kantian Philosophy" and "Kant and the Doctors."
52. Kant, [*Anthropologie-*] *Vorlesung des Wintersemesters 1775/76* (Friedlander), AA, 25:470.
53. Ibid., 472.
54. Steffens, *Anthropologie*, 7.
55. The Jena philosopher professor and Kantian evangelist Karl Leonhard Rheinhold, a student of Platner, attacks Platner's tepid Kantianism. Referring to a dinner with Platner in Naumburg, he writes of the "disgusting presence of the philosopher Platner[, who is] . . . an opponent of the Kantian philosophy." Although Platner remained deferential to Kantian philosophy, and hoped to spend "just eight days" with Rheinhold to discuss it, his hesitance to embrace it led a series of Kantians to dismiss him as a competitor who could only be considered a popular philosopher who "completely misunderstood" Kant's philosophy. Quoted in Kosenina, *Ernst Platners Anthropologie und Philosophie*, 18–22.

56. Platner, "Vorrede," in *Neue Anthropologie*.
57. Wood, "Kant and the Problem of Human Nature," 41.
58. Kant, [*Anthropologie-*] *Vorlesung des Wintersemesters 1784/85* (Mrongovius), AA, 25:1211.
59. Mellin, *Encyclopädisches Wörterbuch der kritischen Philosophie*, 1:277–79.
60. Schmid, *Wörterbuch*, 63.
61. Kant, [*Anthropologie-*] *Vorlesung des Wintersemesters 1784/85* (Mrongovius), AA, 25:1213.
62. Kant, [*Anthropologie-*] *Vorlesung des Wintersemesters 1772/73* (Collins), AA, 25:9.
63. Kant, *Pädagogik*, AA, 9:443.
64. Kant, *Anthropologie in pragmatischer Hinsicht*, AA, 7:324.
65. Ibid., 120.
66. Kant, [*Anthropologie-*] *Vorlesung des Wintersemesters 1784/85* (Mrongovius), AA, 25:1209.
67. Kant, [*Anthropolgogie-*] *Vorlesung des Wintersemesters 1772/73* (Collins), AA, 25:9.
68. On Kant's anthropology as a political anthropology, see Hess, *Reconstituting the Body Politic*, 189–210.
69. Kant, *Logik*, AA, 9:23.
70. Ibid.
71. Kant, *Kritik der reinen Vernunft*, A839/B867.
72. Quoted in Fenves, *Peculiar Fate*, 106.
73. Wilson, *Kant's Pragmatic Anthropology*, 111.
74. Kant, *Reflexionen zur Anthropologie*, AA, 15:800.
75. Ibid., 801.
76. Kant, [*Anthropologie-*] *Vorlesung des Wintersemesters 1781/82* (Menschenkunde), AA, 25:856.
77. Quoted in Wilson, *Kant's Pragmatic Anthropology*, 114. See Kant, *Reflexionen zur Logik*, AA, 16:862.
78. Kant, *Reflexionen zur Logik*, AA, 16:862.
79. Kant, *Anthropologie in pragmatischer Hinsicht*, AA, 7:121.
80. In "Introduction," Foucault notes the centrality of the dinner table as a center for exchange as well.
81. Kant, *Anthropologie in pragmatischer Hinsicht*, AA, 7:278 (Louden, 378).
82. This element continues to frustrate critics of Kant's anthropology. We will see this in our discussion of Schleiermacher, but the attacks, as Zammito notes, have not let up. See Zammito, *Kant, Herder, and the Birth of Anthropology*, 298–99; see also, Brandt and Stark, "Einleitung," xviii.
83. See Louden, *Kant's Impure Ethics*, 176–77.
84. Kant, [*Anthropologie-*] *Vorlesung des Wintersemesters 1775/76* (Friedlander), AA, 25:471.
85. Ibid.
86. Kant, "Recensionen von J. G. Herders *Ideen*," AA, 8:56.
87. Kant, *Anthropologie in pragmatischer Hinsicht*, AA, 7:328 (Louden, 423).
88. Ibid., 331 (Louden, 426).
89. Herder, *Ideen*, in *Herders Sämtliche Werke*, 13:342.
90. Kant, "Recensionen von J. G. Herders *Ideen*," AA, 8:65. This translation follows "Review of J. G. Herder's *Ideas for the Philosophy of the History of Humanity. Parts 1 and 2*," in Kant, *Anthropology, History, and Education*, 141.
91. On the exchange between Herder and Kant over the former's *Ideen*, see Zammito, *Genesis*, 178–88.
92. Wood, *Kant's Ethical Thought*, 229.
93. For more on Herder's critique of Kant's philosophy of history and his reaction to Kant's reviews, see Haym, *Herder*, 277–90, and Zammito, "Herder and Historical Metanarrative."
94. Allen Wood makes this point as well. See Wood, *Kant's Ethical Thought*, 389.
95. Arendt, *Lectures on Kant's Political Philosophy*, 77. Quoted in Wood, *Kant's Ethical Thought*, 389n. For other formulations of this charge, see Stern, "Problem of History," and Fackenheim, "Kant's Concept of History." Allen Wood offers his rebuttal to these charges in *Kant's Ethical Thought*, 389n.

96. Kant, "Recensionen von J. G. Herders *Ideen*," AA, 8:65. This translation follows "Review of J. G. Herder's *Ideas for the Philosophy of the History of Humanity. Parts 1 and 2*," in Kant, *Anthropology, History, and Education*, 121–42.

97. This discussion follows in important respects Wood's discussion of the Herder-Kant debate. See Wood, *Kant's Ethical Thought*, 233.

CHAPTER 4

1. Kant, *Grundlegung*, AA, 4:422–23.
2. Louden, *Kant's Impure Ethics*, 102.
3. Kant, *Anthropologie in pragmatischer Hinsicht*, AA, 7:325 (Louden, 420, trans. modified).
4. For examples of this, see the collection of eighteenth-century essays in Hinske, *Was ist Aufklärung?*
5. This and the next paragraph follow Brandt's discussion of destiny in "Guiding Idea."
6. Moses Mendelssohn, "Ueber die Frage: was heißt aufklären?" quoted in Ciafardone, *Die Philosophie der deutschen Aufklärung*, 14.
7. Moses Mendelssohn, quoted in Abbt, *Vermischte Werke*, 2:14.
8. Kant, *Anthropologie in pragmatischer Hinsicht*, AA, 7:324 (Louden, 419).
9. This section includes comments on physiognomy and temperaments. For Kant physiognomy is the "art of judging the inside of a person—that is, his way of being or way of thinking—according to his visible form, thus from the outside" (ibid., 295). Kant bases his discussion of temperaments on the four medieval humors: sanguine, melancholic, choleric, and phlegmatic.
10. Kant suggests that his comments on the character of peoples are more empirical than philosophical—that is, he considers the characteristics of these varieties contingent rather than necessary. They are the purview of geographers who classify according empirical criteria, in contrast to philosophers who "classify according to principles of reason" (ibid., 312n).
11. Ibid., 312.
12. Kant is referring to Christoph Girtanner, *Über das Kantische Prinzip für die Naturgeschichte* (Göttingen, 1796).
13. Kant, *Anthropologie in pragmatischer Hinsicht*, AA, 7:120.
14. Ibid., 320.
15. Translations of these essays taken from Kant, *Anthropology, History, and Education* (hereafter "*AHE*") will be cited by German title and volume and page number in the Akademie Ausgabe (AA) and by page number in *AHE*. For an overview of Kant's theory of race, see Bernasconi, "Who Invented the Concept of Race?" On race and teleology, see McCarthy, "On the Way to a World Republic?"
16. See M. Neumann, "Philosophische Nachrichten."
17. The secret instructions of the British admiralty, for example, to Samuel Wallis, who discovered Tahiti in 1767, were to clarify the Southern Continent or *Terra australis incognita* question, that is, to confirm or disprove the existence of a southern continent in the South Seas. See Bitterli, *Alte Welt—neue Welt*, 180–82.
18. Bitterli, *Die Wilden und die Zivilisierten*, 28.
19. Ibid., 29. See also Parry, *Age of Reconnaissance*. Parry distinguishes the sixteenth century as an age of "original exploration" marked by a "geographical curiosity," while he characterizes seventeenth-century travel as more concentrated on "distant trade and commerce."
20. Bitterli, *Alte Welt—neue Welt*, 186.
21. Forster, *Cook, der Entdecker*, in *Werke*, 5:259.
22. Bitterli, *Alte Welt—neue Welt*, 195. In Germany the first "völkerliche Fragebogen" appears in 1762 when the orientalist Johann David Michaelis of the Göttingen Society of Sciences provided Carsten Niebuhr a questionnaire for his Arabian journey of 1762.

23. Kant, "Bestimmung des Begriffs einer Menschenrace," AA, 8:92 (*AHE,* 146).
24. On this, see, for example, Zantop, *Colonial Fantasies,* 68–70.
25. Kant, *Reflexionen zur Anthropologie,* AA, 15.2:877–79.
26. Zammito, "Policing Polygeneticism in Germany," 35–54.
27. While we cannot definitively establish whether Kant read Kames, Zammito convincingly concludes that Kames and the broader polygenetic debate "triggered" Kant's first essay. For more on the history of polygeneticism, see Bernasconi, "Who Invented the Concept of Race?"
28. Zammito, "Policing Polygeneticism in Germany," 40.
29. For more on what Kant considered the conflation of the human being and nature, see Zammito, *Genesis,* 189–213.
30. Kant, "Von den verschiedenen Racen," AA, 2:429 (*AHE,* 84). On Buffon's rule, see Roger, *Buffon,* 459–60.
31. Kant, "Von den verschiedenen Racen," AA, 2:429 (*AHE,* 84).
32. Roger describes the goal of Buffon's lifelong work *Histoire naturelle:* "It was not . . . through classing morphologies but in systematizing our knowledge of living beings as they live, through comparing their physiologies, their 'habits,' according to the climates in which they live, that we could read 'that high degree of knowledge where we can see how particular effects, where we can compare Nature with herself in her great operations'" (*Buffon,* 90).
33. Sloan's claim that with Buffon we see the first robust entrance of time into nature is a bit confusing. He claims that his account of historicism differs from merely genetic accounts, but I fail to see the fundamental difference. Sloan writes that Buffon proposes "physical networks of historical filiations." See Sloan, "Buffon," 118. I would suggest that Buffon's temporalization of organic beings is not synonymous with a historicization of organic beings. The former simply suggests that organic beings endure within time—that is, species are the "constant succession of similar individuals" throughout a linear temporality (Buffon, cited in Eddy, "Buffon's Histoire naturelle," 648). The latter implies a more complicated notion of time that involves making sense of origins and the anticipation of future events, something completely beyond the scope and claims of sheer temporality. This difference is key, because as we shall see, Kant, while appealing to Buffon's temporalization of organic beings, extends his account of nature to a more robust historization of nature in the form of a teleology. On differing accounts of Buffon's historicism, see Eddy, "Buffon's Histoire naturelle."
34. As Sloan explains, Buffon's concern with the "separation of the 'abstract' from 'real' orders . . . underlie[s] [his] attack on taxonomy, particularity Linnaean taxonomy." Citing Buffon, Sloan writes: "[The Linnaean system] is not a science, and is at most only a convention, an arbitrary language, a means of understanding; from it results no real knowledge." See Sloan, "Buffon," 109–53.
35. Ibid., 117.
36. For an enlightening article on Kant's appropriation and application of late eighteenth-century notions of embryonic generation, see Sloan, "Preforming the Categories."
37. Ibid., 238.
38. Kant, "Von den verschiedenen Racen," AA, 2:435 (*AHE,* 95).
39. Mark Larrimore makes the astute observation that both Kant's diagram and argument in this essay seem "to imply that the white brunettes are not part of any race, but are the surviving members of the stem genus [*Stammgattung*]." See Larrimore, "Sublime Waste."
40. Kant, "Von den verschiedenen Racen," AA, 2:440 (*AHE,* 95).
41. On this hierarchy, see, for example, McCarthy, "On the Way to a World Republic."
42. Kant, *Reflexionen zur Anthropologie,* AA, 15:878; see also Kant, [Anthropologie-] *Vorlesung des Wintersemesters 1781/82* (Menschenkunde), AA, 25:1187.
43. Kant, "Von den verschiedenen Racen," AA, 2:429 (*AHE,* 84).
44. Kant, "Bestimmung des Begriffs einer Menschenrace," AA, 8:94. On this point, see Larrimore, "Sublime Waste," 106.

45. See also Louden, *Kant's Impure Ethics*, 98, and Kleingeld, "Kant's Second Thoughts on Race."

46. Kant, "Bestimmung des Begriffs einer Menschenrace," AA, 8:99.

47. Even this disarticulation, however, is confounded by various remarks that seem to associate physical with moral characteristics. For an overview of such remarks, see Louden, *Kant's Impure Ethics*, 98–100.

48. Kant, "Bestimmung des Begriffs einer Menschenrace," AA, 8:91.

49. Kant draws on, for example, the English physician James Lind, *An Essay on Diseases Incidental to Europeans in Hot Climates* (London, 1768).

50. Kant, "Von den verschiedenen Racen," AA, 2:435 (*AHE*, 90).

51. Louden, *Kant's Impure Ethics*, 105.

52. For similar accounts, see Hill and Boxill, "Kant and Race," and McCarthy, "On the Way to a World Republic?"

53. See Bernasconi, "Kant as an Unfamiliar Source of Racism"; Eze, *Achieving Our Humanity*; and Mills, "Kant's *Untermenschen*."

54. See Kleingeld, "Kant's Second Thoughts on Race." Kleingeld also gives a very helpful overview of the recent scholarship on the issue from which I draw here.

55. Kant, "Bestimmung des Begriffs einer Menschenrace," AA, 8:91.

56. Ibid., 98 (*AHE*, 151).

57. Kant, "Von den verschiedenen Racen," AA, 2:435.

58. Quoted in Sadji, *Der Negermythos*, 215.

59. Forster, "Noch etwas über die Menschenraßen," in *Werke*, 8:132.

60. Forster to Soemmering, *Briefe, 1784–1787*, in *Werke*, 14:293.

61. Forster, "Noch etwas über die Menschenraßen," in *Werke*, 8:142.

62. I am indebted to Thomas Strack's excellent discussion of this point. See Strack, "Philosophical Anthropology."

63. Sloan makes a similar point in "Buffon," 132.

64. Forster, "Noch etwas über die Menschenraßen," in *Werke*, 8:143.

65. Susanne Zantop makes the important point that both monogeneticists and polygeneticists "seem to share the conviction that the white male is the primeval man, who possesses the most harmonious countenance and has therefore rightfully achieved cultural superiority." See Zantop, *Colonial Fantasies*, 78.

66. Forster, "Noch etwas über die Menschenraßen," in *Werke*, 8:139.

67. Kant, "Über den Gebrauch teleologischer Principien in der Philosophie" (hereafter "Über den Gebrauch"), AA, 8:160.

68. Forster begins his essay with an appeal to Linnaean taxonomy, whose greatest achievement, he claims, is the exact delineations of the levels of relation. See Forster, *Reise um die Welt*, in *Werke*, 2:132.

69. Sloan, "Buffon," 133.

70. Kant, "Über den Gebrauch," AA, 8:163 (*AHE*, 199).

71. Ibid., 160.

72. See Beiser, *Fate of Reason*, 44–91.

73. Kant, "Was heißt: Sich im Denken orientiren?" AA, 8:136.

74. On this, see Shell, *Embodiment of Reason*, 197–99.

75. Kant, "Über den Gebrauch," AA, 8:160 (*AHE*, 197, trans. modified).

76. As recent scholars have pointed out, the possible coincidence of the physical and moral realms, combined with Kant's racial hierarchy, suggests that his teleology ultimately excludes non-whites from the progress of human history. Larrimore, to whom I am indebted here, makes this case well. See Larrimore, "Sublime Waste," 166–125, and Engelstein, *Anxious Anatomy*, 229–30.

77. For a discussion of this essay and his debate with Forster in relationship to Kant's broader thinking on the organism, especially in relationship to the *Kritik der Urteilskraft*, see Zammito,

Genesis, 207–11. Zammito argues, however, that Kant's essay "Über den Gebrauch" was actually an attack on Herder.
78. Kant, "Über den Gebrauch," AA, 8:179 (*AHE*, 214).
79. Larrimore, "Sublime Waste," 117.
80. Kant, *Sachliche Erläuterungen*, AA, 8:468.
81. Quoted in Shell, *Embodiment of Reason*, 163.
82. Kant, "Idee zu einer allgemeinen Geschichte," AA, 8:29.
83. Shell, *Embodiment of Reason*, 174.
84. Kant, "Idee zu einer allgemeinen Geschichte," AA, 8:30.
85. Ibid., 29.
86. Kant's language here—"absurd" and "strange"—underlines the provisional character of Kant's idea for a universal history. He is not laying out a scientific discipline of history in this essay. On this point, see Guyer, *Kant on Freedom, Law, and Happiness*, 372–497. For more detailed treatments of Kant's philosophy of history, see Kleingeld, *Fortschritt und Vernunft*, and Yovel, *Kant and the Philosophy of History*.
87. Kant, *Anthropologie in pragmatischer Hinsicht*, AA, 7:208.
88. Koselleck, *Vergangene Zukunft*, 53.
89. Theisen, "Memories of the Future," 61.
90. Novalis, *Fragmente und Studien, 1799–1800*, in *Schriften*, 3:648.
91. Koselleck, *Vergangene Zukunft*, 62.
92. Kant, "Idee zu einer allgemeinen Geschichte," AA, 8:29.
93. Ibid., 29n.
94. Kant, *Grundlegung*, AA, 4:437n (Gregor, 86n).
95. On this point, see Zammito, *Genesis*, 323–25.
96. Kant, *Kritik der Urteilskraft*, AA, 5:447–48.
97. Kant, "Idee zu einer allgemeinen Geschichte," AA, 8:21.
98. Kant, *Kritik der Urteilskraft*, AA, 5:431.
99. Kant, "Idee zu einer allgemeinen Geschichte," AA, 8:26.
100. Kant, *Anthropologie in pragmatischer Hinsicht*, AA, 7:322.
101. Ibid., 324.
102. Brandt discusses the teleological orientation of Kant's anthropology, beginning with the 1773 lectures, as well (Brandt and Stark, "Einleitung," xlv). Holly Wilson makes an extended argument for the teleological orientation of the Kant's anthropology. See Wilson, "Kant's Integration of Morality and Anthropology"; see also Wilson, *Kant's Pragmatic Anthropology*, 35–42.
103. Shell, "Kant's Concept of a Human Race," 65–66.
104. Kant, *Anthropologie in pragmatischer Hinsicht*, AA, 7:122.
105. See also, Cheah, *Inhuman Conditions*, 96.
106. Kant, *Anthropologie in pragmatischer Hinsicht*, AA, 7:323.
107. Ibid., 331.
108. Kant, [*Anthropologie-*] *Vorlesung des Wintersemesters 1775/76* (Friedlander), AA, 25:472.
109. Kant, "Idee zu einer allgemeinen Geschichte," AA, 8:29.
110. Forster, *Reise um die Welt*, in *Werke*, 2:146.
111. Forster to Jacobi, *Briefe, 1787–1789*, in *Werke*, 15:208.
112. Forster, "Noch etwas über die Menschenraßen," in *Werke*, 8:141.
113. On this, see Uhlig, *Georg Forster*, 268.
114. Forster, "Noch etwas über die Menschenraßen," in *Werke*, 8:78.
115. Forster to Jacobi, *Briefe, 1787–1789*, in *Werke*, 15:235.
116. Neumann, "Philosophische Nachrichten," 533.
117. Forster, *Reise um die Welt*, in *Werke*, 2:10.
118. Forster, "Über lokale und allgemeine Bildung," in *Werke*, 7:45.
119. Forster, "Noch etwas über die Menschenraßen," in *Werke*, 8:139.

120. Ibid.
121. Forster, "Versuch einer Naturgeschichte des Menschen," in *Werke*, 8:159.
122. Ibid.
123. Forster, *Kleine Schriften*, in *Werke*, 5:345.
124. Forster, "Noch etwas über die Menschenraßen," in *Werke*, 8:134.
125. Forster, *Geschichte der Reisen seit Cook: Ankündigung*, in *Werke*, 5:392.
126. Forster, *Cook, der Entdecker*, in *Werke*, 5:194.
127. Forster, *Geschichte der Reisen seit Cook: Ankündigung*, in *Werke*, 5:383.
128. For Forster this point in time will perhaps be accompanied by an "odd revolution" in the "thought and action" in the peoples of India and China, whose character, he claimed, had "essentially remained unchanged" (*Cook, der Entdecker*, in *Werke*, 5:293).
129. Schlegel, *Kritische Schriften und Fragmente*, 1:194.
130. Forster, *Cook, der Entdecker*, in *Werke*, 5:192–93.
131. Kant, *Anthropologie in pragmatischer Hinsicht*, AA, 7:120.
132. Kant, *Kritik der reinen Vernunft*, B4.

CHAPTER 5

1. Dilthey, *Leben Schleiermachers*, 224.
2. Ibid., 227.
3. Alexander, graf von Dohra, to Schleiermacher, Letter 356, in *Kritische Gesamtausgabe* (hereafter "*KGA*"), 5.2:67. *KGA* is cited by volume and part, followed by page.
4. For more details on Schleiermacher's relationship to Schlegel and the German romantics, see Nowak, *Schleiermacher*. For more classical studies, see Haym, *Die Romantische Schule*, 412–555, and Dilthey, *Leben Schleiermachers*, 183–312.
5. A. W. Schlegel to Schleiermacher, Letter 933, in *KGA*, 5.4:218.
6. Friedrich Schlegel to Schleiermacher, Letter 791, in *KGA*, 5.3:379.
7. Specifically, "Zur Siedlungsgeschichte Neuhollands" (1799–1802), "Rezension von Immanuel Kant: *Anthropologie*" (1799), and *Über die Religion: Reden an die Gebildeten unter ihren Verächtern* (1799).
8. Schleiermacher, "Rezension von Immanuel Kant: Anthropologie" (hereafter "Rezension"), in *KGA*, 1.2:369.
9. Ibid., 365.
10. Schleiermacher to F. Schlegel, Letter 910, in *KGA*, 5.4:151.
11. Having reached New Holland's east coast on August 22, 1770, James Cook claimed it for King George III and renamed it New South Wales. Throughout this chapter, however, I refer to New Holland, since that is the most common reference in Schleiermacher's text.
12. Fülleborn, "Abriss," 156.
13. Schleiermacher, *Monologen*, in *KGA*, 1.3:9.
14. Kant, *Anthropologie in pragmatischer Hinsicht*, AA, 7:120–21.
15. Schleiermacher, "Rezension," in *KGA*, 1.2:365.
16. Kant acknowledges this problem as well. See Kant, *Anthropologie in pragmatischer Hinsicht*, AA, 7:130.
17. Schleiermacher, "Rezension," in *KGA*, 1.2:366.
18. Marina, "Schleiermacher on the Philosopher's Stone," 213–14. Schleiermacher develops his critique of Kant's notion of transcendental freedom in a series of unpublished essays from 1788 to 1794. His essays on Kant include "Über das höchste Gut" (1789), "Über die Freiheit" (1790–92), and "Über den Wert des Lebens" (1792/93). On these essays, see Blackwell, *Schleiermacher's Early Philosophy of Life*. Schleiermacher resists Kant's dualistic image of the human being as belonging to two different worlds. By at least the winter of 1793–94, Schleiermacher's response to Kant's dualism is

shaped by his work on Spinoza: "Spinozismus" and "Kurze Darstellung des Spinozistischen Systems" (1793–94). On these essays, see Lamm, "Early Philosophical Roots" and, especially, *Living God.* Also see Meckenstock, *Deterministische Ethik und kritische Theologie.*

19. Schleiermacher, "Rezension," in *KGA*, 1.2:367.
20. Schleiermacher, *Über die Religion: Reden an die Gebildeten unter ihren Verächtern* (hereafter "*Über die Religion*"), in *KGA*, 1.2:208. Translations of *Über die Religion* are either mine or are taken from *On Religion: Speeches to Its Cultured Despisers,* translated by Richard Crouter (hereafter "Crouter").
21. Schleiermacher, "Rezension," in *KGA*, 1.2:369.
22. Friedrich Schlegel to Schleiermacher, Letter 791, in *KGA*, 5.3:380.
23. The reconstruction of the publication history of the New Holland materials draws on Gunter Meckenstock's historical introduction to vol. 1, pt. 3 of the *KGA*, lxxxii–xciii.
24. Schleiermacher to Spener, Letter 565, in *KGA*, 5.3:13.
25. Schleiermacher to Spener, Letter 699, in *KGA*, 5.3:189.
26. Schleiermacher, "Zur Siedlungsgeschichte Neuhollands" (hereafter "Siedlungsgeschichte"), in *KGA*, 1.3:664.
27. Schleiermacher to Spener, Letter 646, in *KGA*, 5.3:108.
28. Schleiermacher, "Siedlungsgeschichte," in *KGA*, 1.3:269–70.
29. Ibid., 271.
30. Phillip, *Voyage of Governor Phillip to Botany Bay,* 54.
31. Schleiermacher, "Siedlungsgeschichte," in *KGA*, 1.3:279.
32. Schleiermacher, "Rezension," in *KGA*, 1.2:368.
33. Tench, *Nachricht von der Expedizion nach Botany-Bay,* 85.
34. Collins, *An Account of the English Colony,* 141–42, 65.
35. I refer to the version of *Über die Religion* published in 1799, not to the revised editions of 1800 and 1821.
36. Haym, *Die Romantische Schule,* 420.
37. The literature on this aspect of the *Über die Religion* is voluminous. On the relationship of *Über die Religion* to Schleiermacher's early essays on Spinoza, see Lamm, *Living God.* On *Über die Religion* and Schleiermacher's early essays on Kant and in relation to Fichte, see Blackwell, *Schleiermacher's Early Philosophy of Life;* Hertel, *Das theologische Denken Schleiermachers,* 145–82; and Meckenstock, *Deterministische Ethik und kritische Theologie.*
38. Barth, "Nachwort," 300. Barth mocks this anthropological character as the "glorious elimination of the subject-object distinction." Barth's characterization of Schleiermacher's theology as anthropological assumes the incompatibility of the anthropological and the religious. For Barth, it is precisely this anthropological-historical character that leads nineteen-century theology into a "dead end" by allowing the religious and the historical to coexist. See Barth, *Die protestantische Theologie im 19. Jahrhundert,* 461.
39. Reynolds, "Religion Within the Limits of History," 52–53.
40. Schleiermacher, *Über die Religion,* in *KGA*, 1.2:208. As numerous scholars have noted, the exemplary metaphysical system that Schleiermacher wants to challenge is Fichte's Wissenschaftlehre. On the relationship between Schleiermacher and Fichte, see Meckenstock, *Deterministische Ethik und kritische Theologie,* and Nowak, *Schleiermacher.*
41. Schleiermacher, *Über die Religion,* in *KGA*, 1.2:211 (Crouter, 22).
42. This concept of the immanence of the infinite within the finite stems from Schleiermacher's earlier work on Spinoza. See Lamm, *Living God,* 57–94, and Seifert, *Die Theologie des jungen Schleiermacher,* 45–48.
43. Kant, *Kritik der reinen Vernunft,* A49/B33.
44. Ibid., A51/B75.
45. Schleiermacher, *Über die Religion,* in *KGA*, 1.2:213 (Crouter, 24).
46. Schleiermacher, *Gedanken,* in *KGA*, 1.2:25.

47. For more on the relationship of religion and history in Schleiermacher, see Nowak, "Geschichte."
48. Schleiermacher, *Über die Religion*, in *KGA*, 1.2:261.
49. Schleiermacher, "Rezension," in *KGA*, 1.2:367.
50. Schleiermacher, *Über die Religion*, in *KGA*, 1.2:255 (Crouter, 62; trans. modified).
51. Schlegel, *Kritische Schriften und Fragmente*, 1:249.
52. Andreas Arndt argues that for both Schleiermacher and Schlegel the dialectic is "the poetic element of philosophy" that makes possible the "mediation" of the finite and infinite. See Arndt, "Zur Vorgeschichte," 328–33. A discussion of Schleiermacher's own systematic dialectic is beyond the scope and aims of the present discussion. Although he never edited a version of his dialectic, he delivered lectures at the University of Berlin on a systematic dialectic beginning in 1811 and again in 1814, 1828, 1831, and 1832. Arndt has edited versions of these lectures for the *KGA*, sec. 2, vol. 10, pts. 1 and 2.
53. Schleiermacher, *Über die Religion*, in *KGA*, 1.2:243.

CHAPTER 6

1. Zammito, *Kant, Herder, and the Birth of Anthropology*, 350–51.
2. Kant, *Logik*, AA, 9:25.
3. Pölitz, *Populäre Anthropologie*, xxxvii.
4. Kant, *Anthropologie in pragmatischer Hinsicht*, AA, 7:122.
5. Theisen, "Macroanthropos."
6. Novalis, *Das Allgemeine Brouillon*, in *Schriften*, 3:286, 3:359.
7. Ibid., 3:457.
8. Ibid., 3:356. For a more extensive account of these historical relations, see Saul, "Poëtisirung d[es] Körpers"; see also Stadler, "Zur Anthropologie Friedrich Hardenbergs (Novalis)."
9. Foucault, *Order of Things*, 65.
10. See, for example, Mähl, *Die Idee des goldenen Zeitalters*. Herbert Uerlings's recent work on Novalis is one of the few exceptions. See his *Friedrich von Hardenberg, genannt Novalis*.
11. "Welcher Lebendige, Sinnbegabte, liebt nicht vor allen Wundererscheinungen des verbreiteten Raums um ihn, das allerfreuliche Licht—mit seinen Farben, seinen Strahlen und Wogen; seiner milden Allgegenwart, als weckender Tag? Wie des Lebens innerste Seele atmet es der rastlosen Gestirne Riesenwelt, und schwimmt tanzend in seiner blauen Flut—atmet es der funkelnde, ewigruhende Stein, die sinnige, saugende Pflanze, und das wilde, brennende, vielgestaltete Tier—vor allen aber der herrliche Fremdling mit seinen sinnvollen Augen, dem schwebenden Gange, und den zartgeschlossenen, tonreichen Lippen." Novalis, *Hymnen an die Nacht*, no. 1, in *Schriften*, 1:132. Aside from minor changes, I use Dick Higgins's translation in *Novalis: Hymns to the Night*.
12. On an Enlightenment hierarchy of the senses that privileges the eye over other organs of sense, see Braungart, *Leibhafter Sinn*, 55–99.
13. "Abwärts wend ich mich zu der heiligen, unaussprechlichen, geheimnisvollen Nacht. Fernab liegt die Welt—in eine tiefe Gruft versenkt—wüst und einsam ist ihre Stelle. In den Saiten der Brust weht tiefe Wehmut. In Tautropfen will ich hinuntersinken und mit der Asche mich vermischen.—Fernen der Errinerung, Wünsche der Jugend, der Kindheit Träume, des ganzen langen Lebens kurze Freuden und vergebliche Hoffnungen kommen in grauen Kleidern, wie Abendnebel nach der Sonne Untergang. In andern Räumen schlug die lustigen Gezelte das Licht auf. Sollte es nie zu seinen Kindern wiederkommen, die mit der Unschuld Glauben seiner harren?" Novalis, *Hymnen an die Nacht*, no. 1, in *Schriften*, 1:132.
14. Ibid., 1:133.
15. Novalis, *Fragmente und Studien, 1799–1800*, in *Schriften*, 3:682.

16. For an extensive overview of the intellectual-historical context and composition history of the *Fichte-Studien*, see Frank, *Unendliche Annäherung*, 785–801.

17. For a consideration of this problem within the larger context of Novalis's *Fichte-Studien*, see Waibel, "Innres, äußres Organ."

18. Novalis, *Fichte-Studien*, in *Schriften*, 2:272.

19. In this passage Novalis uses *Seele* instead of *Geist*. For Novalis, the *Seele* is the individualized *Geist*: "the soul is nothing but bound, restrained [mind]" [die Seele ist nichts als gebundener, gehemmter (Geist)] (Novalis, *Das Allgemeine Brouillon*, in *Schriften*, 3:316). Novalis tends to use *Seele* when speaking of the individual and *Geist* when speaking of more general relations, but he is not always consistent in his use of the terms. On these terms, see Senckel, *Individualität und Totalität*, 79–84.

20. Novalis, *Fichte-Studien*, in *Schriften*, 2:272.

21. Novalis does not adopt one particular physiological model; instead, he draws on various eighteenth-century sources. Albrecht von Haller, whose 1752 lectures initiated debates on stimulation (*Reitz*) and vital forces for the remainder of the century, distinguished sensibility and irritability as the two primarily forces of organisms. He argued that sensibility was a nervous phenomenon associated with the mind and soul and irritability, in contrast, was a disposition to movement inherent to bodily fibers and muscles. Novalis was particularly interested in the work of the Scottish physician John Brown (1735–88), who introduces the notion of "excitability," which refers to processes of mental and sensual reactions to outside stimuli. On Novalis and Brown, see Neubauer, *Bifocal Vision*. On the history of these physiological debates in general, see Richards, *Romantic Conception of Life*, 307–24; see also Jantzen, "Physiologische Theorien."

22. Novalis, *Logologische Fragmente I*, in *Schriften*, 2:540.

23. Novalis, *Das Allgemeine Brouillon*, in *Schriften*, 3:317.

24. Ibid., 318–19.

25. Novalis, *Fragmente und Studien, 1799–1800*, in *Schriften*, 3:574.

26. Novalis, *Logologische Fragmente II*, in *Schriften*, 2:550.

27. Novalis, *Fragmente und Studien, 1799–1800*, in *Schriften*, 3:598.

28. Kant, *Anthropologie in pragmatischer Hinsicht*, AA, 7:144.

29. Novalis, *Fichte-Studien*, in *Schriften*, 2:214.

30. Horkheimer and Adorno, *Dialectic of Enlightenment*, 25. For more on this reading of Novalis in terms of Adorno and Horkheimer, see Utz, *Das Auge und das Ohr*, 19–24.

31. Locke, *Correspondences*, 651.

32. For more on the Molyneux problem, see Jay, *Downcast Eyes*, and Morgan, *Molyneux's Question*.

33. These speculative musings did, however, take on a more tangible character in the eighteenth century through the increased interest in actual cases of "recovery from blindness" following the removal of cataracts. On this, see Morgan, *Molyneux's Question*, esp. chap. 2.

34. See, for example, Jay, *Downcast Eyes*, 83–148.

35. The literature on Herder and the senses is extensive. For a recent overview, see Zeuch, *Umkehr der Sinneshierarchie*, 1–34.

36. Herder, *Viertes kritisches Wäldchen*, in *Herders Sämtliche Werke*, 4:68, 80. Here, I translate *Gefühl* as "touch," since it is clear in the context of use that Herder is referring to feeling as touch.

37. Ibid., 103–4.

38. Herder, "Sinn des Gefühls," in *Herders Sämtliche Werke*, 4:244.

39. Novalis, *Studien zur Bildenden Kunst*, in *Schriften*, 2:650.

40. Novalis, *Fragmente und Studien, 1799–1800*, in *Schriften*, 3:663.

41. Novalis, *Das Allgemeine Brouillon*, in *Schriften*, 3:317–18.

42. This intensification of opposites or poles until they merge is a trope of romantic *Naturphilosophie* that is especially evident in Schelling. On this, see Daiber, *Experimentalphysik des Geistes*.

43. Novalis, *Logologische Fragmente II*, in *Schriften*, 2:547–48.

44. For an overview of eighteenth-century distinctions among the terms "sense," "sensations," and "feeling," see Frank, *Selbstgefühl*, 11–25.

45. Novalis, *Das Allgemeine Brouillon*, in *Schriften*, 3:250.

46. Ibid., 3:429.

47. Novalis, *Anekdoten*, in *Schriften*, 2:578.

48. Novalis, *Die Lehrlinge zu Sais*, in *Schriften*, 1:96–97.

49. Caroline Welsch reads these same passages on attention; but while my reading is indebted to hers, she considers attention strictly in terms of its physiological function. See Welsch, "Die Physiologie der Einbildungskraft um 1800." On the history of attention in the Enlightenment, see Steigerwald and Watzke, *Reiz, Imagination, Aufmerksamkeit*.

50. Novalis, *Die Lehrlinge zu Sais*, in *Schriften*, 1:97.

51. Novalis, *Anekdoten*, in *Schriften*, 2:578.

52. "Sie [die Thoren] fühlen dich nicht in der goldenen Flut der Trauben—in des Mandelbaums Wunderöl, und dem braunen Safte des Mohns. Sie wissen nicht, daß du es bist der des zarten Mädchens Busen umschwebt, und zum Himmel den Schoß macht." Novalis, *Hymnen an die Nacht*, no. 2, in *Schriften*, 1:133; Novalis, *Hymns to the Night*, 15.

53. In his short but provocative essay, Michel Chaouli notes the expressive force of these phrases as well. See his "Intimations of Mortality," 481–85.

54. Pfau, *Romantic Moods*, 63.

55. Novalis, *Hymnen an die Nacht*, no. 2, in *Schriften*, 1:133.

56. Novalis, *Fichte-Studien*, in *Schriften*, 2:127.

57. Novalis, *Studien zur Bildenden Kunst*, in *Schriften*, 2:650.

58. Novalis, *Fragmente und Studien, 1799–1800*, in *Schriften*, 3:650. Novalis's definition of imagination here recalls Kant's in the *Kritik der reinen Vernunft*: "Imagination is the faculty to represent an object even without it being immediately perceptible" [Einbildungskraft ist das Vermögen einen Gegenstand auch ohne dessen Gegenwart in der Anschauung vorzustellen] (B151).

59. Novalis, *Anekdoten*, in *Schriften*, 2:574. Novalis even speaks of an understanding "expanded" through the imagination (2:270).

60. Novalis, *Fichte-Studien*, in *Schriften*, 2:167.

61. Novalis, *Studien zur Bildenden Kunst*, in *Schriften*, 2:650.

62. See Herder, *Plastik*, in *Johann Gottfried Herder Werke*, 4:257.

63. Saul, "Poëtisirung d[es] Körpers," 164–65.

64. Novalis, *Die Lehrlinge zu Sais*, in *Schriften*, 1:80.

65. See, for example, his essay "Versuch über den Zusammenhang der tierischen Natur des Menschen mit seiner geistigen."

66. Novalis, *Fichte-Studien*, in *Schriften*, 2:273.

67. Novalis, *Heinrich von Ofterdingen*, in *Schriften*, 1:210.

68. In the *Kritik der Urteilskraft*, Kant writes that reflective judgment "gives itself . . . and not nature a law" (AA, 5:180).

69. Novalis, in *Fichte-Studien*, in *Schriften*, 2:252.

70. Hegel, *Vorlesungen über die Ästhetik*, in *Werke*, 15:417.

71. Pfau, *Romantic Moods*, 67.

CHAPTER 7

1. In a letter to Christian Ludwig Neuffer, Friedrich Hölderlin, for example, writes of Fichte's popularity: "Fichte is now the soul of Jean. And thank God he is!" Quoted in Frank, *Philosophical Foundations*, 114.

2. W. Humboldt, *Briefe an Friedrich August Wolf*, 107.

3. A. Humboldt, *Die Jugendbriefe*, 428, 433. On the Humboldt brothers' anatomical studies in Jena, see Jahn, "Die anatomischen Studien der Brüder Humboldt," 91–92; see also Müller-Sievers, *Self-Generation*.

4. As far as I can tell, "Plan einer vergleichenden Anthropologie" and "Das achtzehnte Jahrhundert" were first published in *Wilhelm von Humboldts Gesammelte Schriften*, edited by Albert Leitzmann.

5. W. Humboldt, "Das achtzehnte Jahrhundert," in *Werke*, 1:390.

6. W. Humboldt, "Plan einer vergleichenden Anthropologie," in *Werke*, 1:337.

7. For a more explicit account of Goethe and the discourse of eighteenth-century anthropology, see Bell, *Goethe's Naturalistic Anthropology*.

8. Quoted in Förster, "Die Bedeutung"; see Goethe, *Briefe, Tagebücher und Gespräche*, 629. Goethe is citing Spinoza's *Ethics*, pt. 2, prop. 40, scholium 2. See Parkinson's translation of Spinoza's *Ethics*, 149.

9. Dippel, *Wilhelm von Humboldt*, 109.

10. Goethe, *Schriften zur Morphologie*, 24:227, 228. In translating Goethe's writings on natural science, I have consulted Bertha Mueller's translations in *Goethe's Botanical Writings* and Douglas Miller's translations in *Goethe's Scientific Writings*.

11. Goethe, *Schriften zur Morphologie*, 24:228.

12. See Böhme, "Lebendige Natur."

13. Goethe, *Schriften zur allgemeinen Naturlehre*, 25:29–30.

14. For an excellent analysis of these revisions and their relationship to Goethe's morphology, see Mücke, "Goethe's Metamorphosis."

15. Goethe, *Schriften zur Morphologie*, 24:449.

16. See Lepenies, *Das Ende der Naturgeschichte*, 52–77.

17. Blumenbach even visited Goethe in Weimar in October 1796. See Goethe's letter to Schiller on October 14, 1796, in Schiller and Goethe, *Briefwechsel*, 244. For overviews of this debate, see Larson, *Interpreting Nature*. For a discussion of this debate in relation to Wilhelm von Humboldt, see Reill, "Science and the Construction of the Cultural Sciences."

18. Lenoir, *Strategy of Life*, 19.

19. Blumenbach, *Über den Bildungstrieb*, 12–13.

20. On this section, see Zukert, *Kant on Beauty and Biology*, esp. 87–170.

21. Kant, *Kritik der Urteilskraft*, AA, 5:371; Kant, *Critique of the Power of Judgment* (hereafter "Guyer and Matthews"), 243. Translations of the *Kritik der Urteilskraft* are either mine, or are taken from Kant, *Critique of the Power of Judgment*, edited by Paul Guyer and translated by Paul Guyer and Eric Matthews.

22. Goethe, *Schriften zur Morphologie*, 24:393.

23. For a detailed study of the romantic notion of the organism, see Köchy, *Ganzheit und Wissenschaft*.

24. Quoted in Lenoir, *Strategy of Life*, 21.

25. Goethe, *Schriften zur Morphologie*, 24:451.

26. Kant, *Kritik der Urteilskraft*, AA, 5:180.

27. Goethe, *Schriften zur Morphologie*, 24:447.

28. See Richards, *Romantic Conception of Life*, 470–71.

29. Goethe, *Schriften zur Morphologie*, 24:595.

30. Förster, "Die Bedeutung," 184–85.

31. The following discussion draws heavily on Förster, "Die Bedeutung." For more on Goethe's scientific method, see my "Goethe's Morphology of Knowledge."

32. Goethe, *Schriften zur allgemeinen Naturlehre*, 142.

33. Goethe, *Schriften zur Morphologie*, 24:230. On Goethe's *Typus*, see Kuhn, "Grundzüge der Goetheschen Morphologie." Kuhn also makes the point that Goethe's *Typus* is not simply a transcendental idea absent of empirical content.

34. Förster, "Die Bedeutung," 186–87.
35. Goethe, *Schriften zur Morphologie*, 24:392.
36. W. Humboldt, *Theorie der Bildung des Menschen*, in *Werke*, 1:236.
37. W. Humboldt, "Plan einer vergleichenden Anthropologie," in *Werke*, 1:350.
38. Blumenbach, *Über den Bildungstrieb*, 12–13.
39. Mendelssohn, "Ueber die Frage: was heißt aufklären?" 3.
40. Ibid., 4.
41. W. Humboldt, *Über die Innere und Äußere Organisation der höheren Anstalten in Berlin*, in *Werke*, 4:235–36.
42. Ibid., 237.
43. Recent work has argued convincingly that concepts, in the German tradition at least, like *Ethnographie, Ethnologie, Völkerkunde*, and *Volkskunde* emerged in the early 1770s and 1780s. See, for example, Vermeulen and Roldán, *Fieldwork and Footnotes*, 1–59.
44. W. Humboldt to Schiller, in Leitzmann, *Briefwechsel*, 114.
45. W. Humboldt, "Plan einer vergleichenden Anthropologie," in *Werke*, 1:350.
46. Bunzel, "Franz Boas and the Humboldtian Tradition," 12–13.
47. W. Humboldt, "Plan einer vergleichenden Anthropologie," in *Werke*, 1:358.
48. W. Humboldt, "Das achtzehnte Jahrhundert," in *Werke*, 1:502.
49. For a more extensive account of Humboldt's aesthetics, especially in relation to imagination, see Müller-Vollmer, *Poesie und Einbildungskraft;* see also Trabant, *Apeliotes*.
50. W. Humboldt, "Das achtzehnte Jahrhundert," in *Werke*, 1:434.
51. W. Humboldt, *Aesthetische Versuche*, 121.
52. Quoted in Trabant, *Apeliotes,* 29.
53. Ibid.
54. In the fall of 1798 Humboldt visited Johann Caspar Lavater, the Swiss theologian and philosopher whose *Von der Physiognomika* argued that inner characteristics of a person could be discerned from bodily forms and features. In this letter to Forster, Humboldt criticizes Lavater's commitment to "the form and the exterior." Humboldt writes that he is much more interested in how the outer is a manifestation of the imperceptible: "A great deal of *Schwärmerei* may lie in attempts to see the entire perceptible world as a way in which the imperceptible appears, as only an expression of a cipher of it, which we must solve" (Humboldt to Forster, in *Briefe an Forster*, in Forster, *Georg Forsters Werke*, 18:362–63).
55. See, for example, Humboldt's letter to Wolf of August 1796, in *Briefe an Friedrich August Wolf,* 158.
56. Sweet, *Wilhelm von Humboldt*, 231–38.
57. W. Humboldt to Schiller, in *Werke*, 5:196.
58. Esterhammer, *Romantic Performative,* 124.
59. W. Humboldt, "Über Denken und Sprechen," 3. Esterhammer alerted me to this passage.
60. Esterhammer, *Romantic Performative,* 115.
61. For more on Humboldt's philosophy of language, see Esterhammer, *Romantic Performative,* 106–43; Scharf, "Das Verfahren der Sprache"; and Trabant, "Habermas liest Humboldt."
62. W. Humboldt to Schiller, in Leitzmann, *Briefwechsel,* 276–77.
63. Sweet, *Wilhelm von Humboldt,* 240.
64. On its publication history, see Leitzmann, "Einleitung," in W. Humboldt, *Gesammelte Schriften,* 13:195.
65. W. Humboldt, *Die Vasken oder Bermerkungen auf einer Reise durch Biscaya und das französische Basquenland*, in *Gesammelte Schriften* (hereafter "*Die Vasken*"), 13:14.
66. See Esterhammer, *Romantic Performative,* 109–12.
67. W. Humboldt, *Die Vasken*, in *Gesammelte Schriften,* 13:128.
68. W. Humboldt, "Ankündigung einer Schrift über die Vaskische Sprache und Nation" (hereafter "Ankündigung"), in *Gesammelte Schriften*, 3:290.

69. Humboldt's *Berichtigungen und Zusätze zum ersten Abschnitte des zweiten Bandes Mithridates über die Cantabrische oder Baskische Sprache* (1817) corresponds to the anticipated second section.
70. W. Humboldt, *Briefe an Friedrich August Wolf*, 88.
71. W. Humboldt, "Ankündigung," in *Gesammelte Schriften*, 3:223.
72. Ibid., 230.
73. Schleiermacher, *Hermeneutik und Kritik*, 167.
74. For more on this reading of Schleiermacher's hermeneutics, see Frank, *Das Sagbare und das Unsagbare*.
75. W. Humboldt, "Ankündigung," in *Werke*, 5:122.
76. W. Humboldt, *Über das Sprachstudium*, in *Werke*, 5:111.
77. For a discussion of Kantian spontaneity and Humboldt's linguistic spontaneity, see Esterhammer, *Romantic Performative*, 117–20.

CONCLUSION

1. Wenzel, *Menschenlehre*, iii.
2. Kant, *Anthropologie in pragmatischer Hinsicht*, AA, 7:331.
3. Ibid., 333.
4. Novalis, *Blüthenstaub*, in *Schriften*, 2:412.
5. Goethe, *Schriften zur Morphologie*, 24:582.
6. Kant, *Anthropologie in pragmatischer Hinsicht*, AA, 7:331.
7. Ibid.
8. Translation adapted from "Hyperion's Song of Fate," trans. Christopher Middleton, in Browning, *German Poetry from 1750 to 1900*.

Bibliography

Abbt, Thomas. *Vermischte Werke*. 4 vols. Hildesheim: G. Olms, 1978.
Adorno, Theodor. *Gesammelte Schriften*. 20 vols. Frankfurt am Main: Suhrkamp, 1997.
———. *Negative Dialektik*. Frankfurt am Main: Suhrkamp, 1973.
Agamben, Giorgio. *Homo Sacer: Sovereign and Bare Life*. Translated by Daniel Heller-Roazen. Palo Alto: Stanford University Press, 1998.
Allen, Amy. "Foucault and Enlightenment: A Critical Reappraisal." *Constellations* 10, no. 2 (2003): 180–98.
Allison, Henry F. *Kant's Theory of Freedom*. Cambridge: Cambridge University Press, 1990.
———. *Kant's Transcendental Idealism*. New Haven: Yale University Press, 1983.
Ameriks, Karl. *Kant's Theory of Mind*. Cambridge: Cambridge University Press, 1982.
———. "Kant und das Problem der moralischen Motivation." In *Kants Ethik,* edited by K. Ameriks and D. Sturma, 97–116. Paderborn: Menthis, 2004.
Arendt, Hannah. *Lectures on Kant's Political Philosophy*. Chicago: University of Chicago Press, 1992.
Arndt, Andreas. "Zur Vorgeschichte des Schleiermacherschen Begriffs von Dialektik." In *Schleiermacher und die wissenschaftliche Kultur des Christenthums,* edited by Günter von Meckenstock. Berlin: Walter de Gruyter, 1991.
Barker-Benfield, G. J. *The Culture of Sensibility: Sex and Society in Eighteenth-Century Britain*. Chicago: University of Chicago Press, 1992.
Barth, Karl. "Nachwort." In *Schleiermacher-Auswahl,* edited by Heinz Bolli. Gütersloh: Gütersloher Verlagshaus Gerd Mohn, 1968.
———. *Die protestantische Theologie im 19. Jahrhundert*. Zurich: Evangelischer Verlag, 1947.
———. *Die Theologie Schleiermachers*. In *Karl Barths Gesamtausgabe,* edited by Hinrich Stoevesandt and Hans Anton Drewes, vol. 2, pt. 5. Zurich: Theologischer Verlag, 1978.
Beck, Lewis White. *Early German Philosophy*. Cambridge: Harvard University Press, Belknap Press, 1969.
Beiser, Friedrick C. *The Fate of Reason: German Philosophy from Kant to Fichte*. Cambridge: Harvard University Press, 1987.
———. *The Romantic Imperative: The Concept of Early German Romanticism*. Cambridge: Harvard University Press, 2003.
Bell, Matthew. *Goethe's Naturalistic Anthropology*. Oxford: Clarendon Press, 1994.
Benjamin, Walter. *Der Begriff der Kunstkritik in der deutschen Romantik*. Frankfurt am Main: Suhrkamp, 1973.

Bernasconi, Robert. "Kant as an Unfamiliar Source of Racism." In *Philosophers on Race,* edited by T. Lott and J. Ward, 145–66. Oxford: Blackwell, 2002.

———. "Who Invented the Concept of Race? Kant's Role in the Enlightenment Construction of Race." In *Race,* edited by R. Bernasconi. Oxford: Blackwell, 2001.

Bezold, Raimund. *Popularphilosophie und Erfahrungsseelenkunde im Werk von Karl Philipp Moritz.* Würzburg: Königshausen und Neumann, 1984.

Bitterli, Urs. *Alte Welt—neue Welt: Formen des europäisch-überseeischen Kulturkontakts von 15. bis zum 18. Jahrhunderts.* Munich: Beck, 1986.

———. *Die Wilden und die Zivilisierten: Grundzüge einer Geistes- und Kulturgeschichte der europäisch- überseeischen Begegnung.* Munich: Deutschen Taschenbuch Verlag, 1982.

Blackwell, Albert L. *Schleiermacher's Early Philosophy of Life: Determinism, Freedom and Phantasy.* Chico, Calif.: Scholars Press, 1982.

Blumenbach, Johann Friedrich. *Über den Bildungstrieb und das Zeugungsgeschäfte.* Stuttgart: Gustav Fischer Verlag, 1971.

Bödeker, Hans Erich. "Anthropologie." In *Lexicon der Aufklärung,* edited by Werner Schneiders, 38–39. Munich: Beck, 1995.

Böhme, Harmut. "Lebendige Natur: Wissenschaftskritik, Naturforschung, und allegorische Hermetik bei Goethe." In *Natur und Subjekt.* Frankfurt am Main: Suhrkamp, 1988.

Bowie, Andrew. *Aesthetics and Subjectivity from Kant to Nietzsche.* Manchester: Manchester University Press, 2003.

Brandt, Reinhard. "Ausgewählte Probleme der Kantischen Anthropologie." In *Der ganze Mensch: Anthropologie und Literatur im 18. Jahrhundert,* edited by Hans-Jürgen Schings, 14–32. Stuttgart: Metzler, 1994.

———. "The Guiding Idea of Kant's Anthropology and the Vocation of the Human Being." In *Essays on Kant's Anthropology,* edited by Brian Jacobs and Patrick Kahn, 85–104. Cambridge: Cambridge University Press, 2003.

Brandt, Reinhard, and Werner Stark. "Einleitung." In *Vorlesungen zur Anthropologie.* Vol. 2 of *Kants Vorlesungen,* in Immanuel Kant, *Gesammelte Schriften,* vol. 25. Berlin: Walter de Gruyter, 1998.

Braungart, Georg Braungart. *Leibhafter Sinn: Der andere Diskurs der Moderne.* Tübingen: Max Niemayer Verlag, 1995.

Brown, Marshall. *The Gothic Text.* Palo Alto: Stanford University Press, 2005.

Browning, Michael, ed. *German Poetry from 1750 to 1900.* New York: Continuum, 1984.

Bunzel, Matti. "Franz Boas and the Humboldtian Tradition: From *Volksgeist* and *Nationalcharakter* to an Anthropological Concept of Culture." In *Volksgeist as Method and Ethics: Essays on Boasian Ethnography and the German Anthropological Tradition,* edited by George W. Stocking Jr. Madison: University of Wisconsin Press, 1996.

Chaouli, Michel. "Intimations of Mortality." In *A New History of German Literature,* edited by David Wellbery et al., 481–85. Cambridge: Harvard University Press, 2004.

Cheah, Pheng. *Inhuman Conditions: On Cosmopolitanism and Human Rights.* Cambridge: Harvard University Press, 2006.

Ciafardone, Raffaele, ed. *Die Philosophie der deutschen Aufklärung.* Stuttgart: Reclam, 1983.

Collins, David. *An Account of the English Colony in New South Wales: With Remarks on the Dispositions, Customs, and Manners of the Natives of That Country*. 1798. Facsimile. Adelaide: Library Board of South Australia, 1971.

Connolly, William E. *Why I Am Not a Secularist*. Minneapolis: University of Minnesota Press, 1999.

Crouter, Richard. "Introduction." In Friedrich Schleiermacher, *On Religion: Speeches to Its Cultured Despisers*, translated by Richard Crouter. Cambridge: Cambridge University Press, 2004.

Daiber, Jürgen. "Experimentalphysik des Geistes—Novalis als Experimentator an Außen- und Innenwelt." In *Colloquia Academica: Akademische Vorträge junger Wissenschaftler*, edited by Akademie der Wissenschaft und der Literatur. Stuttgart: Franz Steiner, 1999.

Dilthey, Wilhelm. "Die Funktion der Anthropologie in der Kultur des 16. und 17. Jahrhunderts." In *Gesammelte Schriften*, edited by Georg Misch, vol. 2. Göttingen: Vandenhoeck und Ruprecht, 1960.

———. *Leben Schleiermachers*. Berlin: Walter de Gruyter, 1970.

Dippel, Lydia. *Wilhelm von Humboldt: Ästhetik und Anthropologie*. Würzburg: Königshausen und Neumann, 1990.

Eddy, John H. "Buffon's Histoire naturelle: History? A Critique of Recent Interpretations." *Isis* 85, no. 4 (1994): 644–61.

Engelstein, Stefani. *Anxious Anatomy*. Albany: State University of New York Press, 2008.

Erdmann, Benno. "Zur Entwicklungsgeschichte von Kants Anthropologie." In *Reflexionen Kants zur kritischen Philosophie*, edited by Benno Erdmann, 37–64. Leipzig: Fues's R. Reisland, 1882.

Esterhammer, Angela. *The Romantic Performative*. Palo Alto: Stanford University Press, 2000.

Eze, E. C. *Achieving Our Humanity: The Idea of the Postracial Future*. New York: Routledge, 2001.

Fackenheim, Emil. "Kant's Concept of History." *Kant-Studien* 48 (1956/57): 381–98.

Faull, Katherine M., ed. *Anthropology and the German Enlightenment*. Lewisburg: Bucknell University Press, 1995.

Fenves, Peter. *A Peculiar Fate: Metaphysics and World-History in Kant*. Ithaca: Cornell University Press, 1991.

Fichte, J. G. *Grundlage der gesammten Wissenschaftslehre*. In *J. G. Fichte—Gesamtausgabe*, edited by Reinhardt Lauth and Hans Jacob. Stuttgart: Friedrich Frommann Verlag, 1965.

Förster, Eckhart. "Die Bedeutung von 76, 77 der Kritik der Urteilskraft." *Zeitschrift für philosophische Forschung* 56 (2002): 169–90.

Forster, Georg. *Georg Forsters Werke*. 20 vols. Edited by Gerhard Steiner. Berlin: Akademie der Wissenschaft der DDR, 1958–82.

Foucault, Michel. *The Birth of the Clinic*. Translated by A. M. Sheridan Smith. New York: Vintage, 1994.

———. "Introduction à la Traduction de l'*Anthropologie du Point de Vue Pragmatique* de Kant. These Complémentaire de Michel Foucault." Xerox copy of typescript. Centre Michel Foucault, Paris.

———. *The Order of Things*. New York: Vintage, 1990.

———. "What Is Enlightenment?" In *The Foucault Reader*, edited by Paul Rabinow. New York: Pantheon Books, 1984.
Frank, Manfred. *Einführung in die Ästhetik Vorlesungen*. Frankfurt am Main: Suhrkamp, 1989.
———. *The Philosophical Foundations of Early German Romanticism*. Translated by Elizabeth Milán-Zaibert. Albany: State University of New York Press, 2004.
———. *Das Problem der Zeit in der deutschen Romantik*. 2nd ed. Paderborn: Schöningh, 1990.
———. *Das Sagbare und das Unsagbare*. Frankfurt am Main: Suhrkamp, 1989.
———. *Selbstgefühl*. Frankfurt am Main: Suhrkamp, 2002.
———. *Unendliche Annäherung*. Frankfurt am Main: Suhrkamp, 1997.
Frierson, Patrick R. *Freedom and Anthropology in Kant's Moral Philosophy*. Cambridge: Cambridge University Press, 2003.
Frietsch, Ute. "Michel Foucaults Einführung in die Anthropologie Kants." *Paragrana* 11 (2002): 11–37.
Frye, Lawrence O. "Spatial Imagery in Novalis' 'Hymnen an die Nacht.' " *Deutsche Vierteljahrschrift* 41 (1967): 568–91.
Fülleborn, Georg Gustav. "Abriss einer Geschichte und Literatur der Physiognomik." *Beyträge zur Geschichte der Philosophie* 8 (1797).
Garber, Daniel. *Descartes Embodied*. Cambridge: Cambridge University Press, 2001.
Garber, Jörn, and Thomas Heinz, eds. *Zwischen Empirisierung und Konstruktionsleistung: Anthropologie im 18. Jahrhundert*. Tübingen: Max Niemeyer, 2004.
Gardner, Sebastian. *Kant and the Critique of Pure Reason*. London: Routledge, 1999.
Geertz, Clifford. *The Interpretation of Cultures*. New York: Basic Books, 1973.
Geschichtliche Grundbegriffe: Historisches Lexicon zur politisch-sozialen Sprache in Deutschland. Vol. 3. Stuttgart: Klett-Cotta, 1982.
Gibbons, Sarah. *Kant's Theory of Imagination: Bridging Gaps in Judgment and Experience*. Oxford: Clarendon Press, 1994.
Goethe, Johann Wolfgang. *Briefe, Tagebücher, und Gespräche*. Edited by Hartmut Reinhardt. In *Sämtliche Werke*, vol. 2, pt. 2. Frankfurt am Main: Deutscher Klassiker Verlag, 1997.
———. *Goethe's Botanical Writings*. Translated by Bertha Mueller. Woodbridge, Conn.: Ox Bow Press, 1989.
———. *Goethe's Scientific Writings*. Translated by Douglas Miller. New York: Suhrkamp, 1988.
———. *Schriften zur allgemeinen Naturlehre, Geologie, und Mineralogie*. Edited by Wolf von Engelhardt and Manfred Wenzel. Frankfurt am Main: Deutscher Klassiker Verlag, 1989.
———. *Schriften zur Morphologie*. Edited by Dorothea Kuhn. In *Sämtliche Werke*, vol. 24. Frankfurt am Main: Deutscher Klassiker Verlag, 1987.
Goy, Ina. "Immanuel Kant über das moralische Gefühl der Achtung." *Zeitschrift für philosophische Forschung* 61, no. 3 (2007): 337–60.
Gruithuisen, Franz von Paula. *Anthropologie oder von des Natur der menschlichen Lebens und Denkens für angehende Philosophien und Aerzte*. Munich: Joseph Lentner, 1810.
Guyer, Paul. *Kant on Freedom, Law, and Happiness*. Cambridge: Cambridge University Press, 2000.

Habermas, Jürgen. "Taking Aim at the Heart of the Present." In *Foucault: A Critical Reader*, edited by David Couzens Hoy. Oxford: Blackwell, 1986.
Hadot, Pierre. *Philosophy as a Way of Life: Spiritual Exercises from Socrates to Foucault*. Translated by Michael Chase. Oxford: Oxford University Press, 1995.
———. *What Is Ancient Philosophy?* Translated by Michael Chase. Cambridge: Harvard University Press, Belknap Press, 2004.
Han, Béatrice. *Foucault's Critical Project*. Translated by Edward Pile. Palo Alto: Stanford University Press, 2002.
Hatfield, Gary. "Remaking the Science of Mind." In *Inventing Human Science*, edited by Christopher Fox. Berkeley and Los Angeles: University of California Press, 1995.
Haym, Rudolf. *Herder: Nach seinem Leben und seinen Werken*. Berlin: Aufbau-Verlag, 1958.
———. *Die Romantische Schule: Ein Beitrag zur Geschichte des deutschen Geistes*. 1870. Darmstadt: Wissenschaftliche Buchgesellschaft, 1961.
Hegel, G. W. F. *Werke*. 20 vols. Edited by Eva Moldenhauer and Karl Markus Michel. Frankfurt am Main: Suhrkamp, 1970.
Heine, Heinrich. *Sämtliche Werke: Historisch-kritische Gesamtausgabe der Werke*. Edited by Manfred Windfuhr. Hamburg: Hoffmann und Kampe Verlag, 1979.
Heinroth, Johann Christian August. *Lehrbuch der Anthropologie*. Leipzig: Friedrich Christian Wilhelm Bogel, 1831.
Heintel, Erich. "Einleitung." In Johann Niclaus Tetens, *Sprachphilosophische Versuche*, edited by Erich Heintel. Hamburg: Felix Meiner Verlag, 1971.
Heinz, Jutta. "Doppelrolle: Die *anthropologische* Wende der Aufklärung, konstruktivistisch gewendet." *IASL Online*, April 4, 2005. http://iasl.uni-muenchen.de/rezensio/liste/Heinz.htm.
———. *Wissen vom Menschen und Erzählen von Einzelfall: Untersuchungen zum anthropologischen Roman der Spätaufklärung*. Berlin: Walter de Gruyter, 1996.
Hennings, Justus Christian. *Anthropologische und pneumatologische Aphorismen*. Halle, 1777.
Henrich, Dieter. "The Concept of Moral Insight and Kant's Doctrine of the Fact of Reason." In Dieter Henrich, *The Unity of Reason*, edited by Richard L. Velkley. Cambridge: Harvard University Press, 1994.
———. "Hutcheson und Kant." *Kant-Studien* 49 (1957/58): 49–69.
———. *Selbstverhältnisse*. Stuttgart: Reclam, 1982.
Herder, Johann Gottfried. *Herders Sämtliche Werke*. Edited by Bernhard Suphan. 33 vols. Berlin: Weidmann, 1893.
———. *Johann Gottfried Herder Werke*. Edited by Martin Bollacher et al. 10 vols. Frankfurt am Main: Deutscher Klassiker Verlag, 1994.
Herdt, Jennifer A. *Putting on Virtue: The Legacy of the Splendid Vices*. Chicago: University of Chicago Press, 2008.
Herms, Eilert. *Hernkunft, Entfaltung und erste Gestalt des System der Wissenschaft bei Schleiermacher*. Güttersloh: Verlagshaus Gerd Mohn, 1974.
Hertel, Friedrich. *Das theologische Denken Schleiermachers untersucht an der ersten Auflage seiner Reden "Über die Religion."* Zurich: Zwingli Verlag, 1965.
Herz, Marcus. "D. Ernst Platner, der Aerzneykunst Professors in Leipzig, *Anthropologie für Aerzte und Weltweise*. Erster Theil. Leipzig, in der Dyckischen Buchhandlung, 1772.8.292 Seiten." *Allgemeine Deutsche Bibliothek* 20, no. 1 (1773): 25–51.

Hess, Jonathan. *Reconstituting the Body Politic.* Detroit: Wayne State University Press, 1999.
Heydenreich, Karl Heinrich. *System der Aesthetik.* Leipzig: Georg Joachim Gösher, 1790.
Hill, T. E., Jr., and B. Boxhill. "Kant and Race." In *Race and Racism,* edited by B. Boxhill, 448–71. Oxford: Oxford University Press, 2001.
Hinske, Norbert, ed. *Was ist Aufklärung? Beiträge aus der Berlinischen Monatsschrift.* Darmstadt: Wissenschaftliche Buchgesellschaft, 1977.
Hissmann, Michael. *Psychologische Versuche: Ein Beitrag zur esoterischen Logik.* Hannover: Gebrüder Helwig, 1788.
Hodgen, Margaret. *Early Anthropology in the 16th and 17th Centuries.* Philadelphia: University of Pennsylvania Press, 1964.
Horkheimer, Max, and Theodor Adorno. *Dialectic of Enlightenment.* Translated by John Cumming. New York: Continuum, 2000.
Hufeland, Christoph Wilhelm. *Makrobiotik, oder die Kunst das menschliche Leben zu verlängern.* 1805. Reprint, Stuttgart: Hippokrates-Verlag, 1958.
Humboldt, Alexander. *Die Jugendbriefe Alexander von Humboldts, 1787–1799.* Berlin: Akademie Verlag, 1973.
Humboldt, Wilhelm von. *Aesthetische Versuche.* Translated from the French, *Essais Aesthétiques,* into German by Kurt Müller-Vollmer. In Kurt Müller-Volmer, *Poesie und Einbildungskraft,* 120–212. Berlin: Metzlersche Verlag 1967.
———. *Briefe an Friedrich August Wolf.* Berlin: Walter de Gruyter, 1990.
———. "Über Denken und Sprechen." In *Schriften zur Sprache.* Stuttgart: Reclam, 1992.
———. *Werke in fünf Bänden.* Edited by Andreas Flitner and Klaus Giel. 5 vols. Darmstadt: Wissenschaftliche Buchgesellschaft, 1960.
———. *Wilhelm von Humboldts Gesammelte Schriften.* Edited by Albert Leitzmann. 17 vols. Berlin: Behr, 1903–36.
Hunter, Ian. "The Morals of Metaphysics: Kant's *Groundwork* as Intellectual Paideia." *Critical Inquiry* 28, no. 4 (2002): 908–29.
———. *Rival Enlightenments: Civil and Metaphysical Philosophy in Early Modern Germany.* Cambridge: Cambridge University Press, 2001.
Iser, Wolfgang. *The Fictive and the Imaginary: Charting Literary Anthropology.* Baltimore: Johns Hopkins University Press, 1993.
Ith, Johann. *Versuch einer Anthropologie oder Philosophie des Menschen nach seinen körperlichen Anlagen.* Bern: Emanuel Haller, 1794.
Jacobs, Brian, and Patrick Kain, eds. *Essays on Kant's Anthropology.* Cambridge: Cambridge University Press, 2003.
Jahn, I. "Die anatomischen Studien der Brüder Humboldt unter Justus Christian Loder in Jena." *Beiträge zur Geschichte der Universität Erfurt* 14 (1968–69): 91–92.
Jakob, Ludwig Heinrich. *Grundriß einer Erfahrungs-Seelenlehre.* Grätz, 1795.
Jantzen, Jörg. "Physiologische Theorien." In Friedrich Wilhelm Joseph Schelling, *Historische-kritische Gesamtausgabe,* edited by Hans-Michael Baumgartner and Wilhelm Jacobs, *Ergänzungsband zu Werke Band 5 bis 9: Wissenschaftshistorischer Bericht zu Schellings naturphilosophischen Schriften, 1797–1800.* Stuttgart: Frommann Verlag, 1994.
Jay, Martin. *Downcast Eyes: The Denigration of Vision in Twentieth-Century French Thought.* Berkeley and Los Angeles: University of California Press, 1993.

Johnson, Laurie. " 'Wozu überhaupt ein Anfang?' Memory and History in *Heinrich von Ofterdingen*." *Colloquia Germanica* 31, no. 1 (1998): 21–35.
Kant, Immanuel. *Anthropology, History, and Education*. Edited by Robert B. Louden and Günter Zöller. Cambridge: Cambridge University Press, 2007.
———. *Anthropology from a Pragmatic Point of View*. Translated by Robert B. Louden. In Immanuel Kant, *Anthropology, History, and Education*, edited by Robert B. Louden and Günter Zöller, 227–429. Cambridge: Cambridge University Press, 2007.
———. *Critique of Pure Reason*. Translated and edited by Paul Guyer and Allen W. Wood. Cambridge: Cambridge University Press, 1998.
———. *Critique of Pure Reason*. Translated by Norman Kemp Smith. New York: Palgrave Macmillan, 2007.
———. *Critique of the Power of Judgment*. Edited by Paul Guyer. Translated by Paul Guyer and Eric Matthews. Cambridge: Cambridge University Press, 2000.
———. *Gesammelte Schriften*. Edited by the Königlich-preußischen Akademie der Wissenschaften. 29 vols. to date. Berlin: Walter de Gruyter, 1902–. Referred to as "AA" (= "Akademie Ausgabe") in text and notes.
———. *Practical Philosophy*. Translated by Mary J. Gregor. In *The Cambridge Edition of the Works of Immanuel Kant*, edited by Paul Guyer and Allen W. Wood. Cambridge: Cambridge University Press, 1996.
———. *Religion and Rational Theology*. Translated and edited by Allen W. Wood and George di Giovanni. In *The Cambridge Edition of the Works of Immanuel Kant*, edited by Paul Guyer and Allen W. Wood. Cambridge: Cambridge University Press, 1996.
Käuser, Andreas. "Anthropologie und Ästhetik im 18. Jahrhundert: Besprechung einiger Neuerscheinungen." *Das achtzehnte Jahrhundert* 14 (1990): 190–206.
Kittler, Friedrich. "*Heinrich von Ofterdingen* als Nachrichteneinfluß." In *Novalis Beiträge zu Werk und Persönlichkeit*, edited by Gerhard Schulz. Darmstadt: Wissenschaftliche Buchgesellschaft, 1986.
Kleingeld, Pauline. *Fortschritt und Vernunft: Zur Geschichtsphilosophie Kants*. Würzburg: Königshausen und Neumann, 1995.
———. "Kant on the Unity of Theoretical and Practical Reason." *Review of Metaphysics* 52 (December 1998): 311–39.
———. "Kant's Second Thoughts on Race." *Philosophical Quarterly* 57 (2007): 573–92.
Klügel, Georg Simon. *Encyklopädie oder zusammenhängender Vortrag der gemeinützigsten Kenntnisse. Erster Theil welcher die Gewächskunde, Thierkunde, Anthropologie und Mathematik enthält*. Berlin: Friedrich Nicolai, 1782.
Köchy, Kristian. *Ganzheit und Wissenschaft: Das historische Fallbeispiel der Romantischen Naturforschung*. Würzburg: Königshausen und Neumann, 1997.
Kondylis, Panajotis. *Die Aufklärung im Rahmen des neuzeitlichen Rationalismus*. Stuttgart: Klett-Cotta, 1981.
Korsgaard, Christine M. *The Sources of Normativity*. Edited by Onora O'Neill. Cambridge: Cambridge University Press, 1996.
Koselleck, Reinhart. *Vergangene Zukunft: Zur Semantik geschichtlicher Zeiten*. Frankfurt am Main: Suhrkamp, 1989.
Kosenina, Alexander. *Ernst Platners Anthropologie und Philosophie*. Würzburg: Königshausen und Neumann, 1989.

Krauss, Werner. *Zur Anthropologie des 18. Jahrhunderts.* Frankfurt am Main: Verlag Ullstein, 1987.

Kuhn, Dorothea. "Grundzüge der Goetheschen Morphologie." *Goethe-Jahrbuch* 95 (1978): 199–211.

Kuzniar, Alice. *Delayed Endings: Nonclosure in Novalis and Hölderlin.* Athens: University of Georgia Press, 1987.

Lamm, Julia. "The Early Philosophical Roots of Schleiermacher's Notion of *Gefühl.*" *Harvard Theological Review* 87, no. 1 (1994): 67–105.

———. *The Living God: Schleiermacher's Theological Appropriation of Spinoza.* University Park: Pennsylvania State University Press, 1996.

Larrimore, Mark. "Sublime Waste: Kant on the Destiny of the 'Races.'" In *Civilization and Oppression,* edited by Catherine Wilson. Suppl. vol., *Canadian Journal of Philosophy* 25 (1999): 99–125.

Larson, James L. *Interpreting Nature: The Science of the Living Form from Linnaeus to Kant.* Baltimore: John Hopkins University Press, 1994.

Lenoir, Timothy. *The Strategy of Life: Teleology and Mechanics in Nineteenth-Century German Biology.* Chicago: University of Chicago Press, 1982.

Leitzmann, Albert, ed. *Briefwechsel zwischen Schiller und Wilhelm von Humboldt.* Stuttgart: Cotta, 1900.

Lepenies, Wolf. *Das Ende der Naturgeschichte: Wandel kultureller Selbstverständlichkeiten in den Wissenschaften des 18. und 19. Jahrhunderts.* Munich: Suhrkamp, 1976.

Lilla, Mark. "Kant's Theological-Political Revolution." *Review of Metaphysics* 52, no. 2 (1998): 397–434.

Linden, Mareta. *Untersuchungen zum Anthropologiebegriff des 18. Jahrhunderts.* Bern: Lang, 1976.

Locke, John. *The Correspondences of John Locke.* Edited by Esmond Samuel De Beer. Oxford: Clarendon Press, 1981.

———. *An Essay Concerning Human Understanding.* London: Penguin Books, 1997.

Loder, Justus Christian. *Anfangsgründe der medizinischen Anthropologie und der Staatsarzneikunde.* 2nd ed. Weimar, 1793.

Louden, Robert. *Kant's Impure Ethics: From Rational Beings to Human Beings.* Oxford: Oxford University Press, 2000.

———. "Kant's Virtue Ethics." *Philosophy* 61 (1986): 473–89.

Luhmann, Niklaus. "Frühneuzeitliche Anthropologie: Theorietechnische Lösungen für ein Evolutionsproblem der Gesellschaft." In *Gesellschaftsstruktur und Semantik.* Franfurt am Main: Suhrkamp, 1993.

———. "A Redescription of 'Romantic Art.'" *MLN* 111, no. 3 (1996): 506–22.

MacBeath, A. Murray. "Kant on Moral Feeling." *Kant-Studien* 64 (1973): 283–314.

Mack, Michael. *German Idealism and the Jew: The Inner Anti-Semitism of Philosophy and German Jewish Responses.* Chicago: University of Chicago Press, 2003.

Mahmood, Saba. *Politics of Piety: The Islamic Revival and the Feminist Subject.* Princeton: Princeton University Press, 2004.

Mähl, Hans-Joachim. *Die Idee des goldenen Zeitalters im Werk des Novalis. Studien zur Wesensbestimmung der frühromantischen Utopie und zu ihren ideengeschichtlichen Voraussetzungen.* Heidelberg: Winter, 1965.

Markus, Gyorgy. "Culture: The Making and the Make-Up of a Concept." *Dialectical Anthropology* 18 (1993): 3–29.

Marina, Jacqueline. "Schleiermacher on the Philosopher's Stone: The Shaping of Schleiermacher's Early Ethics by the Kantian Legacy." *Journal of Religion* 79, no. 2 (1999): 183–215.
Marquard, Odo. "Anthropologie." In *Historisches Wörterbuch der Philosophie*, vol. 1, edited by Joachim Ritter. Darmstadt: Wissenschaftliche Buchgesellschaft, 1971.
———. *Schwierigkeiten mit der Geschichtsphilosophie*. Frankfurt am Main: Suhrkamp, 1988.
McCarthy, Thomas A. "On the Way to a World Republic? Kant on Race and Development." In *Politik, Moral und Religion: Festschrift zum 65. Geburtstag von Karl Graf Ballestrem*. Berlin: Duncker und Humboldt Verlag, 2004.
Meckenstock, Günter. *Deterministische Ethik und kritische Theologie: Die Auseinandersetzung des frühen Schleiermacher mit Kant und Spinoza, 1788–1794*. Berlin: Walter de Gruyter, 1988.
Mellin, G. S. A. *Encyclopädisches Wörterbuch der kritischen Philosophie*. 6 vols. Jena and Leipzig, 1801. Reprint, Aalen: Scientia Verlag, 1971.
Mendelssohn, Moses. "Über die Frage: was heißt aufklären?" In *Was ist Aufklärung*, edited by Ehrhard Bahr. Stuttgart: Reclam, 1998.
Menninghaus, Winnfried. *Unendliche Verdopplung. Die frühromantische Grundlegung der Kunsttheorie im Begriff absoluter Selbstreflexion*. Frankfurt am Main: Suhrkamp, 1987.
Mills, C. W. "Kant's *Untermenschen*." In *Race and Racism in Modern Philosophy*, edited by A. Valls. Ithaca: Cornell University Press, 2005.
McGinn, Bernard. "The Language of Inner Experience in Christian Mysticism." *Spiritus* 1 (2001): 156–71.
Moravia, Sergio. *Beobachtende Vernunft: Philosophie und Anthropologie in der Aufklärung*. Translated by Elisabeth Preis. Munich: Carl Hanser Verlag, 1973.
———. "The Enlightenment and the Sciences of Man." *History of Science* 18 (1980): 247–68.
———. "From Homme Machine to Homme Sensible: Changing Eighteenth-Century Models of Man's Image." *Journal of History of Ideas* 39, no. 1 (1978): 45–60.
Morgan, Michael J. *Molyneux's Question: Vision, Touch, and the Philosophy of Perception*. Cambridge: Cambridge University Press, 1977.
Mücke, Dorothea von. "Goethe's Metamorphosis: Changing Forms in Nature, the Life Sciences, and Authorship." *Representations* 95 (Summer 2006): 27–53.
Mühlmann, Wilhelm E. *Geschichte der Anthropologie*. Frankfurt am Main: Athenäum Verlag, 1968.
Müller, Ernst. "Religion als 'Kunst ohne Kunstwerk.' F. D. E. Schleiermachers 'Über die Religion und das Problem ästhetischer Subjektivität.'" In *Ästhetische und religiöse Erfahrungen der Jahrhundertwenden I: um 1800*, edited by Wolfgang Braungart, Gotthard Fuchs, and Manfred Koch. Paderborn: Schöningh, 1997.
Müller-Sievers, Helmut. *Self-Generation. Biology, Philosophy, and Literature Around 1800*. Palo Alto: Stanford University Press, 1997.
Müller-Vollmer, Kurt. *Poesie und Einbildungskraft*. Berlin: Metzlersche Verlag 1967.
Munzel, G. Felicitas. *Kant's Conception of Moral Character*. Chicago: University of Chicago Press, 1999.
Nadler, Steven, ed. *Causation in Early Modern Philosophy*. University Park: Pennsylvania State University Press, 1993.

Neiman, Susan. *The Unity of Reason*. Oxford: Oxford University Press, 1994.
Nelkin, Dana. "Two Standpoints and the Belief in Freedom." *Journal of Philosophy* 97 (2000): 564–76.
Neubauer, John. *Bifocal Vision: Novalis's Philosophy of Nature and Disease*. Chapel Hill: University of North Carolina Press, 1971.
Neumann, Gerhard. "Naturwissenschaft und Geschichte als Literatur: Zu Goethes kulturpoetischen Projekt." *MLN* 114, no. 3 (1999): 471–502.
Neumann, Michael. "Philosophische Nachrichten aus der Südsee: Georg Forsters *Reise um die Welt*." In *Der Ganze Mensch: Anthropologie und Literatur im 18. Jahrhundert*, edited by Hans-Jürgen Schings. Stuttgart: Metzler, 1994.
Novalis [Friedrich von Hardenberg]. *Novalis: Hymns to the Night*. Translated by Dick Higgins. Kingston, N.Y.: McPherson, 1988.
———. *Schriften. Die Werke Friedrich von Hardenbergs*. Edited by Paul Kluckhohn and Richard Samuel. 6 vols. Darmstadt: Wissenschaftliche Buchgesellschaft, 1960–88.
Nowak, Kurt. "Geschichte—der höchste Gegenstand der Religion: Schleiermachers Beitrag zur Historik in den Reden *Über die Religion* (1799)." *Theologische Literaturzeitung* 124, no. 6 (1999): 584–96.
———. *Schleiermacher: Leben, Werk, Wirkung*. Göttingen: Vandenhoeck und Ruprecht, 2002.
———. *Schleiermacher und die Frühromantik*. Göttingen: Vandenhoeck und Ruprecht, 1986.
Nowitzki, Hans-Peter. *Der wohltemperierte Mensch*. Berlin: Walter de Gruyter, 2003.
O'Brien, William Arctander. *Novalis: Signs of Revolution*. Durham: Duke University Press, 1995.
Parry, J. H. *The Age of Reconnaissance*. New York: Praeger, 1969.
Patsch, Hermann. *Alle Menschen sind Künstler: Friedrich Schleiermachers poetische Versuche*. Berlin: Walter de Gruyter, 1986.
Pfau, Thomas. *Romantic Moods: Paranoia, Trauma, and Melancholy, 1790–1840*. Baltimore: John Hopkins University Press, 2005.
Pfotenhauer, Helmut. *Literarische Anthropologie*. Stuttgart: J. B. Metzler, 1987.
———. *Um 1800: Konfigurationen der Literatur, Kunst-literatur, und Ästhetik*. Tübingen: Max Niemeyer, 1991.
Phillip, Arthur, and John Stockdale. *The Voyage of Governor Phillip to Botany Bay: With an Account of the Establishment of the Colonies of Port Jackson and Norfolk Island*. 3rd ed. London, 1790.
Pinkard, Terry. *German Philosophy, 1760–1860: The Legacy of Idealism*. New York: Cambridge University Press, 2002.
Pippin, Robert. *Idealism as Modernism: Hegelian Variations*. Cambridge: Cambridge University Press, 1997.
———. *Modernism as a Philosophical Problem*. London: Blackwell, 1999.
Platner, Ernst. *Anthropologie für Aerzte und Weltweise*. Leipzig: Dyck, 1772.
———. *Neue Anthropologie für Aerzte und Weltweise: Mit besonderer Rücksicht auf Physiologie, Pathologie, Moralphilosophie, und Aesthetik*. Leipzig: Siegfried Lebrecht Crusius, 1790.
Pölitz, Karl Heinrich Ludwig. *Populäre Anthropologie oder Kunde von dem Menschen nach seinen sinnlichen und geistigen Anlagen*. Leipzig: Johann Wilhelm Kramer, 1800.

Prickett, Stephen. "Coleridge, Schlegel and Schleiermacher: England, Germany (and Australia) in 1798." In *1798: The Year of the Lyrical Ballads,* edited by Richard Cronin. London: Macmillan, 1998.
Probst, Peter. "Sinnlichkeit und Endlicht: Zum Problem romantischer Anthropologie im Ausgang von J. Chr. Heinroth." *Philosophisches Jahrbuch* 82 (1975): 90–102.
Proß, Wolfgang. "Herder und die Anthropologie seiner Zeit." In Johann Gottfried Herder, *Werke,* edited by Wolfgang Proß, 2:1128–1216. Darmstadt: Wissenschaftliche Buchgesellschaft, 1987.
Purdy, Daniel. "Immanuel Kant and the Anthropological Enlightenment." *Eighteenth-Century Studies* 38, no. 2 (2005): 329–32.
Rabbow, Paul. *Seelenführung: Methodik der Exercitien in der Antike.* Munich: Kösel-Verlag, 1954.
Rawls, John. *John Rawls: Collected Papers.* Edited by Samuel Freedman. Cambridge: Harvard University Press, 1999.
Reill, Peter Hans. "Anthropology, Nature, and History in the Late Eighteenth-Century: The Case of Friedrich Schiller." In *Schiller als Historiker,* edited by Otto Drait. Stuttgart: Metzler, 1995.
———. "Science and the Construction of the Cultural Sciences in Late Enlightenment Germany: The Case of Wilhelm von Humboldt." *History and Theory* 33, no. 3 (1994): 345–66.
Reynolds, Thomas E. "Religion Within the Limits of History: Schleiermacher and Religion—A Reappraisal." *Religion* 32 (2002): 51–70.
Richards, Robert J. *The Romantic Conception of Life: Science and Philosophy in the Age of Goethe.* Chicago: University of Chicago Press, 2002.
Riedel, Wolfgang. *Die Anthropologie des jungen Schiller.* Würzburg: Königshausen und Neumann, 1984.
———. "Anthropologie und Literatur in der deutschen Spätaufklärung: Skizze einer Forschungslandschaft." *Internationales Archiv für Sozialgeschichte der Literatur* 3 (1994): 93–157.
———. "Erkennen und Empfinden: Anthropologische Achsendrehung und Wende zur Ästhetik bei Johann Georg Sulzer." In *Der ganze Mensch: Anthropologie und Literatur im 18. Jahrhundert,* edited by Hans-Jürgen Schings. Stuttgart: Metzler, 1977.
———. "Erster Psychologismus: Umbau des Seelenbegriffs in der deutschen Spätaufklärung." In *Zwischen Empirisierung und Konstruktionsleistung: Anthropologie im 18. Jahrhundert,* edited by Jörn Garber and Thomas Heinz. Tübingen: Max Niemeyer, 2004.
Ritter, Joachim, ed. *Historisches Wörterbuch der Philosophie.* 13 vols. Darmstadt: Wissenschaftliche Buchgesellschaft, 1971–2007.
Roe, Shirley. *Matter, Life, and Generation: Eighteenth-Century Embryology and the Haller-Wolff Debate.* Cambridge: Cambridge University Press, 1981.
Roger, Jacques. *Buffon: A Life in Natural History.* Ithaca: Cornell University Press, 1997.
———. *The Life Sciences in Eighteenth-Century French Thought.* Edited by K. R. Benson. Translated by R. Ellrich. Palo Alto: Stanford University Press, 1997.
Sadji, Uta. *Der Negermythos am Ende des 18. Jahrhunderts in Deutschland.* Frankfurt am Main: Peter Lang, 1979.
Saul, Nicholas. "*Poëtisirung* d[es] Körpers. Der Poesiebegriff Friedrich von Hardenbergs (Novalis) und die anthropologische Tradition." In *Novalis—Poesie und Poetik 3.*

Fachtagung der Internationalen Novalis-Gesellschaft, edited by Herbert Uerlings. Tübingen: Max Niemeyer, 2004.

Saurette, Paul. *The Kantian Imperative: Humiliation, Common Sense, Politics.* Toronto: University of Toronto Press, 2005.

Scharf, Hans-Werner. "Das Verfahren der Sprache: Ein Nachtrag zu Chomskys Humboldt-Reklamation." In *History of Semiotics*, edited by Achim Eschenbach and Jürgen Trabant. Amsterdam: Benjamin, 1983.

Schiller, Friedrich. "Versuch über den Zusammenhang der tierischen Natur des Menschen mit seiner geistigen." In *Schiller Werke und Briefe*, 8:119–63. Frankfurt am Main: Deutscher Klassiker Verlag, 1992.

Schiller, Friedrich, and Johann Wolfgang Goethe. *Der Briefwechsel zwischen Schiller und Goethe.* Edited by Siegfried Seidel. Munich: C. H. Beck, 1984.

Schings, Hans-Jürgen, ed. *Der ganze Mensch: Anthropologie und Literatur im 18. Jahrhundert.* Stuttgart: Metzler, 1994.

———. "Der Philosophische Arzt. Anthropologie, Melancholie, und Literatur im 18. Jahrhundert." In *Melancholie und Aufklärung*. Stuttgart: Metzler, 1977.

Schipperges, Heinrich. *Kosmos Anthropos: Entwurf zu einer Philosophie des Leibes.* Stuttgart: Klett-Cotta, 1981.

Schlegel, Friedrich. *Kritische Schriften und Fragmente.* Edited by Ernst Behler and Hans Eichner. Paderborn: Schöningh, 1988.

Schleiermacher, Friedrich. *Friedrich Daniel Ernst Schleiermacher Kritische Gesamtausgabe.* Edited by Hans-Joachim Birkner et al. 11 vols. to date. Berlin: Walter de Gruyter, 1979–.

———. *Hermeneutik und Kritik.* Edited by Manfred Frank. Frankfurt am Main: Suhrkamp, 2001.

———. *On Religion: Speeches to Its Cultured Despisers.* Translated by Richard Crouter. Cambridge: Cambridge University Press, 2004.

Schmid, Carl Christian. "Einleitung." In Cureau de la Chambre, *Anleitungen zur Menschenkenntniß*, translated by Carl Christian Schmid. Jena: Akademisches Buchhandlung, 1794.

———. *Wörterbuch zur leichtern Gebrauch der Kantischen Schriften.* 1798. Darmstadt: Wissenschaftliche Buchgesellschaft, 1996.

Schmidt, James, and Thomas Wartenberg. "Foucault's Enlightenment: Critique, Revolution, and the Fashioning of the Self." In *Critique and Power*, edited by Michael Kelly. Cambridge: MIT Press, 1994.

Schneiders, Werner. "*Deus est philosophus absolute summus:* Über Christian Wolffs Philosophie und Philosophiebegriff." In *Christian Wolff, 1679–1754: Interpretationen zu seiner Philosophie und deren Wirkung*, edited by Werner Schneiders. Hamburg: Felix Meiner, 1983.

Schott, Robin May, ed. *Feminist Interpretations of Kant.* University Park: Pennsylvania State University Press, 1997.

———. "The Gender of Enlightenment." In *What Is Enlightenment? Eighteenth-Century Answers and Twentieth-Century Questions*, edited by James Schmidt, 471–86. Berkeley and Los Angeles: University of California Press, 1996.

Schulz, Gerhald. "'Mit den Menschen ändert die Welt sich.' Zu Friedrich von Hardenbergs 5. *Hymnen an die Nacht*." In *Gedichte und Interpretationen: Klassik und Romantik*. Stuttgart: Reclam, 1998.

Seifert, Paul. *Die Theologie des jungen Schleiermacher.* Gütersloh: Gütersloher Verlagshaus Gerd Mohn, 1960.
Senckel, Barbara. *Individualität und Totalität: Aspekte zu einer Anthropologie des Novalis.* Tübingen: Max Niemeyer, 1983.
Shell, Susan Meld. *The Embodiment of Reason: Kant on Spirit, Generation, and Community.* Chicago: University of Chicago Press, 1996.
———. "Kant's Concept of a Human Race." In *The German Invention of Race,* edited by Sara Eigen and Mark Larrimore. Albany: State University of New York Press, 2006.
———. "Kant's True Economy of Human Nature: Rousseau, Count Verri, and Human Happiness." In *Essays on Kant's Anthropology,* edited by Brian Jacobs and Patrick Kain, 194–229. New York: Cambridge University Press, 2003.
Sixel, Friedrich W., and Baldev R. Luther. *Die Natur in unserer Kultur: Eine Studie in der Anthropologie und Soziologie des Wissens.* Würzburg: Königshausen und Neumann, 2003.
Sloan, Phillip. "Buffon, German Biology and the Historical Interpretation of Biological Species." *British Journal for the History of Science* 12, no. 41 (1979): 109–53.
———. "The Gaze of Natural History." In *Inventing Human Science,* edited by Christopher Fox. Berkeley and Los Angeles: University of California Press, 1995.
———. "Preforming the Categories: Eighteenth-Century Generation Theory and the Biological Roots of Kant's A-Priori." *Journal of the History of Philosophy* 40, no. 2 (2002): 229–53.
Sokoloff, William W. "Kant and the Paradox of Respect." *American Journal of Political Science* 45, no. 4 (2001): 768–79.
Sommer, Manfred. *Historisches Wörterbuch der Philosophie.* Vol. 6. Darmstadt: Wissenschaftliche Buchgesellschaft, 1984.
Spinoza, Baruch. *Ethics, Demonstrated in Geometrical Order.* Translated by G. H. R. Parkinson. Oxford: Oxford University Press, 2000.
Stadler, Ulrich. "Zur Anthropologie Friedrich Hardenbergs (Novalis)." In *Novalis und die Wissenschaften,* edited by Herbert Uerlings, 2:87–105. Tübingen: Schriften der Internationalen Novalis-Gesellschaft, 1997.
Stark, Werner. "Historical Notes and Interpretive Questions About Kant's Lectures on Anthropology." In *Essays on Kant's Anthropology,* edited by Brian Jacobs and Patrick Kain. Cambridge: Cambridge University Press, 2003.
Steffens, Heinrich. *Anthropologie.* Breslau: Joseph Max, 1822.
Steigerwald, Jörn, and Daniela Watzke, eds. *Reiz, Imagination, Aufmerksamkeit. Erregung und Steuerung der Einbildungskraft im klassichen Zeitalter (1680–1830).* Würzburg: Königshausen und Neumann, 2003.
Stern, Paul. "The Problem of History and Temporality in Kantian Ethics." *Review of Metaphysics* 39 (March 1986): 505–45.
Strack, Thomas. "Philosophical Anthropology on the Eve of Biological Determinism: Immanuel Kant and Georg Forster on the Moral Qualities and Biological Characteristics of the Human Race." *Central European History* 29, no. 3 (1996): 285–308.
Strube, Werner. "Die Geschichte des Begriffs 'schöne Wissenschaften.'" *Archiv für Begriffsgeschichte* 33 (1990): 136–216.
Sulzer, Johann Georg. *Eine allgemeine Theorie der schönen Künste.* Vol. 4. Leipzig, 1794.

———. *Kurzer Begriff aller Wissenschaften und andern Theile der Gelehrsamkeit.* Leipzig: Langenheim, 1759.
Sweet, Paul R. *Wilhelm von Humboldt: A Biography.* Columbus: Ohio State University Press, 1978.
Tench, Watkins. *Nachricht von der Expedizion nach Botany-Bay nebst Bemerkungen über Neu-Südwallis.* Translated from English. Frankfurt am Main: Johann Georg Fleischer, 1789.
Tetens, J. N. *Philosophische Versuche über die menschliche Natur und ihre Entwicklung.* Leipzig: Weidmann and Reich, 1777.
Theisen, Bianca. "Chaos-Ordnung." In *Ästhetische Grundbegriffe: Historisches Wörterbuch in sieben Bänden,* vol. 1, edited by Karlheinz Barck. Stuttgart: Metzler, 2000.
———. "Macroanthropos: Friedrich von Hardenberg's Literary Anthropology." *REAL: Yearbook in English and American Literature: The Anthropological Turn in Literary Studies,* edited by Jürgen Schlaeger, 12 (1996): 243–55.
———. "Memories of the Future: The Temporalization of History in Romantic Narratives." In *The Poetics of Memory,* edited by Thomas Wägenbauer. Tübingen: Stauffenburg, 1998.
Trabant, Jürgen. *Apeliotes, oder der Sinn der Sprache.* Munich: Fink, 1986.
———. "Habermas liest Humboldt." *Deutsche Zeitschrift für Philosophie* 41 (1993): 639–51.
Uerlings, Herbert. *Friedrich von Hardenberg, genannt Novalis: Werk und Forschung.* Stuttgart: Metzlersche Verlagsbuchhandlung, 1991.
———, ed. *Novalis und die Wissenschaft.* Tübingen: Max Niemeyer, 1997.
Uhlig, Ludwig. *Georg Forster.* Tübingen: Max Niemeyer, 1965.
Utz, Peter. *Das Auge und das Ohr im Text.* Munich: Fink, 1990.
Velkley, Richard L. *Freedom and the End of Reason.* Chicago: University of Chicago Press, 1989.
Vermeulen, Han F., and Arturo Alvarez Roldán, eds. *Fieldwork and Footnotes: Studies in the History of European Anthropology.* London: Routledge, 1995.
Wagner, Michael, ed. *Beyträge zur philosophischen Anthropologie.* Wien: Joseph Stahel, 1794.
Waibel, Violetta L. "Innres, äußres Organ: Das Problem der Gemeinschaft von Seele und Körper in den *Fichte-Studien* Friedrich von Hardenbergs." *Athenäum* 10 (2000): 159–81.
Weikard, Adam. *Der philosophische Arzt.* Frankfurt am Main, 1799.
Wellbery, David. *Lessing's Laocoön: Semiotics and Aesthetics in the Age of Reason.* Cambridge: Cambridge University Press, 1984.
Wellmon, Chad. "Goethe's Morphology of Knowledge, or the Overgrowth of Nomenclature." *Goethe Yearbook* 17 (2010): 153–77.
Welsch, Caroline. "Die Physiologie der Einbildungskraft um 1800." In *Die Grenzen des Menschen. Anthropologie und Ästhetik um 1800,* edited by Maximilian Berngenruen and Roland Borgands. Würzburg: Königshausen und Neumann, 2001.
Wenzel, Gottfried Immanuel. *Menschenlehre oder System einer Anthropologie nach der neuesten Beobachtungen, Versuchen, und Gründsätzen der Physik und Philosophie.* Leipzig, 1802.
———. *Vollständiger Lehrbegriff der gesamten Philosophie dem Bedürfnisse der Zeit gemäß: Metaphysik der Natur und der Anthropologie.* Leipzig, 1804.

Wezel, Johann Karl. *Versuch über die Kenntniß des Menschen*. 1784–85. Frankfurt am Main: Athenäum, 1971.
Wilson, Holly L. "Kant's Integration of Morality and Anthropology." *Kant-Studien* 88 (1997): 87–104.
———. *Kant's Pragmatic Anthropology: Its Origin, Meaning, and Critical Significance*. Albany: State University of New York Press, 2006.
Wintsch, Hans Ulrich. *Religiosität und Bildung: Der anthropologische und bildungsphilosophische Ansatz in Schleiermachers Reden über die Religion*. Zurich: Juris Druck, 1967.
Wokler, Robert. "From *l'homme physique* to *l'homme moral* and Back: Toward a History of Enlightenment Anthropology." *History of the Human Sciences* 6 (1993): 121–38.
Wood, Allen W. *Hegel's Ethical Thought*. Cambridge: Cambridge University Press, 1990.
———. "Kant and the Problem of Human Nature." In *Essays on Kant's Anthropology*, edited by Brian Jacobs and Patrick Kain. Cambridge: Cambridge University Press, 2003.
———. *Kantian Ethics*. Cambridge: Cambridge University Press, 2008.
———. "Kant's Compatibilism." In *Self and Nature in Kant's Philosophy*, edited by Allan W. Wood. Ithaca: Cornell University Press, 1984.
———. *Kant's Ethical Thought*. Cambridge: Cambridge University Press, 1999.
———. "Unsocial Sociability: The Anthropological Basis for Kant's Ethics." *Philosophical Topics* 19 (1991): 325–51.
Yovel, Yirmiahu. *Kant and the Philosophy of History*. Princeton: Princeton University Press, 1981.
Zammito, John H. *The Genesis of Kant's Critique of Judgment*. Chicago: University of Chicago Press, 1992.
———. "Herder and Historical Metanarrative: What's Philosophical About History?" In *A Companion to the Works of Johann Gottfried Herder*, edited by Hans Adler and Wulf Koepke. Rochester, N.Y.: Camden House, 2009.
———. *Kant, Herder, and the Birth of Anthropology*. Chicago: University of Chicago Press, 2002.
———. "Policing Polygeneticism in Germany, 1775: (Kames,) Kant, and Blumenbach." In *The German Invention of Race*, edited by Sara Eigen and Mark Larrimore. Albany: State University of New York Press, 2006.
Zantop, Susanne. *Colonial Fantasies: Conquest, Family, and Nation in Pre-colonial Germany, 1770–1870*. Durham: Duke University Press, 1997.
Zedler, Johann Heinrich. *Grosses Vollständiges Universallexicon aller Wissenschaften und Künste*. Halle: Johann Heinrich Zedler, 1732.
Zeuch, Ulrike. *Umkehr der Sinneshierarchie: Herder und die Aufwertung des Tastsinns seit der frühen Neuzeit*. Tübingen: Max Niemayer Verlag, 2000.
Zukert, Rachel. *Kant on Beauty and Biology: An Interpretation of the Critique of Judgment*. Cambridge: Cambridge University Press, 2007.

Index

Abbt, Thomas, 140
Adorno, Theodor, 19, 72
aesthetics, 15, 35, 182, 194, 211, 234, 246, 260, 261, 276
analogy, 20, 36, 40, 168, 224, 236, 247, 260
analogical reasoning, 23
anatomy, 26, 41, 236–38, 240
anthropology
    comparative, 7, 184, 186, 236–37, 250–60, 264–73, 276
    crisis of, 2, 7, 42, 44, 107, 213
    as discipline, 1, 16, 107, 119, 127, 259, 272
    empirical, 214
    and hermeneutics, 11, 212, 272–73
    medical, 8
    moral, 108, 123
    physiological, 44, 121–25, 213, 225, 287
    practical, 54–55, 123–25
    pragmatic, 55, 98, 99, 101, 103, 106, 108, 119
    proto-, 16, 119, 123, 133, 145, 176, 183, 194, 203, 213, 218, 237, 274
    of the senses, 12, 213, 220, 227, 233, 276
    and teleology, 10, 137, 139, 163, 171, 187, 259
    as unity of empirical and philosophical, 258, 259, 264
anthropomorphism, 250
antinomy of pure reason, 61, 63
apperception, 114–16, 131
apprehension, 114–16
Arendt, Hannah, 135
attention, 215, 225, 228

Barth, Karl, 299
Basque country, 12, 237, 265–72
Baumgarten, Alexander Gottlieb, 35, 109
Bildung, 40, 113, 178, 250, 254
Bildungstrieb, 242, 245
Blumenbach, J. F., 254
Buffon, Georges-Louis Leclerc de, 145–47, 177

causality
    and *Bildung*, 254
    efficient, 68, 159, 254
    final, 18
    of freedom, 61–62, 67
    natural or mechanistic, 61–62, 66, 67, 72, 79, 243
    purposive, 242, 254
    of reason, 59, 64, 84
    teleological, 163
character, 59, 70, 86, 88, 90, 102, 171, 251–52
classification, 142, 149
common sense, 97, 290
comparison, 23, 36, 41, 84, 89, 150, 183, 187, 239, 259, 269
contingency, 76, 175, 214, 276, 278
Cook, James, 143
critique, 3–5
culture
    concept of, 37–38, 99, 100
    Herder on, 39–40
    Humboldt on, 266, 270, 272, 273
    Kant's theory of, 89, 90, 169, 171–78

de Bougainville, Louis Antoine, 143
destiny (*Bestimmung*), 149, 153, 162, 188, 259, 275, 277
dietetics, 49
discursive thought, 223, 234, 247
    vs. non-discursive thought, 248
dreaming/dreams, 114, 134

empiricism, 118, 159, 180, 240, 242, 248, 253
epigenesis, 242, 246
ethnography, 9, 139, 143, 154, 198–203, 209, 256, 266
exemplarity, 90
experience, 22, 24, 42, 54, 58, 101

feeling(s), 114, 160, 206
  moral, 33, 51, 83, 92, 288
  of reason, 52, 160
  of respect, 58, 75–82, 84–85, 91
  sensible, 50
Fichte, J. G., 218, 227, 234, 236
finitude, 4, 28, 54, 71, 86, 116, 130, 141, 258, 275
Forster, Georg, 144, 153–63, 176–86
freedom, 10, 18, 42, 52, 57, 118, 124, 137, 174, 198, 204, 229, 246, 257
  practical, 59, 60–68
  as presupposition of reason, 58, 69, 71–72, 86, 106
  as transcendental idea, 60–68
Foucault, Michel, 2–6, 292, 293, 300
Fülleborn, Georg Gustav, 16

Geertz, Clifford, 1
germs (*Keime*), 36–37, 39, 40, 122
Geschichte vs. *Historie*, 168
Goethe, Johann Wolfgang von, 2, 3, 9, 12, 236, 237, 250, 252, 253, 256, 264, 269, 271, 276, 277, 278
  and Blumenbach, 242
  and comparative anatomy, 238–41
  and Kant, 246–50
  and the organism, 244–46

Habermas, Jürgen, 5, 6
Hadot, Pierre, 51, 59
Hegel, G. W. F., 23, 52, 72, 235
Heine, Heinrich, 53
Henrich, Dieter, 73
Herder, Johann Gottfried, 34, 35, 39–41, 49, 107, 133–37, 171, 186, 207, 223, 232, 257
Herz, Markus, 119, 120
history, 39, 134, 137, 153, 156, 159, 252, 259, 272
  and anthropology, 37, 163–71, 207
  Kant's philosophy of, 207
  natural, 17, 146, 148, 150–51, 159, 194, 239, 242
  and religion, 203–4, 209
  of the senses, 35, 220
Horkheimer, Max, 222
Hufeland, Christoph Wilhelm, 38, 49, 51, 99
humanity, 37, 40, 59, 96, 131, 133, 141, 143, 145, 147, 169, 175, 181, 194, 202, 203, 206, 207, 212, 225, 256, 260, 269, 277
Humboldt, Alexander von, 179, 262
Humboldt, Wilhelm von, 8, 12, 36, 121, 179, 235
  on *Bildung*, 254

and ethnography, 265–70, 271–72
  on history, 259
  on language, 262–64
  on natural science, 259
Hunter, Ian, 51, 282, 283, 286

imagination, 32, 185, 219, 235, 261
innate ideas/impressions, 22
intuition, 72, 74, 84, 101, 116, 160, 203, 205, 206, 208, 209, 248

Jakob, Ludwig Heinrich, 42
judgment, 58, 68, 73, 92

Kant, Immanuel, 23, 37, 212, 213, 233, 237, 252, 257, 261, 265, 277–78
  and anthropological observation, 112–19
  and Buffon, 145–46
  and cosmopolitanism, 128–31
  and critique, 4–5
  critique of Platner, 122–23
  and the destiny of the human, 138–41
  and dietetics, 49
  and ethical exercises, 90–94
  and feelings of reason, 52
  and Forster, 153–63
  and Foucault, 5
  and Goethe, 246–50
  and Herder, 135–37, 207
  and the novel, 27, 167
  on the organism, 233–34
  and physiological anthropology, 121–23, 213
  and pragmatic anthropology, 119–21
  on the presupposition of freedom, 58, 69, 71–72, 86, 106
  and Schleiermacher, 196–98
  and the sources of anthropology, 110
  on the theory of culture, 171–72
  and travel literature, 145, 158, 180
  and *Weltkenntnis* vs. Scholasticism, 126–28

Leibniz, Gottfried, 21, 25
Linnaeus, 156, 158
Locke, John, 214, 222
Loder, Justus Christian, 36, 38, 236

marionettes, 70, 76
materialism, 29, 145
memory, 32, 128, 261, 270
Mendelssohn, Moses, 140, 160, 255

metaphysics, 4, 18, 20, 21, 23, 30, 31, 35, 42, 52, 54, 55, 56, 107, 123, 161, 195, 198, 204–5, 240
mind-body problem, 15, 18, 25, 29, 31, 35, 106, 120, 131, 183, 184, 217, 276
Molyneux problem, 214, 222, 225, 231, 301
monogeneticism, 145
moral disposition, 51, 54, 58–60, 69–72, 81, 83, 85, 90, 96, 103, 125
moral economy, 60, 84, 85, 97

narration, 11, 161, 164, 166, 172, 185, 187, 268
necessity, 57, 61, 67
New South Holland, 11, 194, 200
normativity, 9, 18, 39, 41, 44, 45, 57, 68, 95, 106, 175, 186, 213, 221, 234, 235, 251, 273, 275–77
Novalis (Friedrich von Hardenberg), 3, 9, 11, 168, 261, 276, 278
  on analogy, 23
  Fichte-Studien, 218–20, 234
  Hymnen an die Nacht, 215–17, 224–26, 231
  and perception, 220
novel, the, 37, 110, 167–68, 193, 198

organism, 29, 39, 147, 151, 162, 163, 242–45, 252, 254, 259

pedagogy, 8, 17, 125, 194
philology, 261–62
philosophical physicians, 7, 29, 30
physiognomy, 102, 208, 262
physiology, 8, 26, 31, 35, 41, 109, 128
Pippin, Robert, 3, 71, 96
Platner, Ernst, 7, 22, 24, 26, 27, 30, 31, 42, 99, 119, 121, 122, 123, 145, 214, 217, 218
polygeneticism, 145
predispositions, 37, 98, 121, 122, 125, 141, 145, 147, 150–55, 163, 171, 183
preformationism, 242
psychology, 8, 15, 21, 26, 31, 33, 35, 77, 109, 128
purposiveness, 85, 151, 159–63, 166, 170, 187, 189, 242, 244

race, 11, 132, 139, 141–63, 187, 189, 197, 242
Rawls, John, 52
reflexivity, 16, 18, 19
respect (*Achtung*), 52, 58, 78–85
Riedel, Wolfgang, 30, 281, 284
Rousseau, Jean-Jacques, 73, 74, 76, 77

Schiller, Friedrich, 49, 233, 256, 262, 263, 264

Schlegel, Friedrich, 1, 2, 3, 9, 18, 184–86, 193, 198, 211, 212, 221
Schleiermacher, Friedrich, 9, 11, 60, 182, 235, 260, 261, 276, 277, 278
  and aesthetics, 207–12
  and ethnography, 200–203
  on Kant's *Anthropologie*, 194–98
  on language, 271–72
Schmid, Carl C. E., 42, 43, 44, 124
scholastic knowledge (*Schulkenntnis*), 126, 128
self-reflection, 113, 115, 196
sensation, 23, 24, 27, 32–35, 50, 76, 80, 93, 114, 128, 224, 226, 229, 231, 235, 262, 284
sense, 23, 223–27, 230, 231, 233, 234–35, 261
  aesthetic, 193, 204, 210, 211
  inner/outer, 33–34, 114–15, 225, 227, 228–29
  moral, 63, 73, 74
senses, the, 9, 12, 32, 33, 34, 55, 81, 84, 222–27, 274, 276
sensibility, 12, 19, 29, 31–36, 75, 80, 94, 104, 179, 215, 217, 218, 220–22, 224, 229–30, 248, 261, 276, 284, 301
sight, sense of, 215, 222, 223, 230
skin color, 149, 151, 162, 189
Soemmering, Samuel Thomas von, 154, 155, 157, 187
solipsism, 51, 78, 82
soul, 7, 22, 26, 29, 30, 217–20, 227
South Sea Islanders, 138, 155, 275
Spalding, Johann Joachim, 140
Spinoza, Baruch, 25, 203, 238
spontaneity, 55, 62, 64, 65, 67, 185, 211, 234, 255, 305
stimulation (*Reitz/Reiz*), 29, 75, 219, 220, 232, 284, 301
subreption, 79
Sulzer, Johann Georg, 33, 34
synesthesia, 216

teleology, 106, 118, 137, 139, 153, 158
  moral, 143, 162, 163–71
  natural, 143, 161, 162
Tetens, Nicholas, 22
Tischgesellschaft, 131, 151
touch, sense of, 215, 217, 222, 223
translation, 199, 262
travelogues, 110, 111, 138, 143, 144, 145, 158, 183, 193, 200, 201, 208, 250, 256, 266, 268
Typus, 249

Unzer, Johann August, 30

virtue, 50, 51, 85–88, 96, 105, 121, 248
vision, sense of, 215–17, 219, 223, 230, 232

Wagner, Michael, 24, 34, 35
Weikard, Adam, 29, 30

Wenzel, Johann Karl, 15, 16, 23
Witz, 32
Wolff, Christian, 21, 29, 30, 31, 32, 33

Zammito, John H., 107, 282, 283, 284, 285, 291
Zimmermann, Johann Georg, 29, 30

www.ingramcontent.com/pod-product-compliance
Lightning Source LLC
Chambersburg PA
CBHW021353290426
44108CB00010B/222